to base that award in part upon its desire to punish the defendant for harming persons who are not before the court (e.g., victims whom the parties do not represent). We hold that such an award would amount to a taking of "property" from the defendant without due process.

This lawsuit arises out of the death of Jesse Williams, a heavy cigarette smoker. Respondent, Williams' widow, represents his estate in this state lawsuit for negligence and deceit against Philip Morris, the manufacturer of Marlboro, the brand that Williams favored. A jury found that Williams' death was caused by smoking; that Williams smoked in significant part because he thought it was safe to do so; and that Philip Morris knowingly and falsely led him to believe that this was so. The jury ultimately found that Philip Morris was negligent (as was Williams) and that Philip Morris had engaged in deceit. In respect to deceit, the claim at issue here, it awarded compensatory damages of about $821,000 (about $21,000 economic and $800,000 noneconomic) along with $79.5 million in punitive damages.

The trial judge subsequently found the $79.5 million punitive damages award "excessive," see, e.g., *BMW of North America, Inc. v. Gore*, 517 U.S. 559 (1996), and reduced it to $32 million. Both sides appealed. The Oregon Court of Appeals rejected Philip Morris' arguments and restored the $79.5 million jury award. Subsequently, Philip Morris sought review in the Oregon Supreme Court (which denied review) and then here. We remanded the case in light of *State Farm Mut. Automobile Ins. Co. v. Campbell*, 538 U.S. 408 (2003). The Oregon Court of Appeals adhered to its original views. And Philip Morris sought, and this time obtained, review in the Oregon Supreme Court.

Philip Morris then made two arguments relevant here. First, it said that the trial court should have accepted, but did not accept, a proposed "punitive damages" instruction that specified the jury could not seek to punish Philip Morris for injury to other persons not before the court. In particular, Philip Morris pointed out that the plaintiff's attorney had told the jury to "think about how many other Jesse Williams in the last 40 years in the State of Oregon there have been.... In Oregon, how many people do we see outside, driving home ... smoking cigarettes? ... [C]igarettes ... are going to kill ten [of every hundred]. [And] the market share of Marlboros [i.e., Philip Morris] is one-third [i.e., one of every three killed]." In light of this argument, Philip Morris asked the trial court to tell the jury that "you may consider the extent of harm suffered by others in determining what [the] reasonable relationship is" between any punitive award and "the harm caused to Jesse Williams" by Philip Morris' misconduct, "[but] you are not to punish the defendant for the impact of its alleged misconduct on other persons, who may bring lawsuits of their own in which other juries can resolve their claims ..." The judge rejected this proposal and instead told the jury that "[p]unitive damages are awarded against a defendant to punish misconduct and to deter misconduct," and "are not intended to compensate the plaintiff or anyone else for damages caused by the defendant's conduct." In Philip Morris' view, the result was a significant likelihood that a portion of the $79.5 million award represented punishment for its having harmed others, a punishment that the Due Process Clause would here forbid.

Second, Philip Morris pointed to the roughly 100-to-1 ratio the $79.5 million punitive damages award bears to $821,000 in compensatory damages. Philip Morris noted that this Court in *BMW* emphasized the constitutional need for punitive damages awards to reflect (1) the "reprehensibility" of the defendant's conduct, (2) a "reasonable relationship" to the harm the plaintiff (or related victim) suffered, and (3) the presence (or absence) of "sanctions," e.g., criminal penalties, that state law provided for comparable conduct. And in *State Farm*, this Court said that the longstanding historical practice of

setting punitive damages at two, three, or four times the size of compensatory damages, while "not binding," is "instructive," and that "[s]ingle-digit multipliers are more likely to comport with due process." Philip Morris claimed that, in light of this case law, the punitive award was "grossly excessive."

The Oregon Supreme Court rejected these and other Philip Morris arguments. In particular, it rejected Philip Morris' claim that the Constitution prohibits a state jury "from using punitive damages to punish a defendant for harm to nonparties." And in light of Philip Morris' reprehensible conduct, it found that the $79.5 million award was not "grossly excessive." Philip Morris then sought certiorari. It asked us to consider, among other things, (1) its claim that Oregon had unconstitutionally permitted it to be punished for harming nonparty victims; and (2) whether Oregon had in effect disregarded "the constitutional requirement that punitive damages be reasonably related to the plaintiff's harm." We granted certiorari limited to these two questions.

For reasons we shall set forth, we consider only the first of these questions. We vacate the Oregon Supreme Court's judgment, and we remand the case for further proceedings.

This Court has long made clear that "[p]unitive damages may properly be imposed to further a State's legitimate interests in punishing unlawful conduct and deterring its repetition." *BMW, supra,* at 568. At the same time, we have emphasized the need to avoid an arbitrary determination of an award's amount. Unless a State insists upon proper standards that will cabin the jury's discretionary authority, its punitive damages system may deprive a defendant of "fair notice … of the severity of the penalty that a State may impose," *BMW, supra,* at 574; it may threaten "arbitrary punishments," i.e., punishments that reflect not an "application of law" but "a decisionmaker's caprice," *State Farm, supra,* at 416, 418 (internal quotation marks omitted); and, where the amounts are sufficiently large, it may impose one State's (or one jury's) "policy choice," say as to the conditions under which (or even whether) certain products can be sold, upon "neighboring States" with different public policies, *BMW, supra,* at 571–572.

For these and similar reasons, this Court has found that the Constitution imposes certain limits, in respect both to procedures for awarding punitive damages and to amounts forbidden as "grossly excessive." Because we shall not decide whether the award here at issue is "grossly excessive," we need now only consider the Constitution's procedural limitations.

In our view, the Constitution's Due Process Clause forbids a State to use a punitive damages award to punish a defendant for injury that it inflicts upon nonparties or those whom they directly represent, i.e., injury that it inflicts upon those who are, essentially, strangers to the litigation. For one thing, the Due Process Clause prohibits a State from punishing an individual without first providing that individual with "an opportunity to present every available defense." *Lindsey v. Normet,* 405 U.S. 56, 66 (1972) (internal quotation marks omitted). Yet a defendant threatened with punishment for injuring a nonparty victim has no opportunity to defend against the charge, by showing, for example in a case such as this, that the other victim was not entitled to damages because he or she knew that smoking was dangerous or did not rely upon the defendant's statements to the contrary. For another, to permit punishment for injuring a nonparty victim would add a near standardless dimension to the punitive damages equation. How many such victims are there? How seriously were they injured? Under what circumstances did injury occur? The trial will not likely answer such questions as to nonparty victims. The jury will be left to speculate. And the fundamental due process concerns to which our punitive damages cases refer—risks of arbitrariness, uncertainty and lack of notice—will be magnified. *State Farm,* 538 U.S., at 416, 418; *BMW,* 517 U.S., at 574.

Finally, we can find no authority supporting the use of punitive damages awards for the purpose of punishing a defendant for harming others. We have said that it may be appropriate to consider the reasonableness of a punitive damages award in light of the potential harm the defendant's conduct could have caused. But we have made clear that the potential harm at issue was harm potentially caused the plaintiff. See *State Farm, supra,* at 424, ("[W]e have been reluctant to identify concrete constitutional limits on the ratio between harm, or potential harm, *to the plaintiff* and the punitive damages award" (emphasis added))....

Respondent argues that she is free to show harm to other victims because it is relevant to a different part of the punitive damages constitutional equation, namely, reprehensibility. That is to say, harm to others shows more reprehensible conduct. Philip Morris, in turn, does not deny that a plaintiff may show harm to others in order to demonstrate reprehensibility. Nor do we. Evidence of actual harm to nonparties can help to show that the conduct that harmed the plaintiff also posed a substantial risk of harm to the general public, and so was particularly reprehensible—although counsel may argue in a particular case that conduct resulting in no harm to others nonetheless posed a grave risk to the public, or the converse. Yet for the reasons given above, a jury may not go further than this and use a punitive damages verdict to punish a defendant directly on account of harms it is alleged to have visited on nonparties.

Given the risks of unfairness that we have mentioned, it is constitutionally important for a court to provide assurance that the jury will ask the right question, not the wrong one. And given the risks of arbitrariness, the concern for adequate notice, and the risk that punitive damages awards can, in practice, impose one State's (or one jury's) policies (e.g., banning cigarettes) upon other States—all of which accompany awards that, today, may be many times the size of such awards in the 18th and 19th centuries—it is particularly important that States avoid procedure that unnecessarily deprives juries of proper legal guidance. We therefore conclude that the Due Process Clause requires States to provide assurance that juries are not asking the wrong question, i.e., seeking, not simply to determine reprehensibility, but also to punish for harm caused strangers....

The instruction that Philip Morris said the trial court should have given distinguishes between using harm to others as part of the "reasonable relationship" equation (which it would allow) and using it directly as a basis for punishment. The instruction asked the trial court to tell the jury that "you may consider the extent of harm suffered by others in determining what [the] reasonable relationship is" between Philip Morris' punishable misconduct and harm caused to Jesse Williams, "[but] you are not to punish the defendant for the impact of its alleged misconduct on other persons, who may bring lawsuits of their own in which other juries can resolve their claims ..." And as the Oregon Supreme Court explicitly recognized, Philip Morris argued that the Constitution "prohibits the state, acting through a civil jury, from using punitive damages to punish a defendant for harm to nonparties."

The court rejected that claim. In doing so, it pointed out (1) that this Court in *State Farm* had held only that a jury could not base its award upon "dissimilar" acts of a defendant. It added (2) that "[i]f a jury cannot punish for the conduct, then it is difficult to see why it may consider it at all." And it stated (3) that "[i]t is unclear to us how a jury could 'consider' harm to others, yet withhold that consideration from the punishment calculus."

The Oregon court's first statement is correct. We did not previously hold explicitly that a jury may not punish for the harm caused others. But we do so hold now. We do

not agree with the Oregon court's second statement. We have explained why we believe the Due Process Clause prohibits a State's inflicting punishment for harm caused strangers to the litigation. At the same time we recognize that conduct that risks harm to many is likely more reprehensible than conduct that risks harm to only a few. And a jury consequently may take this fact into account in determining reprehensibility. Cf., e.g., *Witte v. United States*, 515 U.S. 389, 400 (1995) (recidivism statutes taking into account a criminal defendant's other misconduct do not impose an "'additional penalty for the earlier crimes,' but instead ...'a stiffened penalty for the latest crime, which is considered to be an aggravated offense because a repetitive one'" (quoting *Gryger v. Burke*, 334 U.S. 728, 732 (1948))).

The Oregon court's third statement raises a practical problem. How can we know whether a jury, in taking account of harm caused others under the rubric of reprehensibility, also seeks to punish the defendant for having caused injury to others? Our answer is that state courts cannot authorize procedures that create an unreasonable and unnecessary risk of any such confusion occurring. In particular, we believe that where the risk of that misunderstanding is a significant one—because, for instance, of the sort of evidence that was introduced at trial or the kinds of argument the plaintiff made to the jury—a court, upon request, must protect against that risk. Although the States have some flexibility to determine what kind of procedures they will implement, federal constitutional law obligates them to provide some form of protection in appropriate cases.

As the preceding discussion makes clear, we believe that the Oregon Supreme Court applied the wrong constitutional standard when considering Philip Morris' appeal. We remand this case so that the Oregon Supreme Court can apply the standard we have set forth. Because the application of this standard may lead to the need for a new trial, or a change in the level of the punitive damages award, we shall not consider whether the award is constitutionally "grossly excessive." We vacate the Oregon Supreme Court's judgment and remand the case for further proceedings not inconsistent with this opinion.

It is so ordered.

STEVENS, J. (dissenting). The Due Process Clause of the Fourteenth Amendment imposes both substantive and procedural constraints on the power of the States to impose punitive damages on tortfeasors. I remain firmly convinced that the cases announcing those constraints were correctly decided. In my view the Oregon Supreme Court faithfully applied the reasoning in those opinions to the egregious facts disclosed by this record. I agree with Justice Ginsburg's explanation of why no procedural error even arguably justifying reversal occurred at the trial in this case. See *post*, p. 1068–1069.

Of greater importance to me, however, is the Court's imposition of a novel limit on the State's power to impose punishment in civil litigation. Unlike the Court, I see no reason why an interest in punishing a wrongdoer "for harming persons who are not before the court," should not be taken into consideration when assessing the appropriate sanction for reprehensible conduct.

Whereas compensatory damages are measured by the harm the defendant has caused the plaintiff, punitive damages are a sanction for the public harm the defendant's conduct has caused or threatened. There is little difference between the justification for a criminal sanction, such as a fine or a term of imprisonment, and an award of punitive damages. In our early history either type of sanction might have been imposed in litigation prosecuted by a private citizen. See *Steel Co. v. Citizens for Better Environment*, 523 U.S. 83, 127–128 (1998) (Stevens, J., concurring in judgment). And while in neither context would the sanction typically include a pecuniary award measured by the harm that the

conduct had caused to any third parties, in both contexts the harm to third parties would surely be a relevant factor to consider in evaluating the reprehensibility of the defendant's wrongdoing. We have never held otherwise.

In the case before us, evidence attesting to the possible harm the defendant's extensive deceitful conduct caused other Oregonians was properly presented to the jury. No evidence was offered to establish an appropriate measure of damages to compensate such third parties for their injuries, and no one argued that the punitive damages award would serve any such purpose. To award compensatory damages to remedy such third-party harm might well constitute a taking of property from the defendant without due process, see ante, at 1060. But a punitive damages award, instead of serving a compensatory purpose, serves the entirely different purposes of retribution and deterrence that underlie every criminal sanction. *State Farm*, 538 U.S., at 416. This justification for punitive damages has even greater salience when, as in this case, see Ore.Rev.Stat. §31.735(1) (2003), the award is payable in whole or in part to the State rather than to the private litigant.

While apparently recognizing the novelty of its holding, ante, at 1065, the majority relies on a distinction between taking third-party harm into account in order to assess the reprehensibility of the defendant's conduct—which is permitted—from doing so in order to punish the defendant "directly"—which is forbidden. This nuance eludes me. When a jury increases a punitive damages award because injuries to third parties enhanced the reprehensibility of the defendant's conduct, the jury is by definition punishing the defendant—directly—for third-party harm. A murderer who kills his victim by throwing a bomb that injures dozens of bystanders should be punished more severely than one who harms no one other than his intended victim. Similarly, there is no reason why the measure of the appropriate punishment for engaging in a campaign of deceit in distributing a poisonous and addictive substance to thousands of cigarette smokers statewide should not include consideration of the harm to those "bystanders" as well as the harm to the individual plaintiff. The Court endorses a contrary conclusion without providing us with any reasoned justification.

It is far too late in the day to argue that the Due Process Clause merely guarantees fair procedure and imposes no substantive limits on a State's lawmaking power. See, e.g., *Moore v. East Cleveland*, 431 U.S. 494, 544 (1977) (White, J., dissenting); *Poe v. Ullman*, 367 U.S. 497, 540–541 (1961) (Harlan, J., dissenting); *Whitney v. California*, 274 U.S. 357, 373 (1927) (Brandeis, J., concurring). It remains true, however, that the Court should be "reluctant to expand the concept of substantive due process because guideposts for responsible decisionmaking in this unchartered area are scarce and open-ended." *Collins v. Harker Heights*, 503 U.S. 115, 125 (1992). Judicial restraint counsels us to "exercise the utmost care whenever we are asked to break new ground in this field." Today the majority ignores that sound advice when it announces its new rule of substantive law. Essentially for the reasons stated in the opinion of the Supreme Court of Oregon, I would affirm its judgment.

GINSBURG, J. (dissenting) (joined by SCALIA and THOMAS, JJ.). The purpose of punitive damages, it can hardly be denied, is not to compensate, but to punish. Punish for what? Not for harm actually caused "strangers to the litigation," the Court states, but for the reprehensibility of defendant's conduct. "[C]onduct that risks harm to many," the Court observes, "is likely more reprehensible than conduct that risks harm to only a few." The Court thus conveys that, when punitive damages are at issue, a jury is properly instructed to consider the extent of harm suffered by others as a measure of reprehensibility, but not to mete out punishment for injuries in fact sustained by nonparties. The Oregon courts did not rule otherwise. They have endeavored to follow our decisions, most recently in *BMW of North America, Inc. v. Gore*, 517 U.S. 559 (1996), and *State*

Farm Mut. Automobile Ins. Co. v. Campbell, 538 U.S. 408 (2003), and have "deprive[d] [no jury] of proper legal guidance." Vacation of the Oregon Supreme Court's judgment, I am convinced, is unwarranted.

The right question regarding reprehensibility, the Court acknowledges, would train on "the harm that Philip Morris was prepared to inflict on the smoking public at large." See also 340 Ore., at 55, ("[T]he jury, *in assessing the reprehensibility of Philip Morris's actions*, could consider evidence of similar harm to other Oregonians caused (or threatened) by the same conduct" (emphasis added).). The Court identifies no evidence introduced and no charge delivered inconsistent with that inquiry.

The Court's order vacating the Oregon Supreme Court's judgment is all the more inexplicable considering that Philip Morris did not preserve any objection to the charges in fact delivered to the jury, to the evidence introduced at trial, or to opposing counsel's argument. The sole objection Philip Morris preserved was to the trial court's refusal to give defendant's requested charge number 34. The proposed instruction read in pertinent part:

> If you determine that some amount of punitive damages should be imposed on the defendant, it will then be your task to set an amount that is appropriate. This should be such amount as you believe is necessary to achieve the objectives of deterrence and punishment. While there is no set formula to be applied in reaching an appropriate amount, I will now advise you of some of the factors that you may wish to consider in this connection.
>
> (1) The size of any punishment should bear a reasonable relationship to the harm caused to Jesse Williams by the defendant's punishable misconduct. Although you may consider the extent of harm suffered by others in determining what that reasonable relationship is, you are not to punish the defendant for the impact of its alleged misconduct on other persons, who may bring lawsuits of their own in which other juries can resolve their claims and award punitive damages for those harms, as such other juries see fit....
>
> (2) The size of the punishment may appropriately reflect the degree of reprehensibility of the defendant's conduct—that is, how far the defendant has departed from accepted societal norms of conduct.

Under that charge, just what use could the jury properly make of "the extent of harm suffered by others"? The answer slips from my grasp. A judge seeking to enlighten rather than confuse surely would resist delivering the requested charge.

The Court ventures no opinion on the propriety of the charge proposed by Philip Morris, though Philip Morris preserved no other objection to the trial proceedings. Rather than addressing the one objection Philip Morris properly preserved, the Court reaches outside the bounds of the case as postured when the trial court entered its judgment. I would accord more respectful treatment to the proceedings and dispositions of state courts that sought diligently to adhere to our changing, less than crystalline precedent.

For the reasons stated, and in light of the abundant evidence of "the potential harm [Philip Morris'] conduct could have caused," (emphasis deleted), I would affirm the decision of the Oregon Supreme Court.

Note

In *Bullock v. Philip Morris USA, Inc.*, 159 Cal.App.4th 655, 693–94 (2008), a California district court held that it was reversible error for a trial judge to have refused the same

defendant's proposal to instruct the jury that: "You are not to impose punishment for harms suffered by persons other than the plaintiff before you." The court reasoned:

> The fact that [the] proposed instruction ... did not include the qualification that evidence of harm caused to others could be considered to determine the reprehensibility of the conduct that harmed Bullock did not render the instruction incomplete or misleading. *Williams* made it clear that imposing punishment for harm caused to others, which is prohibited, is separate and distinct from determining the degree of reprehensibility by considering evidence of harm caused to others, which is permitted. A jury that considers evidence of harm caused to others to determine the reprehensibility of a defendant's conduct toward the plaintiff, for the purpose of determining the amount of a punitive damages award, is not imposing punishment for harm caused to others. It is therefore appropriate to state without qualification that a jury may not "impose punishment" for harms suffered by nonparties to the litigation ...
>
> Philip Morris had no duty to qualify its proposed instruction in order to encompass a rule of law favorable to Bullock concerning the permissible use of evidence of harm caused to others. Each party in a civil case has a duty to propose instructions that accurately state the law supporting its own theory of the case, and need not qualify its proposed instructions for the benefit of an opposing party.

Since the jury's award of compensation to be paid by the defendant was unimpeachable, the case was remanded for a new trial limited to determining the amount of punitive damages in a manner consistent with the court's opinion.

Questions

1. Are awards of punitive damages in torts cases any business of the Supreme Court?

2. What, if any, should be the appropriate limits to an award of punitive damages, and (if there are such limits) how should they be imposed?

3. Does the line of Supreme Court cases on punitive damages suggest that such awards are outdated and serve no useful purpose?

Index

Folk Linguistics

Folk Linguistics

by
Nancy A. Niedzielski
Dennis R. Preston

Mouton de Gruyter
Berlin · New York   2003

Mouton de Gruyter (formerly Mouton, The Hague)
is a Division of Walter de Gruyter GmbH & Co. KG, Berlin.

The hardcover edition was published in 2000 as volume 122 of the series
Trends in Linguistics. Studies and Monographs.

ISBN 3 11 017554 1

Bibliographic information published by Die Deutsche Bibliothek

Die Deutsche Bibliothek lists this publication in the Deutsche
Nationalbibliografie; detailed bibliographic data is available in the
Internet at <http://dnb.ddb.de>.

Disk conversion: Readymade, Berlin.
Printing and binding: Werner Hildebrand, Berlin
Cover design: Sigurd Wendland, Berlin.
Printed in Germany.

For Keith Denning – Linguist, colleague, mentor, friend

Preface to the paperback edition

In *Folk Linguistics* we hope to have shown that the beliefs about, reactions to, and comments on language by what we call "real people" (i.e., nonlinguists) are interesting, illuminating, and empowering from ethnographic, linguistic, and practical (or applied linguistic) points of view. We still believe so, and we are delighted to see in the literature and at many conferences that others apparently agree with us.

So what's new? On a positive note, we believe that the final chapter of *Folk Linguistics* has pointed and continues to point the way to a great deal of as yet unexplored potential – the careful consideration of the underlying presuppositions and beliefs which lie behind the discourses and actions that constitute the primary data of folk linguistics. What are the folk theories of language held by real people, and how can we extract them from discourses and actions? In *Folk Linguistics* we explored several approaches to acquiring and interpreting relevant data, but we are all too aware, as we confess in our last chapter, that much of what we did could be called "ostensive discourse analysis." We acquired the discourses of real people about language, transcribed them, held them up to the view of the reader, and said what we thought they meant and how they contrasted and/or converged with the belief(s) of "real linguists." Except for some of the operational tasks which we assigned respondents, that procedure was our general plan, and we are not unhappy with it. We think the data reported in *Folk Linguistics* are still the richest repository of linguistic lore from various members of a speech community yet collected and interpreted.

As we suggest in the final chapter, however, techniques that allow researchers to look at discourse even more sensitively are developing. For example, some of those suggested in Preston (1993, 1994) offer ways of investigating the patterns of a discourse in relation to its subject matter, and we expect that these techniques and others will allow future work in the field to delve even more deeply into the conceptual realms which lie behind folk comment about and reaction to language. Although we do not believe that there is a straight and easy path from the content of, or underlying belief systems inherent in utterances to the structural elements which encode them, we do think that some aspects of language structure, perhaps discourse structure in particular but by no means exclusively, may be profitably examined to help characterize what mental constructs speakers bring to bear on a linguistic topic.

For example, in a recent investigation of Japanese attitudes towards the English and Japanese languages, Imai (2000) provides a careful analysis of discoursal structure. She triggered the conversation she analyzed by asking, simply, 'What do you think about the differences and similarities between Japanese and English?' She analyzed the conversation as an 'argument' (following Schiffrin 1985 and Preston 1993, 1994), a discourse genre which consists essentially of *positions*, *disputes*, and *supports*.

Imai shows that a young female respondent, "Y," bases her linguistic comments on a theory of what might be called "social use." Briefly, she regards those aspects of a language not used in ordinary conversation to be somehow outside the language proper. Evidence for this interesting folk theory comes mostly from the respondent's support moves rather than from any positions she takes in the argument. Her interlocutor, for example, asserts that English has more words than Japanese, but Y disputes that position and supports her dispute with the claim that "Americans don't use difficult words." When her interlocutor asks if it isn't the case that books can be linguistically difficult, Y notes that she is concerned only with conversation. Later she also notes that she does not consider phone calls from salespersons to be authentic language either, since scripted calls are also filled with difficult and incomprehensible language, the sort she has not encountered in face-to-face interaction.

What is most interesting to us, however, is Imai's eventual interpretation of Y's folk theory when it turns evaluative. Y's continuing support for the notion that authentic language is based on conversational usage leads her to be critical of what she sees as an American insensitivity to demands for flexibility in language use.

> Y: This is not about the words and probably it is because of the national traits, but, well, I don't know how to say this, but sometimes if I said something and they didn't understand, they say they don't understand, right? And if they say 'say it again', a Japanese would change the words or make it simpler=
>
> S: ((laughter))

Y: =We try to make it simpler and explain, don't we? Americans repeat exactly the same thing.

All: ((laughter))

Y: They are not very flexible, you know?

Imai suggests that Y's theory of good language includes sensitivity to the needs of the interlocutor, and she clearly finds Americans lacking in this respect. This is an extremely interesting notion to us since, as we have shown in *Folk Linguistics*, the prescriptive notion attached to language among our U.S. respondents nearly always hinges on versions of correctness and is not based on usage. Y's argument moves suggest that Japanese respondents may base evaluative notions of language more in the area of speaker and hearer rights and responsibilities. If that is so, it may even prove to be the case that the underlying representation of language itself for Japanese speakers is not the idealized, cognitively external code held to be the essence of language by many of our U.S. respondents.[1]

Whatever the viable Japanese folk linguistic notions turn out to be, we are encouraged by such research which relies on discourse structure. Imai's investigation was fruitful because she carried out a painstaking analysis of the argument which her respondents were involved in – outlining each position, support, and dispute as it arose. This careful analysis allowed situationally and culturally sensitive interpretations of the beliefs behind the conversational moves to be made. We look forward to further detailed analyses of talk about language, making use of the entire arsenal of discourse and conversation analytic tools now available to us.

Less positively, we may have characterized too neatly the conscious versus unconscious dichotomy of folk linguistics, particularly as it contrasts with so-called language attitude study. It is odd that we made this error, for we summarized in Chapter 1 a rather detailed characterization of the kinds of "awareness" involved in the field (Preston 1996). Although we must accept complete responsibility, we were perhaps misled by the principal earlier reference to the field:

... we should be interested not only in (*a*) what goes on (language), but also in (*b*) how people react to what goes on (they are persuaded, they are put off, etc.) and in (*c*) what people say goes on (talk concerning language). It will not do to dismiss these secondary and tertiary modes of conduct merely as sources of error. (Hoenigswald 1966: 20)

From this, we fashioned our "triangle" (Figure 1.4. in *Folk Linguistics*), which we repeat here for convenience.

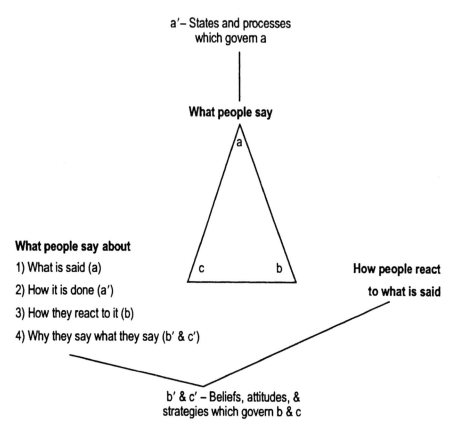

Figure 1.   The place of folk linguistics in the general study of language

We meant to distinguish between the fairly unconscious sorts of reactions tapped in traditional matched guise language attitude studies (in the *b* corner) and the conscious sorts of expressions we sought to tease out in folk linguistics (the *c* corner). In both cases, we make a connection to the underlying beliefs (*b′* and *c′*) which stand in the same relation to folk linguistic and attitudinal performances that the empowering cognitive underpinnings of language (*a′*) do to language production (*a*).

It is more likely that our two corners (*c* and *b*) are actually extremes of a continuum (*b1* through *bn*), one which reaches from the most conscious, deliberate statements about language all the way to the most automatic, least-controlled reactions to it. Perhaps a re-drawing of our triangle will help us as we proceed.

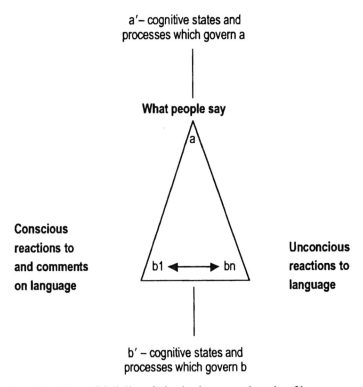

Figure 2. The place of folk linguistics in the general study of language, revised

We regard the leftmost (*b1*) corner of this triangle as the territory most characteristic of folk linguistics; it represents best what we set out to do in this book. We recognize, however, that it would be fool-ish to say that folk linguistics stops precisely at *b23* (or *b48*, or any other position along the continuum) and that everything to the right of it belongs to the social psychology of language, language attitude study, or some other subdisciplinary approach.

From this revised point of view, as one goes about doing folk lin-guistics, it is important to keep the diversity of the objects of research (i.e., the data from *a* and *a'*), the levels of awareness (i.e., the *b*-continuum), and the means of data collection and analysis in mind. For example, one may investigate folk linguistics based on 1) any aspect of *a* or *a'* (from phonetics through pragmatics and interaction, including all cognitive or psycholinguistic aspects of the storage, acquisition, and implementation of all structural levels of language), 2) the most overtly conscious commentary about language (i.e., near or at $b1$) to the most deeply subconscious reaction to a language fact (i.e., near or at bn), and 3) methodological perspectives ranging from the carefully controlled experimental presentation of data to free-wheeling conversations on linguistic topics and the appropriate interpretive mechanisms which follow such data-collecting procedures.

This diversity of data types, levels of awareness, and methodologies suggests that even those data which come from the conscious end of the continuum are open to investigation which may reveal the b' features which lie behind them. In fact, this is the primary reason we have encouraged investigation of the discoursal side of folk linguistics, hoping such data will reveal, perhaps better than any others, the folk theory of language held by nonlinguists (exemplified briefly above from Imai's work on Japanese folk linguistics).

As we noted in the final chapter of *Folk Linguistics*, we are also aware of the need for the investigation of language detail, perhaps particularly at the bn corner. Consider the following. Niedzielski (1999) studied the local Detroit awareness of "Canadian raising" (in which the onsets of the /aw/ ("house") and /ay/ ("night") diphthongs are raised before voiceless consonants). She played a Detroit female speaker's pronunciation of the word "house" in which the onset of /aw/ was considerably raised. Although Detroiters associate this pronunciation with Canadians (even caricaturing it with an inaccurate /hus/ imitation), they quite regularly perform it themselves. She asked Detroit respondents to match this vowel with one of three others (synthesized tokens, which they had heard several times). The first (#2 in Table 1) is called "ultra-low" since it represented an onset considerably below the norm (for F1) for /a/ in local speech. The second is called "canonical" /a/ and represented the height of /a/ as given in Peterson and Barney (1952), an acoustic study of "General American" vowels. The third token to which the sample was to be matched is called "actual," and was the same token used in the sample itself, one in which the onset was considerably raised. Respondents heard these tokens mixed with others, but the presentation was significantly different for the two groups of respondents; one received an answer sheet which had the word "Canadian" prominently printed (in red) at the top of the page; the second group received an answer sheet with the word "Michigan" at the top. Any difference in token-matching by the two groups, therefore, can be attributed to that apparent regional identification.

Table 1. Influence of nationality labels on token selection (for "house")
(Niedzielski 1999)

token label		#2 ultra- low	#3 canonical /a/	#4 actual token	Total
CANADIAN		15%	25%	60%	
	n =	6	10	24	40
MICHIGAN		38%	51%	11%	
	n =	15	20	4	39

$$\chi^2 = 23.48$$
$$p < .001$$

As Table 1 shows, the labeling had a strong effect. Sixty percent of the forty respondents who had the word "Canadian" printed on their response sheets matched the token presented with the "actual" one (i.e., accurately) in contrast to only eleven percent of the thirty-nine who had sheets with "Michigan" written on them. Fully fifty-one percent of the respondents with the "Michigan" written cue heard the token as "canonical /a/" and thirty-eight percent even heard it as "ultra-low." It is obvious that the exterior identification of the home site of the sample voice exerted an enormous effect on the sound which was "heard" by the respondents.

So how do the results of this experiment fit our triangle? First, and almost inconsequentially, as it turns out, although Detroit-area respondents are aware of Canadian Raising (an *a* corner fact), they do not imitate it correctly (they say /hus/ instead of /hʌws/). So they have a *b1* corner consciousness of an *a* phenomenon, but an inaccurate one. That will not surprise folk linguistic investigators. Second, they make use of the false regional information supplied to them on their answer sheets (the voice they hear is identified as being from Michigan or from Canada when it is, in fact, always the same Michigan speaker), bringing it to bear on an apparently purely *a* task – the matching of two vowel sounds. Finally, and, of course, most interestingly, how does the *b1* corner awareness of region cause such inaccuracy in an *a* corner task? The *b'* information is not hard to locate in this case. As we have suggested most strongly in *Folk Linguistics*, a dominating concern among our respondents (all Michiganders, just like the ones Niedzielski has investigated here) is with prescription, and, of all places in the U.S., they regard themselves as the best speakers, residents of the mythic "heartland," where no dialect is spoken. Understanding this, the folk imposition on vowel perception is easy to understand. If Michiganders are speakers of standard English, then the most standard-like vowel is the one the Michigan speaker pronounced, regardless of acoustic reality.

In conclusion, the empowering folk beliefs of *b'*, the ultimate goal in our quest, not only influence the conscious and unconscious reflections on and reactions to language which are a part of the continuum we have suggested at the base of our redrawn triangle, but also interact with our perception of language data itself, the very stuff of *a*. We remain, therefore, convinced that a linguistics without folk linguistics does not explore the breadth and depth of language in communities – the regard in which it is held and even the ways in which it is processed and eventually modified in the progress of language change.

We hope readers of this new edition of *Folk Linguistics* will find in it the sorts of data and interpretations which will encourage them to explore similar data in their own speech communities, leading to comparisons with and challenges to our interpretations. Although we are most optimistic about the likely productivity of discoursal investigation on the one hand and experimentation with linguistic detail on the other, we encourage exploratory, wide-ranging investigations of the sort provided here. It's simply dangerous not to know what real people believe about language and how they respond to it – dangerous to general linguistics, dangerous to applied linguistics, and even debilitating to the desire for a complete account of language and its users. We hope new readers will find *Folk Linguistics* safe territory, for we hope to have ignored none of these dangers.

January 2003   Dennis R. Preston and Nancy Niedzielski

Note

1. We do not mean to suggest when we say that our U.S. respondents find language to be "cognitively external" that they believe there are no cognitive facts associated with language. They believe that adult second language learning requires intelligence, that nonstandard speakers are "lazy" or lack self-pride, that children cannot afford the psycholinguistic luxury of acquiring more than one language at a time, and so on. Nevertheless, they believe that "good language" resides somewhere outside human mental structures, waiting to be acquired (although with no great effort) by those who care. The political repercussions of such a belief are obvious. Those who have not bothered to improve themselves linguistically have only themselves to blame (e.g., Preston 2002).

References

Hoenigswald, Henry
   1966   A proposal for the study of folk linguistics. In William Bright (ed.), *Sociolinguistics*. 16–26. The Hague: Mouton.
Imai, Terumi
   2000   Folk linguistics and conversational argument. A paper presented at New Ways of Analyzing Variation (NWAV). East Lansing, MI, October.
Niedzielski, Nancy
   1999   The effect of social information on the perception of sociolinguistic variables. *Journal of Language and Social Psychology* (Lesley Milroy and Dennis R. Preston, (guest eds.), Special Issue: Attitudes, Perception, and Linguistic Features) 18.1: 62–85.
Peterson, G. and H. Barney
   1952   Control methods used in a study of the vowels. *Journal of the Acoustical Society of America* 24 (2): 175–184.
Preston, Dennis R.
   1993   The uses of folk linguistics. *International Journal of Applied Linguistics* 3: 181–259.
   1994   Content-oriented discourse analysis and folk linguistics. *Language Sciences* 16: 285–330.
   1996   "Whaddayaknow": The modes of folk linguistic awareness. *Language Awareness* 5: 40–74.
   2002   The story of good and bad English in the United States. In Richard Watts and Peter Trudgill (eds.), *Alternative Histories of English*. 134–151. London: Routledge.

Schiffrin, Deborah
  1985   Everyday argument: the organization of diversity in talk. In Teun A. van Dijk (ed.), *Handbook of Discourse Analysis 3*: 35–46. London: Academic Press.

Foreword

One of the most exciting things that is happening in the academic world today is the small steps we are beginning to make towards destroying ... elitism. Although the trend for many years was toward ever-increasing degrees of specialization with concomitant scorn for all that was not specialized, such a position is less well received in today's world. (Shuy 1973:313)

This is a book of *stankos*, a term Leonard Bloomfield's family used to describe the language beliefs of nonlinguists.[1] It is no accident that it looks like a noun form of *stank*, for Bloomfield held the opinion of nonlinguists in low regard; many linguists have shared and continue to share that opinion.

We have sought out and even encouraged stankos, for we believe that what the folk believe about language deserves careful consideration. This is justified along several lines:

1. The study of folk beliefs about language is one of the ethnographies of a culture. In ethnobotany one wants to learn (at least) a culture's beliefs about the naming of, relationships among, and uses for plants. Ethnolinguistics should do the same, but the contrast between folk and scientific linguistics will be more complex than that between many other ethnosciences and their academic partners, particularly in a nonhomogeneous, post-modern society.

The role of language and its attendant beliefs ought to be set in the larger framework of the culture under investigation, for ethnolinguistics may not be just more complex than ethnobotany or ethnogeology, but more complex in subtle ways. If it is believed (and reported) that a certain plant is good for settling the stomach, it would be odd to find it seldom used for that purpose (unless some taboo restricted its use). A contrast between belief and use in language, however, is not an uncommon state of affairs; this apparent mismatch requires greater subtlety in combining an ethnolinguistics with a study of language in use.[2]

2. In the general area of applied linguistics, folk linguistics surely plays a most important role. When professionals want to have influence, they are, we believe, ill-advised to ignore popular belief, and, as we have discovered in our fieldwork for this book, popular belief about language is both ubiquitous and strong. It is surely as risky for a linguist to try to influence the public as it is for a doctor to try to

treat a population without knowing that *the sugar* is their local folk term for diabetes.

3. Finally, folk linguistic beliefs may help determine the shape of language itself. It would be unusual to discover that what nonlinguists believe about language has nothing to do with linguistic change; in one sense, of course, that has been a principal focus of investigation in the more than thirty year old tradition of quantitative (or "Labovian") sociolinguistics.

Penultimately, a word about the folk in this book. We use *folk* to refer to those who are not trained professionals in the area under investigation (although we would not for one moment deny the fact that professional linguists themselves are also a folk group, with their own rich set of beliefs). We definitely do not use *folk* to refer to rustic, ignorant, uneducated, backward, primitive, minority, isolated, marginalized, or lower status groups or individuals. That is an outdated use in folklore and an absolutely useless one for our purposes. We intend to study the texture of folk belief about language in a speech community, and we include the beliefs of respondents from a great variety of backgrounds. To do otherwise would be to assume that folklore and cultural anthropology are not doable where we live. We also adopt from modern folklore the notion that folk belief is simply belief, its folk character being no indication of its truth or falsity.

Finally, we hold to the notion that the study of folk behavior is dynamic as well as static. We have observed the routes the folk follow in thinking through problems about language as well as the contents of their prepackaged items and structures of belief.

Acknowledgments

The authors are first of all grateful to their colleagues who served as fieldworkers during the two-semester seminar in sociolinguistics and folk linguistics held at Eastern Michigan University during the 1987-88 academic year. Without their good contacts, thoughtful interviews, and careful transcriptions, this work could never have been done. Next in line come our respondents – all those who put up with the silly questions and demands of linguists; they have been patient and forthcoming. We hope only that our open-ended style of interviewing gave them some fun as well as us some profit.

The authors gratefully acknowledge the support of the National Science Foundation (BNS-8711267) and the Graduate School and Office of Research Development of Eastern Michigan University; of course, they are not responsible for the conclusions reached here, only for the subvention of some of the time and wherewithal to reach them.

Our colleagues at Eastern Michigan University, The University of California at Santa Barbara, and Michigan State University have put up with folk linguistics for a long time. We thank them for their patience as well as their insights. We are especially grateful to Patricia M. Clancy of UCSB who gave us important advice for 4.1 (First-language acquisition.)

Werner Winter, the Editor of this series, read the manuscript for this book with great care. We are indebted to him for both substantive and stylistic suggestions.

Carol Preston read every word in this book. She is more than a little responsible for whatever clarity and stylistic panache it has; we will have to claim responsibility for the rest.

Contents

List of figures

List of tables

Transcription conventions

1. [[simultaneous utterances (A and B start talking at the same time)

    A: [[I used to party a lot when I was younger
    B: [[I used to study linguistics until

2. [overlapping utterances (B begins to talk while A is talking)

    A: I had a lot of trouble with morphology
    　　　　　　　[
    B:　　　　I see

3.]   end of overlapping or simultaneous utterance (not used unless
         the duration of the overlap is not well represented by the
         physical size of the transcription)

    A: I had a lot of trouble with - uh - morphology.
    　　　　　　　[ ]
    B:　　　　Oh! Did you really?

4. =   linked or continuing utterances (no overlap, but no pause between
         utterances)

    a. for different speakers

        1) single

            A: I like functionalism=
            B: =No wonder.

        2) more than one (in either first or second position)

            A: I like functionalism=
            B: =[[No wonder.
            C: =[[So do I!

    b. for the same speaker (a continuation device based only on page width
    limitations; see also 10. below)

A: I wanted to study a non-Indo-European language before=
           [
B: You did.
A: =starting my Ph.D.

5. Intervals

a. -   untimed (brief), within utterances (See also 6.j. below)

A: I thought - uh - I would go home.

b. **((pause))**   untimed (brief), between utterances

A: What do you think.
   ((pause))
B: Well. - I don't know.

c. 1.0, 3.0, 0.5, etc… times within and between utterances (in tenths of a second)

6. Delivery

a. : length (repeated to show greater length)

A: Way to go:.
B: Yeah. Way to go::.

b. . falling ("final") intonation (followed by a noticeable pause, not based on grammatical considerations)

A: By the way.

c. , continuing ("list") intonation (a slight rise or fall followed by a short pause, again, not based on grammatical considerations)

A: I saw Bill,

d. ? rising ("question") intonation (followed by a noticeable pause, again not based on grammatical considerations)

A: He left?

e. **CAPS** emphasis (emphatic or contrastive stress — "I" is underlined)

A: He LEFT?

f.   **(hhh)**   breathe out and **(.hhh)** breathe in

A: (.hhh) Oh, thank you.
B: (hhh) That's a break.

g.   **(( ))**   noises, kinds of talk, comments

A: I used to ((cough)) smoke too much.
      ((telephone rings))

h.   **!**   animated talk

A: Look out for that rock!

i.   **(h)**   breathiness (usually laughter)

A: I wou(h)ldn't do that.

j.   **-**   abrupt cutoff (glottal stop, always attached to what precedes; N.B.: when - is used for pause [5.a above] it is never attached to what precedes)

A: Look ou-

7.   **( )**   transcriber doubt

a. a guess at the words in question

A: I (suppose I'm not)

b. a guess at some part of the words in question

B: We all (t-   )

c. no guess at the words in question

A: (   )

d. two equally reasonable guesses at the words in question

A: I $\left\{ \begin{array}{l} \text{(spoke to Mark)} \\ \text{(suppose I'm not)} \end{array} \right.$

8. [ ]   phonetic transcription

   A: I saw the dog [dag]

9. --------------------------- omitted material from the same conversation

   A: I used to smoke too much.

   A: My uncle Harry died of lung cancer.

10. Enumeration: In some conversations analyzed and cited here, "lines" are numbered each time there is a speaker change associated with a line change. These numbers, therefore, mark no grammatical or discoursal units of text. In the following, for example, 72 R and 74 R are part of the same utterance but have different numbers because they are interrupted by the beginning of the 73-75 D contribution, itself separated in the same way.

   72 R: So it's h- it's hard for me to rem- think you know (of) Black=
                                 [
   73 D: Course you did cause your - =
   74 R: =dialect.
   75 D: =brothers, your brothers used it quite a bit. (#35)

11. Citation form: When the conversations collected for this study are cited, participants are identified by an initial following the number, if any (see above); the conversation itself is identified by a number in parentheses at the end of the quotation (see above). The appendix provides more complete identification of the participants and the conversational settings. Since initials may be repeated across (but not within) conversations, it will be important to note the conversation number to keep identities straight.

12. Spelling: When pronunciation is focused on, phonetic transcription is used; we particularly avoid (and deplore) the "folk respellings" employed in some conversation studies. In our opinion, they serve only to caricature respondents and/or detract from readability (Preston 1982b, 1983, 1985).

Chapter 1: Introduction

Folk linguistics has not fared well in the history of the science, and linguists have generally taken an "us" versus "them" position. From a scientific perspective, folk beliefs about language are, at best, innocent misunderstandings of language (perhaps only minor impediments to introductory linguistic instruction) or, at worst, the bases of prejudice, leading to the continuation, reformulation, rationalization, justification, and even development of a variety of social injustices.

There is no doubt that comments on language, what Bloomfield called "secondary responses," may both amuse and annoy linguists when they are made by nonprofessionals, and there is no doubt, as well, that the folk are not happy to have some of these notions contradicted (Bloomfield's "tertiary response"):

> A physician, of good general background and education, who had been hunting in the north woods, told me that the Chippewa language contains only a few hundred words. Upon question, he said that he got this information from his guide, a Chippewa Indian. When I tried to state the diagnostic setting, the physician, our host, briefly and with signs of displeasure repeated his statement and then turned his back on me. A third person, observing this discourtesy, explained that I had some experience of the language in question. This information had no effect. (Bloomfield 1944 [1970:418])

Although Bloomfield is perhaps most annoyed by Dr. X's misinformation, he is also unhappy with his inability to accept expert advice (and, perhaps, the emotional manner with which it was rejected).[1]

It is, however, what Bloomfield calls "the diagnostic setting" which concerns us. Bloomfield doubtless has a complete understanding of the linguistic facts (Chippewa has more than a few hundred words!), but his account of the social and psychological impulses which influence the beliefs of Dr. X are speculative. We must infer what Bloomfield believes to be "the diagnostic setting," but it is not hard for a professional linguist to do so:

1. Nonlinguists often believe some languages are primitive, impoverished in various ways, including vocabulary size.
2. Nonlinguists often believe in an ethnic or racial genetics of language; therefore, a Chippewa guide can speak Chippewa.

3. Nonlinguists often believe there is no such thing as a science of language; therefore, native speakers (the guide) and intelligent laypersons (Dr. X) are authorities.

Our concern is that Bloomfield, as we have here, has imagined rather than discovered this set of folk-linguistic beliefs. They may be the proper inferences to have been drawn from Dr. X's behavior, but we have very little evidence to go on. The complex set of beliefs Dr. X holds about language and linguistics is not further investigated. From an ethnographic point of view, Bloomfield has carried out a participant-observation study of a few minutes and reached a conclusion. Folk linguistics surely requires more time. We hope to show how the data of linguistic folk belief may be more systematically collected and interpreted, and this first chapter sets our study in a broader historical framework and describes the way we went about collecting our data.

1.1 Background

The tradition is much older,[2] but we shall date interest in folk linguistics from the 1964 UCLA Sociolinguistics Conference and Hoenigswald's presentation there entitled "A proposal for the study of folk-linguistics" (Hoenigswald 1966).

> ... we should be interested not only in (*a*) what goes on (language), but also in (*b*) how people react to what goes on (they are persuaded, they are put off, etc.) and in (*c*) what people say goes on (talk concerning language). It will not do to dismiss these secondary and tertiary modes of conduct merely as sources of error. (Hoenigswald 1966:20)

Hoenigswald lays out a broadly-conceived plan for the study of talk about language, including collections of the folk expressions for various speech acts and of the folk terminology for, and the definitions of, grammatical categories such as *word* and *sentence*. He proposes uncovering folk accounts of homonymy and synonymy, regionalism and language variety, and social structure (e.g., age, sex) as reflected in speech. He suggests that particular attention be paid to folk accounts of the correcting of linguistic behavior, especially in the context of first-language acquisition and in relation to accepted ideas of correctness and acceptability. He recommends asking what sorts of language and speech styles are admired and what sorts have special status under the general rubric of taboo. He urges researchers to seek historical folk-linguistic accounts as well as folk accounts of language abnormalities (e.g., stuttering, muteness).

1.1.1 Objections to folk-linguistic study

This wide-ranging set of suggestions has been taken up very little in subsequent work, at least in any general or systematic way, and we shall deal first with reasons for that failure before exploring some precursors to the work reported on here. That folk-beliefs are simply unscientific and worthy only of disdain is an opinion we have already illustrated in our citation of Bloomfield above and dismissed in our Foreword[3]; here we turn to two more sophisticated objections, one which suggests that folk linguistics is impoverished, another which suggests it is largely inaccessible.

1.1.1.1 Impoverishment of data. The impoverishment issue is raised by Labov immediately following Hoenigswald's 1964 presentation:

> The overt responses in American and English society generally are quite poor as far as vocabulary is concerned. "Poverty-stricken" would be the best term for this vocabulary. The inadequacy of people's overt remarks about their own language is directly reflected in the fact that there are only a few words that they use to convey the subjective response that they feel. ... But some of the references made here today show that there are highly institutionalized folk attitudes toward language which are much richer than those which we are accustomed to meeting in the U.S. and England. (Labov, discussion of Hoenigswald 1966:23)

That a folk vocabulary is inadequate is a strange notion. If one could show that there is a strong pattern of responses which the folk are interested in talking about but are incapable of doing so due to vocabulary deficiency, then one might say that a language or variety was inadequate. We believe, however, that a language would not long languish in such inadequacy; if the concept has worked its way out into the open, it will surely get a word. (The Bloomfields had no trouble coming up with *stanko*!) In his own work, Labov singles out features which rather obviously do have labels and makes the point that they are linguistic *stereotypes*, items which are the subject matter of speech-community comment (e.g., Labov 1972a:248). If Labov means only to say that the folk lack a vocabulary to describe that of which they are not aware, we do not object, although, as suggested above, we shall have more to say about *aware*, especially in 1.1.2.

Perhaps Labov's judgment of Anglo-American folk linguistic impoverishment reflects the focus in his New York City studies; his two examples of the vocabulary he characterizes come from phonology (*nasal* and *twang*). From the point of view of linguistic structure, he does not speak of folk terminology (or concern) for morphology, lexicon (including meaning), grammar, semantics, or higher levels of discourse organization or genre type. From other perspectives still central to general linguistics, he does not speak of folk notions of language origin, spread, and change, nor of those of acquisition (first or second), multilingualism, and intelligibility. He does not comment, either, on whether a rich or minimal terminology exists for a host of social linguistic phenomena (many of which are so carefully elaborated in his own work): region, age, ethnicity, status, and the like along with attendant interactional and situational characteristics of formality, power, setting, solidarity, and so on. (See Preston 1986b for an attempt to gather together the range of such concerns.) In short, if phonological folk-linguistic terminology is small in the Anglo-American tradition (a conclusion with which we tend to agree; see below), that is no reason to abandon the rest of the field.

We also believe that Labov has been too hasty in dismissing what folk-linguistic information he *has* uncovered. His account of *nasal* is as follows:

> Frequently, if you ask somebody what he thinks of this style of speech (nasalized), he'll say it's very "nasal"; and if you produce a speech of this sort (denasalized), he'll say that's very "nasal" too. In other words, the denasalized speech characteristics of some urban areas and extremely nasalized speech are treated in the same way. (Labov, discussion of Hoenigswald 1966:23-4)

Disregarding this folk account overlooks both its sophistication and the clues it carries for further investigation.

It is sophisticated phonetically, for the respondents Labov describes use *nasal* to describe a nasal phenomenon; whether over- or underemployed, it is that feature (accurately) they hit upon.[4] More importantly, the hint for further research is buried by the contention that nasalized and denasalized speech are "treated in the same way." There are two problems lurking here: 1. Does the fact that they are labeled in the same way mean that they are treated in the same way? The attitudinal responses to denasalized speech might be considerably different from those to nasalized speech. If that is so, then Labov's complaint that the folk terminology is limited might be correct, as we acknowledge above; respondents might react differently to nasalized and denasalized forms, but have no terminology to differentiate these perceptually distinct stimuli, for the specific linguistic features which influence the behavior are not analytically known. That does not entail, however, that the different stimuli are "treated in the same way." 2. Does the ambiguous folk-phonetic terminology mask other unambiguous terminology which might consistently differentiate nasalized and denasalized speakers (e.g., *whiney* versus *doltish*, respectively)?[5] The misunderstandings lurking here may spring from linguists and/or the folk having missing terms in their accounts, sharing terms with different meanings, or even constructing systems in different ways. Figure 1.1 contrasts two models.

At level 1, terminological richness is greater for the linguists, who have a name for the phenomenon in general, but the first component of level 2 is a draw; neither linguists nor the folk have a term which refers specifically to appropriately nasalized speech, although that is undoubtedly one of the requirements for such generalized folk evaluations as *pleasant* or *normal*. In the second component of level 2, there is a folk term. What is "nasal" is "inappropriately nasalized," a describable concept for the linguist, but one without a specific term. Level 3 is also a draw; both linguists and nonlinguists have terms for the subcategories of inappropriately nasalized speech. Although this examination suggests that the folk vocabulary may be as large as the linguistic one for some of the elements it covers, it may also differ considerably from the technical one.

For example, the terminological mismatch which bothers Labov occurs between component two of level 2 in the folk taxonomy and component one of level 3 in the linguistic one: the folk use "nasal" for inappropriate amounts of nasality on either end of the scale; linguists use the form most like it ("nasalized") for only the excessive end.[6]

Of course, the folk have been permitted to change point of view (at least from a scientific perspective) in order to fill out their taxonomy. What began as a discussion of raised or lowered velum turned to one of personality or attitude. One of the styles of characterizing data demanded and admired by science is a consistent point of view; no such stringent demand is made on the folk. Such shifts, however, make folk taxonomies elaborate and overlapping, and the elicitation, characterization, and interpretation of folk belief is made both more complex and rewarding as a result. We shall refer to the need to examine the shifting perspective of folk respondents throughout.[7]

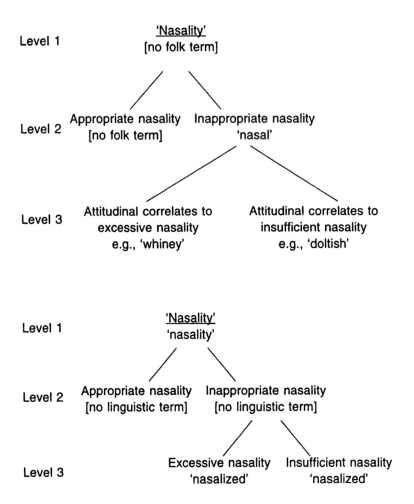

Figure 1.1 Folk (top) and linguistic (bottom) taxonomies of "nasality"

Our treatment of folk-linguistic data takes these complex shifts into consideration and tries to set them in a dynamic context of actual use, not in a static one of folk linguistic knowledge. This point of view has allowed us to find an abundant traditional and creative folk linguistics, one operating at many levels of linguistic structure and in many areas of language concern. Although his focus is on vocabulary, Sherzer reflects this general attitude in the following:

... terms for talk ... are communicative resources which vary from person to person and from context to context and are used strategically in the course of speaking. In addition, there are significant features of ... language and speech that are not labeled, and there are labels that are ambiguous without reference to contextualization in concrete instances of usage. (Sherzer 1983:16)

1.1.1.2 Inaccessibility of data. The second impediment to folk linguistic research has been the touted inaccessibility to the folk consciousness of linguistically interesting matters. Although we agree that there is much that is not available to folk awareness, that concern has been overworked. There are at least four such research traditions which cast doubt on ordinary speakers' abilities to bring linguistic phenomena into awareness:

1. General linguistics: Attempting to discover the hidden organizational principles of language design, linguists have teased out information from native speakers. Observing that people in a speech community respond differently to, say, the two phonetic strings [pʰit] and [pʰIt], the linguist begins to ask if a number of pairs such as [bit] – [bIt] and [lid] – [lId] are the same or different. The native speaker notes that they are all different, for, indeed, one may dig *peat* [pʰit] from a *pit* [pʰIt] but not vice versa, and so on. Thus the linguist discovers and is able to give a verbal account of the fact that the speakers of this language distinguish phonemically between the high front tense vowel [i] and the high front lax vowel [I], a terminology representing a set of concepts apparently not available to the awareness of the native speakers. Similar operations may expose other levels of structure. In attempting to discover the status of /swIm/, the linguist finds from native speakers that it is insertable into frames such as *I can* _____ *and I* _____ *every morning* but not into those such as *I know* _____ *or* _____ *know you*. Eventually some such technical term as *verb* is used to describe the membership class to which this item belongs. Traditional linguistic theory, therefore, is an attempt to *know about* what the native speaker simply knows how to do. Generally speaking, home-grown attempts of the speakers themselves to know about language are disregarded.

With the advent of interest in semanto-syntax, the areas of knowing about became so abstract compared to the earlier interest in the closed sets of phonemes and word classes that nonlinguist native speakers were often circumvented. Linguists began to focus more deeply on their own languages and tested their intuitions concerning marginal constructions which pushed the limits of their growing understanding of the operating principles of language itself. It simply took too much explanation or "respondent training" to get a naive native speaker to avoid consideration of social and other influences not at stake in the linguist's judgment of grammaticality. For example, it takes considerable pains to get a nonlinguist to admit that *He sent a letter to himself* is ungrammatical (or not well-formed) if the intended reading is one in which *he* and *himself* are not coreferential. They *are* coreferential for the nonlinguist, and the idea that that sentence is in any sense an exemplar of their noncoreferentiality (and is, therefore, ungrammatical) is a heady exercise in abstraction. Attempts to short-cut the abstraction in psycholinguistic experiments using cleverly constructed sample sentences which contrasted at just the points of concern have often proved unwieldy, and many modern grammarians are happy to be their own sources of information on grammaticality.[8]

2. Social psychology: Attitudinal responses to the nonpropositional aspects of linguistic performance have been elicited from the folk. In the classic model of this research (Lambert et al. 1960), one speaker (to avoid voice-quality influences) provides two performances (hidden among others and at some distance from one another) – the *matched guise* technique. The two performances vary the feature under investigation (e. g., the first performance is French, the second English; the first performance contains no [or fewer] examples of a post-vocalic /r/, the second no deletions [or fewer], and so on). The respondents rate these performances along scales like the following:

ugly _____ _____ _____ _____ _____ _____ _____ pretty

The polar opposites for these scales have been drawn from surveys in which respondents have been asked to list adjectives which describe speech and language (a step often skipped, since many researchers rely on lists derived from earlier work). Means scores and factor analyses of the judgments of these pairs are then computed. A finding common to many speech communities is that respondents value local, nonstandard varieties for honesty, sincerity, and the like, and superposed, standard varieties for intelligence, industry, and so on (e.g., Ryan, Giles, and Sebastian 1982).

The degree of awareness of the linguistic variable is not really at stake in such studies. In some cases (e.g., French versus English), the respondents obviously have a folk awareness and terminology to describe the variation. In others, they have a folk awareness of the variable, but specific post-task interviews (of ratings of more or less stop versus fricative performances of /θ/ and /ð/ in New York City, for example) show that in some cases they cannot name the variable being manipulated in the performance on which their evaluations were based (Labov 1966:315). In still others, respondents can characterize the global difference between varieties (e.g., regional differences) but cannot name specific lower-level features, and in still others, respondents have neither global nor specific labels to attach to varieties or features which they, nevertheless, show a consistent pattern of differentiated responses to.

What is sought in language attitude research is, therefore, not any linguistic level. One does not ask if French is *nicer* than English or if post-vocalic /r/ deletion is *less intelligent* than its presence. Those underlying questions are submerged in a search for responses to a wide variety of evaluations which mediate between the speakers or sorts of speakers to whom such evaluations might be assigned and the linguistic facts which guide them. A language attitude is, after all, not really an attitude to a language feature; it is an awakening of a set of beliefs about individuals or sorts of individuals through the filter of a linguistic performance, although, admittedly, association with a linguistic feature and a group may be so long-standing that the attitude appears to be to the linguistic feature itself (e.g., Milroy and McClenaghan 1977).

Such matched-guise and other tests presumably circumvent respondent tendencies in more direct questioning to take positions which present an optimum image of self to the interviewer (even if the interviewer is hidden behind a paper-and-pencil task). In general, language attitude research seeks folk information but tries to get around the conscious, reflective processes of folk reasoning and/or interaction. It avoids a report of the attitude, inferring it from responses to samples of use.

3. Quantitative sociolinguistics: Sociolinguists have made use of attitude studies, often modified to measure specific rather than global features and often used in conjunction with scales of social status (e.g., job titles) rather than with paired adjectives. The more general suspicion of folk awareness in quantitative sociolinguistics, however, runs deeper. The reasoning goes as follows: When people are aware that their speech is being investigated, their self-monitoring devices are turned up. The resulting performances are a combination of their unconscious, most systematic (*vernacular*) language rules and superposed models of schooling, proscription, prescription, erudition, deference, defensiveness, formality, and who knows what else. Observed language is, therefore, least like systematic, unreflective rule-oriented behavior, the description of which is, presumably, the goal of linguistics. Since recordings of actual language use awaken this

monitor and since surreptitious collection is difficult, illegal, and/or unethical, sociolinguists are confronted with the *observer's paradox* (e.g., Labov 1972a:209).

This sociolinguistic rubric which addresses use seems to have rubbed off on accounts of use. It is likely that when respondents are questioned about language, those same influences which are at play in the performance monitor are highlighted, and the account given reflects them rather than vernacular attitudes and opinions.

4. Ethnographic approaches: It may seem unusual for ethnographic approaches to be listed among those lines of research which devalue folk opinion, but, no matter how broadly conceived the modern ethnography of speaking has become, there remains in it a decided prejudice for getting at the meaning of behavior not open to the folk. Ethnosensitive participant-observers are able to see through superficial activity (and folk accounts of it) and come up with interpretations of the structure and covert meanings of behavior. Some such scholarship includes contrasts of folk accounts with observation and interpretation, and a grounded ethnography specifically uses folk explanation of behavior. In the long run, such work still seeks a contrast between the folk account and the trained observer's account, the latter intended to seek levels unknown to the former.

Since, however, talk about talk is itself a behavior, ethnographers have been forced to attend to the subject matter of this book, and we shall have a little more to say about some of these successful enterprises later.

1.1.2 Folk-linguistic awareness

If the folk talk about language, they must, of course, know (or at least believe they know) about it. Silverstein (1981) attempts to describe the sorts of linguistic detail which are more (and less) likely to be available to folk scrutiny (or awareness). He suggests five conditions which predict (or enhance) such awareness: 1. unavoidable referentiality, 2. continuous segmentability, 3. relative presuppositionality, 4. decontextualized deducibility, and 5. metapragmatic transparency. Since these are not folk-linguistic terms themselves, we provide the following glosses:

1. Linguistic units either point to something (in a real or ideational world) or they do not; that is, they either do or do not have "reference." Silverstein illustrates "unavoidable referentiality" with the deference-to-hearer versus solidarity-with-hearer pragmatic system of many European languages – e.g., German *Sie* (deferential)

versus *du* (solidary); French *vous* (deferential) versus *tu* (solidary). These items are unavoidably referential, for, although they carry the pragmatic meaning of deference and solidarity, at the same time, they refer to individuals – e.g., *du* does not just "mean" solidarity (in the pragmatic system); it also "means" *you* (in the referential system) (Silverstein 1981:5). In contrast, the raising of the low-front vowel (i.e., [æ] to [ɛ] or even [I]) in northern U.S. cities (e.g., Labov 1994) is also richly pragmatic, carrying at least such speaker and situational characteristics as gender, status, area (rural versus urban), and degree of formality. On the other hand, the low-front vowel (in any of its guises), is not in itself referential. That is, the low-front vowel – or, as sociolinguists prefer to say, the variable (æ), for it may be pronounced in a non-low front position – does not by itself pick out or refer to anything in the real or ideational world.

Silverstein suggests that the pragmatic meanings of unavoidably referential forms are more likely to be a part of folk-linguistic awareness, and in the case of the examples given above, he is correct. Europeans are aware of the pragmatic system symbolized by alternative forms of the second-person singular pronoun; they even discuss it, we are told, when linguists are not within earshot. On the contrary, residents of such places as Detroit, where the low-front vowel raising described above is going on, are overtly aware of neither the change in progress nor of the pragmatic meanings the change supports.

It is possible to think of folk-linguistic exceptions to Silverstein's predictions. For example, the items *can* and *could*, which clearly bear some referential load, are part of a pragmatic politeness system (Brown and Levinson 1987); past-marked modal auxiliaries (e.g., *could*, *would*) are "more polite" than non-past-marked forms (e.g., *can*, *will*). Native speakers of English, who unconsciously apply the system and even rate the forms appropriately on "scale of politeness" tests, are not, however, usually overtly aware of the pragmatic opposition. Perhaps the low-level or "abstract" referentiality of such forms as modals (and other "structure" words) contributes to their subconscious rather than overt realization as members of pragmatic systems.

On the other hand, the presence or absence of nonprevocalic /r/ in New York City speech, although highly symbolic in the pragmatic system (i.e., /r/-presence symbolizing higher social class membership and greater formality and /r/-absence symbolizing the opposite), is not, in itself, referential. In this case, however, /r/ has become a linguistic "stereotype" (Labov 1972a), an item which, regardless of its referentiality, is fully available to the awareness of speech-community members. It is impossible, therefore, to predict accurately on the basis of linguistic status alone which items *may* play a part in the folk linguist's conscious repertoire, and the remaining four of Silverstein's predictors will have similar probabilistic rather than categorical values.

In some other cases, however, a nonreferential linguistic level (e.g., phonology) may be available to folk awareness, but in a general or "global" way. Folk respondents are aware, for example, of some undifferentiated non-native accents, dialect varieties (often those which awaken no strong attitudinal responses), temporary speech disturbances (e.g., colds, drunkenness), superposed prescriptions, and so on. What is interesting about just these examples is that, although phonology is the area referred to in the account, specific items are usually not available to the folk.

> B: A friend of mine was from North er yeah she's from North Dakota and when she came here she lived here for several years and she had a funny? way of describing the way midwesterners talk.
> M: Um hum.
> B: And she'd say you guys talk real funny. She said you talk up and down. And she said out in North Dakota we talk sideways. I said D. Explain that to me what is up and down and sideways talk. She said that's the only way I can describe it. (#38)[9]

Here we may be tempted to agree with Labov that, at least in the Anglo-American tradition, folk terms for phonological matters (intonation?) are lacking. Another of our respondents says her older relatives spoke with a strong Polish accent, but she could offer no details. Such general references to pronunciation contrast sharply with specific accounts of items usually when the folk view has been shaped by a strong attitudinal caricature:

> J: (imitating "New Jersey" speech) Twe- [twi] tree little boids, sitting on a coib - eating doity woi(h)- - eating doity woims and saying=
>   [[
> M: ((laughs))   ((laughs))
> J: =doity woids. (#38)

Here J, although he may not be able to articulate it in the following terms, is clearly "aware" of a rule which substitutes the diphthong $[\partial^{\text{i}}]$ for a syllabic [r] in New York City speech. It seems extremely unlikely, in the face of the variety of words in the above little poem and in other instantiations of this rule we have in our data, that this is a lexical (hence referential) rule.

We have strayed, however, from our explication of Silverstein's probabilistic conditions for folk awareness, and we return to that list and reserve for later comment the levels and types of awareness which play a role in the folk characterization of language.

2. The second of Silverstein's requirements is "continuous segmentability." Linguistic units which the folk are most likely to be aware of are not interrupted by other material. In "I am going to town," the entire sentence, each word, phrases such as *to town*, and even inseparable morphemes such as *-ing* are all continuously segmentable. The form which refers to the progressive aspect, however, is *am -ing* (or, more abstractly, *be -ing*) and always displays discontinuity in English (Silverstein 1981:6).

In our data, however, in a rather lengthy discussion of the passive, an equally discontinuous phenomenon (i.e., *be + -en*), several respondents provide evidence for considerable folk awareness (5.3.2). That the speakers involved are well-educated does not, as we have already stated, deter us from describing the data gleaned from this interaction (and others like it) as folk linguistics. Subject-verb agreement (a clearly discontinuous dependency) and split infinitives are also frequently discussed phenomena, but, like the non-referential items discussed above, they all seem to qualify as exceptions to Silverstein's rules on the basis of their status as linguistic stereotypes, further evidence, perhaps, of the dominating concern of prescription (and proscription) in folk comment.

3. "Relative presuppositionality" refers to the degree to which a pragmatic function of language depends on other factors to realize its meaning. The higher the relative presuppositionality, the greater the chance for folk awareness. At the high end of this scale are such items as *this* and *that*, which successfully function only if there is a physical reality to which they can be linked, a relative physical (or metaphoric mental) distance which supports the choice between them, or a prior mention of some entity (Silverstein 1981:7). It is important not to confuse this strict dependency which is a feature of items with high relative presuppositionality with the more general notion of context sensitivity. An item like *here*, with very high relative presuppositionality, is, in fact, not very context sensitive, neither to the surrounding linguistic nor nonlinguistic context. *Here* means the same thing in a wide variety of tense-aspect configurations ("He's on his way here"; "I've been here before") and in a church or in a saloon.

At the other end of the scale, phonological matters have no dependency on a specific element in the surrounding linguistic or nonlinguistic world. A nonprevocalic /r/, for example, is always just a nonprevocalic /r/. Nothing like "a locus" (necessary for *here*) or "previous mention of a female person" (necessary for *she*) provides "meaning" to nonprevocalic /r/.

Although there is considerable evidence that the folk are aware of the sort of creative pragmatic marking made by speakers who use more or less of one form or another, even at the level of phonology (where relative presuppositionality is lowest), it is also the case that such awareness, as we have already suggested, appears to develop from associated attitudes about speakers, attitudes which make stereotypes out of linguistic elements. The same might be said of lower-level grammatical features (e.g., agreement) whose referentiality is low, particularly in a language such as English.

4. "Decontextualized deducibility" refers to those linguistic items which can be given a ready meaning by folk respondents without extensive reference to context. Here Silverstein apparently means to refer to the general sort of context excluded from the strict dependencies described in 3) immediately above. The more elaborate the context one needs to differentiate an opposition or pragmatic contrast, the less likely it will be available to folk awareness. Nevertheless, Silverstein claims that when the folk comment on linguistic objects, they tend to specify the "deducible entailed presuppositions," which, he says, is the equivalent of stating the meaning. In other words, providing the contexts in which the use of the form in question fits or is true is a common folk linguistic activity (Silverstein 1981:13-4).

We encounter this approach often among the folk, particularly in discussions of the meaning of words. The fit between increasingly specified contexts and the conditions under which the word can be said to belong is a ploy explicitly remarked on by D in the following:

[In a discussion of Christmas customs, H (the fieldworker) has asked if there is any difference between *gift* and *present*; D has said earlier there is not, but he returns to the question.]

D: Oftentimes a gift is something like you you go to a Tupperware party and they're going to give you a gift, it's- I think it's more=
                                                           [
H: Uh huh.
D: =impersonal, - than a present.
              [
G: No, there's no difference.
                                  [
D: No? There's real- yeah there's
really no difference.
      [

G:　　　　　There is no difference.
D: That's true. Maybe the way we use it is though.
U: Maybe we could look it up and see what "gift" means.
　　　　　　　　　　　　[
D:　　　　　　　　　　　　　I mean technically
there's no difference. (#28)
((They then look up *gift* and *present* in the dictionary.))

D's distinction between "technical" meaning[10] and "use" points in the direction of "decontextualized deducibility"; that is, although he feels the words mean the same at some definitional level which is open to expert knowledge, the fit of the words into different contexts may reveal distinctions. After some time passes in the conversation, he comes up with an appropriate frame:

D: In advertising sometimes they'll say: you know, "We have a gift for you." Or- or something.
　[
H: Yes, yes.
H: But they don't use "present."
D: Um: - I don't think as much. (#28)

D goes on to say that his bank offers a *gift* if one opens an account; *present* would be unlikely in that context. The finely-tuned characterization of meaning is determined through the folk activity of matching the item to those contexts which meet the required characteristics.

5. Finally, "metapragmatic transparency." When the folk characterize what went on, they are more likely to reproduce exactly what was said only if the performance was a "metapragmatically transparent" one. Suppose that Wanda is cold and that Karla is near the thermostat. Wanda has a number of options:

Brrrrrrrrr!
I'm freezing.
Aren't you cold? I wonder if the furnace is broken?
Would you mind if we had a little more heat in here?
Turn up the heat.
etc.

"Turn up the heat" has the greatest metapragmatic transparency. Accounts of the interaction between Wanda and Karla are more likely to result in an observation that "Wanda asked Karla to turn up the heat" than in an embedding of any of the other request forms. ("Wanda said 'Aren't you cold?' and by that meant for Karla to turn up the heat" would be a strange folk report.) In other words, folk awareness seems to focus on direct rather than indirect speech acts.

Although we have little occasion in our data to observe such translated reports of speech activities, we do have evidence of folk awareness of indirection. In one case the fieldworker relates a story of a foreign student's cool reception at the home of a US student who had asked her to "Come and see me sometime." A respondent tells the fieldworker that "Yeah, sometimes what is necessarily SAID, is not – what is actually meant." (G, #36a)

Except for these occasional counterexamples, however, we agree in general with Silverstein's generalizations about those cognitive and linguistic aspects of language which are likely to hinder or advance accessibility. We believe, as we have already hinted, however, that nearly all of them can be overcome (or exaggerated) by factors yet to be discussed. We do not discuss here, however, other ("nonlinguistic") concerns which may influence accessibility: memory, attentiveness, and other such cognitive factors and their correlation with both simple (e.g., part of speech, linguistic level) and complex (e.g., "transformational complexity") linguistic factors. Doubtless these are important matters, and they deserve attention (Preston 1996).

1.1.2.1 Communicative primacy. We add to these considerations of Silverstein's a more general account of the accuracy of folk report, for we believe that the straight path from linguistic facts (of any sort, at any level) to folk report is a very rocky one, impeded by the nature of communication itself. If attitudinal factors (i.e., the sorts of social prejudices which create linguistic stereotypes) do not intervene to foreground some structural element, such elements appear to be overwhelmingly subservient to communicative function.

In several years of training transcribers of conversation, one of the authors has offered prizes (within the severe limits of a professorial salary, of course) to students who can provide two pages of error-free double-spaced transcription. Everything is loaded in favor of the students' winning. Most are linguists in training; they are informed of the prize before the work; and error-free is generously defined. (Noisy sections of tape or disputable interpretations are not used to discredit a transcription, and the students themselves are used as judges.) No one has yet claimed the prize.

How can linguists whose focus is on form (and who are teased with reward) err so badly? An inspection of typical mistakes shows that even multiple listenings by linguistically sophisticated transcribers miss (or supply) facts; they are not detected because the communicative (propositional) core of the language event flows freely. "I said that he left" may be listened to many times and still appear in a transcript as "I said he left" (or vice versa). "Bill took the dog out for a walk" might be rendered as "Bill took the dog for a walk" (or vice versa). In every case, the report is informationally accurate, but the details are off.

The students are always amazed at their silly mistakes, but the point is straightforward. Even settings which focus on the details of form may be subverted by the fulfillment of the communicative function. This communicative power may be so great as to submerge apparently glaring differences. One of the authors once told a new acquaintance (a Slavic linguist with no information about United States varieties) that he was from northwestern Ohio. The amazed Slavist allowed that that was so, and wanted to know the arcanities on which the identification was based. One of the telling facts was his use of such constructions as "My shoes need shined" (opposed to the more widely distributed "My shoes need to be shined" or "My shoes need shining.") Linguist though he was, he had never noticed that his structure differed. (In fact, he went away to check and returned shattered, for he was a prescriptivist, to find that many speakers of United States English found his construction weird, nonnative, and the like; we return to those observations in a moment.) It is important to note that the linguist under discussion is from a section of the United States known in regional dialectology as the "North Midland," an area little caricatured, perhaps even the seat of the fictional home of Standard American English (where national radio and television announcers and newspersons are supposed to come from.) It is an area of high linguistic security, so our linguist would have little reason to believe that anything he did was out of the ordinary (see Chapter 2.1.1.2 below). His inaccurate first response, then, on being told this construction was used to identify his regional speech, was that "Everyone says that." Since his own performance, distinct as it was, awakened no caricatures of region or status, he simply translated the performance of all speakers of educated varieties into his own. Given that he had only negative evidence to go on (in his adult life, surrounding speakers did not use the construction), it is not surprising that he emerged from graduate school (in an area where the construction is not used), worked overseas (with a considerable variety of English speakers), and reached his thirties before he became aware of the "oddness" of his construction.

It is important to notice, however, that even our linguist's positive evidence (his use of the odd construction) apparently awakened no comment in years of contact with non-users. Recall that he is a North Midland speaker; his phonology awakens no caricatures, and his auditors simply could not believe, therefore, that his syntax could be so strange. That is, they must have assumed that what he said was normal, partly overcome by the rest of his unremarkable performance, partly by the overwhelming communicative function of interaction, and partly, doubtless, by his status.

In short, we believe that the communicative function of language (in caricature-free environments) is so strong that it overcomes the ability to give an accurate report of performance whether of self or of others and whether of general or restricted phenomena. The inaccuracy of self and other report when person stereotypes are engaged is well-known – near-southerners claim there is nothing southern about their speech; speakers of African-American Vernacular English (AAVE) claim not to know it, etc.[11]

1.1.2.2 Prescription. We shall go further here in distinguishing what the folk perceive as even the proper content of observations about language itself. Nonlinguists use prescription (at nearly every linguistic level) in description; linguists, on the other hand, find the sources for prescription in power, esteem, tradition, and the like, not in the underlying nature of language itself. In other words, for linguists some language facts acquire special status due to their association with certain segments of society. To be sure the folk associate language facts and social groups, but they reject the cause-and-effect relationship: good language is not good just because it is (and has been) used by good speakers. Good language for the folk is a much greater abstraction; it is good because it is logical, clear, continuous (in an etymological sense), and so on. For the folk this notion of good language extends itself even to the boundaries of what the language is or may contain. What is not a part of that logical, continuous entity is not really language at all. (*"Ain't* ain't a word, is it?"*) Appeals to the dictionary and grammar books are, therefore, not really appeals to trusted authorities on usage; they are appeals to pundits and sages who have insight into the Platonic abstraction that is the language. If these guardians of the public linguistic trust fail in their responsibility to provide access to the abstraction by, for example, basing their work on usage, they may be open to public outcry.[12]

Recall that D (#28, cited above) contrasts "the way we use it" with "technically" in determining the difference between *gift* and *present*. Many linguists will find this naive, for "the way we use it" is the determiner of the sense. D, like other folk linguists, however, knows that there is an abstract reality (one only glimpsed in dictionaries and grammars) in which, apparently, these two words mean the same thing, and that this abstraction lurks behind use. The introductory linguistics battle against prescriptivism is often seen as a social or human contest, one which tries to instill linguistic relativism by defeating folk beliefs about the language of the poor or marginalized. There is a deeper philosophical position involved in the confusion of prescription and description, however. For the folk, social stratification provides only another exemplification of the distribution of goods in a society; it is not the source of the shape of the goods themselves. A real language exists in folk belief, and even enfranchised speakers themselves may stray from it for any number of reasons.

What many folk linguists have to say about the nature of language will, therefore, appear to professional linguists to be filtered through reactive, attitudinal factors. Folk observations, however, may often reflect only the difference between a belief in a technical abstraction (the language itself) and what is actually done – the latter, in the folk mind, of apparently little interest to language professionals.

It is important to note that this philosophical (or Platonic) prescriptivism[13] is not the outpouring of an overactive linguistic insecurity. The area where this research was done has no such self-image (e.g., Preston 1989a and 2.1 below), and many of the respondents in this survey felt no such linguistic embarrassment.

Figure 1.2 contrasts a folk versus linguistic taxonomy of some of these issues. Many linguists agree that although such phenomena as drunken speech, interference from other systems, and slips of the tongue may be interesting, they need to be edited out in constructing a grammar of a language, which leads back to the guiding cognitive principles on which it is constructed. The X in the linguistic taxonomy is, therefore, a perfect reflection of the language, the performance which reflects the competence of Chomsky's famous ideal native speaker-hearer:

> Of course, it is understood that speech communities in the Bloomfieldian sense – that is, collections of individuals with the same speech behavior – do not exist in the real world. Each individual has acquired a language in the course of complex social interactions with people who vary in the ways in which they speak and interpret what they hear and in the internal representations that underlie their use of language. ... We abstract from these facts ..., considering only the case of a person presented with uniform experience in an ideal Bloomfieldian speech community with no dialect diversity and no variation among speakers. (Chomsky 1986:16-7)

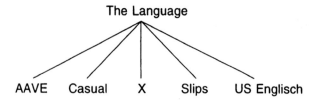

a. A folk taxonomy of competence and performance

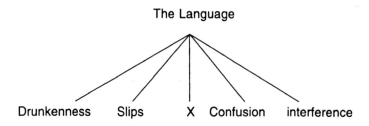

b. A linguistic taxonomy of competence and performance

Figure 1.2   Folk (a.) and linguistic (b.) taxonomies (partial) of
"competence" and "performance"

In terms of Figure 1.2b, it is at the level "The Language" itself where
dialectal, stylistic, and even individual diversity are edited out for the
linguist. "The Language" is a cognitive, internal reality of an individual speaker, and linguists often pretend, for the sake of science,
that a mass of linguistic clones exists.[14] To show all the concerns of
the folk taxonomy in a linguistic one, we would have to show a much
grander scheme – Figure 1.3. In an attempt to get to the principles of
human language, many linguists cut through the mass of diversity in
Figure 1.3 and simply pretend that the individual performance isolated at X is the performance of an ideal Bloomfieldian speech community. Figure 1.3 shows that the difference between the folk and
linguistic taxonomies of Figure 1.2 is more radical than it first appears. Linguists have created an agreed-on abstraction ("The Language") by pretending that there is a group of error-free, monodia-
lectal, monostylistic speakers. They know that such a group does not

exist. The folk, however, appear to believe in their abstraction ("The Language" in Figure 1.2a), and they rate a considerable array of factors as deviations from it.

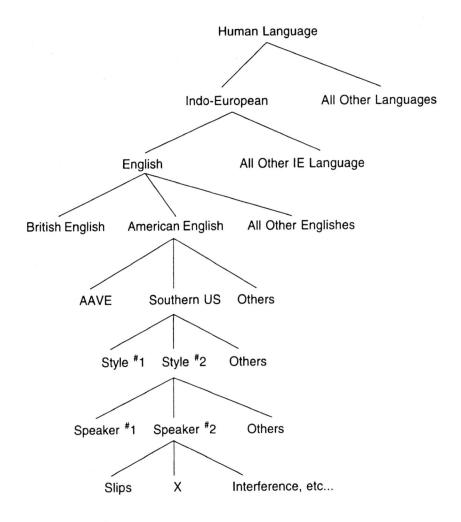

Figure 1.3 A more elaborate (linguistic) taxonomy of "competence" and "performance"

Linguists agree with the folk that slips, interference, and the like are deviations, but other varieties are treated by linguists as alternative examples of "The Language." A linguist is happy to write the rules of AAVE, Coastal Southern English, or lower-class New York City English. Any of these specific varieties might be the basis for an abstraction; for the folk, however, varieties deviate from the single abstraction.

Teachers of introductory linguistics will recognize an instantiation of this folk belief which is incredibly difficult to overcome. The abstraction is rule-governed; the deviations are not. The linguist's so-called rules of AAVE or lower-class New York City English are, therefore, nonsense. What rules could there be when the forms under discussion are simply failures to observe the rules of "The Language"? In more linguistically familiar terms, such varieties for the folk are performance deviations from competence, not alternative competencies.

Although we shall offer reminders from time to time of this considerable difference in the basic, underlying philosophical definitions of language itself by the folk and linguists, we are sure we will not do it frequently enough or as elaborately as it might be done. We ask readers, therefore, to treat our occasional reminders of the "prescriptive" bases of folk linguistics as a short-form substitute for this fuller discussion, and we ask that readers keep this basic distinction in mind even when we fail to offer such a reminder.

What then are the actual types and levels of the folk awareness of language in light of this variety of responses and characterizations? We do not quibble much with Silverstein's account of the probability of folk awareness of linguistic structure, for he is unconcerned with the mediating influences of language attitudes. We believe, however, that discussions of awareness have been muddied partly by the use of a number of terms (*subconscious, covert, unmonitored*, and so on) and partly by more serious shifts in meaning (*automaticity, inaccuracy, unanalyzability*, and so on). We hope to keep these straight in what follows, and to do so propose the following definitions (Preston 1996):

1. *Availability*: As we have suggested, not all facets of language (whether of performance, ability, or reaction) have equal availability to the folk. We rank them as follows:

    a) *Unavailable*: the folk not only do not but will not comment on such topics (e.g., specific phonological features of some so-called accents).

b) *Available*: the folk will discuss some matters carefully described by a fieldworker (e.g., some of the sample, deviant sentences of 5.3.1), but they do not normally do so.

c) *Suggestible*: although seldom initiated in ordinary conversation, the folk will comment on topics if they arise, and they do not require elaborate description from a fieldworker.

d) *Common*: topics of usual folk linguistic discussion.

2. *Accuracy*: Although it has no bearing on the value of the data, folk descriptions of every aspect of language may be inaccurate or accurate.

3. *Detail*: A linguistic object may be characterized with great specificity or none.

a) *Global*: in 1. a) above, for example, we indicate that the phonological detail of an accent might be unavailable; that does not limit comment on the accent.

b) *Specific*: in some cases, linguistic characterization is detailed (e.g., accounts of speakers who are said to drop their g's in -*ing* forms).

4. *Control*: In both account and performance, folk linguists may or may not control the variety (or an aspect of it) under consideration. This cuts across the first three considerations in unexpected ways. A speaker who reports on only the global aspects of an accent might nevertheless give a detailed imitation of it (which might be in part accurate, in part inaccurate, e.g., white imitations of African-American English and African-American imitations of white English, Preston 1992).

Note that all the above categories are clines or continua (although some, e.g., 1 and 4, seem to have discrete categories and others, e.g., 2 and 3, appear to be simply dichotomized). In all cases, however, those representations are merely prose conveniences expressing extremes on the one hand or "settings" along a continuum on the other.

It makes little sense to us to say that respondents who have reacted to, considered, or performed linguistic activity are "unaware" unless every aspect of that reaction, consideration, or performance is "unavailable." Our concerns, therefore, reach much more broadly across the spectrum of "awareness" than do those of Silverstein, for we believe he is interested in the ultimate ability of a respondent to provide an (accurate) account of a linguistic phenomenon (whether or not such an account is a part of the traditional repertoire of the community). In working with respondents in an attempt to uncover linguistic aspects of previously unrecorded or little-studied languages, it is helpful to have "guideposts" such as those Silverstein provides. Where will one need to resort to "covert" collection and where will overt questioning do?

This outline of the folk modes of awareness of language and their relative independence leads, we believe, to the following conclusion: we must not limit what we call language awareness (or "attention to language") to one class or type of behavior. Those who can globally characterize a variety (e. g., a "Polish accent") have a gross categorization of language difference available, even though, admittedly, their failure to characterize (or produce) any detail does not allow us to measure the degree of accuracy of the observation. Furthermore, although we might test them to discover the degree to which they are adept at identifying authentic Polish-accented English, that would simply test another level of perceptual skill, for even if the results showed that they could not tell German-accented English from Polish, we could hardly deny the perceptual salience of the notion "Polish accent." Laferriere (1979), for example, shows that Boston Jews identify the use of a less-prestigious (o) variable in Boston as "Irish," when, in fact, her own work on the ethnic distribution of the form in Boston shows that Italian-Americans use the nonprestige form with the greatest frequency. Her explanation is simple; "Boston Irish" is a folk term available for a wide range of social stereotypes; "Boston Italian" is not.

In short, the folk awareness of language is not only a matter of degree but also one of mode or type. When one characterizes (however generally, however badly) a linguistic fact, we cannot say that he or she is "unaware." Conversely, when one mimics a variety perfectly but cannot provide any overt detail of what it is that one controls in that imitation, we would also not want to say that he or she is "unaware." For every act of language production and language perception (including attitudinal as well as "processing" perception), then, the mode and degree of awareness is an open question.

A word about 1. b) ("available") is especially in order, for some may wonder how the folk can have a folk linguistics about matters they are led into. We reject, however, the notion that folk belief is a static set of wisdoms trotted out at opportune or culturally caricaturistic moments. Folk belief is also the dynamic process which allows nonspecialists to provide an account of the environment. Some parts of the environment have been so frequently focused on in traditional reasoning that the results have come down neatly pre-packaged. We have not ignored these, but we have, as well, presented our respondents with problems and areas which expose the processes of their thinking about language, perhaps even taking them down paths which they have not trod before. We believe this is a productive way to discover folk concepts, for we think it is more like the real world of problem-solving than an artificial world of static responses both to and in caricaturistic contexts. What we believe about the folklore of language is stated concisely for the field in general by Toelken:

> ... we might characterize or describe the materials of folklore as "tradition-based communication units exchanged in dynamic variation through space and time." *Tradition* is here understood to mean not some static immutable force from the past, but those pre-existing culture-specific materials and options that bear upon the performer more heavily than do his or her own personal tastes and talents. We recognize in the use of *tradition* that such matters as content and style have been for the most part passed on but not invented by the performer.
>
> *Dynamic* recognizes, on the other hand, that in the processing of these contents and styles in performance, the artist's own unique talents of inventiveness *within* the tradition are highly valued and are expected to operate strongly ... Folklore is made up of informal expressions passed around long enough to have become recurrent in form and content, but changeable in performance. (Toelken 1979:32)

1.1.3. The position of folk linguistics

We shall try to elaborate on our own approach to folk linguistics and its relation to other approaches to the study of language in Figure 1.4. The points of the triangle are the three areas of concern Hoenigswald describes – *(1) what goes on, (2) how people react to what goes on, and (3) what people say about all this* (1970:20, cited above). We have added primes (') for the explanatory backgrounds to these three areas and a few other revisions which we comment on in the following discussion.

We recognize at the outset that there are classificatory problems in Figure 1.2, since not all linguists chop up the world in the same way. Recall that Hoenigswald exemplifies "reactions" (**b** in Figure 1.4) with "They are persuaded" and "They are put off" (1966:20, cited above). The second of these is ambiguous, at least for us, between **a** and **b**. Imagine that on their first date Josie observes casually to Serge that "Some yahoo who believes the earth is flat came into the office today." This romance is nipped in the bud, for, as it turns out, Serge is president of the local Flat Earth Society. Josie did not know Serge's flat-earth leanings and made her report with the most general of intents (making *small talk*, obeying Malinowski's requirement for "phatic communion" [1923] between like species members).

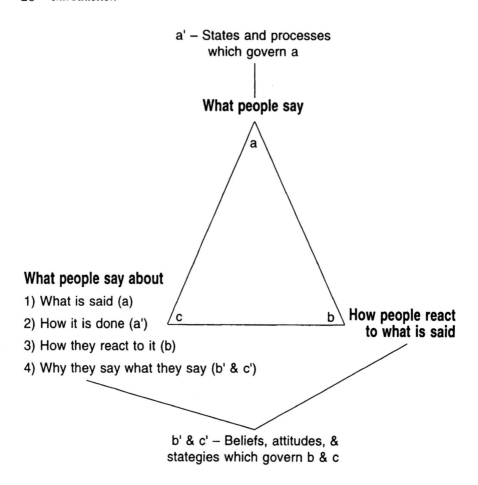

a' – States and processes
which govern a

What people say

a

What people say about

1) What is said (a)

2) How it is done (a')

3) How they react to it (b)

4) Why they say what they say (b' & c')

c

b

**How people react
to what is said**

b' & c' – Beliefs, attitudes, &
stategies which govern b & c

Figure 1.4   The place of folk linguistics in the general study of language

What interests us is that Josie's sentence has three linguistic levels, all of which we shall include at **a**. First, it is a *locutionary act* made up of noises, phonemes, words, phrases, syntactic structures, and so on. Second, it is an *illocutionary act*, as we indicated, a *report*. (Other illocutionary acts include *promises, requests, invitations*, and the like.) Third, it is a *perlocutionary act*, here, as we suggest above, *small talk*. (Others include *belittling, teasing, praising*, and the like). Serge, regardless of Josie's perlocutionary intent, has the perlocutionary uptake of, as Hoenigswald puts it, being "put off."

That there is a mismatch between intent and uptake does not require us to junk the model. If Josie had wanted to put Serge off and known his position on the earth's shape, the same report would have had the same effect, and there would have been a match between perlocutionary intent and uptake. All this – locution, illocution, perlocution – we classify in **a** of Figure 1.4.

We can imagine another putting off, however, which is clearly a reaction (**b** in Figure 1.4). Hannah has spotted Daniel at a party and finds him more than a little attractive; she sets out to seduce him (a perlocutionary intent). Hannah is no slouch at seduction; she has a repertoire of illocutionary acts (and nonlinguistic behaviors) which should effectively lead Daniel into the correct perlocutionary uptake. (Note that a correct perlocutionary uptake does not mean that the uptaker performs the perlocutionary intent of the intender, only that it is understood.) Unluckily for Hannah, however, she is a low-front vowel raiser, and Daniel finds that vowel positioning debilitating in romantic relationships. Although he has the correct perlocutionary uptake (understanding that he is being seduced), the Hannah-Daniel romance goes no further than the Josie-Serge one, but for reasons of what we shall refer to as language attitude (**b** in Figure 1.4). Daniel's attitude towards low-front vowel raising has guided the outcome (but not the identity) of his perlocutionary uptake.

We can imagine yet another scenario in which even the identity of the uptake might be derailed by the attitude. Hannah pops into Daniel's field of awareness with "Hi, haven't we met before." Unluckily, the second word contains an exemplar of the offensive low-front-vowel, raised considerably in Hannah's performance. In this case, Daniel's eventual rebuff of Hannah is perhaps even more puzzling to her, for she senses that her seduction (her perlocutionary intent) is not even being understood. Indeed, it is not. It is inconceivable to Daniel that any person with such a debilitating linguistic feature as low-front vowel raising could even enter the romantic fray. His perlocutionary uptake of Hannah's skilled advances must have been that of responding to chit-chat (or small talk). In this case, the language attitude has reached out to shape the identity of the perlocutionary uptake.

Although these anecdotes show that we include illocutionary and perlocutionary intents and uptakes as parts of **a**, they do not yet address the central concern of piecing out what is available in language to folk awareness. Theoretically anything in **a** is available to **b** or **c** – anything people do may awaken an attitude and/or be commented on. Practically, we know this not to be the case. The loss of the /I/ versus /ε/ distinction before nasals (in the speech of one of the authors) awakens no attitudes when he is home in southern Indiana. Additionally, it raises no comments there about a failure to distinguish between pens with which one writes and pins with which one sticks.

That situation does not obtain, however, in the same author's current location in southeastern Michigan. Both **b** and **c** responses abound. "Hillbillies don't make any difference between the sounds in words like *pin* and *pen*" (apparently a **c** response, unless one takes the use of pejorative labels to be sure indicators of attitude), and "People who say *pin* when they mean *pen* must be dumber than shit" (pretty certainly a **b** response). In the *South Midland* (or *Outer Southern*) area where the author under discussion is from, the vowel conflation mentioned is categorical – speakers of all reputes, education, ethnicities, and social classes do it, and they do it when they are being extremely formal as well as extremely casual. No wonder it does not trigger attitudes or comments there. In the *Inland North* (and other areas), however, there is a caricature of South Midland speakers as rustic, poorly-educated, and the like. The /ɛ/-/I/ neutralization must be striking to Michigan speakers who have the pair well separated, and it has become a triggering device for the attitudes and comments caricatured above.[15]

That language attitudes come from just such associations (and are not the product of linguistic form itself) makes the explanatory **b'** & **c'** in Figure 1.4 necessary. We must know that Appalachians are believed to be rustic, uneducated, unintelligent, and the like for the attitudinal reaction to be triggered. Michiganders lose just as much linguistic information when they conflate /ɔ/ and /o/ before /r/ (*horse* versus *hoarse*), a conflation not made by many Appalachians, but they do not comment on it, and it awakens no attitudes.

This /ɛ/-/I/ story should make it clear that a primary route to **c** is through **b**. That is, an awareness of what people do and, therefore, its availability for comment is often based on attitudinal factors. It will often be difficult, therefore, to distinguish between those **c** responses which focus on **a** and those which focus on **b**. Below we offer a subclassification of **c** responses which may help clarify this confusion.

We turn now to folk accounts of **a'**, a possibility not considered by Hoenigswald. It seems obvious that the folk will have theories about cognitive or psycholinguistic issues, but the folk will have a more difficult task than the linguist in this area. The linguist needs to show how individuals have learned the rules of their speech communities, but the folk will be required to account for the numerous class-, region-, and ethnic-based deviations from "The Language" in their psycholinguistic theories. Therefore, reactions (i.e., **b**-like characterizations) find their way into accounts of **a'** as well as accounts of **a**. In folk linguistics, people may not acquire the rules of "The Language" for complex social reasons:

> M: It's laziness and probably - maybe it is you know, because they are low class and they just don't know how to bring themselves up or they just don't want to. (#9)

On the other hand, there are straightforward folk accounts of **a'** matters which are not complicated by prescription and/or other factors from **b**. They include those of acquisition (of first and second languages [4.1 and 4.3]) and deeper concerns about the degree of control one has over language.

Finally, we enlarge **c** of Figure 1.2 to include not only Hoenigswald's original concern for reports of what is done (and our addition of reports of how it is possible to do what is done) but also folk comments on reactions to language (i.e., **c** remarks about **b**). An example from outside language may help clarify the difference between attitudes and their reports. Some recent studies have turned up depressing information about men's attitudes towards women's rights. A number of married men were surveyed, and many of the well-educated, younger ones were dream spouses: they said that women should have equal rights, opportunities, and encouragement to fulfill the entire breadth of society's promises. At a mundane level, they said that women should not uniquely shoulder dreary housework activities. Their behavior, however, was no better than that of their more poorly-educated counterparts: all talk, but an apparent revulsion for sharing time for a spouse's professional plans and training or even dishwashing.

What these men said was not meant to be an account of what people do (a **c** response describing **a**), for they were asked to characterize their attitudes (a **c** response describing **b**). It is furthermore not itself a **b** response, for we would apparently have to devise some much cleverer experiment if we wanted to get to their reactions – perhaps measuring their pulse rates when shown photographs of men ironing or sweeping.

Folk linguistics will include accounts of what people say about reactions to language. Since such reactions are often embedded in other language, it will often be difficult (perhaps unnecessary) to distinguish between a reaction and a report of one: " ... if you heard somebody talking like that you'd probably think they had lots of money or something." (S, describing slow, carefully enunciated speech, #23.) In other cases, however, the report is clearly of an attitude and not an example of it.

G: You- you want to communicate to the group that you're (a) part of the group, that you're not trying to put them down. And sometime to speak - correct, proper, completely proper English, (.hhh) makes them think that you're trying to PUT them down. (#36a)

In summary, our characterization of **c** in Figure 1.4, expanding on Hoenigswald, has included the following:

1. What people say about what is said;
2. what people say about how it is done;
3. what people say about how they react to what is said; and
4. what people say about
   a) why they say what they do, and
   b) why they react the way they do

The reports in **c** – whether of 1., 2., 3., or 4. – are seldom pure, for, as we have shown above, much that is said in **c** is influenced by **b** or subverted by stereotypes of communicators and communicative functions. That impurity, however, is a part of the folk wisdom and reasoning we seek to discover.

We turn now, very briefly, to some of the specific lines of research which have fostered ours, although the prior mention of dynamism in folklore studies in general already touches on one such area and may be taken to be an important influence on the work reported on here.

Folk dialectology: What nonspecialists believe about dialect differences has been a relatively well-tilled field. Although some of the previous research is rejected as valueless (even by those who carried it out, since the folk opinions turned up are not the same as linguistic ones [e.g., Grootaers 1959]), a number of techniques have been developed to determine folk notions of dialect differences. An extensive survey of this work is presented in 2.1.1 below. Although folk dialectology pointed the way to a need for an even more encompassing account of folk linguistic notions, it is still a prominent topic in its own right (2.1).

Sociolinguistics: In spite of sociolinguistic emphasis on change from below (i.e., from below the level of conscious awareness), covertness (i.e., nonmainstream values taken up unconsciously by even mainstream individuals), and the observer's paradox (i.e., the scholar's inability to ethically record authentically casual behavior), there is a limited tradition among its adherents of folk linguistic collection and interpretation. In addition to what he regards as limited folk phonology (see above), Labov has collected valuable folk commentary in his early work in New York City in a number of areas:

1. New Yorkers on the recognition of New York City speech by outsiders: "It's the first thing you open your mouth." "I know I sound like a New Yorker. I've been spotted instantly innumerable times" (1966:341).

2. New Yorkers on the opinions of New York City speech by outsiders: "They think we're all murderers." "To be recognized as a New Yorker – that would be a terrible slap in the face." "Somehow the way they say 'Are you a New Yorker?', they don't care so much for it." (1966:341-2)

3. New Yorkers' attitudes towards New York speech: "It's terrible." "Distorted." "Terribly careless." "Sloppy." (1966:344)

I'll tell you, you see, my son is always correcting me. He speaks very well – the one that went to [two years of] college. And I'm glad that he corrects me – because it shows me that there are many times when I don't pronounce my words correctly. (1966:246)

4. New Yorkers' awareness of the need to use local, casual speech:

... most of the people that I associate with in this area are men with very little schooling ... mostly Italian-American ... so that these are the men I've gone out drinking with, the ones I go out to dinner with, and when I talk to them, my speech even deteriorates a little more, because I speak the way they speak ... (1966:347)

5. New Yorker attitudes towards southern speech:

(Typical white respondent:) I like the sound of it. A girl in the office comes from Kentucky, and people get me mixed up with her. (1966:352)

(African-American respondent:) When I was very young, and used to hear about some of the things that happened in the South, I had a physical reaction, as if my hair was standing on end ... and I would hear a white Southerner talk, I was immediately alerted to danger, and so I could never see anything pleasant in it ... (1966:352)

Labov's use of folk-linguistic data is enterprising, for he tries to show how they are consistent with and shed further light on variable performance data and subjective reaction test results. Later sociolinguistic projects which might be noted for their mention of folk linguistic data include Feagin (1979) and Macaulay (1977). Although both focus nearly exclusively on the folk perception of linguistic norms, as we have suggested earlier, that is a ubiquitous folk linguistic topic. We believe all sociolinguistic projects (including those social psychological ones which try to tease out subjective reactions) would be aided by healthy doses of respondent talk about language along a wide range of topics, but we recognize here those pioneering few which have even considered such data.

Folklore and ethnography: Although ethnography is listed above as one of those areas which contributes to the scholarly devaluation of folk opinion, not all studies and not all practitioners have held that attitude. It is unfortunately the case, however, that very few of these exemplary studies (e.g., those listed in note 2 to the Foreword) are set in western, post-technological, heterogeneous cultures. Like these ethnographic investigations and unlike the sociolinguistic and dialectological traditions outlined above, this work treats qualitative, exemplary data from a "convenience" sample of respondents. Such samples are ordinary in investigations of non-Western, non-post-technological cultures and in the ethnomethodological tradition of conversation analysis which has focused on Western European societies, and their value here is not intended to reach farther than the usual representativeness which such intensively investigated data reveal.

It is not our intent, however, to simply collect folk opinions about language. Like other studies in the ethnography of speaking, ours seeks to know the organizing principles behind belief, and some parts of our introductory chapter have been decorated with such attempts. Our intellectual and procedural debt, therefore, is to those ethnographers of speaking whose work with a variety of data from a variety of contexts leads, we believe, to an enriched understanding of language. Hymes puts it simply and directly:

> If the community's own theory of linguistic repertoire and speech is considered (as it must be in any serious ethnographic account), matters become all the more complex and interesting. (Hymes 1972:39)

We know what we have dug up is complex, and we find it interesting. We hope our interpretations of it help begin the account of linguistic folk belief in a United States setting.

1.2 Methodology and fieldwork

The data collection for this study was carried out by eleven members of a graduate-level sociolinguistics seminar held during the 1987-88 academic year at Eastern Michigan University in Ypsilanti. Five of the student fieldworkers were native speakers of English, and, of the remaining six, five were native speakers of a non-European language. There were six women and five men. Seven were linguistics majors, two TESOL majors, and two majors in composition and rhetoric. The general preparatory work included study of the ethnography of speaking (and associated fieldwork procedures) and a review of the likely breadth of folk-linguistic topics, at least partly accomplished by considering those outlined in Preston 1986b (see below).

Of the fieldwork conventions available, we decided that the network model (Bortoni-Ricardo 1985, Burton 1978, Labov 1984:31, Milroy 1980) would best suit our needs. Each fieldworker became a member of a group of associated individuals (or of several groups of such individuals). We determined that suitable networks for this study would be made up of current residents of southeastern Michigan but not necessarily local-born natives. We were only secondarily interested in filling quotas of demographic subdivisions representative of the area. Since the fieldworkers discussed their choices of networks with one another and with us, we were assured a suitably varied group. The sixty-eight respondents eventually surveyed comprised a demographically varied group of southeastern Michigan residents (see the Appendix). There were forty-one females and twenty-seven males; nine were African-Americans (the remainder white, although other ethnic backgrounds of some of the respondents, e.g., Polish, German, had some influence on the data). Half the respondents were long-time southeastern Michigan residents, but a third of these had been reared in other states. Most were adults, between twenty and sixty, although fifteen were older and three were younger. (A number of younger children who were often present but did not contribute are not counted in this tally.) Two-thirds of the respondents had attended college and an additional five were currently-enrolled college students.

Once a network was approved for study, a fieldworker became a part of it, hoping to create the situation Milroy describes concerning Labov's Philadelphia neighborhood studies:

> The intention here was to allow the interviewer to simulate a conversation and over a period move towards a more symmetrical interactive relationship so that the interviewing style came to resemble participant observation. (Milroy 1987:69)

Even though it was not our intention to utilize the face-to-face interview style (Labov 1984:30), much of our data could be so classified. Since we were not overly concerned with the possibly damaging influences associated with *asking* people for their overt, perhaps rehearsed opinions about language, our goals were met whether or not interviews developed into the more natural conversational settings Milroy describes. Perhaps the fact that we have some stretches of interaction which are interview-like and others obviously relaxed and conversational (in many cases with the same participants) suggests that we have been partly successful in avoiding the difficult or impossible dual role of the investigator implied in Burton's suggestion that the network method leads to "empathetic and analytic immersion into a social world" (1978:165).

It was originally planned not to tell the participants that we were interested in their ideas about language. This plan faded, and many of the fieldworkers inadvertently (or on purpose) let the cat out of the bag, either by focusing too obviously on specific questions, becoming too excited by certain topics, or working with respondents who knew them to be students of language and linguistics. Since the opinions sought were those overtly held by the respondents, and since the subject matter appeared to them to be one open to public opinion, we do not believe this failure to conceal the primary intent impeded or sullied the research.

Part of our rationale for originally concealing our topic stemmed from the hope that our respondents would be interested enough in language to discuss it naturally. Fortunately, it often required no more than a little leading on the part of the fieldworker to elicit such talk, and how to so lead the respondents was a focus of our fieldworker training. Example suggestions included the fieldworkers' telling language-related narratives of their own or their bringing a small child to the recording session (so that some sort of first-language acquisition beliefs might be triggered). Suggestions were developed for a broad range of topics, and the fieldworkers prepared and rehearsed a number of conversation starters or icebreakers in connection with the categories of linguistic variation suggested in Preston 1986b (Table 1.1).

Table 1.1 Topics referred to in the conduct of the research (Preston 1986b)

I. PARTICIPANTS	II. INTERACTION	III. CODE
A. Ascribed	A. Setting	A. Status
1. age	11. time	31. autonomy
2. sex	12. place	32. historicity
3. nativeness	13. length	33. standardized
4. ethnicity	14. size	34. vitality
5. area	B. Content	35. source
B. Acquired	15. situation	36. currency
6. role	16. topic	37. duration
7. specialization	17. genre	38. frequency
8. status	C. Relation	39. value
9. fluency	18. solidarity	40. magic
10. individuality	19. network	41. taboo
	20. power	42. publicity
	D. Function	B. Organization
	21. purpose	43. phonology
	22. outcome	44. syntax
	23. goal	45. semantics
	E. Tenor	46. text
	24. distance	
	25. emotion	IV. REALIZATION
	26. tone	47. body
	27. stance	48. voice
	28. manner	49. mode
	F. Participation	50. channel
	29. speaker	
	30. hearer	

The strategies for triggering respondent comments worked with varying degrees of success. For instance, the fieldworkers had to be careful when telling a story of their own not to make it too lengthy or involved, so that the respondents would not conclude that the fieldworkers were authorities or conclude that nothing more need be said. There were several instances in which a fieldworker did relate a long and detailed story, and the respondents merely agreed, adding little or nothing of their own:

K: ((the fieldworker)) OK OK, did you guys like - did you notice any difference between as you went down from northern Germany - did you have any problems understanding going down to southern

Germany or Austria=I know - like when I first went to Swabia ((English pronunciation with [we])) Schwabia ((German pronunciation with [vɑ])) to go to work as a Gastarbeiter I couldn't understand anybody on the train. These people were talking - like one of the things I liked to do when I was learning a language is listen to people talking on the train, listen to people's conversations, or I'd be sitting in a cafe just listening to the people talk. And I went to the train you know - I was going to work. This was the first day of work, I hadn't met anybody at work or anything. I got on the train and I listen to these people talking, and I think oh my God I can't understand what they're saying. It was like a new language or something and I got to work and everything and my boss=I could understand him because he spoke VERy HIGH GERman=you KNOW REALLy eNUNciated EVEry SINGle WORD even though he was Swabian a Schwab ((see above)) - you know he'd have a little bit of accent=his words were like ( ) enunciated. So then am I going to understand my coworkers now and I couldn't. It was horrible they'd talk to me - and I'd have to ask them five times what they said and everything like that and it was like - I don't know I had a real hard time. Did you feel you ran into any difficulty like this?
S: ((the respondent)) Oh yeah. In southern Germany. (#3)

Unfortunately, that is all S has to say about this topic so elaborately led up to by the fieldworker. On the other hand, it was important in some cases for fieldworkers to share experiences so that the respondents felt comfortable telling those of their own. In conversation #42, for example, fieldworker M succeeds in getting the respondents to relate experiences of their own with southern speakers by telling one about her own southern husband. There are many such successes.

The idea of bringing a small child to the interview, although good in theory, was disappointing in practice. There were in fact three fieldworkers with small children, and, while it was true that a few folk ideas were developed in the interviews in which they were present, the incidence of such performances was often more dependent on whether or not the *respondents* had children of their own, and, in particular, whether or not those children were present.

In general, however, language proved such a ubiquitous and engaging topic that talk about it was abundant. Perhaps more importantly, since many respondents did not treat those aspects of it which they chose to discuss as the domain of specialists, the talk was unfettered. Of course, even when folk comment was filtered through, or made in reference to, technical information, we consider it no less interesting and no less folk.

The fieldworkers were also trained in one of the aspects of ethnographic grounding – asking respondents for explanations and interpretations of their own comments. This took place on the spot in some of the recorded interactions, but since many of the networks were recorded more than once, the review of earlier comment was also more traditionally carried out in later sessions.

These follow-up interviews often produced apparent changes in folk belief. For example, one of the fieldworkers asked a respondent, an African-American, about his dialect. He reacted uncomfortably (perhaps defensively) to the suggestion that he might have one:

C: (fieldworker): So could you tell me - a little bit about - your dia-
lect?
D (respondent): Dialects.
C: Heh yeah.
All: ((laugh))
      [
D: Well, uh: - well - see the world's getting smaller. There's=
         [[
C: ((laughs)) I- I mea- do you have-
D: =not even among all ethnic groups we're- we're getting- getting
less and less of dialectual in- inFLUence. (.hhh) Uh I'm- happen -
not to be - from the South, uh: uh u- du- There is a certain
aMOUNT of Black English that's (.hhh) spoken. There's a certain-
certain uh: forms and uh certain idioms that uh uh- blacks use
that's indigenous to blacks. (#35)

Confronted with the issue, D begins to deal with the numerous feel-ings he has about the existence of AAVE, his status as a speaker of it, and the like. By the next interview, however, D has worked out a comfortable definition of dialect, so when another respondent asks the fieldworker to explain the term, D jumps in:

D: OK. Uh when we- when we talk (.hhh) among the saints we
don't use the street talk neither do we use a very proper form of
English - you see - so, uh what's our every- everyday talk he's=
      [   ]
V: [[Yeah.
R: [[Uh huh.
        [
C: Yeah, that's good ((laughs))
D: =talking about well, then what do you use, when he talks about
dialect he's talking about (.hhh) what do you use like around the
house. Just your normal conversational English. (#51)

In the time between interviews, D has formulated a new definition of dialect, possibly in anticipation of the same subject's being discussed again. (A definition is required here since there is a new respondent at this interview.) D begins his statement with an "OK," almost certainly a turn-getting device which also signals "Let me handle this; I have the information," and he is clearly more comfortable with the subject than in the previous interview. We are aware that such changes are not necessarily developmental but may reflect, as we have already suggested, altering points of view.

Other variation found in both the style and content of our data results from the fact that six of the fieldworkers were not native speakers of English (one of Japanese, four of Mandarin [three Taiwanese, one Mainland Chinese], and one of Serbo-Croatian). Although some differences resulted from the fact that the native speaker fieldworkers were often members of their networks before the study (as the nonnatives were not) and from the fact that the nonnatives were assigned a sentence structure correction task (see below), other striking differences resulted.

Nonnative speakers were allowed to ask direct questions: "Do you use the passive construction in English?" (Chapter 5.3.2) "Where in the United States is standard English spoken?" Native speakers would have had great difficulty posing such questions or would have elicited strikingly different responses. First, respondents would have realized that native speakers would be just as likely as them to know the answer to such inquiries, making them (in folk linguistic terms) silly questions. Second, perhaps worse, a respondent might have felt that the fieldworker was the expert and that the question was a trick or test, intended to expose the respondent's naiveté, ignorance, or prejudice. Such questions are neither threatening nor silly from nonnatives, for they can be assumed to have neither information nor expertise.

The fact that some fieldworkers were nonnative speakers seems to override the fact that they were graduate students in language or linguistics. Their respondents considered themselves experts, knowledgeable about a broad variety of nontechnical aspects of English which could not have been elicited by a native fieldworker.

On the other hand, the networks chosen by the native speaker fieldworkers were usually those which they already belonged to. The beliefs that they could elicit, then, were often more emotionally charged. The fieldworker was a trusted other, and the respondents felt comfortable revealing beliefs and attitudes which might not always put them (or the larger and smaller cultures they represented) in the best light. For example, conversations among native speakers often included heated discussions about the inappropriateness of AAVE in the schools or its total unacceptability. Interestingly, the nonnative speaker who chose a church group network to which he previously belonged was also able to elicit emotionally charged responses, but they were the opposite of the prejudicial positions revealed in many native-native interactions.

These emotionally charged topics may not have been taken up in the nonnative-native interviews because the respondents were hesitant to reveal negative or embarrassing aspects of their own culture. Often the respondents appear overconcerned with portraying a positive view of United States society. H (a Taiwanese fieldworker) has expressed his surprise that in English there is no obligatory distinction between the labels for older and younger siblings. G takes the opportunity to expound on the fairness in the United States system this implies:

```
G:                              Like in different places it might make a
difference, cause maybe the older brother inherits or something
like that? And that's not true in the United States.=
         [
H:        Uh huh.
G: =Every child has equal rights. It's not just the oldest. And so to=
                                                       [
W:                                                      Oh!
                                                              [
H:                                                            Oh.
G: =the youngest- a girl has as much rights as a guy. I- it makes=
            [
H:          ((laughs))
G: =no difference. And so i- it's not a matter of who's the eldest.
(#1)
```

Such elaborate descriptions of what is good about the United States would be unlikely to occur in a native-native setting.

Variation due to fieldworker gender was difficult to detect since there was considerable imbalance between the large amount of data contributed by the native speaker female fieldworkers and the smaller amount collected by their male counterparts. Among the nonnative speakers, the situation was reversed, but in this setting gender influences would be difficult to detect due to the overwhelming influence of ethnolinguistic difference. We are more prepared, however, to offer some generalizations on the basis of respondent gender. On the one hand, as many early discourse studies of male-female interaction suggest, men seem to dominate conversation (see, e.g., West and Zimmerman 1983); in our data, men often speak for lengthy stretches (even when back-channeling cues to them are absent). On the other hand, women are significant contributors to both content and structure in these conversations, supporting alternative interpretations of the relationship between gender roles and language use (as in, e.g., Fishman 1983 and a large number of subsequent studies of gender roles in conversation).

Fieldworker age was not a significant factor; all but one were young adults (25-33). Respondent age did not as caricaturistically predict liberal versus conservative attitudes as might have been expected, although there were certainly examples of such contrasts (e.g., in #9 between T [a college undergraduate] and M [her mother] concerning the validity of AAVE).

Finally, the nonnative fieldworkers were given a list of sentences drawn from contemporary theoretical work in syntax and asked to get native speaker reactions to them. We suspected that nonnatives might be able to get finely-tuned, descriptive, structural comments rather than the prescriptive ones (or worse, none) that the native speaker might receive. The original intention was to have the nonnative fieldworkers present these data in some apparently natural situation (e.g., as an example of their own writing which had been criticized by a professor), hoping to elicit detailed correction and explanation.

In practice, the sample sentences were sometimes presented by the nonnative fieldworkers as intended, sometimes not. Often the fieldworker simply said "I'd like you to look at these," providing no imaginary context. In spite of this direct technique, the questioning often produced rich results, although some respondents gave up after responding to only a few sentences. This task served, in addition to providing folk grammatical information, to reveal prescriptivist ideas held by the respondents (such as "Don't end a sentence with a preposition") as well as beliefs about certain ethnic varieties of speech. For example, several respondents attributed examples from this list of sentences to AAVE. The general results of this "approach" to theoretical syntax with folk respondents (and a list of the sentences submitted for judgment) are given in 5.3.1.

The remainder of what went on with whom and why will be discussed in place as we provide a more detailed account of the topics which preoccupied our folk linguists and of our approaches to and interpretations of what they said.[16]

Chapter 2: Regionalism

In Chapter 1 we suggested that the folk studied here believe that "The Language" is an idealized abstraction; therefore, it should not be surprising that the degree to which a social group is seen as users (or non-users) of that ideal will play a strong role in its own and in others' social regard for the group. That is, since the folk do not hold to the relativistic notion that language varieties are "just different," we will find that variation in language which reflects differences in ethnicity, region, gender, and other social subdivisions will most often entail evaluation.

Dialectologists have been principally concerned with differences in speaker production and have hoped that studies of such production will help illuminate the principles of language change. Language attitude scholars have included regional variants in their collection of responses to varieties. Overt folk notions of geographical variation, based on neither production nor responses to forms, provide a helpful corollary to both production and attitude studies. Since this area of investigation is, however, the subject of a number of other publications, it will not be treated as thoroughly here as it might, but geographical variety is such an important folk linguistic area that it cannot be overlooked. General results from and some of the most recent work in this area are surveyed; however, the data elicited specifically for this research project are treated more fully. Before we begin the investigation of folk data, however, it will be important here to separate the scientific belief from the folk belief a little more carefully, for the scientists themselves have not been so fastidious.

A commonplace in United States linguistics is that every region supports its own standard variety; no one region is the locus (or source) of the standard. Historically, that is a fair assessment; no center of culture, economy, and government such as Paris or London ever dominated. Therefore, the truth in some texts is as Falk (1978) has it:

> In the United States there is no one regional dialect that serves as the model. What is considered standard English in New York City would not be considered standard in Forth Worth, Texas. Each region of the country has its own standard. (289)

Although there is no doubt that speakers in each region could recognize within their own local varieties which forms were more standard, (the usage of the best-educated speakers), it is not at all certain that they would adhere to a cultural-linguistic relativism that would allow them to admit that a standard exists in every region. More to the point here, it is very doubtful that nonlinguists in the United States believe that there is no region or area which is more (or less) standard than others. Falk's position is clearly a confusion of sophisticated linguistic relativism, deriving from well-intentioned attempts to debunk notions of so-called primitive and deficient linguistic systems, with what she believes to be popular perception. The latter, of course, is the point which deserves investigation, for, at least in the United States (if not everywhere), it is not linguists who define language standards.

Other introductory texts use the national newscaster suggestion or have even proposed a mysterious, nonexistent variety:

> In America, Standard English is the form of the language used on the national media, especially in news programs ... (Akmajian et al. 1979: 181).
>
> SAE [Standard American English] is an idealization. Nobody speaks this dialect, and if somebody did, we wouldn't know it because SAE is not defined precisely. Several years ago there actually was an entire conference devoted to one subject: a precise definition of SAE. This convocation of scholars did not succeed in satisfying everyone as to what SAE should be. The best hint we can give you is to listen to national broadcasters (though nowadays some of these people may speak a regional dialect) (Fromkin and Rodman 1983: 251).

From this it is clear that Fromkin and Rodman contrast the standard with regional varieties, and they earlier show that they find some regional varieties distinctly nonstandard:

> ... it is true that many words which are monosyllabic in Standard American are disyllabic in the Southern dialect: the word *right*, pronounced as [rayt] in the Midwest, New England, and the Middle Atlantic states and in British English, is pronounced [raət] in many parts of the South (249). [N.B.: This pronunciation is, in fact, not disyllabic. Why a centering glide, not there in most varieties of Southern speech anyway, causes Fromkin and Rodman to call it disyllabic and a rising one does not is puzzling.]

Fromkin and Rodman here come much closer to a folk linguistic description of a standard as their own prejudices peek through. SAE is exemplified in the Midwest, New England, and the Middle Atlantic states (and even in British English?) while the South has another variety (by implication, clearly not standard). Falk would have accused Fromkin and Rodman of regional prejudices (and she would be right), but a legitimate search for the source and locus of SAE will have to consider just such prejudices. What linguists believe about standards matters very little; what nonlinguists believe constitutes precisely that cognitive reality which needs to be described – one which takes speech community attitudes and perception (as well as performance) into account. In fact, it is pretty well agreed upon by sociolinguists that the notion *speech community* itself is better defined by the presence of shared *norms* than by that of shared *performance* characteristics; e.g., Labov 1972a:158.

SAE surely cannot be characterized as a simple socioeconomic reality. If it could, why do Fromkin and Rodman make the mistake of contrasting regional vowels in the South (used by the most privileged and impeccably educated) with those of SAE? They have committed the error of stating their personal folk beliefs cloaked in the mantle of linguistic expertise. If they know what attitudes people from different areas hold about varieties, they should make it clear either that they have that information from research or that they cite it as folk linguistic information reflecting their own beliefs. To do otherwise confuses scientific reporting and hypothesizing with stating linguistic prejudices. At least Langacker makes it clear that he is citing what many people may believe (although with no documentation) when he observes the following:

> British English enjoys special favor in the eyes of many Americans. Boston English is considered by many people to be more prestigious than Southern speech or Brooklynese (1973:55).

This must be true for Fromkin and Rodman, for they believe that some Southern vowels, despite their use by educated and uneducated speakers alike, are regional, *therefore* not standard.

To correct even introductory linguistics textbooks, research must be done which studies responses to varieties, and language-attitude studies have explored just such dimensions of diversity, beginning by sampling attitudes towards different languages (Lambert, et al. 1960) and moving on to different varieties of the same language (e.g., Tucker and Lambert 1969). Giles and his associates (summarized in Ryan and Giles 1982) have investigated a large number of such reactions (to taped voices) and have suggested a general pattern: speakers of regional varieties (where that suggests nonstandardness) find speakers of their own varieties warm, friendly, honest, sympathetic, and trustworthy, but often slow, unintelligent, and plodding;

they often regard speakers of a superposed standard as cold, dishon-
est, and unsympathetic, but quick, intelligent, and ambitious. In
short, to the extent that listeners find their own varieties less prestigious, they suffer from what Labov (1966) called "linguistic insecurity." One suspects that some of this insecurity has its direct source
in speakers' awareness of the fact that the local variety will not serve
extra-regionally. That is, it will not convince some outside listeners
that the intelligence, education, and authority of the speaker or writer
are high, and it will not, therefore, inspire confidence in the content
of some messages. Of course, there are notable exceptions; information of the sort most likely to be delivered in a local or nonstandard
variety (street-wise facts, farming information, sports calls and expressions, hunting and fishing facts) might, indeed, be seen as more
trustworthy if delivered in a nonstandard variety, but the evaluation
of other ("intellectual") characteristics of the speaker would not be
improved.

Language-attitude studies confirm, then, that regional varieties are
not all equal, even when only phonological features are contrasted
(that is, when lexicon and grammar are not variables). Such studies
help establish the folk-linguistic base for another perspective on varieties, an essential one for languages with no clear-cut standard model.
What is lacking in such settings is an account of what speakers of various regions (and classes, and sexes, and ethnic groups, and ages, and
so on) believe. While language-attitude surveys hope to avoid the observer's paradox (Labov 1972a) – which here includes the effect
awareness has on respondents' reactions to, as well as on their performances of, language – folk linguistics seeks to discover the overt
categories and definitions speakers have of linguistic matters.

If speakers are presented with the task of identifying the areas of
the United States where the most "correct" English is spoken, for example, how will they respond? If they are all relativists like Falk, they
will simply indicate that the task cannot be done, claiming that each
area supports a standard. If, however, as Fromkin and Rodman show
(surely unintentionally) and Langacker claims, they have clear linguistic prejudices about the locus of SAE, they will readily rank areas of
the country for language correctness. Additionally, if Langacker is
specifically right, there should emerge some preference for "British"
speech (however that may be represented in new world areas) and a
preference for Boston over Brooklyn and the South; if Fromkin and
Rodman's prejudices are widely represented, a preference for Eastern
and Midwestern speech over Southern should emerge.

Additionally, if the studies by Giles and his associates apply to
United States varieties, one might also expect to find that speakers

who consider their accents "regional nonstandards" (i.e., who suffer from linguistic insecurity) will rank their home areas lower for correct speech than some other areas. On the other hand, since Giles and his associates found that there was a decided preference for the local area along affective dimensions (friendliness, honesty, and so on), one should find such a preference for the local area in a ranking task which asks where the most "pleasant" variety is spoken.

Such tasks are distinctly different from typical language-attitude surveys. In the latter, respondents check off attributes which they assign to the speaker based on a short tape-recorded sample. These studies generally conclude that attitudes to voices from here and there are thus and so, but they do not, as a rule, ask the respondents where they thought each voice was from (but see Milroy and McClenaghan 1977). It is possible, then, that research which reports that respondents from, say, Detroit believe that voices from Atlanta are "unfriendly" may be an accurate report of the response to the voice sample but may be that for at least two possible reasons: 1. the respondents did not recognize where the voices were from (or might, in fact, have believed the voices were from somewhere else), and 2. (a not unrelated fact) the respondents might not have a cognitive speech area to which the voice sample might be readily assigned. In short, folk linguistic considerations must be made a part of social psychological studies of language attitude.

2.1 A survey of earlier studies

This survey includes data collected from the United States South and from two other regions – southern Indiana (an area suspected to be linguistically insecure, stemming from its association with caricaturistic South Midland ["hillbilly"] speech) and southeastern Michigan (a typical Inland Northern speech community which should show little or no linguistic insecurity).[1] Although not all tasks and not all subdivisions of the respondents studied are reported on here, the following general research program is the background resource for this section:

    1. Respondents drew boundaries on a US map around areas where they believed the regional speech zones of the United States were; earlier applications of this methodology are reported on and summarized in Preston 1989b; recent techniques developed by Preston and Howe (1987) allow computerized generalizations to be compiled from individual responses (e.g., Preston 1989a and 1993a). Although computer generalizations of

Southern hand-drawn maps have not been done, a number of individual Southern maps are contrasted with the Indiana and Michigan data.[2]

2. Respondents ranked the fifty states on a scale of one to four (1 = "same," 2 = "a little different," 3 = "different," 4 = "unintelligibly different") for the perceived degree of dialect difference from the home area. One version or another of this technique is long-standing in dialect study (e.g., Daan and Blok 1970, Grootaers 1959, Kremer 1984, Rensink 1955, Weijnen 1968) and is reviewed in Preston 1989b and Preston, to appear; the revised version used here is described in Preston 1989a and 1993a.

3. Respondents ranked the fifty states, New York City, and Washington, DC., on a scale of one to ten (1 = "least," 10 = "most") for "correct" and "pleasant" speech; such ratings are common in other areas of cultural geography (e.g., Gould and White 1974). The version of this task used here is reported in Preston 1989a and 1993a.

4. Respondents listened to nine voices from sites on a north to south line down the middle of the United States (from Saginaw, Michigan to Dothan, Alabama); the samples were all of male, well-educated, middle-aged speakers discussing nonspecialist topics. They were presented to the respondents in a scrambled order, and they were instructed to assign each voice to the site where they thought it belonged. This task is also reported in Preston 1989a and 1993a.

5. Respondents were interviewed after they had performed 1. through 4. to determine the etiology of their rankings, mappings, and identifications and to allow the expression of any other of their opinions about language distribution and status. Processing of these data is not yet complete and will be included only incidentally in what follows. (Preston 1993a and 1993b contain fuller accounts of these more ethnographically oriented data.)

2.1.1 Hand-drawn maps

The most straightforward way of discovering what respondents believe about areas is to have them draw maps. In the first attempt to use this technique in dialect study, Preston (1982a) asked undergraduates at the University of Hawaii to "draw maps of the areas of the United States where people speak differently." He also asked them to label the areas they outlined with the name of the variety of English spoken there or, if they did not know or use one, with the label they usually assigned the speakers who lived there.

A word about a false start in this research, one not meant to be critical of students at the University of Hawaii, for it has proved to be a difficulty wherever this work has been done. Since physical and political boundaries may or may not coincide with dialect boundaries, a blank outline map of the United States was first used for elicitation. The resulting confusion was so great that it became necessary to use a map with state lines and allow respondents to consult a detailed road map for orientation. There is a movement to improve geographical

knowledge of at least the United States, but, for the time being, folk
dialectological research is confounded with folk geography.

Figure 2.1 is an example of one young Hawaiian's map and Figure 2.2 of another's. The detail of the first must somehow be combined with the extremely limited information of the second in arriving at a composite; a relatively simple technique was used at first.
Each respondent's boundary for each area was treated as an isogloss.
When the "isoglosses" from all respondents for one area were overlaid by hand drawing, "bundles of isoglosses" were identified and
taken to be that group's mental map outline of the dialect area.

Figure 2.3 shows how thirteen southern Indiana respondents'
overlapping boundaries were used to determine the dialect area
"Northern" for them. There is little disagreement on the eastern and
northern limits; similarly, many respondents set the southern limits at
the Michigan, Wisconsin, and Minnesota southern boundaries, although the majority include a small portion of northern Iowa. The
map does not show it, but a slightly larger number of respondents included all of Minnesota at the western boundary, so the final determination was as is shown in Figure 2.4, in which the results of similar composite-making for all areas are displayed.

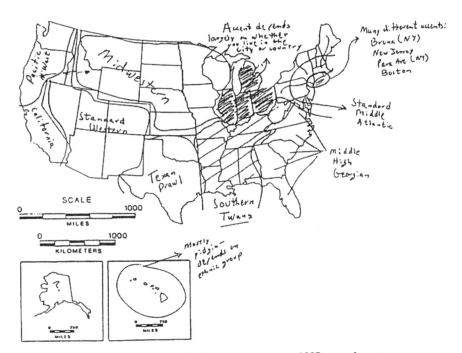

Figure 2.1 A Hawaii respondent's hand-drawn map of US speech areas

Figure 2.2   Another Hawaii respondent's hand-drawn map of US speech areas

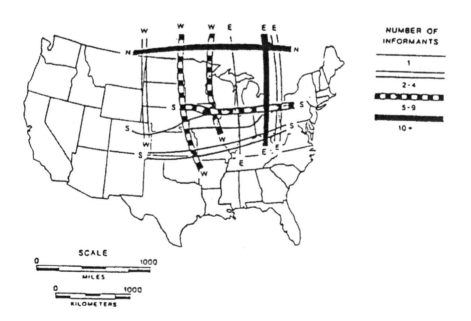

Figure 2.3   The determination of the "Northern" speech area based on thirteen southern Indiana respondents' hand-drawn maps

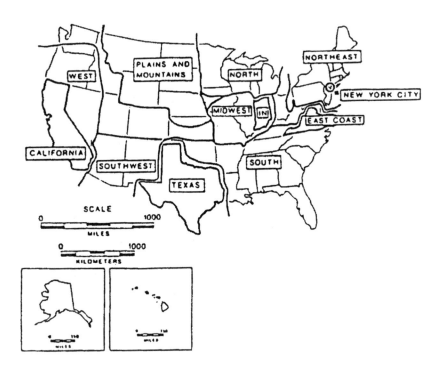

Figure 2.4   The perceived speech regions of the US based on thirty-five southern Indiana respondents' hand-drawn maps

Preston (1986a) compares and contrasts five such maps from the perspectives of Hawaii, southern Indiana, western New York, New York City, and southeastern Michigan with one another, with "production" dialect maps, and with maps of nonlinguistic aspects of cultural geography. These studies suffer considerably, however, from the small number of respondents imposed by the laborious hand-tracing of boundaries, making it impossible, for example, to investigate gender, generation, class, or ethnic differences. Once it was seen that respondents from many areas used the same general cognitive template for area identifications, a way of determining isoglosses for larger numbers of respondents was devised. The outlines of each respondent's areas were traced onto a digitizing pad which fed the co-ordinates activated by this tracing into a program keyed to a standard map. This technique allows automatic compilation of composite maps based on large numbers of respondents and on demographically appropriate subdivisions of them.

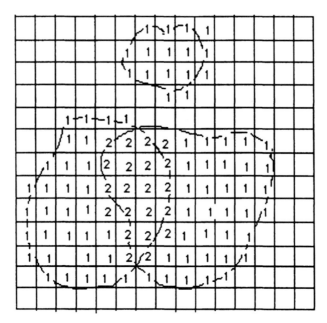

Figure 2.5 Three "dialect region" outlines tallied in the computer record

Figure 2.5 illustrates a hypothetical case to clarify this procedure. Respondent #1 has drawn the circular area to the left to outline a speech region, and respondent #2 has indicated the same area in the partially overlapping circle to the right. The superimposed grid allows the computer to keep track of the number of times a cell has been included in a respondent's outline. A higher "score" inside a cell indicates that a greater number of respondents have included it. It is possible, as seen in the small circular area outlined on the top, drawn by respondent #3, that there could be no agreement about an area. In this case, the cells with a score of "2" represent the best agreement among these three respondents.

The generalizations which emerge from such considerations are not automatic. For example, 138 southeastern Michigan respondents drew some representation of the United States South, and their maps were subjected to the computer analysis outlined above. If we ask the computer to show us the entire territory of the South for which even one respondent included a cell, we get such an uninformative map as Figure 2.6, obviously an exaggeration and most likely the result of one or two sloppy or idiosyncratic drawings.

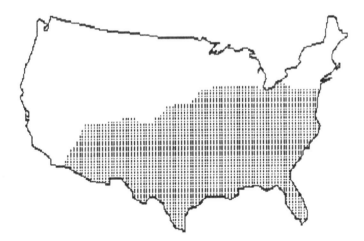

Figure 2.6 Southeastern Michigan respondents' computer-generalized map, showing where even one respondent outlined a "South"

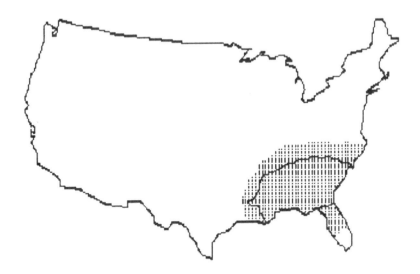

Figure 2.7 Indiana (outlined – 53 of 106) and Michigan (shaded – 69 of 138) respondents' generalizations at the 50% level of the United States "South"

It is necessary, therefore, to seek other patterns of agreement, and the territory outlined by fifty percent of the respondents seems to provide a reasonable generalization, although, to be precise and to provide additional insights (as will be illustrated immediately below), one will want to sample a number of "percentages of agreement." Figure 2.7 shows the area called "South" by both Indiana and Michigan respondents at this fifty percent level of agreement.

As suggested above, this procedure allows interesting questions: For example, 1. Where is the heart or core of a region? In this case, where is the greatest agreement on where the "South" is? 2. Do decreasing percentages of respondent agreement show regularly increasing concentric patterns of area outlining? Figure 2.8 answers this first question about the heart of the South (at least for Michigan respondents). Since some respondents drew outlines which overlapped with no part of an outline drawn by the other respondents (as suggested in Figure 2.5), we cannot, in fact, see 100% agreement.

Figure 2.8 shows, however, that 96% of the respondents find the heart of the South in southeastern Alabama, but Figure 2.9 shows that a regularly spaced series of concentric circles does not emerge from the Alabama heartland. When a 91% reading is taken, a "tail" reaches to the coast, suggesting that although the heart of the South is in southeastern Alabama, its eastern and coastal ties are still significant for many respondents.

Figure 2.8 Michigan respondents' core "South" at the 96% (132 of 138) agreement level

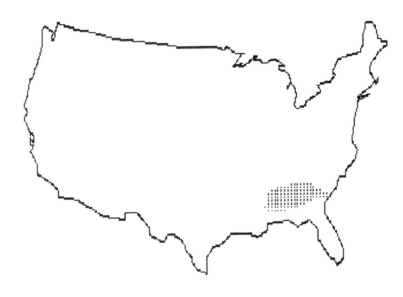

Figure 2.9 Michigan respondents' 91% (126 of 138) agreement for the "South," showing a coastal attachment

As Figure 2.7 shows, the difference between Michigan and Indiana perceptions of the South is not great. For both groups of respondents, the Southern speech area is a generally southeastern phenomenon; it includes none of Texas, little of Arkansas, and no more than one-half of Louisiana; Florida (more dramatically southern Florida for Michigan respondents) is obviously different. We believe it is easy to explain these exclusions. Texas and, less frequently, Louisiana are often singled out as separate speech areas, and Florida is often noted as a haven for Spanish-speakers and "Yankees." (see Figures 2.10 and 2.11). Arkansas is excluded, we believe, both due to its "western" distance from the core and to the fact that the exclusion of Louisiana would have forced respondents to make an extra drawing effort to include it. These interpretations are also based on the study of the details of a number of individual hand-drawn maps which cannot be included here.

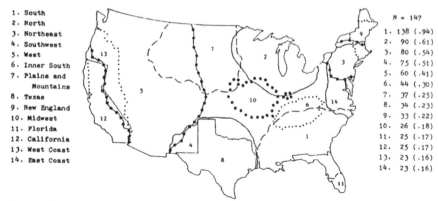

Figure 2.10 Speech regions for southeastern Michigan respondents

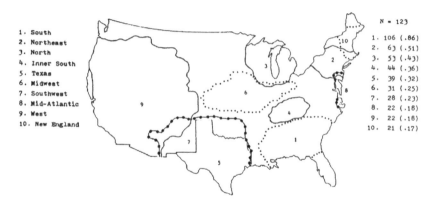

Figure 2.11 Speech regions for southern Indiana respondents

Figures 2.10 and 2.11 show every computer-generalized dialect area drawn by at least fifteen percent of the respondents for both Michigan and Indiana. We have seen above that the South outlines are based on drawings by 138 Michigan and 106 Indiana respondents; here we see that the South is overwhelmingly the most salient area for both groups. The 138 Michigan respondents who actually drew a South represent 94% of the 147 total respondents in the study. The second most salient area (the "North," actually a small Great Lakes area) was drawn by only 61% (90 of the respondents). A similar dramatic pattern exists for the Indiana data. 86% (106 of the 123 total respondents) drew a South. The next most frequently drawn area (the "Northeast") was drawn by only 51% (63) of the respondents. Note that the "Northeast" is also the third most salient area

(54%) for the Michigan respondents. It is also interesting to note that for Indiana respondents the "Outer South" ("Southern Highland" or "Appalachian" area) is a separate zone while for Michigan respondents it overlaps a "deeper" South considerably. Of 163 maps drawn by Southern respondents, 157 (96%) outlined a South, slightly besting even the 94% figure set by the Michigan respondents.

Michigan respondents see their entire state as uniquely in the "Northern" area (sharing space only with Wisconsinites), while Indiana respondents put part of their state in the "North" and part in the "Midwest" – the part where these respondents live, on the very southern edge of this "Midwest."

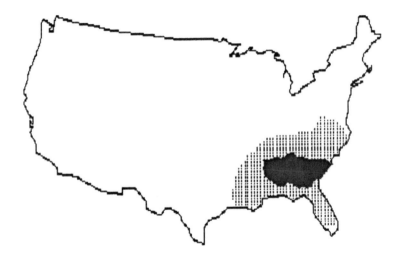

Figure 2.12 Youngest (under 20 – shaded area) and older (over 60 – solid area) Michigan respondent outlines of "Southern"

As suggested above, since computer processing permits a larger sample, subdivisions of populations may be investigated. Figure 2.12, for example, contrasts the youngest and the oldest Michigan respondents' characterizations of "Southern."[3] The fifty-year-old decade stands about half way between these extremes, but there is no significant difference between the youngest respondents' outline and those of the respondents in the twenty, thirty, and forty year old decades. The Indiana respondents reveal a similar (though not quite so dramatic) difference. It remains to be seen if this is an age-graded characteristic (that is, older raters might draw a smaller "South" or they might draw smaller areas in general[4]) or a change in the perception of the extent of the speech area "Southern" for both Indiana and Michigan raters.

Although gender differences in the map-drawing task have not proved interesting, social status provides additional contrasts. Figure 2.13 contrasts lower middle (shaded area) and upper middle (solid area) class perceptions of "Southern" for Michigan respondents. Although working class respondents outline a slightly smaller area than the lower middle class, there is little difference between the middle and lower-middle class representations. Like the oldest respondents, the upper middle class tend to isolate a more core-like area. The interpretation of these social status differences is not immediately clear.

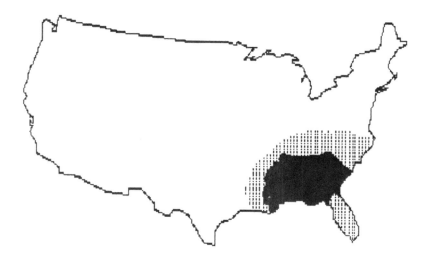

Figure 2.13 Michigan lower-middle (shaded area) and upper middle class (solid area) perceptions of "Southern"

From these comparisons, it appears that the commonplaces determined in production studies (change, age-grading, social stratification) are paralleled in this perceptual task, and continued comparison of subgroups for different regions and with data derived from other studies (see below) may reveal other parallel patterns.

In recognizing regional speech areas, nonlinguist respondents use protocols other than their perception of purely linguistic differences. The Hawaii study of hand-drawn maps (Preston 1982a) cataloged the labels which were assigned to areas and residents of areas and found that midwestern and inland northern speech areas were most often assigned such labels as "standard," "regular," "normal," and "everyday." In fact, all areas except the South were assigned some such positive label at least once. These results suggest the following: 1. regard for language correctness plays a role in areal distinctiveness and 2. areas perceived as least correct have greatest distinctiveness.

Of course, what is outlined as a dialect area by a respondent is understood in folk terms of "different speech," and the term "dialect" itself was scrupulously avoided in all the fieldwork. Nevertheless, it is not surprising, as Figures 2.10 and 2.11 show, that the South is the most frequently drawn area and that the "Northeast," the area which includes New York City, is also often represented. These are precisely the areas referred to by Langacker as less prestigious – certainly not representatives of SAE. Research discussed below will further develop this theme; for the moment, we simply claim that nonrelativistic, evaluative notions of an area's speech, particularly those which are pejorative or devaluing, enhance the area's salience as a distinct linguistic region.

A second, less powerful trend emerged from a more careful examination of labels. Such labels as "standard," "normal," and "everyday" were often contrasted with "high-falutin'," "very distinguished," and "snobby" (the latter usually associated with northeastern varieties). In addition, some positive labels did not refer to correctness at all: e.g., "friendly" and "down-home." These data suggested that respondents were distinguishing between "correct" and "pleasant" varieties, a trend not unlike the pattern of ratings given local versus RP varieties in much of the work carried out in Great Britain (e.g., Ryan, Giles, and Sebastian 1982) – a nonlocal, standard variety may rank high for education, status, competence, industriousness, but low for honesty, warmth, friendliness. A local or nonstandard variety (or varieties) often has these ratings reversed.

Figures 2.14 through 2.16 display three Northern hand-drawn maps which help further illustrate these claims about labels. The Michigan maps shown in Figures 2.14 and 2.15 make it clear that the Southern speech area is not one simply outlined as distinctive. In Figure 2.14 the characterization is of "hicks" and in Figure 2.15 of "hillbillies." The Michigan respondent who produced Figure 2.14 obviously believes that local speech is so ordinary that it deserves no outline at all; the one who produced Figure 2.15 calls the local area "midwestern english" [sic] and observes parenthetically that it is "normal." Here, however, it is important to note that although Indiana is in that larger "normal" circle, it is outlined as a subsection which is identified as having "its own expressions," and the "pronunciation is different." We shall refer to the special status of Indiana as we further develop its Southern ties (and its own futile attempts to deny them).

Figure 2.14 Michigan hand-drawn US dialect map

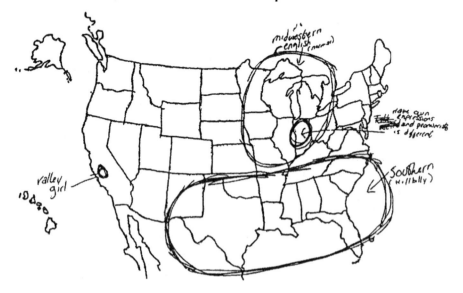

Figure 2.15 Another Michigan hand-drawn US dialect map

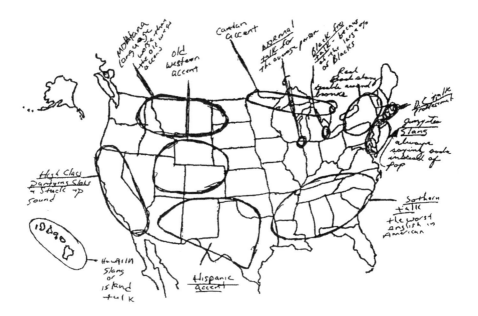

Figure 2.16 A Chicago hand-drawn US dialect map

Figure 2.16, drawn by a Chicago respondent, makes these "hillbilly" and "hick" labels even clearer; he notes that "Southern talk" is, quite simply, "the worst english in American" [sic]. His "normal" talk is extremely localized in Chicago. A number of other regional comments which cannot be examined here could be studied; in Figure 2.16, for example, the most interesting are, perhaps, the California label ("*High Class Partying Slobs* a stuck up sound"), the New Jersey one ("*Jerseyite slang* always saying soda instead of pop"), and the note that Detroit speech is "*Black fro talk* – because of the large % of Blacks." Labels on hand-drawn maps were, therefore, an obvious early clue in this program of research that relativistic outlines of where people simply spoke differently were not foremost in the minds of the respondents.

We do not need to rely on map labels alone to discover that Northerners make Southern speakers aware of the fact that they hold their speech in low esteem. A displaced Southerner (C) who has moved to the Ann Arbor, Michigan, area confesses the following when a fieldworker (M) asks if she can still "speak Southern."

C: ... I can't always do it on cue anymore. (2.0) ((mimics a Southern accent)) As y'all know, I came up from Texas when I was about twenty-one. And I talked like this. Probably not so bad, but I talked like this, you know I said "thi::s" and "tha::t" and all, those things.
M: Uh-huh.
C: And I had to learn rea:l fast how to talk like a Northerner?
M: Uh-huh.
C: Cause if I talked like this people ('ll, 'ld) think I'm the dumbest shit around. ((ends mimicry))
M: ((laughs))
C: So I learned to ta(h)lk li(h)ke a(h) Northerner.
                                          [
M: ((laughs)) Uh-hm.
C: ((rapidly)) Real fast. ((laughs)) (#49)

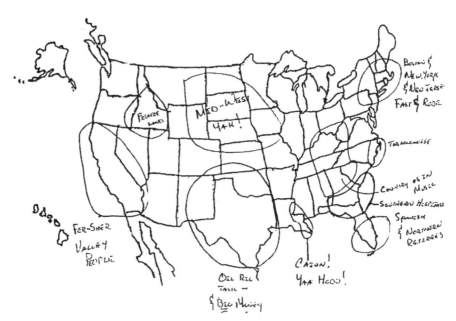

Figure 2.17 A North Carolina hand-drawn US dialect map

It would not be fair to fail to give prejudiced-against areas space for some of their hand-drawn representations. Since Southerners' maps reveal the same general outlines as those drawn by Northerners, we must ask if Southern maps reveal the same pejorative treatment of the South. Figure 2.17, drawn by a North Carolinian, would seem to reverse things. The "core" South (small as this representation is) is characterized by "Southern Hospitality"; the "Upland" or "Outer South" is "Country As In Music" (a gloss designed, we believe, to remove the usual pejoration associated with the plain label "country"). "Boston & New York & New Jersey" are "Fast and Rude," and Midwesterners' speech is "Yak."

Southerners' maps much more often than Northerners' dichotomize North and South on a valued dimension, but accompanying labels do not make it clear that the evaluation is of language variety, although one could make that criticism of any number of labels used by Northerners as well (e.g., "hillbillies"). One map realizes this dichotomy directly in the assignment of "Them – the bad guys" to the Northeast and Great Lakes areas and "Us – the Good People" to a typically southeastern South. Figure 2.18 expresses in even more traditional language exactly what we suspect many of these North-South maps seek to express. (Another map contrasts "Yankees" with "God's people.")

There is no doubt that pride in local cultural values allows many Southerners to escape the self-hate or intense "linguistic insecurity" that so many of Labov's New York City respondents reported (1966), but Northern pejorative trends in Southern maps are not universally absent. Figure 2.19, for example, complains that Southern speech is "very slow hard to comprehend" and that, except for a few caricaturistic labels, the rest of the United States is the "midwest" which "doesn't have accent."

Figure 2.18 A South Carolina hand-drawn US dialect map

Figure 2.19 Another South Carolina hand-drawn US dialect map

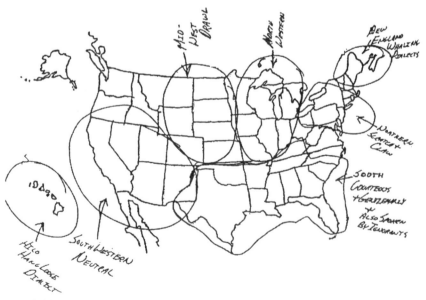

Figure 2.20 Still another South Carolina hand-drawn US dialect map

One might note, however, that comprehension (dealt with more extensively in the "degree of difference" task below) and rate are not the harshest criticisms that could be brought against a variety. Figure 2.20, however, although it continues the caricature of Northeastern speech ("Scratch and Claw"), admits that Southern speech, although it may be "Courteous and Gentlemanly," is "Also Spoken By Ignorants," a devastating blow to the notion that "Southern" is one of the varieties of SAE.

In conclusion, Southerners are certainly aware of Northern caricatures of Southern speech (and culture), and some even seem to have incorporated such negative caricatures into their own folk linguistic belief. Even for them, however, linguistic insecurity appears to be coupled with regional pride, particularly as even speech itself reflects certain cultural strengths ("gentlemanliness," "hospitality") or offers an excuse to outline a region with positive identities ("God's people") or contrast it with one which lacks positive identities (e.g., "Damn yankees"). Even among Southern respondents. however, there is a strong caricature of "Midwestern" speech as "accent free" or, as one respondent noted over a large Plains States area, "No Identity at all."

We shall refer to the composites of the hand-drawn maps as we compare them to other quantitative and conversational studies, and we shall provide a general comparison to professional dialectologists' accounts of United States regional speech in 2.1.4.

2.1.2 "Correct" and "pleasant"

Since geographical identification seemed to be based in evaluation, respondents were asked a more direct question: "Where are the most (and least) 'correct' and 'pleasant' varieties of English spoken in the United States?" As indicated above, such ranking procedures have a long history in cultural geography (e.g., Gould and White 1974). Figure 2.21 is a map of mean scores for "correctness" from southeastern Michigan, Figure 2.22 for southern Indiana, and Figure 2.23 one compiled from Southern responses (N = 36, Auburn University students, principally from Alabama, Georgia [the majority] and South Carolina).[5]

Very few respondents complained about this task. The relativist position taken by linguists, though morally unreproachable, was not taken by the majority of respondents. Although some complained that they did not have information about a state, the ranking of most areas for correctness appeared to be a "reasonable" task.

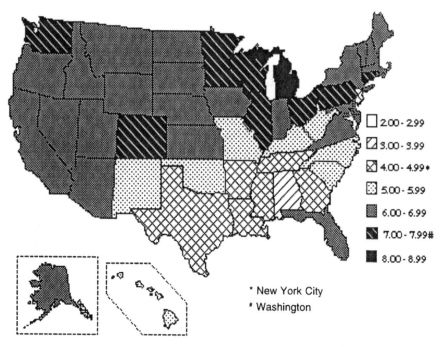

Figure 2.21   Mean scores of Michigan "correctness" ratings

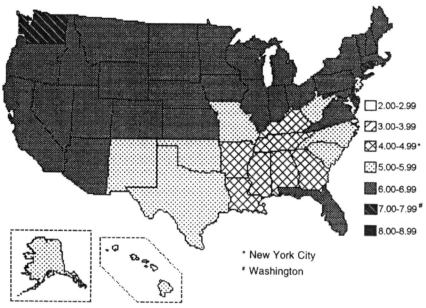

Figure 2.22   Mean scores of Indiana "correctness" ratings

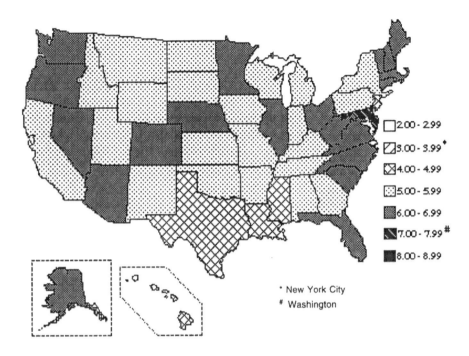

	2.00 - 2.99
	3.00 - 3.99 *
	4.00 - 4.99
	5.00 - 5.99
	6.00 - 6.99
	7.00 - 7.99 #
	8.00 - 8.99

* New York City
# Washington

Figure 2.23 Mean scores of Southern "correctness" ratings

Figures 2.21 and 2.22 show that for both southeastern-Michigan and southern-Indiana respondents the areas most definitely associated with incorrect English are the South and New York City; they are the only areas which have mean scores within the range 4.00–4.99 (Alabama, for Michigan raters, dipping even into the 3.00–3.99 range). Langacker's assessment of what nonlinguists believe about correctness and Fromkin and Rodman's personal prejudices are upheld in this survey on at least two counts; the South and New York City (Langacker's "Brooklynese") are both rated low. In addition, areas which border on the South and New York City are given ratings in the 5.00 to 5.99 range, and their low ratings may be accounted for by noting their proximity to the lowest-rated areas. The other two sites falling in that range, – Alaska (only for Indiana respondents) and Hawaii – must be interpreted differently. It is most likely that for many respondents the caricature of non-native speakers for these two regions may be very high. Unfamiliarity is an unlikely reason for the low rating since these respondents are just as likely to be unfamiliar with some of the plains and mountain states (e.g., Montana and Idaho) which fall in the 6.00–6.99 range.

Turning to the other end of the scale, predictions about linguistic insecurity seem to be borne out. Michigan raters, most strikingly, see themselves as the only state in the 8.00–8.99 range, exposing considerable linguistic self-confidence. Indiana respondents, however, rate themselves in the generally acceptable 6.00–6.99 range, but clearly regard some other areas (Washington, DC, Connecticut, Delaware, and Washington)[6] as superior. This lower ranking of the home area must indicate some (but not rampant) linguistic insecurity. They are clearly different from Michigan raters, who, apparently, see themselves as the only speakers of SAE in the United States. The Michigan ratings suggest at least one of the sources of the Indiana insecurity. Those raters allow surrounding states to bask in the warmth of Michigan's correctness. Wisconsin, Minnesota, Illinois, Ohio, and Pennsylvania (all nearby states) earned ratings in the 7.00–7.99 range. Indiana however, which actually shares a land boundary with Michigan (as Illinois, Minnesota, and Pennsylvania do not) is rated one notch down, in the 6.00–6.99 range. Two interpretations are available: Indiana is seen by Michigan raters as belonging to that set of states farther west which earn ratings in that range, or, much more likely, Indiana is seen as a peculiarly northern outpost of southern speech. It is surely that internal and external perception of Indiana as a site influenced by Southern varieties (an historically and descriptively accurate perception, by the way) which produces its linguistic insecurity. That Indiana respondents classify themselves along with Michigan, Illinois, Wisconsin, and other Great Lakes states in the 6.00–6.99 range in their own rating may be interpreted as their attempt to align themselves with Northern rather than Southern varieties in order to escape the associations which form the basis of their insecurity. Further substantiation of this dialect social climbing may be seen by noting whom Indiana residents do not align themselves with. Their Kentucky neighbors are rated a full two steps lower for correctness, in spite of their considerable linguistic similarity. On the other hand, the narrower range of ratings provided by the Indiana respondents (4.00–7.99) compared to the Michigan raters (3.00–8.99) might indicate a more democratic view of the distribution of correctness in general. That alternative and not necessarily contradictory interpretation will require more investigation. In previous research, however, nonstandard speakers have provided the harshest ratings of nonstandard performances (e.g., Labov 1966).

Other high ratings by both groups do indeed include some of the New England area Langacker indicated might be preferred (and might be associated with British speech). Quite unexpectedly, Washington, DC. earns a high rating from both sets of respondents –

an indication, perhaps, that the center of government is seen as an authority on matters linguistic, although its high rating might represent only a part of the Mid-Atlantic section of SAE believed in by Fromkin and Rodman. Not mentioned by either Langacker or Fromkin and Rodman as a folk site for SAE, however, is the West, but it is assigned generally high ratings by both Indiana and Michigan respondents. There is, doubtless, for both sets of respondents a sense of a leveled, unremarkable (but standard) speech to the West.

The Southerners' map of correctness (Figure 2.23), like comments on their hand-drawn maps, does not reveal a sweeping and unequivocal pattern of linguistic insecurity. In fact, some of these "southeastern Southerners" do not find themselves any less well-spoken than the southern Indiana respondents did, giving South and North Carolina, Virginia, and West Virginia ratings in the 6.00–6.99 range. Parts of the South rated one step down in the 5.00–5.99 range are just like the ratings for most of the country. New York City and New Jersey are the only big Northern losers, but those ratings are expected. The interesting zone of 4.00–4.99 incorrectness seen here is the "western" South – Mississippi, Louisiana, and Texas, the latter two often excluded from the "true" South (for example, in the Indiana respondents' hand-drawn composite – Figure 2.11).

A comparison of the Indiana correctness map (Figure 2.22) with the Indiana map of regional differences (Figure 2.11) shows that correctness evaluations do not necessarily change at the boundaries of perceived regional difference (although, of course, those hand-drawn boundaries which are not at or near state lines will not be reflected in this task). While the low correctness ratings for the South (area #1) and Inner South (area #6) and for the Southwest (area #7) are very good matches between the two representations, the Midwest, North, West, New England, Northeast, and East Coast, all seen as distinct speech areas, differ little in their correctness ratings.

The Michigan map of perceived dialect areas (Figure 2.10) shows little correspondence with the detailed levels of correctness in the Great Lakes area which emerged in the correctness ranking study. Much of Indiana is lumped together with Michigan, Minnesota, Illinois, Wisconsin, and Ohio in a "North" in Figure 2.10. On the other hand, when compared to the Indiana rankings, the greater complexity of rankings in the Michigan correctness study is paralleled by a greater complexity of areal distribution in the hand-drawn map task. Considerably greater overlapping appears in the Michigan map (Figure 2.10), suggesting that areas with less linguistic self-confidence (here Indiana) may show greater uniformity and consistency in perception.

That generalization would appear to be reflected in the Southern correctness map, which, like the Indiana one, contains a much narrower range of rankings. Since a computer generalization was not done of Southern hand-drawn maps, we cannot compare these other quantitative studies with such a composite, but informal observation suggests that there is little correlation between the distinctions made in this correctness map and the sampling of Southern hand-drawn maps provided above (e.g., Figures 2.17 through 2.20).

A factor analysis of ratings often provides a more subtle way of grouping together areas rated similarly. Figure 2.24 shows the factor analysis of the "correct" ratings from Michigan and Figure 2.25 the results for Indiana. Although the strongest factor group (#1) for both groups is the rather large western area to which both assigned high but not the highest ratings,[7] the second strongest factor group for both is the low-rated South, and, for Indiana residents, it reaches up to include the local area, rather strong proof that Indiana linguistic insecurity stems from associations with Southern speech. This same factor group is peculiarly divided for Michigan respondents; in addition to a small group of southern states, there is a continuum of New England, Mid Atlantic, and Great Lakes States in this category. Even these areas are broken up by a small number of idiosyncratic groups. These analyses suggest that the Indiana raters have a greater consistency in their perception of correctness as a geographical phenomenon, a feature already noted in their less-complex hand-drawn composite (i.e., Figure 2.11).

The third factor group for Indiana is a New England – Mid Atlantic stretch, the fourth a generally southwestern group of states, the fifth New York and New York City, and the sixth a possible confirmation of the suggestion that Alaska and Hawaii were rated lower on the basis of their being perceived as sites with a high concentration of non-native speakers. Their being joined by New Mexico in a factor analysis makes that more plausible.[8]

Unfortunately, the smaller number of respondents did not allow a meaningful treatment of the Southern data in a factor analysis mode.

These "correctness" ratings show the predicted differences between the Michigan secure and Indiana insecure raters and even more dramatically confirm the low prestige assigned Southern and New York City varieties. The task further confirms that it is association with Southern speech which gives Indiana its low external and internal regard. On the other hand, the more confused picture of Southern linguistic insecurity remains. These "southeastern" Southern raters were harsher in general, and, although they did not rate themselves high, they did not, as Indiana raters did, place several other areas higher than themselves.[9] On the other hand, they did locate a Southern region of incorrectness, but it was a "western" one, which, with the exception of Mississippi, was often excluded from "core" Southern representations in the hand-drawn maps.

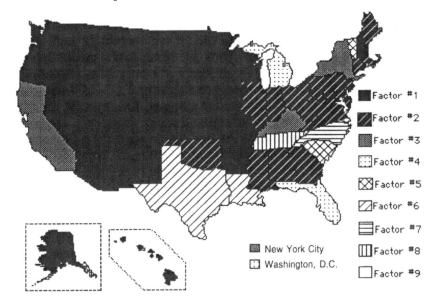

Figure 2.24 Factor analysis of Michigan "correctness" ratings

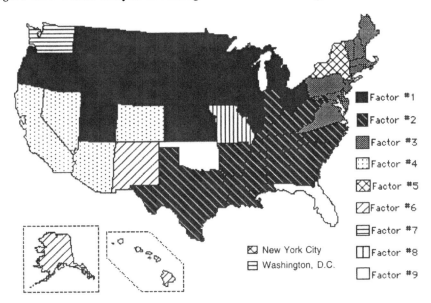

Figure 2.25 Factor analysis of Indiana "correctness" ratings

Figures 2.26, 2.27, and 2.28 display the ratings of Michigan, Indiana, and Southern respondents for "pleasant" speech. The suggestion by Giles and associates that local speech is affectively preferred, regardless of its "correctness," is strongly confirmed. Indiana respondents rate only Indiana in the 7.00–7.99 range for pleasantness, and the Southern raters place the entire Southeast in this high category and elevate Alabama (the site where the ratings were done) to 8.00–8.99, a level paralleled only by Michigan's evaluation of its own correctness. The Michigan raters put only Washington, Colorado, and neighboring Minnesota in the same 7.00–7.99 range along with their home site. These results suggest, further, that the preference for local norms along affective lines is stronger in areas where there is linguistic insecurity. At the other end, only a few areas are rated low by Indiana and Michigan respondents. New York City is the only site put in the 4.00–4.99 range by both Indiana and Michigan raters. More interestingly, the ratings of the South, similar for the Indiana and Michigan groups in the correctness task are very different for this "pleasantness" task. The Michigan respondents continue to rate the South low, giving Alabama a score in the 4.00–4.99 range, but the Indiana raters, although they find the South incorrect, do not find it so unpleasant. In fact, New Hampshire, New Jersey, New York, and Delaware are a much larger pocket of unpleasant speech areas from the point of view of Indiana speakers. For Michigan speakers this eastern unpleasantness is associated only with New York City and its immediate surroundings.

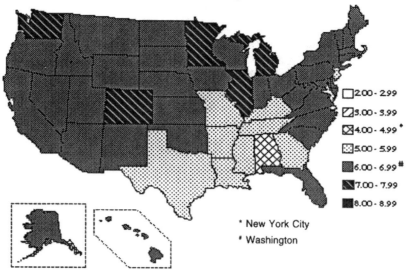

Figure 2.26 Michigan ratings of "pleasant" speech

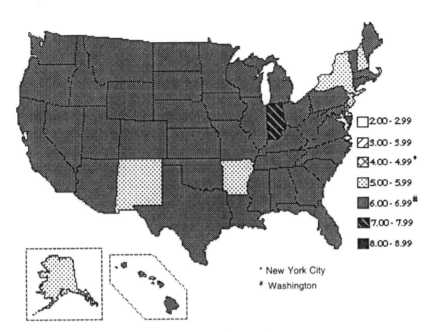

Figure 2.27 Indiana ratings of "pleasant" speech

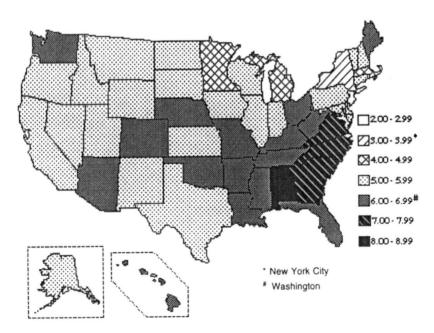

Figure 2.28 Southern ratings of "pleasant" speech

Southern "unpleasantness" ratings are harsher. The only 2.00–2.99 rating in any of these studies shows up for New Jersey; New York City and even New York State are given a 3.00–3.99; Massachusetts, Michigan, and Minnesota are assigned 4.00–4.99, a rating reserved by Michigan raters for only the "worst" Southern state (Alabama) and Indiana raters for only New York City in the same task.

Factor analyses of these "pleasant" ratings (Figures 2.29 and 2.30) show that Indiana speakers do create a little pocket (along with Illinois) for themselves (Figure 2.30, #6), but Michigan raters, more linguistically secure, extend the "pleasant" rating of their home site over the entire Great Lakes area (Figure 2.29, #3). The factor groups for both regions show greater consistency and internal agreement than for the correct task and raise possibilities for interpretation not taken up here. Although the small number of respondents again prevents general consideration of Southern data, the second strongest group in a factor analysis of those data is a central and western South (with a negatively loaded Northeast), suggesting that the "Yankee" – "Southern" contrast is very strong for these respondents, exactly as many of the hand-drawn maps show.

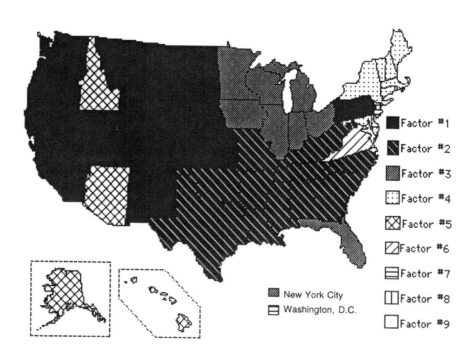

Figure 2.29 Factor analysis of Michigan "pleasant" ratings

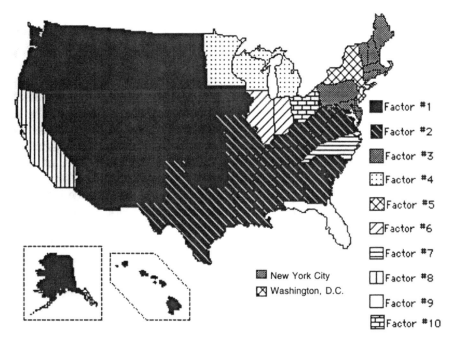

Figure 2.30 Factor analysis of Indiana "pleasant" ratings

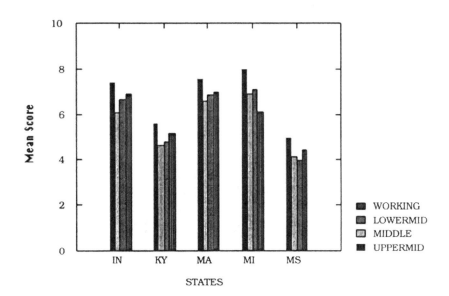

Figure 2.31 Indiana "correctness" ratings by class

Some subgroup behavior in these tasks is revealing. Upper-middle-class Indiana respondents generally give higher correctness ratings and middle and lower-middle-class raters give lower ones, as shown for selected states in Figure 2.31.

This tendency is true for stigmatized (Kentucky and Mississippi) as well as approved (Massachusetts and Michigan) areas and applies to the local area (Indiana) as well. (This tendency also extends to the Indiana "pleasant" ratings.) Such class stratification in correctness ratings may reflect middle and lower-middle-class linguistic insecurity, manifested here in generally lower ratings. Michigan raters, from an area of greater linguistic security, do not show this stratified rating.

Since these data suggest a parallelism to "hypercorrection," it will be important to ask if these tendencies are stable or involved in change. Apparent time scores of Indiana ratings for correctness do not indicate change in progress, suggesting that the mildly hypercorrect patterns of middle and lower-middle-class (and, to a lesser degree, female) raters may be relatively stable phenomena. In fact, the pattern of Indiana ratings for southern speech suggests age-grading rather than change (Figure 2.32). Since neither younger nor older speakers participate in the everyday world of work (Chambers and Trudgill 1980:91-92), the prescriptive attitudes of the community which reflect negative evaluations of southern speech mean least to them, and the amelioration of their rankings on the correctness task follows an age-graded, curvilinear pattern.

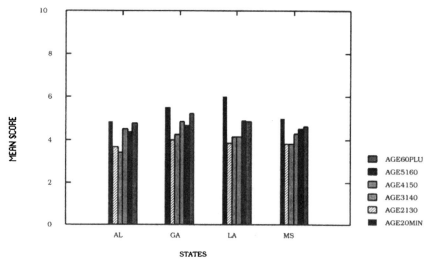

Figure 2.32 Indiana "correctness" ratings by age

In addition to such age, gender, and class variation in performance and attitude, sociolinguists have observed ethnic diversity. African-Americans, for example, were found to have less linguistic insecurity and less awareness that New York City speech was stigmatized by outsiders (Labov 1966: 351-352).

Similarly, African-Americans in southeastern Michigan rate the local area high, even higher than long-term white residents, but their ratings of southern speech, although low, are not lower than white Michigan respondents' ratings of the same areas (Figure 2.33).

From this perspective, African-Americans in Michigan share local attitudes to a greater extent than immigrant Appalachians do. For example, Michigan raters with Appalachian backgrounds assign Michigan itself a rather lower correctness score than do the African-American and long-term European-American residents. In fact, the Michigan Appalachian rating (7.0) is not strikingly different from the assessment of Michigan given by Indiana raters (6.8). In addition, their ratings of southern areas are not as harsh as those assigned by the African-American and long-term European-American Michigan respondents. In this case, attitudinal convergence is stronger across racial lines than across a line which divides recent immigrants who come from a stigmatized speech area (the "Inner" or "Upper" South) from long-term local European-American residents in a relatively prestigious one (Michigan).

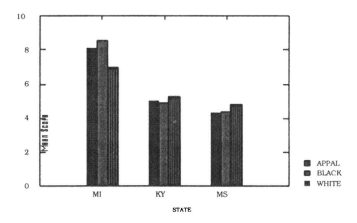

Figure 2.33 Michigan "correctness" ratings by sub-groups

A more careful look at the Appalachian Michigan ratings shows, however, that dramatic change may be beginning. Figure 2.34 is a display of apparent time data for Michigan Appalachians' ratings of those same areas shown above in Figure 2.33.

The youngest Appalachians' high regard for the local variety might be called "contact hypercorrection" and is, perhaps, a painful indicator of their desire for local acceptability. The old home area, here Kentucky, although clearly downgraded by all six age groups, is more dramatically disapproved of by the youngest three, whose scores are even lower than those of their age pairs from Michigan in their ratings of Kentucky.

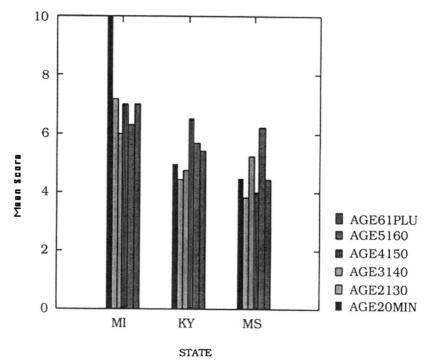

Figure 2.34 Michigan Appalachian "correctness" ratings by age

These "correct" and "pleasant" ratings provide confirmation of the general patterns of linguistic security and insecurity outlined above. Areas with greater linguistic insecurity focus on regional solidarity (as expressed in "pleasantness") to express local identity. Areas with considerable security do not use local speech to express such identity, for its "uniqueness" is already taken up in the expression of status rather than solidarity matters. Finally, of course, details of stereotype and caricature are more definitively cataloged through such tasks.

2.1.3 Degree of dialect difference

In the map-drawing task, unless a respondent refers specifically to comprehensibility or the degree of difference between one area and another, we cannot know the "intensity" of difference intended. Since some areas are not outlined at all, we have no information about them. Additionally, the "correct" and "pleasant" rankings do not directly address this problem. For example, it might be possible for two areas to have very different "correctness" rankings but be perceived as equally "different" from the local area. When respondents are required to rate each state for the degree of its difference from the local area, we overcome some of these handicaps. Although originally rated by the respondents as 1 (no difference), 2 (slightly different), 3 (different), and 4 (unintelligibly different), the derived mean score ratings were divided into four groups as follows: 1.00–1.75, 1.76–2.50, 2.51–3.25, 3.26–4.00.

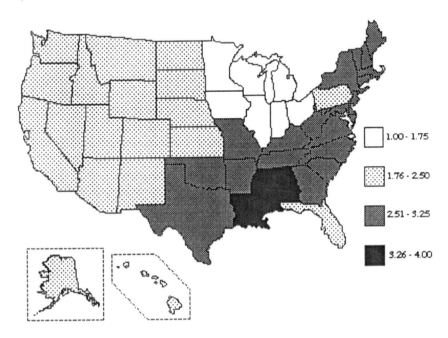

Figure 2.35 Mean degree of difference ratings for Michigan respondents

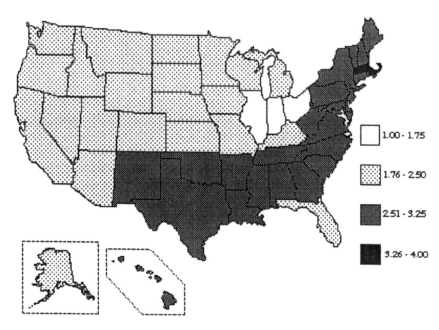

Figure 2.36 Mean degree of difference ratings for Indiana respondents

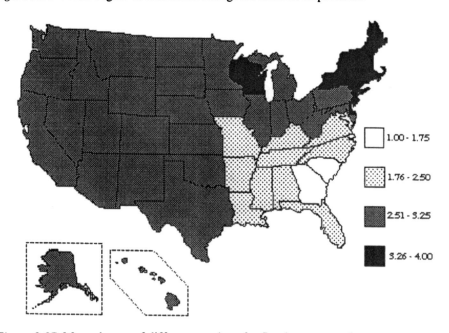

Figure 2.37 Mean degree of difference ratings for Southern respondents

Figure 2.35 shows that when Michigan raters evaluate degree of difference they perceive a larger local area than when they draw dialect maps. The "North" in Figure 2.10 is a more circumscribed Michigan-Wisconsin area than the states rated "1" here, although that may be artificially imposed by the rating of entire states. In fact, all the states rated "1" here are at least partially included in the "North" in Figure 2.10. This task also reveals that Michigan respondents feel their speech is closer to a large western US group of states than to any other region, a fact not revealed in the hand-drawn maps.

Here, however, it is the Michigan South ratings which are of greatest interest. A much larger South than the one drawn in Figure 2.10 emerges as a territory rated "3." Texas, Arkansas, Oklahoma, and Missouri (identified in the map-drawing task as separate speech areas, "Southwestern," or even "Midwestern") are here rated along with obviously Southern states (e.g., Georgia and South Carolina). We cannot tell if the "3" assigned Virginia, West Virginia, Maryland, and Delaware is a result of the raters' desire to make any or all of those states part of a South, or if it is a desire to assign such a rating to the entire Northeast and East Coast (with the exception of Pennsylvania). Even if one adds the "Inner South" area (#6) from Figure 2.10, the South of the map-drawing task is not as large as the one represented here. This larger South, however, does not appear to be due to forced ratings of entire states; Florida, for example, is excluded from this "3" rating, when in fact, as the map-drawing task shows, it is only the southern tip of Florida which causes folk respondents to exclude it from the South. The core South of this task lies clearly in those three states which earn a "4" (Alabama, Mississippi, and Louisiana), an area shifted slightly to the west from the core area established in the map-drawing task (see Figure 2.8) but similar to the correctness map of Southerners themselves, who also located the "most incorrect" areas of the South even farther to the west (see Figure 2.23). These degree-of-difference ratings, unlike the map drawing, then, suggest that the Michigan raters are aware of a much wider area of influence of Southern speech, emanating from an unintelligibly different core. Even though the Northeast and East Coast also earn the "3" rating, there is no similar "unintelligible" core there.

In the correctness task the Indiana raters grouped themselves with areas to the North (Figure 2.22), presumably to avoid connection with the contaminating South. Here, however, insecurity surfaces (as it did in the factor analysis, Figure 2.25), since the Indiana respondents find a degree of difference between themselves and speakers to the North. In fact, the difference ratings from Indiana look more like the Indiana pleasantness ratings (Figure 2.27), since only the two latitudinally contiguous states (Ohio and Illinois) are regarded as exactly similar.[10] Indiana respondents do not, however, associate difference from their own speech with nonstandardness. For example, the South (rated worst) is as different from Indiana speech as is the Northeast (generally rated well, with the obvious exception of New York City and nearby areas). In fact, Massachusetts, rated quite high, is the only area with unintelligibly different speech. Michigan respondents, on the other hand, are much harsher on the South and do seem to associate extreme difference with nonstandardness, but this is hardly surprising since for them the local area is the ultimate in correctness. The core of the South (Louisiana, Mississippi, and Alabama) is rated both most different and most incorrect.

More significantly, it is the Northeast which is apparently the most different for these Indiana raters, for the "unintelligible core," although small, is there in Massachusetts. Although they are from contiguous states, the Michigan and Indiana raters have very different orientations to the Northeast and the South. The Northeast is "most" different for the Indiana raters, the South for the Michigan group. Traditional dialectology would simply affirm that Michigan is, after all, an extension of western New England and upstate New York speech and that Southern speech influences are very strong in Indiana, particularly in the southern part of the State where this research was done.

Figure 2.37, the Southern raters' map of degree of difference, although more like the Indiana map in one important way, is unlike the two earlier difference maps in a number of ways. Like Indiana raters, Southerners find the heart of major differences in the Northeast, but they expand the zone of unintelligibility to include the entire area, and it almost expands West through Michigan to Wisconsin. Like Michigan raters, however, their zone of unintelligibility is large, suggesting that the "Midland" position of Indiana is less likely to produce such radical evaluations. Also like Indiana raters, the Southerners have their own core zone of similarity (Georgia and South Carolina), but, unlike Indiana or Michigan raters, they expand it to a secondary "local" zone. Confirming earlier map generalizations from nearly every area, it excludes Louisiana and Texas, but, unlike some maps presented above, it includes Florida, Missouri, and Arkansas. For Southern raters, the large Western zone of states is all lumped together, but it is a "3," not a "2" as it was in the Indiana and Michigan surveys. The two-level differentiation within the South seems to have promoted more distinctive ratings of all nonsouthern areas – the West, North, and Northeast.

These difference ratings confirm and challenge some of the earlier claims concerning sociolinguistic commonplaces in perception data. Figure 2.38 shows ratings of Kentucky by age for various respondents.

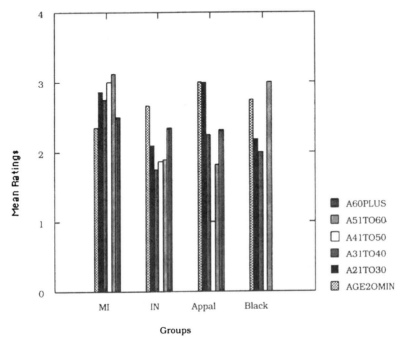

Figure 2.38 Ratings of Kentucky by age

A rather strong age-graded pattern emerges for the three "southern-based" groups (Indiana, Michigan Appalachians, Michigan African-Americans) which, at least for Indiana responses, is not what might have been predicted. Above it was assumed that the age-graded pattern of better correctness ratings for southern areas by younger and older Indiana respondents was based on their failing to participate in working community prejudices, but in Figure 2.38 it appears that working-age groups feel less strongly that Kentucky is different. Perhaps the dominance of Louisville as the local metropolitan area for these Indiana respondents will not allow working people to ignore the similarity of speech on both sides of the river, so the difference ratings are necessarily lower. Paradoxically, the Indiana community prejudice against less prestigious Southern varieties is strongest in those same respondents, as can be seen in Figure 2.32.

Does this reveal a tension between large-scale regional prejudice against Appalachian and Southern speech and a desire to be dissociated from it on the one hand and local recognition of the extensive speech similarity between southern Indiana and northern Kentucky on the other? This apparent disharmony (and perhaps others in such studies) might be reconciled by recent work in vantage theory, which suggests that differential labeling of the same facts may represent different vantage points from which such facts are viewed. In this case, Indiana and Kentucky are different when some domains are activated (hand-drawn maps, correctness, pleasantness) but similar when other protocols are used (degree of difference). That explanation, however, does not at all account for the fact that Michigan African-Americans and Appalachians also show age-graded responses to Kentucky, with youngest and oldest respondents finding a greater degree of difference.

In general, however, the perception of difference task showed less demographic variation than any of the others, but work in other geographical areas and further investigation of these data themselves may reveal patterns worth analyzing.

2.1.4 Placement of regional voices

This last task may seem ill-placed in a folk-linguistic setting, for it would appear to test only a respondent's acuity in the detection of regionally different voices, but we believe that folk caricature expresses itself even here. We seek to discover in this task how accurately respondents can locate voice samples along a US North-South continuum and how the boundaries which emerge correspond to those already established in the above tasks. More importantly, how might such identification patterns supplement conclusions already drawn about "correctness," "insecurity," and the like? Figure 2.39 shows the home sites of the recorded voices; these voices (described in 4 in 2.1 above) were then played in random order, and the respondents were asked to associate each voice with a site. We assigned the sites the values one through nine (from north to south) to allow calculation of mean scores for the task. For example, if a respondent placed the voice from Saginaw, Michigan, at South Bend, Indiana, the value "3" (rather than the correct "1") was tallied for that response. If each voice were assigned its correct site perfectly by each respondent, the scores would read simply, 1.00, 2.00, and so on from north to south. The actual scores are shown in Table 2.1:

Figure 2.39 Home sites of the nine middle-class, middle-aged male respondents' recorded voice samples

Table 2.1   Mean placement scores of the nine regional voices

		'correct'	Michigan	Indiana
Site				
1	Saginaw, Michigan	1	3.66	2.45
2	Coldwater, Michigan	2	3.05	2.63
3	South Bend, Indiana	3	3.46	3.75
4	Muncie, Indiana	4	4.13	5.09
5	New Albany, Indiana	5	5.27	5.83
6	Bowling Green, Kentucky	6	5.52	6.06
7	Nashville, Tennessee	7	6.22	6.38
8	Florence, Alabama	8	6.61	6.31
9	Dothan, Alabama	9	6.95	6.59

What is perhaps most striking, although perhaps not particularly important to the focus here, is the fact that these nonlinguists were very good at arranging these speech samples along a North – South dimension. In fact, each group has "displaced" only one site each; the Michigan respondents have heard site #1 (Saginaw, Michigan) as being farther "South" than it actually is, and the Indiana respondents have switched the order of sites #7 and #8 (but only by .07!). It is interesting that both these "errors" involve the first and the last voices as they were presented in random order to the respondents: Saginaw, Michigan (site #1) was presented last, and Nashville (#7) was presented first. Since the respondents were forced to choose only one site for each voice heard, it was very difficult for them to make corrections as the experiment progressed. The first (Nashville, Tennessee) voice might have been placed a little too far south and not corrected later; the last (Saginaw, Michigan) voice might have been placed farther north if it had been heard earlier, but the northernmost spaces must have been used for earlier voices. Under these rapid forced choice circumstances, however, we continue to believe that these respondents did a remarkable job (on average) of ordering these voices, revealing a folk ability not previously suspected of United States nonlinguists.

We shall use a rough distance gauge to investigate these identifications further. If one assumes that a greater difference between mean scores indicates a greater distinctiveness heard between two samples, then a convention of calling a .50 or greater difference a "minor" boundary and a difference of 1.00 or greater a "major" one seems reasonable. Based on those calculations, maps of the respondents' areas of acoustic differentiation of United States dialects (along this North – South dimension only, of course) are represented in Figures 2.40 and 2.41. In the few cases when the respondents' mean scores result in a site's being displaced, a box is drawn around that site number and an arrow points to the incorrect position which resulted from the faulty identification. For example, in Figure 2.40, the mean score for Michigan raters' placement of Saginaw, Michigan (site #1) moves it from its correct position to one between sites #3 and #4. The difference between mean scores is calculated for the new order of displaced voices. For example, there is a .61 difference between the scores for sites #1 and #2 in the Michigan respondents' data (Table 2.1), but since the site #1 voice has been "displaced" to third position, the mathematical comparison was made between sites #1 and #3 (northwards) and between #1 and #4 (southwards), neither of which produced a difference between mean scores greater than .50.

Figure 2.40 Michigan identification "boundaries"

Figure 2.41 Indiana identification "boundaries"

As Figure 2.40 shows, the Michigan respondents distinguish, with a major boundary, between a large northern territory which extends from their home state about halfway through Indiana. This major boundary cuts off site #5 (the home site of the Indiana respondents in these same studies) and everything farther south from this large northern area. Such a division lends further support to the Indiana respondents' "fear" that they are "Southern," the obvious source of their linguistic insecurity. The Michigan respondents also hear, however, a minor boundary between sites #6 and #7, a division which would seem to distinguish between an "Appalachia" (or "South Midland") and a "Deep South."

In contrast, the Indiana respondents (Figure 2.41) hear sharp subdivisions in the "North," placing major boundaries between sites #2 (Coldwater, Michigan) and #3 (South Bend, Indiana) and between #3 and #4 (Muncie, Indiana). They continue this "northern discrimination" with a minor boundary between #4 and #5 (New Albany, Indiana, their home site). It should be fairly obvious that this identification task has not awakened local insecurity, for the Indiana respondents have placed their own region's voice in a large, undifferentiated "South." In what remains of this section on quantitative studies in folk dialectology, we shall focus on a comparison of these identification findings with the other experiments already reported on and with professional dialectologists' findings.

The North to South dimension of these nine regional voices will, in many professional accounts, result in four major regions – 1. a "North" (or "Upper North"); 2. a "North Midland" (or "Lower North"), 3. a "South Midland" (or "Inner South," "Upper South," or often, inaccurately, "Appalachia"), and 4. a "South" (or "Lower," "Coastal," or "Deep South"). We shall compare our perceptual results with two professional representations of this territory – one based exclusively on phonology, the other on general characteristics of dialect, although it is important to note that dialect vocabulary and grammar played no role in these identifications since the portions of the tape-recordings which were used for the task were specifically selected to exclude such features.

Figure 2.42 shows this four-part division along the path of our stimulus voices: 1. a "North" (in which a vowel change known as the "Northern Cities Shift" is taking place in the largest urban areas) extends from Michigan into about the upper one-fourth of Indiana; 2. a "North Midland" (in which the low vowels [ɑ] and [ɔ] are merging) covers only about one-half of central Indiana; 3. a "South Midland" (which Labov assigns no phonological characteristics undergoing rapid, current change) extends from the lower one-third of Indiana through the northern one-third of Tennessee; 4. finally, a "South" (undergoing the "Southern Vowel Shift") encompasses the rest of Tennessee and all areas farther south. In this taxonomy, our voices would be placed as follows:

> Saginaw and Coldwater, Michigan and South Bend, Indiana – North
> Muncie, Indiana – North Midland
> New Albany, Indiana, Bowling Green, Kentucky – South Midland
> Nashville, Tennessee – South Midland – South border
> Florence and Dothan, Alabama – South

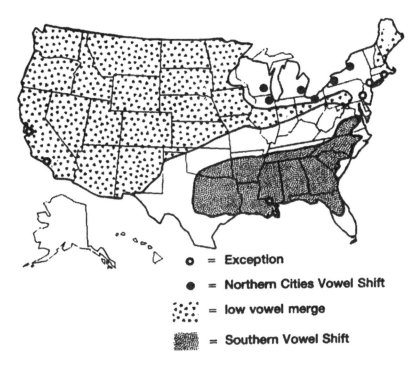

Figure 2.42 The "three dialects of English" (Wolfram 1991:89)

In our test, therefore, major boundary lines *should* have been heard between #3 and #4 and between #4 and #5. Ideally, at least minor boundaries should have been heard between #5 and #6 and between #6 and #7 (distinguishing the "transitional" or "border" nature of Nashville, Tennessee). Both the Michigan and Indiana identifications (Figures 2.40 and 2.41, respectively) show successes and failures in this regard. Michigan respondents do not distinguish a "North" from a "North Midland," for they include #4 (Muncie, Indiana) in their larger "North." They do, however, hear the "North Midland" – "South Midland" distinction very strongly, placing their only major boundary there. This placement suggests, by the way, that the alternative identification of the "North Midland" as a "Lower North" is perhaps to be preferred, an argument suggested by some recent work in dialect lexicography (e.g., Carver 1987, where it is suggested as well that the "South Midland" territory is actually an "Upper South"). The Michigan respondents also place a minor boundary between sites #6 (Bowling Green, Kentucky) and #7 (Nashville, Tennessee), the transitional area where the "South Midland" (or "Upper South") should stop and the "South" (or "Lower South") should begin, according to Figure 2.42. The fact that this is a "weak" boundary does not help us to resolve the "existence of the Midlands" controversy referred to just above.

The Indiana raters, on the other hand, make three distinctions, but they do not completely fulfill the expectations of Figure 2.42, either. First, they hear a "major" distinction between Coldwater, Michigan (site #2) and South Bend, Indiana (site #3) where, according to Figure 2.42, there should be none. They are, however, exactly on target with a strong boundary between sites #3 and #4, strengthening the argument for a "North" versus "Midlands" distinction. That trend would seem to be further supported, since they hear only a "weak" boundary between sites #4 and #5 (the traditional "North Midland" – "South Midland" distinction). In fact, however, their distinctions also support the loss of a "Midlands" territory, for their "South Midland" area (beginning at site #5) is not once separated (even with a minor boundary) from the "South." Moreover, their reversal of sites #7 and #8 makes their failure to make any southern subdivisions more difficult to interpret, although the very small difference in the mean scores of sites #7 and #8 (only .07) makes any further consideration of that point unnecessary. In fact, that reversal suggests the transitional nature of Nashville, Tennessee (site #7) as predicted in Figure 2.42, but since there are no major or minor subdivisions in the Indiana identification from #5 on south, we cannot offer further interpretations.

Michigan raters are, then, accurate in cutting the "South Midland" and "Southern" territory apart, but do not recognize the closer-to-home "North" versus "North Midland" split. Conversely, Indiana respondents separate the "North" from the "North Midland" (and even throw in a "Far North" versus "Not-So-Far-North" for good measure) but make no distinctions from the home site on south.

Figure 2.43 A "conglomorate" of US dialect studies (Lance 1994:338)

Figure 2.43 shows a map prepared from a large conglomerate of professional dialect studies done over the years. We shall not interpret all the details, but we will comment on those divisions (and subdivisions) which have to do with our sample voices. The "A" line is a principal cutoff for "North," and it corresponds to what we have already seen above. The "D" line is also a major division, and it separates sites #4 and #5 exactly as Figure 2.42 does. The "C" line is a weaker boundary and it separates sites #3 and #4 (also as Figure 2.42 does). Although there are a number of minor dialect boundaries in the "Outer South," there is no major subdivision in the southern area except those which separate areas "I" from "K" and "P" from "R" (limiting our attention to only those areas which include our sample voices). Based on this general picture, therefore, our voice samples should be stratified as follows:

Saginaw and Coldwater, Michigan, South Bend, Indiana – "North" (north of line "A")

Muncie, Indiana – "(Southern) North Midland" (between lines "C" and "D")

New Albany, Indiana – "(Northern) Ohio Valley" (south of "D" but north of the Ohio River

Bowling Green, Kentucky – "(Southern) Ohio Valley" (south of "D" and south of the Ohio River)

Nashville, Tennessee, Florence, Alabama – "South Midland" (within area "I" or "K")

Dothan, Alabama – "South" (within area "R")

These major boundary divisions cause quite a different picture of the southern United States from that given in Figure 2.42. This different picture, however, has only little influence on what we have already said about the patterns of identification of our sample voices. The Michigan distinction between sites #6 and #7 is also supported in this representation, but, again, there is no justification for the Indiana placement of a boundary between sites #2 and #3.

In general, therefore, our respondents hear the right order of our north-to-south samples, but they sometimes do and sometimes do not "hear" greater distinctions at those boundaries which have been discovered in the professional study of dialect differences.

How will these identifications supplement the information which has already been seen in the other quantitative studies? Recall that Figures 2.10 and 2.11 represent the composite of hand-drawn maps for Michigan and Indiana, respectively.

For the Michigan respondents, the most noticeable correlation is the failure to differentiate among voices #1, #2, #3, and #4 and the unity of that territory in the hand-drawn composite. All four sites fall within the area defined in Figure 2.10 as "North," and no boundaries are heard by Michigan respondents in that area in the identification task. Figure 2.10 shows that Michigan respondents have an "eastern tail" of their "Midwest" (area #10), but it falls between Muncie, Indiana (site #4) and New Albany, Indiana (site #5), encompassing neither. When the Michigan respondents produce a major boundary between these two areas, then, their hand-drawn composite is very supportive of that identification. One leaves the "North" and crosses the "eastern tail" of the "Midwest" between Muncie, Indiana and New Albany, Indiana.

On the other hand, New Albany, Indiana, does not quite fit into area #6 (the "Inner South" of Figure 2.10) either, a fact which would correspond very well with some professional findings. Carver (1987), for example, distinguishes southern Indiana within what he calls the "Lower North," although he notes strong southern influences there (in what he calls a "Hoosier Apex"). In Figure 2.10, in fact, New Albany, Indiana, lies in a sort of trough between the "Midwest" and the "Inner South," but since the hand-drawn composite shows that there are two boundaries between New Albany, Indiana, and Muncie, Indiana (to the north) and only one between New Albany, Indiana, and Bowling Green, Kentucky to the south, the identification task's major boundary between #4 and #5 strongly correlates with the hand-drawn task from a southern perspective as well.

Figure 2.10 shows an overlapping "Inner South" (area #6) and "South" (area #1). The remaining sample voices are distributed in that territory as follows:

> Site #6 (Bowling Green, Kentucky) – Inner South (#6)
> Site #7 (Nashville, Tennessee) – Inner South (#6) and South (#1)
> Sites #8 and #9 (Florence, Alabama and Dothan, Alabama) – South (#1)

Of course, only one of these boundaries (between sites #6 and #7) is supported, with a minor boundary, in the Michigan identification task.

The Indiana composite of hand-drawn maps (Figure 2.11) shows a slightly different organization of the territory under consideration here. First, site #3 (South Bend Indiana) lies just on a "dual boundary" (the southern limits of area #3 – a "North," and the northern limits of area #6 – a "Midwest"). Interestingly enough, although there is no support for it in professional studies, the Indiana respondents "heard" a major boundary between sites #2 and #3, just where their "North" and "Midwest" collide in Figure 2.11.

Muncie, Indiana, and New Albany, Indiana, also lie on a boundary in Figure 2.11 – the southern edge of the "Midwest" (area #6), an area separated from the "Inner South" (area #4) by a small trough or "empty" territory. In spite of the fact that the hand-drawn map puts the local area on the southern edge of the "Midwest" for Indiana respondents, they hear a difference (a minor boundary) between themselves and Muncie, Indiana. Perhaps the following scenario can explain this discrepancy. When the map-drawing task is proposed, linguistic insecurity causes Indiana respondents to place themselves as far north as they believe will appear reasonable (the lower edge of a "Midwest"). The identification task does not allow that (semi-?) conscious attention to insecurity, and the (accurate) distinction between "North Midland" (Muncie, Indiana) and "South Midland" (New Albany, Indiana) surfaces. Whatever the explanation, the placement of sites #4 and #5 in the same area in the hand-drawn composite and their separation by a minor boundary in the identification task is the most striking discrepancy between these two measures for the Indiana respondents.

In the remaining southern territory, the Indiana hand-drawn composite shows a neat division between an Outer South (area #6) and a "South" (area #1), and the remaining voice samples are divided equally between them – Bowling Green, Kentucky, and Nashville, Tennessee, fall in the "Inner South" and Florence and Dothan, Alabama, fall in the "South." In the identification task, however, Indiana respondents mark no major or minor boundaries in this territory.

Since the "correct" and "pleasant" tasks and the "degree of difference" task used states for rankings, the comparison with the identification task will not be as productive, but we offer the few following comments.

In the "correctness task" (Figure 2.21), the Michigan respondents indicate five gradations in the territory covered by the voice samples of the identification task. The home state is in the 8.00 range, Indiana 6.00, Kentucky 5.00, Tennessee 4.00, and Alabama 3.00. This would suggest the following subdivisions:

> Saginaw and Coldwater, Michigan
> South Bend, Muncie, and New Albany, Indiana
> Bowling Green, Kentucky
> Nashville, Tennessee
> Florence and Dothan, Alabama

In the identification task, however, only one Michigan boundary (the minor one between Bowling Green, Kentucky and Nashville, Tennessee) supports this division. The major boundary (between Muncie and New Albany, Indiana) could not be represented in the correctness task at all (and is, perhaps, a good indication of the artificiality of the state-wide assessment required in that task). On the other hand, the displacement of the Saginaw, Michigan, voice (site #1) to a position between sites #3 and #4 (both in Indiana) completely ignores the considerable correctness distinction made by the same raters between Michigan and Indiana.

The Indiana correctness task, as Figure 2.22 shows, reveals that Indiana raters make only two distinctions in the territory under consideration. All sites in Michigan and Indiana belong to a generally correct (6.00-6.99) northern area, and all sites to the south fall within the generally incorrect (4.00-4.99) region. Similarly, the Indiana identification task observes no major boundaries in the south (from sites #5 through #9), and that almost matches Figure 2.22, except for the fact, of course, that these Indiana raters have put themselves (site #5) in the more correct "North" in this correctness task – the task which rather obviously promotes greatest attention to overt norms. Recall, however, that the factor analysis of Indiana correctness ratings – Figure 2.25 – teased out the Indiana relationship with the South. That more subtle measure parallels the Indiana classification of the local site as "Southern" in the identification task. Where Indiana raters make many identification distinctions (between sites #2 and #3, between #3 and #4, and between #4 and #5), however, there are none in the correctness task, although one could have occurred between sites #2 and #3 (Michigan and Indiana, respectively).

The Michigan "pleasant" task (Figure 2.26) shows almost as many distinctions along the line of voice samples from the identification task as the correct task did. As we have already seen, in fact, the Michigan "correct" and "pleasant" tasks give very similar results. The only minor difference is that Kentucky and Tennessee (which are rated in different categories in the "correct" task, in keeping with the general Michigan tendency to rate states lower for correctness the farther south they are) are rated in the same (5.00–5.99) range in the "pleasant" task. The distinction in the identification task between Nashville, Tennessee, and Bowling Green, Kentucky, (supported by a minor boundary) is, therefore, not paralleled in the "pleasant" task for these respondents. The major Michigan identification boundary (between Muncie, Indiana, and New Albany, Indiana) cannot, of course, be paralleled here since the two sites are in the same state. The factor analysis of the "pleasant" task (Figure 2.29) shows that for the voices under consideration in the identification task, there is only a two-way division between two strong factors – Factor Group #2, a "South," which would contain all the voices from sites #6 through #9 and Factor Group #3, a "North," which would contain all the others (including, of course, the southern Indiana site #5). Again, we cannot see the major Michigan identification boundary between sites #4 and #5 since they are within the same state (Indiana). The minor Michigan identification task boundary (between Bowling Green, Kentucky, and Nashville, Tennessee) is not reflected in the factor analysis of these Michigan "pleasant" task data.

The Indiana "pleasant" task (Figure 2.27) differentiates only two degrees – a "very pleasant" 7.00–7.99 for the home site and a "generally pleasant" 6.00–6.99 for everything to the north and the south along the line of voices used in the identification task. That classification is precisely paralleled in the major identification boundary between Michigan (site #2, Coldwater, Michigan) and Indiana (site #3, South Bend, Indiana) to the north, and would seem to cut Indiana off from surrounding territory exactly as the "pleasant" task did. To the south, however, the picture is muddy. There is a major boundary in Indiana in the identification task (between South Bend, Indiana, and Muncie, Indiana) and a minor one between Muncie, Indiana, and New Albany, Indiana, neither of which, of course, could be reflected in the "pleasant" task. It is interesting, however, that all the Indiana major and minor identification boundaries fall within the state and that the state is isolated in the "pleasant" task. The Indiana factor analysis of the "pleasant" task (Figure 2.30) is slightly more articulated than the mean-score data from the "pleasant" task itself, and it divides the line of voices used in the identification task into three sets: Michigan voices (Factor Group #4), Indiana voices (Factor Group #6), and all voices south of Indiana (Factor Group #2). This articulation again matches the strong Indiana identification boundary between Michigan (Coldwater, Michigan) and Indiana (South Bend, Indiana) but offers no support for the internal divisions of Indiana, as, of course, it could not.

Finally, the "degree of difference" ratings for Michigan respondents (Figure 2.35) show a three-way division along the line of the stimulus voices: Michigan and Indiana voices are all "the same" (1.00–1.75), Kentucky and Tennessee voices are "very different" (2.51–3.25), and Alabama voices are "unintelligibly different" (3.26–4.00). In some ways this is a very close match to the Michigan identification scores. Recall that the Michigan respondents place no boundaries from site #1 (Saginaw, Michigan) through site #4 (Muncie, Indiana). Since site #5 (New Albany, Indiana) is at the southern extreme of Indiana, and since states were not subdivided in the "degree of difference" task, this large undifferentiated stretch in these two tasks is very similar. On the other hand, the minor boundary which Michigan respondents "heard" in the identification task is not paralleled in the "degree of difference" task, where, of course, it might have surfaced. Instead, the "degree of difference" task cuts Alabama off from Tennessee but suggests that Kentucky and Tennessee are similar.

The "degree of difference" task for the Indiana respondents (Figure 2.36) also presents three degrees of difference along the line represented in the stimulus voices for the identification task, but they are organized very differently. To the north, the Indiana respondents rate Michigan as "slightly different" (1.76–2.50), and to the south, they give the same rating for Kentucky. They find both Tennessee and Alabama similarly "very different" (2.51–3.25). Again the major boundary between Indiana (South Bend, Indiana) and Michigan (Coldwater, Michigan) in the identification task is reflected in another quantitative task. We cannot argue as we did above for the Michigan data, however, that the minor boundary between Muncie, Indiana, and New Albany, Indiana, in the identification task is reflected in the Indiana – Kentucky difference shown in the "degree of difference" task. Since these Indiana raters are from the southernmost part of the state and still reckon Kentucky "a little different," we must take them at their word. Doubtless, that is a reflection of the greater "overtness" of the "degree of difference" task and its ability to bring out the linguistic insecurity of these southern Indiana raters, manifested, as we have seen before, in their desire to cut themselves off from contaminating "southern" influences. In all these final comparisons, however, we continue to be handicapped by the fact that the ratings refer to entire states.

2.1.5 Summary of previous research

Southern United States English and New York City English are clearly varieties prejudiced against. Northern speakers are prejudiced against Southern speech even along affective dimensions. There are significant differences in the patterns of pleasantness and correctness when the perceiving groups are divided into one with some degree of linguistic insecurity and another with a generally positive linguistic self-concept. Insecurity may result in exaggerated isolation of the home area in affective evaluation and in exaggerated isolation from nearby "contaminating" areas in evaluations of correctness. Insecure areas also seem to be less harsh in evaluating correctness in general, although Labov reports the opposite tendency for stigmatized speakers' evaluation of others with similar features in his study of attitudes and production differences in New York City (1966). Both secure and insecure areas agree, however, in assigning greater geographical salience to areas seen as incorrect.

The responses from, rather than about, the South, an obviously significant region in these tasks, however, do not fit so neatly into this picture. When given the opportunity for self-loathing on correct speech ratings, Southerners do not express rampant insecurity (or they deflect it to another part of the South, as seen in Figure 2.23). Nevertheless, they rate themselves very high for pleasantness and Northerners very low (Figure 2.28). In fact, they assign Northeasterners, particularly New Yorkers, the lowest mean ratings for any group in any task carried out in this research program. Although they have both shame and pride in local speech, they show very little grudging appreciation of Northeastern "standards" (as there was from both Michigan and Indiana raters); only a "national government" Washington, DC, standard (not all that far from the South) is admitted to by Southern raters.

Variation in folk dialect data reveals many of the characteristics of production data: apparent time change and age grading, social stratification, hypo- and hypercorrection, gender related trends, linguistic insecurity, and divergence and convergence of contact groups. On the other hand, some of these parallels may not precisely mirror specific findings from production sociolinguistics. For example, the similarities in the treatment of regional speech by all three groups studied here may be importations from popular culture rather than reflections of on-going change in perceptions which mirror production changes already in progress. Just such indications, however, may be clues to the factors which lurk behind the social motivations for perceptual change, and those changes may constitute a part of the impetus for later change in production itself.

Most importantly, these several approaches have shown that correctness and related affective dimensions, at least in United States English, are notions which, for nonlinguists, have geographical significance. Though it is not easy to arrive at the folk perception of such concepts, it is important to seek it out, since, at least for United States English, it represents a set of beliefs both strongly held and highly influential in the linguistic life of large and small speech communities. As with other folk-linguistic matters treated in this book, such a multidimensional approach to what are ultimately folk questions provides a surer consideration of the limited data gathered in language attitude surveys and from anecdotal and participant-observer information. It serves, moreover, to help build a more complete and accurate picture of the regard for language use and variety within a speech community, providing questions about such issues as language standards with answers from the communities themselves. Other evidence from the United States and surveys from several other countries may be found in Preston, to appear.

2.2 Conversational evidence

The essentially quantitative approaches summarized above are supplemented and expanded on here from data gathered in interviews for the current project. In this first sample, respondents illustrate one of the more important conclusions from the quantitative studies – that "North" and "South" are the principal distinctions in American English and that the division is supported by prescriptive notions:

H: But which city you think is the - standard English for, I mean,
from-
 [
D: From from well - we think, yeah, we think the Midwest.
 [
S: (   )
 [
G: Detroit. ((laughs))
H: Midwest?
 [
S: The Midwest no, cause dad Cal- I I've been to California=
 [
D: (   )
 [
G: California-
S: =a lot more than you, California talks the same way as here.
There's no accent. I can't tell the difference.
 [
D: Right - that's true I can't either when I'm in California.
 [
S: So like
the the Western - the North, North and the South would=
 [   ]
D: They talk a little slower though.
S: =would basically be the two accents, with little tiny dialects here
and there.
G: That's true.=
S: =Like the New Yorkers ((laughs)).

H: Oh you know what, I've always thought Northern part English is
standard. So, that's wrong right?
G: I think so Northern English.
 [
D: (   ) - Yeah I think so, I think that's correct.
 [
S: Yeah North- Northern English
(   )
 [
H: Northern part English is c- is standard English (   )?
 [

D: Yeah, yeah.
                                                               [
G: That's right=
                                                               [
S: Yeah=
G: =- what you hear around here.
S: -=standard.
                               [
D: Because that's what you hear on the
TV - like newscasters. If you listen to the - the national=
[
H: ((laughs))
D: =newscast of the national news - on Channel 7 som- they=
                                    [
G: Uh huh
D: =sound they sound like we: do, they they sound sort of ( )=
                                                          [
H: ( )
D: =Mid- Midwestern, like we do. (#23)

It is important to note in this exchange that the respondent term
"Midwest" often isolates an area labeled "North" in the maps presented so far (e.g., Figure 2.11). In fact, in #5 the respondents explain
to a Taiwanese fieldworker that although such states as Wisconsin
and Michigan are in the northern part of the country they are called
"Midwest." Although "North" and "South" are the principal American English speech areas and "North" is the land of correctness for
the respondents in #23 cited above, one of the "little tiny dialects" is
New York City. At the hiatus in this passage, all the participants (and
even the fieldworker) participate in their impression of New York
City pronunciations of "New York," a clear indication of the salience
of this also prejudiced-against speech area,[11] and we deal first with
this notion of admired and despised speech regions.

2.2.1 Prescription and region

It is clear from these conversational data that Northern (or
"Midwestern," or Michigan) speech is the norm. One respondent (A
in #4) is amazed that a "dialect recognition entertainer" at a USO
club could identify a speaker who was from Milwaukee: "I mean I
didn't think that anyone from Milwaukee was any different" (see,
e.g., Figure 2.10). G makes this point very explicitly when the fieldworker (H) asks him if there is a standard English in the United
States which is the equivalent of Beijing (Mandarin) Chinese, which
he has just described as the Chinese international standard:

G: I think I think - yeah. I think what n- what what K=
                                          [
H: In the Un-
G: =was talking about was (.hhh) the standard- if you have such a
thing as called standard English other than textbook English, it
would probably be the language that you're hearing right now. As
you listen to the Midwestern. (#36a)

Small wonder, then, that speakers who cite themselves as models of
the national standard would exhibit the intense linguistic security we
find in nearly all the quantitative tasks reported on above for Michigan respondents. They believe, as well, that this standard is the one
appropriate for broadcast:

D: Although the Midwest kind of (1.0) is the voice you hear on television all the time.
N: Uh-huh. Yeah. We were talking about that -
D: Unless it's a particular program where they might have a Southern person or - or somebody from France over there you know
over - here. Mostly I think when you watch television it's it's a Midwest voice on there. (#46)

As surely as the North is the land of correctness, most of our respondents agree with the evaluation of the South outlined in the
quantitative studies reported above (especially in 2.1.2). In #5, for
example, M notes that a relative of hers who just moved to North
Carolina said that the grammar was "incredible." In discussing this,
the respondents recognize that the explanation for Southern bad language is difficult, for the well-educated Southerners are also guilty;
they conclude, nevertheless, that Southerners are simply not as well
educated "as they should be." This relationship between poor education and improper Southern speech is common. K (in #18) notes that
people who came to Kokomo, Indiana from Kentucky and Tennessee
maintained (and even promulgated) "... a VERY: Southern, uneducated, way of speaking... ." This relationship is established even
more directly in the following:

M: I did find that - that the people when
we stopped to eat along the way or stopped for gas, people in
Kentucky didn't seem to be as educated in the- in the back=
N: =Yeah=
M: =parts as the people in- in the Southern people from Tennessee
seemed to be more up, on education than those from the you know
smaller towns in Kentucky. And they spoke well. I mean they still
had an accent but you know, they- they didn't use as many double

negatives and (1.75) the sort of thing that a lot of the others from Kentucky, and we were=
[
T: (   )
M: =talking on the way back and I said because I- na- I'm not per-fect and God, C isn't either. He's terrible. He- he doesn't know how to use - when to use "come" and "came."
[
T: Past tense of verbs.
N: Ummmmmm.
M: I mean he - come and came and every time he talks I go "What?"
[
N: ((laughs))
M: "You what?" ((laughs)) And ah, I know I'm wrong a lot too but (1.0) the people in - in ah, Kentucky didn't seem to (2.75)
N: Either know or didn't care or what?
[
M: No. They didn't. Yeah. And (0.5) they just keep saying it th- it's just so obvious you just se- even someone who doesn't have perfect English themselves and you - you (   ) and C even s- "Did you hear what that guy said?"=
[
N: ((laughs)
M: =And I said "Oh you caught that." ((laughs)) "I didn't know if you would." But he noticed it too and he said "Yeah." it was funny from one- one state to the other=I don't know if there was more (2.75) geographically I don't know where the Appalachian Mountains are I'd have to look on a map to see=are they're more in Kentucky or more in Tennessee.
T: There just could be more people in one area concentrated in that
[
M: Well the Appalachians are where the more the people are the poorest though. And I think that would come (1.75) having poorer language skills (0.75) you know.
[
N: Ummmmm.
M: They don't go to school as much right? (#9)

Within Southern speech areas (although there everyone has an "accent"), one may distinguish poorer speech as a result of greater educational disadvantage (so much so that even T's husband C, a Northern speaker noted for confusing *come* and *came*, was impressed with it). It is not surprising, perhaps, to find that the "Appalachian" caricature is strong, for US popular culture has served up a strong dose of a backward, poor, uneducated Upland Southern population for many years.

An interesting theme emerges here when M notes, however briefly, that "... they just keep saying it." The implication is, of course, that they ought to know better but, for some reason, persist in using the variety which she (and even her husband C) find so strange. The South, for example, even resists the homogenizing influence of the media:

> G: Because of TV though I think - there's kind of a standard English that's evolving.
> D: Yeah.
>   [
> G: And the kind of thing you hear on th- uh - TV is (.hhh)=
>   [
> D: Uh huh.
> G: =something that's broadcast across the country, so most people are aware of that, but (.hhh) there are definite accents in the South, ... (#7)

Almost recalcitrantly, then, Southerners seem to resist the influences of "standard English," and "they just keep saying it" (i.e., their own variety). In #54, S tells of a "Southern" woman who has lived in the North for forty years and is still misunderstood in the service station when she pronounces *oil* as [ɔl]. S observes, "I know she must know better than that by now," although this respondent claimed earlier in the same interview not to associate regional pronunciation with "correctness" at all.

Why speakers "choose" to continue speaking a nonstandard variety when presented with evidence of its nonstandardness (and even of its ill effect on their personal ambitions) has been a puzzle for social psychologists of language (e.g., Ryan 1979). Naturally, those ratings of speech samples which show nonstandard speakers' high affective regard or solidary symbolism for their own variety help explain this otherwise inexplicable attachment to language types which are regarded poorly. The Indiana respondents' high ratings of the "pleasantness" of local speech reported in the quantitative studies summarized above is surely a reflex of the same phenomenon.

The folk, however, do not seem to be aware of this attachment; at least, they do not articulate it. Since these speakers do not rush to correct what even TV should have made obvious to them is incorrect speech, many of our respondents find them intransigent on this matter. Why, in spite of all the evidence, for example, don't Kentuckians, New Yorkers, and African-Americans all simply learn to use Michigan (i.e., "Midwestern, correct") speech? That they do not is interpreted sympathetically (as in the above) as a lack of education and unsympathetically (as we shall see particularly in the case of attitudes towards AAVE) as a lack of industry, intelligence, and even common sense.

2.2.2 *The acquisition and loss of regional varieties*

This unsympathetic interpretation is perhaps all the more understandable from the folk perspective when we consider another very common theme – the ease with which one may acquire another regional variety. This, the folk believe, is particularly easy for children to do:

> B: I - I developed a Southern accent in Texas.= And then, I grew up in the New York City area, went to Texas for two years, by age eight I had a Texas accent, went back to New York, I lost it pretty much in about six months and then, went back to   (   )
> Eastern, East Coast, Northeast, US., New York, type accent. (#8)

Six months seems to be the right amount of time, especially for child learners, as the following will also show, but not all children will change dialects, and the reasons may be complex:

> K: I knew a family that moved from England. And there was a brother and a sister, two years apart. And within six months the boy, had completely lost his English accent. comPLETEly. And the girl: who was, I think, about sixteen at the time: she still spoke with an English accent. I am sure she does toDAY.
> Z: That's amazing. Do you think it has something to do with: her mental development? or something: psychological?
> K: I- I think·it probably had to do with- He was in Junior High and he he wanted very much to fit in, and probably made a conscious effort and she: maybe- I didn't know her that well, but- maybe she preferred being English. And I think just that for a girl, and for a little older, it was something exotic. (#18)

K implies that both age and gender play a role in the younger boy's rapid acquisition of the new variety. While most psycholinguistically-oriented sociolinguistic studies of adaptation to new norms would uphold the age generalization (e.g., Payne 1980), most would also suggest that the gender patterns are reversed (e.g., Chambers 1989). On the other hand, if the American variety had "covert" (tough, masculine, nonstandard) prestige (e.g., Trudgill 1972) rather than a standard appeal for these learners (as might reasonably be taken to be the case in a caricaturistic comparison of British and

American English), then both age and gender are correct as reported by K. In another example, a young woman who moved to Indiana after childhood years in New York (H in #3), for example, did not accommodate to the "hick" speech she encountered, and found more in common with Michigan speakers after she later moved there. Perhaps the "covert prestige" of local Indiana speech did not have appeal to her as it might have to a young man. J's identification of a "hick influence" in Indiana speech confirms, of course, the Southern associations which, we believe, are the clear causes for the linguistic insecurity attributed to Indiana in the quantitative studies outlined above.

A more personal account of child dialect shift is provided in the following:

D: We lived in- we lived in Virginia till I was four. Then we moved to Texas during the Second World War and when I was eight we moved back to Virginia (3.0) and then when I was thirteen we moved to Toledo and then I didn't live in the South anymore.
N: Oh I see.
D: So we moved a whole lot.
N: And so that wo- that would be why you think tha-
D: I would think that may be why I didn't have that much of an accent. I really can't figure.
N: Do- your parents don't - they they do have an accent.
D: They do have some yeah. My mother is from St. Louis and - and she was an adult when she moved to Mobile Alabama, but now my dad was from the South he was born and raised in Birmingham and then lived here in the South most of his adult life until he moved to Toledo. I imagine he was forty you know. Give or take a couple of years. ((laughs))
N: ((laughs))
D: But yeah I would think that would be why I didn't have such an acc- because we moved so much.
N: Do you think you did have one and you lost it. I mean-
D: Yes a little bit but never a whole lot. (3.0). Because I can remember when we moved to Toledo kids teasing me because I had an accent.
N: Well that was nice of them.
D: Hey kids don't change you know. But you know what I do remember by the time I went to high school I must have pretty much lost the accent because I still ca- I don't think I told you this before but my mother always called me D-J ((two full names)), which is a very Southern characteristic to use both of a person's names, and one time she came to the hi- to the h- where I went to high school and she asked the n- it was a Catholic school, and they had this nun who at night after school would be downstairs in an office to keep people from running through the building, you know, you'd have to kind of check in with her before you'd get in the building.

N: Uh-hm.
D: And she asked for D-J (0.5) H ((respondent's full maiden name))
(1.0) and when the nuns saw me the next day she s- she found me
and when she saw me the next day she wondered whether that
was my mother? Or - she couldn't figure out how this woman with a
Southern accent was related to me.
N: Oh really?
D: So she didn't place me as having been from the South at all.
N: Do you think you worked at losing it?
D: I don't know.
     [
N: Did you-
D: That would that would have been about - only about two or=
           [
N: Do you remem-
D: =three years later.
N: Uh-hum.
D: I don't - I don't really know. Maybe kids just change. Faster than
other people do.
(2.0)
N: That would make sense.
D: And the fact that you know I had moved, a Texas accent is dif-
ferent than a normal Virginia accent would be.
N: Well you wouldn- you wouldn't have gotten teased though
probably in Texas.
D: No no. Nor either in Virginia. It would be close enough but (0.5)
it (0.5) would still be a different accent I think because (0.5) I think
some people change different=my grandmother was from New
England and she lived in the South (0.2) fifty years before she died.
I can't remember. You ALWAYS knew she was from New England.
N: Really.
D: Yeah.

D: I'm sure as a kid I didn't really want to sound different so proba-
bly made an effort somewhat to change. (#59)

D believes she lost her Southern characteristics so completely after
two years in Toledo that the nuns were surprised to hear her mother
speak. Like K (in #18, cited just above) she believes that children in
particular want to "fit in." She also believes, however, that her irregular dialect input (Virginia and Texas) caused a sort of leveling
effect on her own speech. B (#8), quoted above, also believes that his
early childhood movement back and forth between Texas and New
York has now left him with what he calls a "polymorphous, poly-
glot" accent. He notes that although the New York City accent is
very distinct, he is not recognized as a speaker of it in Michigan.
(This is a belief the folk hold about second language learning as well,
prizing "consistency" of input – see 4.3). Finally, D's story about her

grandmother suggests that the covert prestige of the South would not appeal at all to a female New Englander, and, as a result, she did not change in fifty years.

Regional varieties, on the other hand, seem to be rather easily acquired by adults in other situations. We have already noted the case of C (#49) above (2.1.1), an Oklahoman who felt she had to learn "Northern" after she moved to Michigan so that she would not sound like "the dumbest shit around," and she reported no particular difficulty in accomplishing this feat. In that case, however, the gender and language prestige relationships were "properly" aligned – the female learner accommodated more rapidly to the Northern (overtly prestigious) speech norm. Northerners who move South may also learn, but, for the usual reasons of covert prestige and regional symbolism, it is more likely that these learners would be male. D's brother-in-law has, apparently, acquired a southern variety, although more slowly.

> D: Now my bother-in-law lives in Tennessee and he was up here at Christmas (0.1) and (0.1) he's probably been down there about five years and I really can hear the accent in him now. We didn't the first couple of years but I really can hear it now and they pick up their particular phrases and sayings but now he's getting quite a bit of Southern (0.1) drawl to his voice. (#46)

D in #46 also says of a Michigan female friend of hers who went to New York and returned that "I don't hear her with any accent at all." This suggests that an already prestigious or secure female speaker will resist accommodation to a variety with only covert prestige appeal. On the other hand, at least one Michigan female reports acquiring Southern speech during military service there:

> R: when I came up here I know: I had the most Southern accent cause you know? I was down there. I was around all those people and my family would go - "jeez" every time I'd call them "God? you sound just like some damn Southerner." You know because of the way I'd talk and now that I'm back up here ((i.e., in Michigan)) and I go down there ((i.e., to the South)) now I go down there and they all seem to talk so: slow: and so: you know really really really really Southern.
> M: So when you were down there they you got to the point where it didn't sound strange.
> R: No: (#16)

But this same respondent's mother picked up none of the accent of southern Illinois even after she moved there permanently among relatives who "really have a Southern drawl."

Even within the South, "native" adults in "professional" or "urban" contexts may try to avoid local speech.

R: I think there's a big difference - between Louisiana and Atlanta
- because Louisiana is- is- you know i- m- much more=
  [
M: ((coughs)) Yeah.
R: =French oriented - and Atlanta's much more uh-=
                  [
M: Uh-huh.
R: =and uh has a lot of professional people that try very very-hard NOT to have Southern accents or Southern drawls=
                                [
M: Uh-huh.
R: =because it has a stigma to it.=
M: Uh-huh.=
R: =People think you're slow when you're from the South, they=
                              [[
M: U-huh.   Uh-huh.
R: =think you know that you're lazy, when you're from the=
                            [
M: Uh-huh.
R: =South, and so people that are professionals there don't want to give that - idea or - or have that you know come from them to other
                                          [
M: Uh-huh.
R: people that you know when they're dealing business with all other parts of the country so (.hhh) a- an- and in Louisiana - you know only one big really big city there's New Orleans, you know and that's known for - in- in Baton=
[
M: Yeah and Baton - he was in Baton Rouge.
R: =and that's known for - in- in Baton Rouge yeah, in that=
                                     ]
M: =Baton - he was in Baton Rouge.
R: =area.
M: So he probably did that deliberately then, didn't he.
R: Yeah, oh I'm serious, yeah I would think so because I=
   [
M: I don't know.
R: =notice when you're in Atlanta i - it's even Atlanta and Colum-bus, Columbus is ninety miles South of Atlanta, and=
      [
M: Uh-huh.
R: =the difference in the way people talk from Atlanta to Columbus is amazing, even though they have a Southern twang in Atlanta=
M: =Yeah it's really light.=
R: =In Columbus it's like a big-time Southern drawl:.(#16)

The folk, therefore, both express and reveal a number of sociolinguistic commonplaces in gender and age-related facts concerning the acquisition of speech norms, particularly when stereotypical evaluations of such a stigmatized region as "Southern" is involved.

A surprising number of our respondents, however, report on "short-term," quickly learned and quickly lost experiences:

> G: And - two of
> my friends uh had relatives down South. And each summer they
> would go down and stay for one month. (.hhh) And after a full
> month of being exposed to it down there they would come back
> and what we would consider talk funny.
> H: Oh you mean they (were) (   )
>   [
> G: And because they had picked up the language as
> it was spoken down there. And so they'd come up and=
>   [
> H: ((laughs))
> G: =they'd talk funny for a while.
> H: Uh huh ((laughs))
> G: (.hhh) And then within about a week or two weeks it would
> slowly start to dwindle, and they would talk to what we considered
> was correct. Got rid of that funny talk.
>   [
> H: Oh ((laughs))
>   [
> G: But - I suspect when they went down, the first
> two weeks or three, while they were just getting accustomed to the
> way English was spoke, uh they were the one with the funny talk, -
> when they started to speak. (#36a)

D (in #46) acquired "kind of that (1) Boston (2) accent or whatever" in just a "few months" when her husband was stationed in Rhode Island in the Navy, but it only lasted "a week or so" after she returned to Michigan. Such sort-term adaptation to local norms has not been studied in the professional literature, but it is very much like the accounts of linguistic accommodation in face-to-face interaction which have been treated to considerable study (Giles and Powesland 1975, Giles and Smith 1979, Giles 1979, Thakerer et al. 1982). Such accommodation (at least to a "previously-known" dialect) is explicit in the following:

> C: I noticed in my own family that my: - that my older sis-
> ter who lived in Kentucky for the longest has a very strong South-
> ern accent, or Kentucky accent. Whereas the rest of us pretty
> much lost it.=One time I noticed that-

Z: So you had?
C: Yes. (   ) And then I noticed when I am around people who have an accent I often speak that way a little more.
Z: Still? So you didn't (   ).
C: It depends on the situation. I: tend to: respond to, I think. Whenever I am around someone who has an accent. Or if: let's see: - It just slips out, sometimes. (#21)

In some cases such short-term accommodation may have more lasting influence. K (in #53) spent only three weeks with her sister in Kentucky but was teased for her "drawl" by her brother when she returned to Michigan. In some cases, one may apparently not even be aware of this continuing influence:

S: L came back from Kentucky being down there only a year and he's got a definitel- definite Southern accent.

S: He- remember him - he's got a Southern accent now, still.
                          [
D: Yeah.
D: Does he?
S: Yeah and he's been back for like a few months he's still got one.=
D: =Hmm.
G: Does he like to keep it? It sort of amuses him.
D: [[(   )
S: [[No, I don't I don't think he even knows he has it really.
G: Oh=
S: =Cause I uh I told him last night, told him it was really funny to hear YOU talking in a Southern accent and he goes "Yeah," (.hhh), "and some people said I do and uh I haven't noticed it." (#23)

G apparently finds it odd that after being back a "few months" L has not dropped whatever Kentucky influence he picked up in his year there. In fact, she seems to believe that only some sort of willful act could have kept him from reverting to "normal" Michigan speech. That L was unaware of his "contamination" is particularly interesting. It is the case, however, that many second-generation Appalachian speakers in southeastern Michigan are completely unaware of the fact that they have not fully acquired local norms, but since L is not of Appalachian heritage, it is difficult to account for his inability to hear in himself evidence of a variety which is strongly (and negatively) caricatured in his own speech community.

In the following, J appears to believe that he has not accommodated but simply recognized the efficiency of another variety and "chosen" to use it.

> J: I was going to say when I was in the service, one of my best=
>   [
> M: Uh huh.
> J: =buddies, - in - Fort Bragg North Carolina was from Algoro Massachusetts.
> M: Uh hum?
> J: And he had that - that Boston accent [bas?n̩] accent
>   [
> M: Yeah.
> M: He dropped the R.
> J: Yeah talking about the [ka:]
>   [
> B: Always talking about the [ya:d]
> M: Uh huh.
> J: And I hung around with this guy so long: I started talking like him because it was simpler: to say [ka] than it was to say "car." (#38)

In light of the typical folk prescriptivist norms outlined in Chapter 1, it is unusual to hear a Michigan speaker admit to change for reasons of economy alone. More interestingly, J, in spite of his admission that he "hung around with this guy for so long" does not attribute any sort of social or interpersonal reasons to his change.

2.2.3 Intelligibility

K (in #36a) believes that newscasters are encouraged to use "Midwestern" speech not only because it is a "standard" but also because it is more universally intelligible, and our conversational data touch on the intelligibility of varieties rather frequently. Recall (Figure 2.35) that Michigan ratings of "degree of difference" place an "unintelligibly different" group of voices in the central South (Mississippi, Alabama, and Louisiana). D, for example, (in #46, see 3.1.1 below) believes she "can understand Black people a whole lot better than some of the white Southern people." G claims to have needed translation help understanding Southern when he was in the service, although a characteristic of the variety was its speed:

> G: uh - I was=
>   [
> H: (   )

G: =stationed in- in- in Georgia for a while, stationed in Fort Mon-
mouth New Jersey, (.hhh) an:d I had to look at two of my buddies to
sometimes figure out what somebody was saying. (.hhh) When=

                                        [

H: Oh this- is-
G: =they- they talk in a Southern draw,[12] (.hhh) and I would   wait
for the words to finally come out because they go real: real: slow.
(#1)

Later, however, (in #36a) both G and K (his spouse) claim that
Northern and Southern varieties are mutually intelligible, G stating,
quite specifically, "Oh there's no problem with that." In spite of
some claims like G's in #1 and the quantitative results outlined
above, therefore, intelligibility among United States regional varieties appears to be a more general opinion. D (in #28) claims that
there are not really very distinct dialects in the United States
(excepting Gullah) and that intelligibility is never a problem if you
"adjust your listening a little bit"; in #7 the same respondent notes
"Southern" is intelligible if you "tune your ears to their accent." Like
G (in #1 and #36a), however, respondents contradict themselves on
this point, in one case even overtly:

J: And sometimes you really don't. ((i.e., understand another dialect)) I told your wife earlier that you CAN understand people in
various parts of the United States, be- because we all do speak
English, but that's not true. Because I remember listening to a man
in - South Carolina, and I really did not understand one wo(h)rd he
sai(h)d.

                       No I can't remember what he said, but he was
standing in back of me, and he was talking to me, and he had such
a deep Southern accent, - or deep Southern drawl. (#25)

Additionally, although the data are not from this research project,
there is some conversational evidence that Indiana speakers regard
Northeastern varieties as difficult (see Figure 2.36).

R: Well, I was in New York City, - right after rush hour time, five
o'clock. (.hhh) And uh - was lost. - So I stopped uh this gentleman
on the street, and asked him how to get to the Island, Long Island, I
- had to go there. And uh - he(h) ju(h)st commenced to uh -
((mimics)) So you take you know thirty-third and third, and go down
here and you here here and that ((ends mimicry)) and I just
couldn't understand it. I could NOT=

          [

F: ((laughs))
R: =understand it.[13]

2.2.4 Specific features

In spite of their general claim that they have no trouble with Southern speech, some Northern explanations of "Southern" are not so good. In #42, DH gives the following account of the putative Southern lexical item *var*.

> DH: Our painters on the site are all Southern guys and one guy's from uh Kentucky you know I was talking to him the other and he's so bad it's like "Yeah. I went over [vɑɹ] and when we got over var" and he- and exactly, he used that word for everything. "We go over=
>   [
> M: ((laughs))
> DH: =var, I was drinking that moonshine," and it's bad. A-
>   [
> M: You mean like
> s- say "over there" he's going "over var"?
>   [
> DH: "Over var."
>   [
> SH: ((laughs)) "Var" (what is that) ((laughs)) (#42)

What DH's Kentucky painter acquaintance has said is not *over var* at all, and they need not have puzzled over the odd lexical item. The process is actually pretty simple:

> 1. *over there* ——> *over thar* from a regular historical vowel alternation [ɛ]~[ɑ] (e.g., *bear* and *bar*)
> 2. *over thar* ——> *ov thar* [ovðɑɹ] from weak (unstressed), syllable loss
> 3. *ov thar* ——> *ovvar* [ov:ɑɹ] from total assimilation of the [ð] by the preceding [v] (and compensatory lengthening)

The geminate or "long [v]" which results from this process lets the Northern speakers "hear" the entire word *over* and assume that the second item is *var*. Although the semantic interpretation is correct, and, one assumes, intelligibility is not really the issue, the mishearing is striking.

Mimicry appears to be the most productive means of eliciting the details of varieties from the folk. We turn, therefore, to evidence from these conversational data concerning the details of US dialects – the actual linguistic details which the folk use to identify (and caricature) regional differences. Often when they actively try to retrieve such matters, they are at a loss. In some cases they simply seem to disregard (or just forget) the relevance of linguistic levels other than the one on which they are currently focused:

H: So you can tell this guy from
uh what maybe I mean - just listen his accent. Like ( )
                                            [
S: (.hhh) You can tell
whether he's from the North or the South but not which=
                                       [
D: Yeah - yeah
S: =particular area,
D: Although- although- although some Western States have=
H: Oh it's just the part, North part, South part.
                                       [
S: Right.
D: =particular ways of talking too.
                            [
G: But they're kind of southern.
D: Yeah, that's true.
G: I mean you wouldn't think of North Dakota or something would
you.=
D: =Usually Texas is pretty distinct.
G: Colorado's not very distinct.
D: No, Colorado isn't.
G: Texas is, but that's Southern.
D: Yeah.
H: Texas is Southern part, yeah?.
G: Yeah.
H: But you say that California English is the same uh accent=
                                               [
S: As here
H: =here?
S: Yeah. - California is the same accent
              [
D: Yeah, pretty much.
                 [
H: So in in this case how do you - distinguish from=
                                               [
S: You couldn't tell=
H: =this guy for instance he may be from California ( )
                              [
S: =the difference.   OH: You could possibly tell the
difference from the slang words they use.

S: Yeah they they might have the
same accent but use different terms for things, like s- "pop," we call
it like "pop" here, (.hhh) Andrea's from- my sister's been in California for a long time, they call it "soda" out there. (#23)

D pushes the idea that "Western" is salient, but "North Dakota" and
"Colorado" are used as examples of places no different from Michi-
gan (see Figure 2.35). "Texas" is different, it is admitted, but it is
"Southern." The fieldworker reminds the respondents that they

claimed earlier that California was also the same as Michigan and asks if there is no way to tell these regions apart. Oddly enough, especially in light of claims about the primacy of vocabulary in folk awareness, only after this prodding does S come up with the idea of lexical difference, the previous discussions being restricted, apparently, to phonology (or "accent" – the term preferred by nearly every folk respondent for pronunciation differences).

Since the respondents in the hand-drawn map task reported on above (2.1.1) were given instructions to draw boundaries around areas where people "speak differently," it is worth wondering, in light of this interview evidence, what linguistic level was guiding the task. The assumption that a general consideration of features (from phonetic ones through discourse conventions) might be operative is not borne out by such discussions as these.

Although we have already cited a number of specific dialect caricatures, we will provide a few more here, particularly since it has been claimed that the folk (at least in the United States) are not sensitive to such matters (see 1.1). Of course, we shall not seek systematic accounts of dialect features, but the following, coupled with examples already given, should make it clear that folk imitations and accounts are not in the least impoverished.

Vowels appear to mean more to the folk than consonants, at least in overt comment. Only a fieldworker-generated discussion of aspirated versus unaspirated (and tapped) *t* focused extensively on consonants, and it was not obvious that the respondents ever got the point (#5). One respondent-generated "regional" consonant feature was the "intrusive *r*" (in, e.g., *Warshington*), which S (in #56) says is used by speakers in Ohio and Pennsylvania and J and H (in #5) attribute to people who are "really incorrect," the result of a "lack of education." Interestingly enough, however, even mention of this consonant feature in #56 devolves into a discussion of the quality of the first vowel of *Washington*. This generalization concerning the relative importance of consonants and vowels has only to do with overt comment; as we shall see, imitations of other varieties may not exclusively focus on vowels at all.

As one might expect from much of what has been said, Southern vowels in particular are a common topic. J, for example, is sensitive to Southern diphthong reduction and imitates her husband's pronunciation of *oil*:

J: "Oil." Have you heard him say "oil"?
M: Huh-uh.
J: [ɔl]

M: For what?
J: "Oil."
M: Oh "oil oil." (#41)

The item *oil* appears to be a caricature of both the diphthong reduction reported here and of the *r* pronunciation (presumably homophonous with *Earl*) cited above in S's (#54) account of a "Southern" woman. In the dialect-sociolinguistic film "American Tongues," diphthong reduction (and subsequent vowel quality) is the source of a Southerner's anecdote about Northerners', reception of his pronunciation of *ice*. They tease him because they find it homophonous with *ass*; perturbed at mocking requests for repetition, he finally calls them *ice-holes*. We have, however, little characterization of the typical Southern fronting of the first element of the diphthong [aw] (to [æ]), in spite of such elocutionary caricatures as "*How now brown cow.*" Only N's imitation (in #48) seems to successfully realize this fronting in both *down* and *South*.

There does occur, however, a limited if not perfectly represented, awareness of another aspect of Southern front vowel differences. When S (in #23) is describing a "Southern accent" to H (the fieldworker), he notes that "Their *a*'s are like [ɑ] than [e] – in a lot of places." Southern lowering (and even wider diphthongization) of the front tense vowels is a process in which [iy] becomes [ey] (e.g., *beat* is lowered to *bait*) and [ey] becomes [ay] (e.g., *bait* is lowered to *bite*) (see Wolfram 1991:87). Although S cites only the first element of the diphthong which results from the [ey] to [ay] shift and offers no examples, it would seem that he has this phenomenon in mind.

As suggested in Chapter 1, however, even confidently delivered imitation, may not always be accurate, although it is important to investigate such performances to see what features they do incorporate. J (#38) comments that local newscasters whom he heard while he was Gatlinburg, Tennessee, had no Southern speech unless they interviewed a local person. He imitates their shift to local norms with the string "Y'all know what I'm talking about now, don't you?" Phonetically:

[yæw:lnowʌhɑmtʰɔkn̩bɑwtnɑwdontʃu]

The following analysis will show this is both good and bad. Again, our focus is on the vowels.

1. The diphthong [æw:] in 'y'all' is an authentic Southern diphthong (replacing the more widely spread [ɑw]), but it is not the vowel of 'all' (which, in all Southern varieties is never farther forward than [a] and in

many is even farther back and raised). To J's credit, however, the vowel in many Southern varieties of 'all' is strongly diphthongized (towards [w]).

2. The final [l] in 'y'all' is neither reduced nor vocalized, a feature common to most Southern varieties.

3. The [o] in 'know' is neither fronted nor strongly diphthongized, either of which would have made the form more acceptably 'Southern.'

4. The first element of 'what' is [w], although a voiceless or even aspirated (i.e., [hʍ]) form is common in some Southern varieties.

5. The vowel he uses in 'what' is simply [ʌ], and, like the vowel in 'know,' is not fronted, a feature in some Southern varieties.

6. The end of 'what' and transition to 'I'm' is unusual. There is no final consonant (not even a glottal catch) at the end of 'what.' Such total final apical stop deletion is not uncommon in allegro speech in Southern (and African-American) varieties, but it is oddly followed by a strong [h] before the following vowel (in 'I'm'). Perhaps J is familiar with such (limited) Southern caricatures as 'hit' (for 'it') and believes that an [h] before 'I'm' is justified. If so, this is simply an overgeneralization.

7. The vowel J uses in 'I'm' is the authentic Southern [ɑ]. Although it is not commented on by the respondents themselves, we suspect that this is the most common vocalic caricature of Southern speech, perhaps limited to a small set of lexical items.

8. The vowel of 'talk' is appropriately [ɔ], as it would be in many Southern varieties. Although this might be a candidate for imitation for many Northern speakers, it almost certainly is not for J. He is from rural northern Michigan and has spent only the last fifteen years or so in the more urban southeastern part of the state. He is almost certainly not, therefore, a participant in the recent Northern vowel change (i.e., the so-called 'Northern Cities Shift,' see, e.g., Wolfram 1991:85-90) which would have changed his [ɔ] to [ɑ]. When he uses an [ɔ] in 'all,' therefore, he is simply using his own vowel.

9. The substitution of [n] for [ŋ] in 'talking' and the loss of the initial syllable of 'about' may be parts of J's caricature, but both are common in the informal speech of all regional varieties. Since informality is often confused with standardness, however, such general changes may simply be a part of an imitation strategy which would have Northern speakers use whatever 'nonstandard' elements are available to them when they imitate 'Southern.' (See Preston 1992 for a similar strategy in White imitations of African-American speech.)

10. The diphthongs in 'about' and 'now' are [ɑw]; J does not front the first element to [æ] nor is the diphthong reduced. This failure to imitate is perhaps a little odd since an 'accurate' Southern version of this diphthong was used (inappropriately) in 'y'all' (see 1) above).

11. The [o] vowel of 'don't' is not modified (see 3 above).

12. The proximity of [t] and [y] in 'don't you' result in the coalesced form [tʃ]; as in 9 above, however, we feel this is simply an informal, allegro speech phenomenon common to all regional areas but employed here as a part of the general nonstandard caricature of Southern speech (and even further evidence of the folk confusion of informality with nonstandard, discussed more fully below).

Segment-by-segment, then, this imitation is technically inept. Nevertheless, the impression it leaves is successful (as the laughter after J's performance indicates), because a successful imitation need be neither complete nor accurate. Students of the representation of dialects in literature have long been aware of the value of the limited use of "authentic" material in "artistic" performance.

> It may be safely put down as a general rule that the more faithful a dialect is to folklore [i.e., linguistics], the more completely it accurately represents the actual speech of a group of people, the less effective it will be from the literary point of view. (Krapp 1926:523)

If this rubric is also known to folk performers, however unconsciously, it will be difficult to decide when a folk imitation is "inaccurate" due to lack of knowledge and/or ability and when it is inaccurate because the folk performer feels that he or she has done enough to effectively establish whatever point is being made by the imitation. A more folkloristically oriented study of the data we are treating here would catalog the folk linguistic conventions used to imitate different varieties (by different speakers, for different purposes, in different settings, etc ...). Following Krapp's rubric stated above, J's use of such items as [ɑ] for [ɑy] in *I'm* (and, perhaps, his faulty [æw] in *y'all*) may be sufficient "peppering" of the segmental stream to "Southernize" his imitation, although, as suggested above, we leave it to folklorists and/or students of popular culture to catalog the identity and intensity of features which result in successful performance.

Indicating the percentage of items which have been modified does not, however, answer all the questions of folk imitation from a more linguistically oriented point of view. In the case of the skilled dialect writer, we assume, perhaps falsely, that he or she is a skilled user of the dialect in question and that every opportunity to use a dialect feature is a decision-point i.e., each time there is an opportunity to use the dialect, the writer makes a decision whether or not to employ it. Of course, we make no such assumption about the folk. The fact is that some caricatures (e.g., reduction of [ɑy]), although themselves not consistently used, are the *only* ones used. Other elements of the imitated variety which might have been used (e.g., the substitution of [ɛ] for [I] before nasals) never occur at all, and we may conclude (assuming we have enough evidence) that they are not a part of the possible repertoire of the folk performer.

Additionally, imitation does not answer questions about the level of awareness. For example, we never encounter overt discussion of the reduction of [ɑy] in any of the many discussions our respondents have about Southern speech. One might conclude, therefore, that the item is available only in the imitation "mode" of folk linguistic awareness. This overlooks, we believe, the common folk process of definition by ostentation. That is, Labov (1.1.1.1) may be right in his complaint that the folk lack words which describe phonological features (at whatever level), but that lack does not necessarily mean that a certain feature is available only to the most covert levels of folk awareness.

In fact, the relation between imitation and comment is complex. For example, *r*-lessness, a most frequently studied phenomenon in the professional literature, is never once commented on in our conversations; nevertheless, it is a feature of several imitations. In a discussion of Southern speech, the main topic of which is *you all*, both R and J in #25 (neither of whom claims to be a good imitator) offer the caricaturistic Southern phrase *Y'all come back now, you hear* with clear *r*-deletion (or schwa vocalization) in the last item. Recall, also, that in J's (#38) imitation of "Joisy" speech cited in 1.1.2, *birds* is *boids* and *words* is *woids* and that this same respondent was the one who adopted his military buddy's Boston *r*-less pronunciation of *car* because it was "easier" (cited above).

Also to our surprise the Southern caricature *help* [hɛp] was not mentioned, nor any other case of *l* loss or vocalization, further proof, perhaps, that consonants have played a minor role here. There were, however, a few cases of word-level phonology, and one did involve *l*, but the family of the respondent referred to was small-town Michigan rather than Southern and the phenomenon discussed is "intrusive *l*," not *l*-loss:

> SH: It's like D's family they all talk funny I think.
> DH: My family?
> SH: Uh huh. Like we DH we had a big problem about one word that he said.
> M: Oh yeah?
> DH: What word was that.
> SH: The word "iDEa." Er you used to say "iDEAL"=whenever he would be saying something he'd say "I have an ideal." I'd be like DH it's "I have an idea." And that used to dri:ve me: nuts. (#42)

We cannot be so sure, however, as we have already suggested, that even the diphthongal reduction in *I'm* in J's imitation (#38), which we have examined in such detail, is not a lexical caricature. Unfortunately, the limited number of imitative phrases in these data will not allow us to pursue this. A large number of cases might let us assert that certain lexical items were "principal carriers" of this or other imitative phonological strategies, and richer data might even allow investigation of the possibility that imitators are sensitive to phonological environments.

It is mostly nonsegmental characteristics, however, which allow J and his interlocutors to "appreciate" his performance as Southern. That performance, comments already cited, and many other imitations studied illustrate, predictably, the slower tempo or rate of Southern speech. The most common label for this phenomenon is "drawl," (although, as we have noted above, a number of respondents have folk-etymologized this item to "draw"). H and S (in #3) refer to it as a "cadence" and a "rhythm," and H illustrates it with the word *temperature*, giving an especially elongated final vowel to it – tempətyʊːɹ].[14] Although it is not overtly commented on, these imitations seem to make it clear that the "drawling" aspect of Southern speech is to be located in the vowels, a perception supported by professional investigation and comment (e.g., Feagin 1985). Linguists' investigations of "drawling" in Southern speech, however, focus on it as a variable, stylistic phenomenon, one related to such factors as status, age, gender and the like. Folk linguists simply identify all Southern speech as "drawled."

J's performance does not give us an opportunity to investigate it, but one might have expected greater comment on Southern stress shift to the initial syllable, particularly in light of such caricatures as *PO-lice*, but mention of this feature occurred only rarely.

> M: The girl that
> just started working with us this summer, there are some words
> that she says (0.5) you know when she pronounces the words=I
> forget what they are- Oh (1.25) "Monroe" [mən'ɹo]. The city of
> Monroe. We have a rental office in Monroe. She calls it
> ['manɹo].
> N: Oh really?
> M: And we laugh every time she says it. We say "Oh, MONroe is
> on the phone" and- and you know, she laughs right along with=
>   [
> N: Uh huh.
> M: =us- and I said "Why do you say MONroe instead of monROE
> and she said (1.75) "I don't know. That's just the way people
> around" - She's from Cl- the Cleveland area and she said people a
> lot of people just pronounce it that way. (#9)

Of course, M's acquaintance does not say *MONroe* because she is from Cleveland, a decidedly nonsouthern speech area. The "people around" whom she learned it from are Monroe, Michigan, natives, and why they have a Southern stress-shift feature is much easier to account for – many of them are Southern or only one generation removed from Southern. Apparently the respondents in #9 do not know that Monroe is one of the southeastern Michigan sites which has a (deserved) reputation for a concentration of Appalachian immigrants. Due to the intense development of the post-World War II automobile industry and to limited employment opportunities in parts of Appalachia at that time (coupled with a lengthy coal strike), many Appalachians migrated (and have continued to migrate) to southeastern Michigan for employment. Although no history or careful social survey of this population has been done, their presence is still well-known. The east side of Ypsilanti, Michigan, a small city with major automobile industry plants, is so recognized for this population that it is called "Ypsitucky."[15]

We believe that much of the earlier work described above makes it clear that the South is linguistically very salient for all Northern speakers, but there is an immediate relevance for our southeastern Michigan respondents because of the population we have characterized here. Since many of our respondents are from Ypsilanti (or nearby communities), this fact may have enhanced their awareness of Southern speechways and, perhaps, fed their imitative abilities. After R and H's imitations of Southern speech in #25, for example, R says "But you can hear this [i.e., Southern speech] in Ann Arbor, Ypsilanti." It is clear that J, whose imitation from #38 we have been looking at more carefully, has this information, for earlier in the same interview he (and B) respond to the fieldworker's query about "Ypsituckians."

M: I keep hearing about these Ypsituckians.
B: Oh yeah that was World War II.
M: Are they - I mean do you know any Ypsituckian people=
J: =Yeah, there're a lot of them.
                     [
B: There's a lot of people.
J: (Well-)
B: We work with them.
M: You d(h)o? What do you mean THEM. Are they - I mean=
          [
B: See we work with (   )
M: =are they- - Do they still sound like they're=
         [
B: Well this town was (   ) small and=
J: =Yeah.
M: Do they still sound like they're from the South?
J: I swear to God when you talk to them, - and they still got the uh=

B: [I don't notice that (   )
B: =the twang=
J: =You know, the twang
                 [
M: Uh huh.
           [
B: A twang. And a lot of them have been here - you know
like from- - forty-five. (#38)

Another respondent is impressed with the fact that even lifelong Ypsilantians have Southern speech:

> N: The reason it's called "Ypsitucky" is, because there's a lot of people - that live in Ypsilanti, that have lived in Ypsilanti all their life, that speak with a Kentucky uh, Kentuckian uh: slang. Very Southern, very Southern. (#48a)[16]

We turn now to elements beyond what the folk call "accent." Recall that the first item in J's performance in #38 is *y'all*, and there is no doubt that this is the Southern caricature par excellence. It is, as well, the subject of considerable overt discussion. Our respondents are even involved in one of what Michael Montgomery (1992) refers to as the two principal questions about the form – "... whether *you all* is ever used as a singular" (356). For R (in #2) it is apparently his interpretation of it as a singular which makes it so striking:

> R: Like uh in the South, if I were addressing you, - an:d - J was with you, I might say "you all." "You" as opposed to: you or or J=
>   [
> H: (   )
> R: =in this· case directing it to you, I say "you all." (#2)

In fact, *you all* as a singular appears to be an important matter to R, for he repeats this interpretation to H in another interview (#25). B (the Chicagoan in #56) was in Houston for a short time and believes that *y'all* is a singular, and he has an account of its plural as well:

> B: Well it's funny down there - well first of all up here, if you're=
>   [
> X: Uh huh.
> B: =talking to a bunch of people you say, "Well, do you GUYS want to go - over HERE."
>   [
> X: Uh huh.
> X: Uh huh.

B: Down there, - if you're talking to one person, you say "you all."
X: Uh huh.

     [

B: "If y'all go over here."

          [

X: "If you all go-" Yeah.
B: Then if I'm talking to both of you, I'll say "All you all." (#56)

R (#16), however, who learned her *y'all* from longer exposure in the South, has retained it apparently only as a plural, for she notes that the Northern equivalent is *youse guys* or *guys*. Her excuse for its retention is simply "... I ((laughs)) like it." Although she also cites *hey* as a Southern form for *hi* in greetings, *y'all* may be the only consistent lexical caricature. Others which occur from time to time appear to be "colorful" or "rustic" items which are similar to the proverbialisms and folk speech forms discussed more fully below. J (in #41), for example, tells of her shock at hearing her Southern husband call a boil on her shoulder a *rising*. Even her Southern parents (who, she admits, would have "said it funny" – i.e., with a reduced diphthong, which she imitates) would not have called it a *rising*. She does not pursue it, but this would seem to indicate some awareness of social status or urban versus rural distinctions in Southern speech (as M indicates in #9 above in her distinction between Kentucky and Tennessee speakers). In general, however, such distinctions are not made, and all Southern Speech (or all New York City area speech) is lumped together. We shall elaborate on the folk confusion of style, status, and region below.

There also appear to be grammatical forms which are commonly repeated as part of the Southern-imitation routine. J in #38 is not alone in using a tag at the end of his exemplary sentence (*Y'all know what I'm talking about now don't you*). We have already cited the *r*-less use of the tag *you hear* by R and J in #25, and we believe it is a good candidate for a Southern grammatical caricature. Both casual and nonstandard constructions appear to be part of Northerners' general strategies in imitating Southern speech, and we shall have more to say about that in our discussions of style and status below.

Longer strings or stock phrases are also a part of the Northern imitator's repertoire. R and J in #25 have not just used the tag *you hear*, but have used it at the end of the caricaturistic *Y'all come back now*. It is perhaps also worth noting that the *now* of such stock phrases is also characteristic and is a part of J's performance in #38. For example, in #28, D, imitating Texas speech, says *Do y'all want to go out horseback riding now?* Perhaps there is no better evidence that a folk performer has a stock phrase in mind than a failed attempt to deliver it. G in #36a is, we believe, reaching for some such stereotype as *Y'all come down and see us sometime, you hear*, but he has not quite got it:

> H: Ca- yo- give me an example. ((i.e., of Southern speech))
> G: Y- y'all come down and see you someone else sometimes.
> (#36a)

From a speech-act point of view, it is striking that nearly all these Southern-speech imitations are "offers" or "invitations," perhaps covert recognition of the stereotype of "Southern hospitality." There are a number of discussions about Southern "temperament" and the like (particularly between X, S, and B in #56), but these caricatures would lead us away from our more language-centered concerns.

Beyond these stock phrases, there seems to be considerable agreement that proverbialisms and other brief folk-speech performances are particularly abundant in Southern speech (see Preston 1989d). For example, after M (the fieldworker) in #41 suggests to J that Southerners have "funny little sayings" (and offers "even a blind squirrel finds an acorn every once in a while"), her respondent (J) agrees and cites her Southern husband's use of "busier than a one-armed paper-hanger" and "harder than Chinese arithmetic," although she is "not sure" such expressions are Southern.

S (in #56) is very explicit about the artistic superiority of Southern folk speech:

> S: Whe(h)n No(h)rtherners ge(h)t angry, like, you know - people around - where I lived in Ohio and even back in New York, - =
> X: [
>   Uh huh.
> S: =they they're almo- they're almost - they're quite straightforwards. You know, "You- you're a big dummy and this this this this this this - and this." It's like not using a lot of creativity. - Ju(h)- just being very straightforward and saying boom boom boom. But in the South, - it's mo(h)re like - I- I don't want to use any swear words.
> X: It doesn't matter.
>   [
> S: But it's more creative.
>   [
> B: Heh heh.
> S: It's much more creative.
> B: "You're dumber than a -
>   [
> X: It's-
> S: Yeah. "You're dumber than shit."
> X: ((laughs))

B: They compare you. - You say "You're dumber than a bag=
                [
X: ((laughs))
                [
S: (   )
B: =of rocks," or you know "You're so- that's stupid."
            [
X: No(h) ((laughs))
S: "Get off your ass, you. You ain't doing nothing today. Why you're slower than my uncle's donkey."
X: ((laughs))
     [
B: Yeah, I mean they use examples of uh what you're doing right or wrong. (#56)

2.2.5 A regional summary

We have spent a great deal of time on Southern speech for, as we have reported above in our survey of more quantitatively oriented work, it is, perhaps excepting New York City, the principal, general US speech caricature. We shall not review the history and background of events from slavery and the Civil War through the activity of the Ku Klux Klan, and even more recent civil rights struggles nor the myriad popular culture representations (country and western music, Gone with the Wind, the Beverly Hillbillies, Hee-Haw, etc...) which have contributed to the picture of the South as a distinct area; suffice it to say that none of that has hindered the perception of it as a separate speech area. It is also the case that the caricature, in general, has been a negative one, and most of the representations offered us reflect the picture of a backward, rustic Southerner. It is certainly the case that when our respondents wanted to imitate Southern speech, they said such things as "I'm going down to the creek to catch crawdads, y'all" (S in #56), not such things as "I'm going over to the hospital to perform brain surgery, y'all." Although the cultural caricature is no more accurate than the linguistic one, it is there. Whether for the purely scientific purpose of recording it or for the social purposes of helping us better understand our attitudes towards one another, we suggest that the study of such linguistically-oriented caricature is an important task.

Our respondents' views include, however, notions of a "New South," as suggested in the reference to the differences between Atlanta and Columbus, Georgia, speech outlined above by R in #16. The following exchange even suggests that a more urban, wealthy

South is responsible for a change in what constitutes an acceptable variety for the national news:

B: Dan Rather is very interesting. He's from Texas.
Z: Yes,
((pause))
B: From the South. And that's where he grew up, and he's got a SLIGHT, Southern accent. I have a theory about Dan Rather.=
Z: [Hm.
B: =I believe, you know- the reason they picked him, to be the=
Z: [((laughs))   [Yes.
B: =number one - newsman to replace Walter Cronkite was the big guy, he was the numbe- he was the number one=
Z: [Uh huh, I remem-
B: =announcer. He retired. And so it was a big thing, who are they going to get to replace him, cause - he was the number=
Z: [Uh huh.
B: =one news:caster in the country. I mean- this Dan RAther. -=
Z: [Uh huh.
B: =And I- my theory is tha- that one reason was because he has ((pause)) he speaks- his accent is:: more or less - standard - mainstream but it's- it has a slight, Southern - uh - sound to it.
Z: Hm.
B: He lost most of it. But- from his - growing up in Tex- in the South in Texas, and I think that they- that they picked him - =
Z: [Uh huh.
B: =because th- because this the population of the South is increasing, and they want to appeal to that region of the=
Z: . [Uh huh.
B: =country, which is increasing in population, and there are more people wh- with wealth etcetera, - who have a- who=
Z: [Uh huh.
B: =speak with a Southern accent from that region, than than twenty thirty fifty years ago. You know the economy is boo- and, i- =
Z: [Uh huh.
B: =it's stronger and an- in tha- in that part of the =
Z: [I see.
B: =country. So I think they they liked that idea that he had a slight Southern accent in his voice. To appeal to that region. (#19)

Finally, as all prejudiced-against groups are likely to do, something positive may be made from something negative. When C (in

#49) found that her Baltimore relatives did not like her "country" Oklahoma accent, she used it whenever she wanted to annoy them. In data acquired for another study, a second-generation male Ypsituckian reports that use of Southern speech is especially effective in attracting members of the opposite sex. Below, in our discussion of gender, we will examine how one of our female speakers makes use of "sweet-little-ol'-thang" associations with Southern speech when she finds herself in Northern and male-dominated business situations.

We would like to spend more time on the South, but there is simply not space for it here. There are, for example, interesting comments in our conversational samples about the area which constitutes the South, much of which, for example, confirms those quantitative findings which tend to exclude Texas and Florida, among others. A more complete report on the South as the most significant linguistic area in US dialect perception is provided in Preston 1993a.

We cannot put aside this section, however, without some reference to secondary and tertiary areas of significance to our respondents. We have already cited a few folk comments on the New York City metropolitan area, found to be the second-most prejudiced against speech region in quantitative studies, and Labov 1966 has shown considerable internal dislike (or "linguistic insecurity") among New Yorkers themselves. In these conversations, however, New York City speech was infrequently mentioned. The overwhelming focus on "different" (and nonstandard) speech was the US South.

We have also already cited a number of references to Michigan speech as a "norm," although this theme was also less touched on than the quantitative data reported above might suggest. Nevertheless, as already reported, many respondents mentioned a "Midwestern" if not exclusively Michigan "normal," "standard," or "national broadcast" variety.

Since a few of our respondents have Canadian roots (and since Canada is so nearby), it is not surprising to find references to Canadian speech matters. Also not surprising is the fact that the Canadian tag *ey* is the most frequently mentioned phenomenon. In #4, for example, J reports that Canadians say *ey* "after every sentence"; K in #53 first says it is "just an expression" but finally suggests that it is "More like in a questioning tone, maybe?" and characterizes its use as follows: "They'll ask a question then they'll say 'ey,' expecting you to respond."

The respondents in #4 and #25 who have Canadian backgrounds are also aware of "Canadian raising" and provide effective imitations in both these interviews of their [ɑw] diphthongs as [ʌw] in such items as *shout* and *about*. Additionally J (in #4) reports that Canadians use what she calls a "broad a" in such words as *pass* and *class*. She imitates what she calls the "American" pronunciation as [pæs] and the "Canadian" as [pɑs], although it is unlikely that any but the poshest Ontarians would have a vowel that far back.

There are other brief mentions of dialect preferences of one sort or another: some claim to like Jamaican English, and one even says that Southern speech is fun to listen to. A native Chicagoan says Chicago speech is "nasal," and another native Michigan respondent calls Michigan speech "clear." Most respondents believe that people from the US are good at recognizing broad regional differences, although K in #18 says it is difficult to identify speakers from one's own region.

We will let E (#55) conclude this section for us. When she was asked to characterize US (or other) English varieties outside the North, she said her first thoughts are "What planet did you come from" and "What's wrong with you." In spite of increased personal travel, military service, and the media, US dialects are as intact internally as they were years ago, a fact supported in much technical work but widely disbelieved in popular circles. It is also the case that folk prescriptivist notions which play a large part in the formation and maintenance of attitudes towards regional varieties are still very much a part of the national linguistic life of the US.

Chapter 3: Social factors

3.1 Ethnicity

Ethnicity plays a large role in these interviews, as it did not in the
earlier tasks. In map-drawing, for example, only the Hispanic populations of southern Florida and the Southwest were often referred to,
but in these interviews AAVE was a central theme.

3.1.1 AAVE

Considerable attention is also paid to AAVE in educational settings
in 4.2.3 We focus here on the folk notions of the etiology, provenience, persistence, and components of AAVE and on general folk
impressions of it.

A creole hypothesis or at least connections to African linguistic
forms (e.g., Stewart 1970, Dillard 1972) has reached only a very
small number of our respondents. Although it figures in the discussion cited just below, the conversation begins with a very common
folk linguistic descriptor for AAVE, namely "slang":

G: Yeah Black people have a lot more slang - (.hhh) than - than
whi- not more than white people, but they have a different slang
than white people do, and it's understood, you know, across the
whole (.hhh) age groups of Blacks I think, you know, that's part of
their culture.
H: Oh::. Speaking of Black - uh people uh - I mean - the: - Black-
they use the different English?
                              [
G   Yeah, in fact there's something called
Black English.
H: I heard that- I heard Black English (   ), but I don:'t=
                                        [
D: Yeah.
H: =understan: - Any difference? (You think?)
      [[
D: Well, see th-   Well, one thing, like their
their language - is, they talk about essences of things. And and - =
                                                        [
H: Uh huh.

D: =you know they: they use a lot of - emphasis in their language. So they say like - "We be cool," or "She be talking."="She be talkin'." That means uh that's who that person is, somebody who talks a lot, or "We be cool" means, you know, "I'm some- I'm=

                                      [

H: (   )

D: =somebody here saying really ((snaps fingers)) with it" or something. And so they they put the word "be," - before other words for emphasis.=They also have double negatives.

D: [[(Uh), - yeah as an emphasis. Means it's REALly that way,=

H: [[Double negatives.

D: =like- "I ain't NEVer," you know, that's that to to white people=

      [

H: That way.

D: =think "These people are stupid," but the truth is in African-base languages, - they use double negatives. And they-

                                            [

H: You mean "I ain't never."

D: Yeah. R- right. "I ain't nev-

      [[

G: Right.   Or "I won't never"?

D: Right, and

          [

H: Oh "I won't-" OK.

D: Right. And - they they did they do that as a way of emphasis, an:d that comes from a rule that they used from African-based languages.=Just just like if you started all of your time sentences with "Today I'm" (.hhh) you're using uh a rule from Chinese language - Ther- they use that from an- from a rule from African-based languages. Just and they-

H: Oh:

    [

G: And it's improper in English to use double negatives.

H: Yeah, ( ) be- because if you uh as my knowledge, - if a=

             [

D: Right.

H: =sentence use the two I mean double negative, that will become -

G: It changes and makes it positive.

H: The positive, yeah. The positive, yeah.

       [

G: Just like math, actually. Two negatives make a positive in math.

H: But- they won't- you mean they still still negative.

G: [[(   )

D: [[Right. Right. In African-based languages it's still negative=

                            [

H: (Oh. I see.)

D: = right.

H: Oh so- you- uh you mean uh Black Engi- Black English is uh s- has something to do with uh African languages.

D: [Yeah. Right. And and to this day,
some of those same rules are still used within Black culture.
G: So th- the slang, I don't think Black people could recognize
where it comes from before, but it's just part of their culture.
D: [No. Not mos- not most of them.
D: The educated o(h)nes do(h), but (.hhh).
G: [Uh huh. OK.
H: [Can you - if I mean -
(   ) you (can) understand.
[
G: Sure we can understand
D: Oh yeah. Sure.
H: OK. - But you OK you know that's their language.
G: But that's slang and it's not - it's not proper English. (#7)

At the opening of this stretch of talk, G has to redefine her use of
"slang," for she clearly has two senses of it. Just before this discussion of AAVE, H, D, and G have been talking about teenage (and
other) slang, and G wants to make it clear that her use of it to refer to
AAVE is something different. She accomplishes this second sense by
noting that what she means by AAVE "slang" is known "across the
whole age groups." In short, AAVE "slang" is a variety common to
African-American speakers of all ages, unlike the more restricted
"slangs" which have been the earlier focus of attention.[1]

This similarity of AAVE across regions is mentioned by several
respondents. M in #13, for example, notes that "The regional differences of Black English are closer to each other, than the difference
between Black English [presumably of a Midwestern AAVE
speaker] and Midwest white English, is what I am trying to say." On
the other hand, M also claims that he can detect some regional varieties of AAVE (at least Northern and Southern), but he is not sure of
the features which allow him to do so.

What D means by AAVE speakers referring to the "essences" of
things is difficult but perhaps not impossible to understand. *Be* is,
after all, the verb of "existence," and D may feel that it somehow
emphasizes any attribute it links to an individual. If one says "We be
cool," then one asserts that "cool" is an essential part of their nature.
If this is so, then D reinterprets uninflected *be* as a sort of marked
form of the regular copula (*is, am, are*, etc...) which emphasizes the
attribute in a *be* sentence. If this interpretation is correct, then it is
not difficult to see how D moves from "essences" to "emphasis";

uninflected *be* emphasizes the essential nature of whatever it attributes; i.e., if "We be cool," then we are *really* cool.

At first glance, D's interpretation seems far from the linguistic one. The latter suggests that this uninflected (or "invariant") *be* is part of the AAVE tense-aspect system which is in contrast with a zero copula form and refers to durative or iterative events while the zero form refers to momentary or punctual ones (e.g., Bailey 1993). For example, the adverbials cannot be switched in the following.

He busy right now
He be busy all the time

Perhaps this is, after all, the distinction D is trying to get at (without the linguist's jargon for aspectual systems). "We cool" isolates an instance of our cool behavior while "We be cool" describes our usual, customary, "durative," or, as D might put it, "essential" condition. Although D does not draw the specific contrast with the missing copula form and characterize invariant *be* as a part of the AAVE tense-aspect system, his notion of "essence" and "emphasis" may, in fact, capture some of the truth of invariant *be*.

Although he feels that the function of both invariant *be* and multiple negation is emphatic, D notes that the latter is a structure which AAVE has as a result of its preservation from the African linguistic heritage. It is not clear if the "rule" he refers to is one in which African languages provide for "emphatic" multiple negation or one in which multiple negation is simply a norm. If the latter is the case, then the AAVE emphatic use is a later development, although D says that the "same rules are still used." J (in #25) also suggests that AAVE "probably came from African languages." Another respondent (K in #53) theorizes, however, that AAVE is a more recent cultural product of its users; children and speakers in urban areas in particular "have modified it to fit their needs." This position fits very nicely with the recent work of some linguists who find less continuity with the African (and creole) past in current AAVE (e.g., Bailey 1993). K is, by the way, also adamant that it is not a "dialect" but a separate "language." D in #12 believes that AAVE is the English learned by slaves from Europeans, and B in #8 thinks it is simply Southern English removed to the North.

In several ways, the conversation with D and G (#7) is the most linguist-like of our folk ideas.[2] They attach the use of AAVE (and its African elements) to the culture, but they continue to be adamant, G in particular, that AAVE is not "correct." Whatever their prescriptivist urges, however, they would appear to have a more positive

view of AAVE speakers and their variety than the following perhaps
more typical position:

M: Yeah, ah see that - that's what upsets me. You can see a really
- an educated Black person, I mean I- you know I don't care what
color a person is.
N: Uh huh.
    [
M: It doesn't matter to me. - And you can underSTAND them
and you can TALK to them and - Look at on the news, all the news
broadcasters and everything. They're not talking ((lowered pitch))
"Hey man, ((imitating African-American speech)) hybyayhubyhuby."
You can't understand what they're saying.
[
N: ((laughs))
N: Uh huh.
M: And - I just don't think there's any excuse for it. It's laziness and
probably - maybe it is you know, because they are low class and
they don't know how to bring themselves up or they just don't want
to. (#9)

For this respondent and others, African-Americans (and, as we have
already seen, Southerners and New Yorkers) all appear to be simply
recalcitrant in their refusal to acquire a "standard" variety. The
source of AAVE incorrectness is "laziness," "low class," or an inability (or unwillingness) to perform otherwise. That their performance is itself historically continuous and systematic is a matter not
considered. Another of our European-American respondents who
feels that African-Americans have the ability to speak otherwise provides an anecdote in which this belief is confirmed by an African-
American colleague:

J: And I used to teach Black children. And I had a difficult time understanding what they were saying. And I found out later though
that they were - it was intentional, because they could speak - like
we speak. And they wer- because: I - was having difficulty with this
o(h)ne little bo(h)(h)y. He was twe(h)lve. (.hhh) And - I - was supposed to test him, for uh reading problems. And I couldn't=
                                    [
H: Uh huh.
J: =understand what he was saying. And so I called uh the=
                                  [
H: Oh:?
J: =teacher next to me was Black. (   ) next to me. (.hhh) So I=
                                  [
H: Uh huh.
J: =did go over and get her, and I asked if she would help me.
(.hhh) And she came in and she- - just- said to him, she said "You

straighten up and talk - the right way. She's trying to help you."
((laughs))
      [
H: So uh you mean uh - he shou- can: - I mean, he know=
        [
J: (   ) understood what he mean( ).
H: =how to -
J: talk correctly
      [
H: talk to correctly. But he won't.
          [
J: Well, she said he did, but he wouldn't. (#25)

S (in #54), who several times indicates that she cannot understand AAVE, also notes that that is no problem for her, for her misunderstandings occur only when they are talking "among themselves." They change when they speak to her, particularly, she says, "if they want something." Since many of our respondents believe that African-Americans in general have the ability to switch back and forth easily between AAVE and some more standard variety, they appear to resent uses of AAVE, much, in fact, as people often feel suspicious of or even angry at what they perceive to be "unnecessary" foreign language use in their midst.

Other respondents, however, find such "switching" to be natural and connected to cultural values:

T: When they're around each other and they can- do speak that way, they fall into that pattern. Uh C's old roommate her friends that were in music school, and one was from Jamaica, a- and this other girl's from down South, and they spoke perfect English, but then when they were around their Black friends, you couldn't even understand them. So, yeah that's more=
                [
N: (   )
T: =like a cultural- and I don't mind that, (#9)

B and S (in #56) are both impressed with Jesse Jackson's ability to switch from an African-American "ministerial rhetoric" to a "more conservative" style. They are impressed in general with the importance of dialect switching to African-Americans in a "white world," although they note that if whites use AAVE they are thought of as racists. (This appears to be in sharp contrast to D's claim in #35 that many "blue-eyed soul brothers speak the same jive.")

Our African-American respondents are certainly aware of the value of variety manipulation, and some describe situational switching in great detail:

D: The only thing I may do which is a little different twist because I'm Black and the majority of my bosses are white. Um (0.5) sometimes you sense that they feel a little (0.5) uneasy when they talk to a professional Black. So rather than make them feel uncomfortable you try to make them feel comfortable by talking as much like them as you can. Um don't use the common (0.3) lingo that you'd use to a girlfriend on the telephone on a Saturday morning over a cup of coffee. Talk a little straight up and pronounce your words as clear as possible.
M: Uh huh.
D: That helps to ease the tension.
M: Yeah.
D: Because they tend not to look at you so much as to listen to you.
M: Mmm::: Uh huh?
D: So you have to play that a little bit. (#52)

For some African-Americans, therefore, code-switching is apparently a form of accommodation. D speaks "as much like them" as she can, suggesting that, although she is capable of that sort of performance, it is not her native, ordinary variety. The notion of African-American speech behavior as performed ("you have to play that") accommodation in the presence of whites is discussed in Kochman (1972).

In general, however, many European-Americans cannot understand why AAVE (or other nonstandard varieties) persists – the question taken up specifically in Ryan (1979) and focused on considerably in the early social psychological study of language. The academic answer – that nonstandard varieties (or perceived nonstandards) symbolize solidarity, comfort, honesty, and a host of other values associated with the smaller speech community – is never really broached by our folk respondents (although B in #56 says "I THINK a lot of Blacks – they need identity and they use English as an identity"). The more common opinion appears to be that of S in #54, who simply notes that African-Americans are opposed to change which would "conform to any standard." The closest a number of our respondents come to the more academically oriented position is the general agreement that a person will speak the language of their cultural environment, i.e., "fit in."

Even African-American respondents with strong prescriptivist tendencies are certain of this domination of cultural contexts in the acquisition and maintenance of a variety. D in #12, for example, is annoyed when a school psychologist says she cannot identify some African-American children from their speech alone (when, for example, her back is turned to a class). Since these children, according to D, grew up in an environment where they would not have had the opportunity to learn AAVE, the psychologist's claim seems naive to her, for it fails to note that children will learn the language of their environment.

> D: But (1.0) she could not figure out why it was that Black students sounded like white students in Ann Arbor. I said well the quality of the way you talk is directly influenced by where you grew up and how the people around you speak. (#12)

We turn now to the oft-mentioned theme of variety intelligibility. D and G in #7 cited above are both certain that they can understand AAVE; M in #9 is equally certain that she cannot. Most of our European-American respondents indicate difficulties in understanding AAVE. One pair of respondents argues over this intelligibility issue, and it leads to an interesting anecdote:

> E: I don't really think you'd notice it.
> N: A southern accent?
>   [
> E: Honestly. Unless it's a real deep southern accent. And a Texas accent is not necessarily- really southern.[3] - Not what I=
>   [
> D: Yeah but you=
> E: =consider southern.
> D: =notice people who have an accent. I mean like working at the store people will come there, and I couldn't tell if they were saying "white" or "wide" you know when they were asking for shoes.
> E: Yeah but that's black not white people.
>   [[
> D: They want-   No no. It wasn't black people. It was not black people if I recall they were- they were white people
>   [
> E: You know like the time I was standing outside-
>   [
> D: ((clears throat)) In fact I think I can understand black people a whole lot better than some of the white Southern people.
>   [
> E: But I had that time when I was standing outside the office there and I kep- you know- and he kept saying - you know "Atwood" and here he was saying "Edward."
>   [
> D: Edward
> N: Oh ((laughs))
> E: And I said "No: damn it. X. Edward X.," and he says "That's right. Atwood X." ((The respondent uses his full surname; which we give as simply "X."))

N: Oh ((laughs))
D: But no I- I-

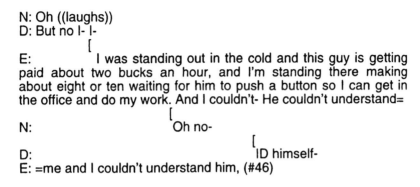

E: I was standing out in the cold and this guy is getting paid about two bucks an hour, and I'm standing there making about eight or ten waiting for him to push a button so I can get in the office and do my work. And I couldn't- He couldn't understand=

N: Oh no-

D: ID himself-
E: =me and I couldn't understand him, (#46)

The details of the above misunderstanding – "Atwood" versus "Edward" – are worth noting. How could E have taken his African-American interlocutor's pronunciation of "Edward" to be "Atwood?"

1. AAVE (like many US Southern and East Coast and Southern British varieties) has no nonprevocalic [ɹ]. E expected the second syllable of his name to sound like [wɚd], but it was more likely pronounced [wət]. (There are also likely vowel quality differences between the schwa represented above and the actual vowel produced by the AAVE speaker, but we ignore them here; suffice it to say that they might result in a vowel which could even more reasonably be interpreted as [U] and therefore closer to E's expectation of "-wood" rather than "-ward.")

2. AAVE has a tendency to devoice (or substitute a glottal catch for or even delete) syllable-final stops, particularly apical ones. Where E expected a [d] at the end of the first syllable of his name, therefore, he heard a [t].

The above two facts are simply those of AAVE, and, taken together, they might be sufficient to account for E's misunderstanding. The third fact, however, has as much to do with E's system than with AAVE, and, from the point of view of deeper folk misunderstandings, may play an even more significant role in the mystery we are trying to unravel here.

3. E is no doubt an early stages Northern Cities Shift speaker – age, status, gender, and suburban background all point to that classification. (If that were not enough evidence, we have heard considerable tape of E's speech and are certain of this categorization.) In the early stages of this vowel rotation, E's low-front vowel (i.e. [æ]) will have raised towards [eə] (eventually even [Iə]). AAVE speakers in the North will have resisted this vowel rotation. It is not at all unreasonable, then, to claim that the AAVE interlocutor reported on by E would have produced an [ɛ] (or [e]) vowel in "Edward" which would have matched E's auditory expectations for the Northern Cities Shift vowel of "Atwood."

To summarize (phonetically): the AAVE speaker may have said [etwət], and any one (or all) of the phonetic differences between that production and E's expectation of what "Edward" (and "Atwood") should sound like produced the confusion.

Of course, all this linguistic detail is not as interesting as the uses E has made of it. First, he has used it as ammunition against his wife's claim that AAVE is not so difficult to understand. (In fact, she claims that Southern white speakers are more difficult to comprehend.) Second, and more sociologically significant, he has used it as a basis to introduce the fact that his AAVE-speaking interlocutor is only a two-dollar-an-hour wage earner while he (E) is an eight (to ten) dollar an hour employee. The moral, although unstated, seems clear: Why should a lower-level employee, who cannot even pronounce "Edward" correctly, keep a more skilled (i.e., higher-paid) employee waiting?

In spite of these generally negative reactions to AAVE, several respondents note the contribution of African-American speech to the general culture. In a discussion of *man* in #36a, A tells the fieldworker that "We picked it up from – the Black people." B in #19 is even more enthusiastic about the loans from AAVE to other varieties:

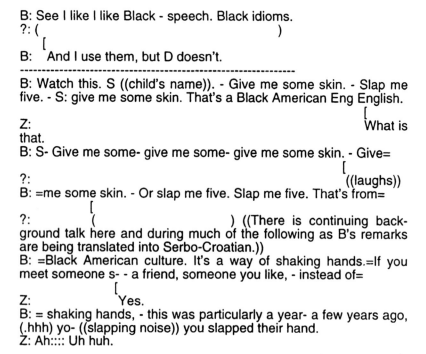

```
B: See I like I like Black - speech. Black idioms.
?: (                                                    )
      [
B:    And I use them, but D doesn't.
----------------------------------------------------------------
B: Watch this. S ((child's name)). - Give me some skin. - Slap me
five. - S: give me some skin. That's a Black American Eng English.
                                                           [
Z:                                                         What is
that.
B: S- Give me some- give me some- give me some skin. - Give=
                                                           [
?:                                                    ((laughs))
B: =me some skin. - Or slap me five. Slap me five. That's from=
      [
?:    (                              ) ((There is continuing back-
ground talk here and during much of the following as B's remarks
are being translated into Serbo-Croatian.))
B: =Black American culture. It's a way of shaking hands.=If you
meet someone s- - a friend, someone you like, - instead of=
                     [
Z:                   Yes.
B: = shaking hands, - this was particularly a year- a few years ago,
(.hhh) yo- ((slapping noise)) you slapped their hand.
Z: Ah:::: Uh huh.
```

B: ((slapping noise)) That- that- i- I don't know exactly where that came from, but that's - come from Black American culture. - And

Z: So you will- - you wil (   )

      [

B: So so I I like that kind of stuff, and I've known Black people. - And it's - crept into white culture. - So uh:: I mean it's=

  [

Z: Uh huh.

B: =fun. So I say, S ((begins to say child's name)) I say- I do that with the kids.

Z: Uh huh.

B: S ((child's name)). Slap me five.

Z: ((laughs))

B: ((quietly)) Slap me five.

Z: Slap me five?

B: Give me some skin.

Z: ((laughs))

B: Give me some skin. - ((rapidly)) She doesn't want to do it.

       [

Z: ((laughs))

B: ((whispers)) Give me some skin.

Z: ((laughs))

B: Give me some skin;

Z: No, she isn't (   ).

B: She won't do it now. - Anyway, that's just an example.

Z: Hm:. But how did you learn.

       [

B: But D- D doesn't talk that way.

Z: You should ask her why.

D: I'm just not with Black people as much.

B: No. It's cause you're a woman. (#19)[4]

B "likes that kind of stuff" and notes that AAVE practices have "crept into white culture." This conversation is also pertinent to our discussion of gender below (3.4), however, for B is apparently aware of the fact that AAVE has "covert prestige" and is more available for male than female use among European-Americans. This situation is similar, of course, to the more likely acquisition of Southern and New York City varieties by men than by women outlined above.

As in their representations of the details of other regional varieties, our respondents are not particularly rich (or accurate) in their characterizations of AAVE.[5] The examples embedded in the quotations already given have provided some indication of the characterizations of linguistic detail in the majority of the interviews in which AAVE was a topic. In addition to G and D in #7 (cited above), L in #31 illustrates multiple negation with "I ain't got no money today." She is also the only respondent who illustrates third person indicative leveling – "She or he don't." The only other grammatical feature mentioned (other than the comments in #51 examined below) was the leveled participial in "I have went" by G in #1. Again, other than the respondents in #51, pronunciation is never exemplified by any respondent as an important feature of AAVE, although several characterize the variety as being "accented." There is support, however, for our earlier claim that some varieties which are thought to be non-standard are simply represented that way by having general nonstandard or even casual features attributed to them. When D in #7 illustrates the invariant *be* form in "She be talking," he "corrects" his performance by saying the same sentence a second time but with an alveolar rather than velar nasal. Many of the above-listed grammatical variants are, in fact, wide-spread nonstandard features, not items unique to AAVE. But just as sociolinguists and dialectologists would not insist that a variety have a large number of elements unique to it for it to be considered a separate variety, we should not insist that folk respondents identify and/or imitate only those features unique to a variety in their representation of it.

One might have expected more "slang" forms or exemplary lexicon offered as examples of AAVE, but such items were also not frequent. D and G in #7 discuss the semantic reversal of *bad* (= "good") in AAVE; we have already cited B's use of "Give me some skin" and "Slap me five" in #19. A in #36a notes that *man* is now used by everybody but was borrowed from African-American use. Only J in #48b comments on ethnically related taboo when he quotes a traditional racist one-liner:

> J: I think the the first word that uh ((sniff)) - you know white people - ((sniff)) uh you know use when when they're babies i- they learn "mother," Right?
>   [
> A: Uh huh.
> A: Uh huh.
> J: And the Black people, they learn "mother f-er." ((pronounced as if it were "effer")) (#48b)

His wife, however, immediately objects, accuses her husband of "prejudice," and claims that European-Americans use the form as much as African-Americans.

Our fieldworker Hwang's work with an African-American family in Detroit was more productive. He has an extended conversation with African-American respondents, however, in #51, and we summarize some of those contributions here.

From folk lexicon, these respondents discuss *yo*, and define it as an "attention getter." D notes that his son (S) uses "me chappie," a form which we attribute to contemporary Caribbean (perhaps Jamaican) influences on AAVE. *Dude* for "person" is also mentioned. More obviously slang items within AAVE itself are also provided. *Geek* is given as the participial *geeked* and glossed as "you're all swelled up, you're all happy" and "You have a big head." *Gump* is glossed as a person who is "goofy," and *psych* [sɑyk] is cited as a form which means to "fool" or to "kid" (i.e., tease). V interestingly folk etymologizes *nerd* as "nerve," but it is not clear that she means to offer that item as an example of AAVE slang. The respondents do mention *dorkie, wimp,* and *Cinderella* as terms for boys who are seen as school-oriented, what some of the linguistic and sociological literature refers to as "lames" (e.g., Labov 1972b), but, again, it is not clear that they mean to suggest that these are AAVE items. It is obvious, however, that when they mention *epic* (which they gloss as "cool") they want to indicate a non-AAVE slang item, for they locate the provenience of it as "the new word now out in the suburbs." In their general discussion of AAVE slang, they note that it is young people who create it and that the older generation does not understand it, contradicting the European-American opinion cited above that AAVE is known "across generations." It should be obvious that these respondents and others have difficulty distinguishing between the elements within a variety which linguists would regard as "slang" (and which would be age and sub-group restricted) and the entire variety itself. That difficulty is exaggerated by the fact that the folk term "slang" refers to both.

R focuses on more conversational elements when she identifies "I hear that" and "You got that right" as typical "back-channel" sorts of phrases used by AAVE speakers. (D argues, by the way, that the correct form is "I heard that.")

Invariant *be* is also discussed in #51, and this conversation also provides an example of hypercorrect *be's* in "It be's that way" and the only interesting examples of phonology – r-less [do] for [doɹ] and a diphthongized vowel in "bed" [bɛəd]). R only briefly mentions and exemplifies the substitution of stops for labiodental fricatives in *that* – "dat."

Also in #51, V, the most authentic AAVE speaker in our data, is especially sensitive to the proscription of AAVE and is determined that her daughter will not use it:

V: You know like when my daughter go around, J's ((her sister's=
 [
S: He (   )

V: =house)), you know K ((V's daughter)) when she go around my
family, they say she talk like - like she's white instead of Black.

S: ((to the dog)) ( ) boy.

R: White.
C: Uh huh.
V: But - what it is Bill ((D and his family and friends know the field-
worker as "Bill")), she talk the proper language.
C: [[Oh, is she your mother?
D: [[(   )
V: My daughter.
C: [[Oh your daughter.
V: [[K.

R: (   )
V: She speak the proper language.
C: Oh really.
V: And you know the rest of us speak that slang: language.=

C: No-   Not- not like you-
C: =Uh huh.
R: Yeah.
C: Why your daughter speaks proper language.
V: Because I don't allow her to speak the slang at our house.

C: Oh really.
V: And plus - it comes from environment. (#51)

Although V confesses to being an AAVE speaker herself, she has
tried to provide the kind of environment which will keep her daughter K from acquiring and using it. She appears to have been successful, at least to the extent that some of their relatives note that her
daughter "sounds white." V herself, on the other hand, was surprised
that people in Cleveland, where she visited once, thought she was
from Mississippi.

In light of the great majority of our European-American comments, it is not surprising that African-Americans should exhibit
considerable linguistic insecurity. Even those of our respondents
(European-American and African-American) who have a more
"linguist-like" sense of the origins, structure, and even social utility
of AAVE seem to agree that it is "not proper English." Worse, many
of our respondents attribute indifference or even recalcitrance to
those who "refuse" to perform in "standard English." We have no
doubt that some of that attitude stems from the experiences cited in
the section above on regional varieties. Learning another variety
seems to be an easy chore to our respondents; a visit to another part

of the country for just a couple of weeks is enough to have one "rub off" on you. Since such acquisition is apparently so easy, why groups or individuals would persist in performing nonstandard varieties when they either know or could easily learn the one which would be most beneficial to them is a folk puzzle. That it even provokes anger in some is doubtless also tied to nonlinguistic caricatures of race in US society. Linguists may be heartened by the apparent fact that information about AAVE seems to be influencing folk knowledge, but all may be disappointed that it has not yet influenced attitudes as strongly as one might have hoped.

3.1.2 Other

In fact, there is little reference to other ethnic groups in our conversations. As Southerners are the major regional group, African-Americans are the major ethnic group of folk linguistic interest. We noted above that Hispanic populations in the Southwest, in some urban areas, and in south Florida were frequently singled out in the map-drawing task. They are a frequent topic in these conversations only in the context of bilingual education, and that matter is treated in 4.2.4. Additionally, some ethnic groups are considered from a purely language-learning point of view, and one might reasonably say that their language rather than the group is the focus in such discussions. These matters are treated in 4.3.

It is not surprising that German linguistic heritage should be mentioned in southeastern Michigan, particularly in the rural areas around Ann Arbor and in Ann Arbor itself. The loss of German language abilities due to Second World War fears is mentioned a few times, and J in #2 notes that R did not learn German because his father "...was afraid to speak his German." Nevertheless, R believes he had problems with English (particularly in reading) because of his father's German accent. R explains that Ann Arbor was inhabited by Swabians early on and that that accounts for the fact that there are many German restaurants there and a continuing influx of Germans into the area, particularly those who work at the University and who "all speak German."

H's mother (in #3) grew up in "Pennsylvania Dutch" territory, and she remembers her pronouncing such items as *gold* as "golt." In the same conversation, H and S are, however, apparently unaware of Germanisms in their own speech. K, the fieldworker, asks if they are familiar with such phrases as "Do you want to go with?," Germanisms which, in non-German influenced English require a nominal or pronominal prepositional object.

> S: "Going with?"
> K: Yeah.
> S: Yeah. What is wrong with that?
> K: ((laughs)) Nothing is wrong with it.
> H: Nothing. (#3)

In such communities as Milwaukee, for example, phrases such as *Do you want to come with?* are used by even non-ethnic Germans with no awareness that such forms represent a substrate influence. Many of the Italian and East European immigrants there would have learned English from earlier immigrated (and more well-to-do) German residents. Since these speakers are from areas of considerable linguistic security, it is often a shock for them to learn that such constructions are not ubiquitous in well-thought-of varieties of US English. DR associates German with some unpleasant childhood memories:

> M: Like what comes to your mind when you think of about - like maybe your mother, or your grand- or your mother. Was she a quiet woman?
> DR: Yeah.
> SR: Very quiet.
> DR: Very quiet, and when she got upset with us kids she spoke German.
> M: Did she really.
> DR: Yeah. (0.5) That we knew.
> M: So do you know any German?
> DR: Oh no I haven't none at all.
> M: But so she spoke German to you.
> DR: Well that's only because we always figured it was because she was MAD at us, and like maybe said some nasty words.=
> SR: =Swear words.=
> DR: =And we didn't know what she was saying.
> M: You never knew what she was saying though.
> DR: But when she started speaking it, - we knew it was time to=
>   [
> M: Uh huh.
> DR: =run and HIDE. ((laughs))
> M: So you're afraid of German. You hear German and you got to run.
> SR: Tell her about the scissors or the shears.
> DR: Oh yeah, she used to hit us on the head with the handle part of the shears.
> SR: When they were bad. ((laughs))
> M: Do you have any fond memories of your mother. (#39)

This is also our only folk account of the "secret" use of a foreign language.

Aside from German, only a very small number of ethnic groups earn any specific mention. R in #25 suggests that the reason that English is spoken "a little differently" in the Upper Peninsula of Michigan is due to Finnish speakers who came there to work in the region's mines. The Upper Peninsula (or "UP") is a well-recognized folk and popular culture region in the state. Bumper stickers even recognize linguistic features, displaying such slogans as *I love da UP, eh*. (*Eh* is the Michigan folk spelling of the ubiquitous Canadian [ey].)

DH in #42 remembers having French-Canadian relatives who moved to the US, including a grandmother who never learned to speak English, but he also notes that his father, who moved to the US when he was four or five, "... knows a little bit (i.e., of French) but he can't fluently speak it." R in #25 also notes that the spelling (but not the pronunciation) of Detroit and other Michigan place names is due to the influence of early French explorers.

K in #53 had Polish relatives and her father spoke "a little." She says she cannot cite any details of Polish-accented English but is sure she would recognize it and other "Slavic" accents (which she exemplifies as German and Russian).

B in #56 comes from a multi-lingual household (a non-Japanese but Japanese-speaking father and a Czech grandfather who spoke seven languages). He strongly believes that second generation immigrants in America preserve European languages. He is also the only respondent to comment extensively on Spanish outside the setting of bilingual education. He claims that Spanish has already become the second language of the US and is on its way to becoming an "official" US language. We will take up the matter of Spanish in the US, particularly in educational settings, in more detail in 4.2.4 and 4.3.4.

Differences among ethnic groups and intolerances towards them from locals is dealt with at some length in the following, although the linguistic details are not as rich as one might have hoped for:

D: X was an international company or is an international company, and so they choose their people from all over the world.
[
M: Uh huh.

D: For example, uh (0.5) here in Ann Arbor? in fact there were (0.5) hundreds? probably. People people who were not native Americans, we had Indians, we had Arabs, we had uh- oh just=

          [

M: Uh huh.

D: from everywhere.

M: Uh huh.

D: Russians uh Yugoslavs, everybody. Chinese they just came from all over the world, but they were qualified, good engineers.

M: Uh huh.

D: And so they came for that reason.

M: Uh huh.

D: They were brought here because of their technical skills.

M: Uh huh.

D: But they brought other things as well. They brought ethnic differences, they brought language differences, they brought uh=

                                                [

M: Uh huh

D: =their own prejudices.=I can remember one of the major problems that we had was uh a situation in which we had a LOT of INdian engineers, uh ethnic Indians. (0.3) And they were very good, extremely good, very capable. Very professional. But we also had a lot of Sikhs, and we found that the the conflicts that=

          [

M: Uh huh.

D: =existed in India they brought with them here, and of course=

                                             [

M: Uh huh.

D: =WE couldn't allow those kinds of conflicts to develop here. So I put together, and it was with the help of people from EMU ((Eastern Michigan University)) as a matter of fact, uh I put together a program (0.5) of cross-cultural uh awareness in order to try to make the Indians. and the Sikhs understand that regardless of what their concerns and differences were, what they what happened back in India, that HERE we had some some concerns which were different.

M: Uh huh.

D: And they had some kind of an obligation to be aware of that.

M: Were there any uh conflicts conflicts dealing specifically with language barriers not transcending into cultural barriers but just language barriers first?

[

D: There were there were language barrier conflicts that that developed? But frequently there were a lot, of language conflicts developed among uh (0.5) local employees and the uh foreigners.

                                                      [

M: Uh huh.

M: Uh huh.

D: Uh and the local employees would be the clerical the administrative the support people.

M: Uh huh.
D: And I- looking back one of the reasons why is because we we have uh- (0.5) what's our cultural base in this area, particularly in Ypsilanti it's blue collar Appalachian or Southern Black.
M: Uh huh.
D: And these are the kinds of people one- once they have established themselves at an economic level they will be less tolerant of people who are not the same as they are.
M: Uh huh.
D: And unfortunately that's the way it is.
M: Uh huh.
D: I mean a REDNECK is a REDNECK. He's going to be an intolerant REDneck.
M: Did-
    [
D: And we found a lot of them.
M: Uh huh. So maybe you had tough situations where staff just refused to do or try to cooperate-
D: That's right, they would belittle those who maybe in their perceptions did not speak English as well as they did.
M: Uh huh.
D: And that caused me problems, as you can imagine. (#44)

As our fieldworker suspects, we are being led rather far from purely linguistic matters here, but it is interesting to note that several ethnic components of the area (African-American, Appalachian, and immigrant) come together in this commentary. That greater intolerance of immigrants (and their language ability) is attributed to lower-status speakers against whom linguistic prejudices are also strong in the community (as we have already shown) is also worth noting. It is also unfortunately true, however, that general prejudices against foreign language use, or "linguistic xenophobia" are common, and we cite only one example from our data since versions of the following are so common that the story-line itself has almost gained the status of an "urban legend."

M: [[But I find myself doing that in a store or in a restaurant.=
T: [[(   )
M: =You're sitting there - and - these people um - I don't know where they're from but you know they're of the Arabic descent or they're from that PART of the country, and they're sitting there and they're saying a few words and you sit down and they say a few words to each other in English, and then they start this ((imitates impression of a foreign language)), you know, and I just want to turn around and go ((imitates same language)) ((laughs)) Speak English you fool.
N: This is America.
M: I don't want to listen to your conversation but I don't want you talking about me either, and that's what it makes you think. (#9)

Attitudes to other languages and reflexes of those attitudes in educational programs are discussed more fully in Chapter 3, and we turn now to other social characteristics which more frequently engaged our folk respondents.

3.2 Status

Status only occasionally shows up in direct comment in these conversations (although it surfaces indirectly in the use of the discourse marker "quote (unquote)").When the folk do talk about status, the linguistic features associated with it do not appear to be those teased out by sociolinguists:

```
G: [[Or and I don't know when I hear people say "soda" I think=
H: [[Oh really.
G: =they're trying to be up- sort of upper crust or snobbish or=
                                                [
S:                                              (          )
G: =something yeah.
H: Oh "upper crust" means the same
            [
G:           Putting on airs:, well I think it's putting on airs really.
S: It could be-
       [
H:      Oh ah this is very interesting, you mean if you - you would
think the people say - "soda" is from upper class (    )?
S: [[I don't - not really
G: [[No not really not the upper class so much as as people who try
to look sophisticated like - traveled a lot or something.
                       [
S:                      When you-
S: When you hear someone using like - no slang, perfect English=
      [
H:     Oh.
S: = you would think of - upper class.
G: Um hum.
        [
S:       (.hhh) You know always talking - in perfect English and
using like their full vocabulary, - always always
                                   [
H:                                 How- how do you define perfect=
                              [
G:                            Very (        )
H: =Engl- I mean.
S: Uh - perfect grammar uh - you wouldn't cut words short, uh=
    [                    [
H:   (   )                oh perfect
                                         [
G:                                       Like=
```

S: =there would probably, yeah, you wouldn't say "goin'," you=
G: =you wouldn't say "goin'"
[
H: Wouldn't say=
S: =would say "going." You'd hear that, you'd hear the "g" at=
[
H: ="going."   "Going"
S: =the end, "going". - (.hhh) You know they'd-
[
W: "Going".
H: Everybody's very clear or something?
S: Yeah, it'd be - very clear - you know - and probably s- semi-slow.
G: Probably, yeah.=
S: =Y- you know to make sure they would get it all out, if you heard someone talking like that you'd probably think they had lots of money or something.(#23)

After G suggests that people who say *soda* are upper-crust, a more thorough discussion of class stratification ensues, and G asserts throughout that there is a kind of pretense in such use. In her discussion, then, the focus on status is really a focus on appropriateness. When she reflects on status and language, the first thing that comes to mind are those who use "snobbish" language to paint a false picture of themselves, i.e., those who inappropriately use it. Perhaps G is characterizing the use of a "superstandard," a stylistic matter which we discuss in 3.3.1, but we shall return in this section to the issue of folk sensitivity to the use of status-related speech which may be taken as "showing off" or "putting on airs."

S, however, appears to believe that the features he enumerates (slower and more distinct pronunciation, large vocabulary, no slang) isolate authentic upper-class speakers, not linguistic social climbers. It is, of course, not the case that upper-status speakers use no slang, for every folk group has its own slang, even slang embedded in technical language (see 3.3.2). It is possible, however, to misinterpret "slang" here, for, as we have pointed out in several places, "slang" is a common folk term for nonstandard use. Even though S provides no specific examples, we suspect that he has nonstandard rather than slang in mind, for immediately after he mentions that upper-status speakers use "no slang" he notes that they do use "perfect English."

Vocabulary is not a common element in the discussion of status and language (nor, in fact, a common topic in sociolinguistics in general outside the specific area of developmental concerns), but S notes that upper-status speakers use "their full vocabulary." We suspect that he simply associates with higher status the use of words which are more likely to be in the active vocabulary of better-educated persons. Although sociolinguists (and sociologists, for that matter) do not uniquely associate status with educational level, it is often an important element in the characterization of status in the United States (e.g., Wolfram and Fasold 1974).

When asked specifically for examples of "perfect English," S notes that upper-status speakers are not likely to "cut words short" and contrasts the velar and alveolar pronunciations of -*ing*. Here, of course, he is at the core of the stuff of quantitative sociolinguistics (e.g., Trudgill 1974). We do not, however, jump to conclude that S is a junior sociolinguist. First, of course, -*ing* ~ -*in* alternation is sensitive to many more determining factors than status alone – gender, age, style, etc... . Second, and more important to our investigation of folk linguistics, such variation in general is known by sociolinguists to be variable within such demographic identities as status while folk respondents assume it is categorically distributed. That is, S believes that upper status speakers "wouldn't say goin'," but quantitative studies (e.g., Trudgill 1974) show that upper-status speakers use less and lower status speakers more of the nonprestige variant of a large number of such alternatives. Labov (1972a) suggests, and we agree, that overt, conscious folk perception is often categorical – speakers of certain "types" either use or do not use certain stereotypical variants. That S chooses such a highly stereotyped item and appears to attribute categorical use to it (at least for upper-status speakers) would seem to confirm this generalization.

Finally, it is important to note that S, although he believes that upper-status speakers are the most frequent users of "perfect English," does not attribute the etiology and existence of standards to status-related issues. We assume that he, like most of our folk respondents, believes in the abstraction we spent some time characterizing in Chapter 1. Upper-status speakers are not the source of a standard; they are simply those who are the most likely users of it. On this final issue, therefore, in spite of whatever sociolinguist-like sensitivities the folk may have, they seem doomed to a Platonic prescriptivism which is, in fact, somehow separate from although involved in social concerns.

These more "technical" aspects of status, however, do not so often concern our folk respondents. As hinted at in G's remarks at the beginning of the section, the folk are more interested in the perception of status which may result from the acquisition of a prestige variety. In #1, G, himself an educator, wants to make sure that learning the standard does not lead to class-like or "snobbish" distinctions:

G: Because you were expected to speak and write - as a college student. And you were not allowed to make the other mistakes.=

    [
H: Uh huh.

       [
W: Uh huh.

G: =And I'm not so sure that's wrong. Because th- that's what (learning) is for. It is to supposedly eduCATE you. (.hhh) Not to make you snobberish, but you know (   ) better than anybody else, because you're not. Everybody's equal. - Uh - but=

                          [
H: Uh huh.

G: =you - i- i- i- if you- if you're - if you're have an opportunity to get - I don't know what, I hate to use the word better education, but if you- if you have a chance to get more education than someone else. Th- then you should use it. - And I think that's a waste if you=

    [
H: Uh huh.
G: =don't. (#1)

He is also aware that those who learn standard English may not be able to use that variety at home:

G: You go to school, and you learn what's called proper English. (.hhh) And this is your written ((G uses an aspirated "t" in "written" here; it is not his normal usage)) English. And it's also what's considered proper. But once you take that=

                          [
H: Uh huh.

                              [
?:   ((whispering))
G: =back home, everybody's home is a little different. And from the culture of economics. What you: how you were raised and all that, (.hhh) y- you may speak different - ly that what- actually wa[s] given to you. (.hhh) You have like we have normally in English you have to match up the appropriate verb with the appropriate tense. Uh there are certain verbs that when we use a helping verb or "have," "has," or "had," (.hhh) we use a special verb, for example.=

           [
H: Uh huh.
G: =(.hhh) When you get back HOME, uh some don't use the=

                    [
H: Uh huh.
G: =corre- some do NOT use the correct verb, with it. But when they're speaking they do not think anything about it. (.hhh) If they would go back into the classroom now, and they were to take that same test, (.hhh) they would have to use the correct verb. But when they go home and SPEAK, they will not use that verb. Because to do so, somebody'll look at you and say "Oh you're=

[[

H: Uh huh.   Uh huh
G: =trying to be uppity, huh." "You're trying to be smart, huh."=
                            [
H: Uh huh(h).
G: =In other words trying to look down on your - on uh on your el-=
[
H: Oh what I-, what I mean i-
G: =elders. Trying look down (.hhh) trying to say that I'm better th-
than uh than you are. (#36a)

This same G has a great deal to say about the unimportance of status in US culture, and we shall investigate some of his ideas along these lines even more carefully in the sections on minority language education (4.2). More than a few respondents touch on this theme of snobbery; recall that J in #38 (2.2.2), who copied his Army buddy's Boston speech, was accused of "trying to be snobbish" by his sister when he came home on leave, suggesting that region and status as well as region and standard are confused among folk respondents.

When asked specifically about language and class, B in #56 can think only of distinctions in Great Britain. He and S say there are two kinds of English in England – "upper class Oxford English" and "Liverpool Beatle's English." B later identifies "Monty Python" speech as being "proper, upper-crust British English," suggesting a linguistic insecurity of the New World in general. He specifically states that there are no such examples of social class dialects in "America," but admits that "snobbery" exists, particularly in "isolated, upper-crust areas."

Ethnicity as well as region play a role in the folk awareness of snobbish speech. D in #12 is also sensitive to being accused of fancifying her English, but she notes that she was brought up in the "first Black middle class community in the United States" and that her use of standard English (or her failure to use AAVE) is understandable – "everybody talked the way that I talked so it was no big thing." It is interesting that the social status of African-American speakers is rarely discussed, although many of our respondents may have simply presupposed that lower-status speakers were being represented in their characterizations of AAVE. When such presuppositions are not stated, however, they may lead to misunderstandings, for they suggest that all African-Americans (or all Southerners, or all New Yorkers) share the same linguistic abilities, but it is possible to accuse professional linguists as well as the folk of this failure (e.g., Morgan 1994).

Some of our respondents, however, see upward mobility rather than snobbishness connected to the desire for "better" language:

S: I think we try so hard to talk like the people do on television.
K: ((laughs))
H: ((laughs))
S: I mean that is our measure.
H: Ted Koppell. Remember that?
S: That is the upper mobile - That is the kind of English that will get you promotions.
H: Right. Upward and mobile.
S: And that is the way - and that's what we try.
K: Uh huh.
S: And we have been doing that for so many years - (#3)

Such higher status has apparently been achieved by some subgroups. There is no doubt, for example, that "yuppies" are standard English speakers:

M: I think one of the things about being a Yuppie is, you're supposed to be pretty educated. And that's fairly
 [
Z: (And speak) standard English?
M: Yeah, I think people who use a slangy kind of grammar probably would not- would be somewhat ( ) by standard issue Yuppies. In a sense that would be a sign of poor education, poor breeding, you know,=I am just guessing. But it would seem that way to me. ( ) I don't know- I mean by definition, the Yuppie is: young, upwardly, young upwardly, mobile professional. ( ) professional, you should speak pretty: - pretty good English, pretty use- pretty correct grammar, not be too slangy. (#13)

Note that here, as for S in #23, cited at the beginning of this section, the principal key to status is education.

In spite of such disclaimers and urges towards asserting that class-ridden distinctions are not common in the United States (and, therefore, not reflected in language), there are overt characterizations of standard versus nonstandard performances clearly related to class structure. In southeastern Michigan, where these data were collected, for example, the small cities of Ann Arbor and Ypsilanti (which adjoin one another) have quite different reputations. Ann Arbor is a white-collar, internationally-oriented, gentrified community with a very small minority population. Much of its cultural life is dominated by the prestigious University of Michigan. Ypsilanti is a blue-collar (auto industry) city with large African-American and Appalachian communities and is home to the less-prestigious Eastern Michigan University, a former "teachers college." According to several of our

respondents, the status distinctions of the two cities are clearly reflected in language use:

> R: But here then you'd have Ann Arbor and the way they talk, and
> you know they don't say "ain't." And you know they REALly you=
>   [
> M: No.
> R: =very rarely hear someone use poor English or bad English or
> English that's not proper. Where I get very very upset when I listen
> to students at this university ((i.e., Eastern Michigan University))
> talk because they put together English in such a way that it just- it's
> just totally wrong.
> M: Yeah?
> R: You know? And you know it and you hear it, and you think how
> can they be a senior or a junior and been through so many years of
> college and have how many English classes and still can't say a
> proper English sentence? And I wish I could think of an example
> because I know there's one that J says, and I'll tell you C's the best
> one of all that does it. You see how they talk and how they say "I'm
> goin' somewhere?" And and it's just very - poor poor English.
>   [
> M: Uh huh.
> M: Can't understand them or is it-
> ((pause))
> R: It's well not that I can't, no no, it's poor English. It's not putting=
>   [   ]
> M: Is it slang or is it-
> R: =the not putting the right verbs with the right nouns and the=
>   [
> M: Yeah.
> R: =right tense.
> M: Oh yeah. I know what you mean. - After four years of college.
> R: Yeah, and you're thinking, why can't they talk, and you don't
> hear: that in Ann Arbor. You don't hear it, you know? And I I have=
>   [
> M: That's true.
> R: =very many friends in Ann Arbor and they don't talk that way.
> M: Uh huh. Do you think it's a- do you think maybe they do it be-
> cause it's cool?
> R: No:.
> M: Do you think people they talk like you know I might I might just
> to emphasize something, I might say "Well, I AIN'T going to do it J."
> You know just to kind of emphasize be a joke you know.
> R: NO, because they're talking in a regular conversation with a
> person, and they can't get the right verb in there. (#16)

The fieldworker tries to give the respondent some "excuses" for nonstandard use (peer pressure, metaphoric shifting), but R is not buying
any. It seems clear to her (although it puzzles her why the people she

is describing can't change their behavior) that the underlying cause of their failure to use the standard lies in the social status differences of the two cities. We note again the theme of "annoyance" with those who, for some reason, cannot or will not acquire the standard variety. Here, however, this annoyance is not connected to ethnicity as it was in our examples in 3.1.1.

The folk do not connect all status and language matters to proper or correct use, however. In #10, S attributes a wider range of topic choice and the choice of "familiar" topics to higher status speakers, particularly in work situations:

S: I think people generally in the higher position are able to be more free and they can talk about whatever they want, because they know people underneath them can really going to (0.1) to comply uh and also the people in the higher position feel it's a good way to make people in a lower position feel relaxed. If you are the manager, you want the people who work for you to feel good, and making them feel good, uh means talking about things other than work and to give them the feeling that you are concerned with their their uh lives and not just work. (#10)

This is a particularly interesting comment, for it deals with what one might call "discourse privileges." A great deal of linguistic work has been done on the structure of discourse (e.g., Schiffrin 1994), and some has been done on contrasts in discourse styles and practices, but the targets have been men and women (e.g., Maltz and Borker 1982), ethnic groups (e.g., Schiffrin 1984), and institutional settings (e.g., education, Sinclair and Coulthard 1975; medicine, Candlin, Leather, and Bruton 1976; and law, O'Barr 1982). Very little work, however, directly addresses the question of organization and strategy in discourse as it may or may not differ among status groups, although Akinnaso and Ajirotutu (1982) focus on the factors of power, ethnicity, and status in job interview settings. Perhaps status and linguistic practice (except in quantitative sociolinguist accounts) gained such a bad reputation from the furor over Bernstein's "restricted" and "elaborated" codes, which originally suggested that the lower-classes suffered from language deficits rather than differences, that many have feared to tread in that territory (e.g., Bernstein 1971). More recently, however, there are objective reports on social class differences in discourse practices (e.g., Kleiner 1993, which shows a difference between middle- and working-class uses of politeness strategies in direction-giving).

In general, the folk do not so directly attach social status to standard English, although some respondents obviously regard "proper" speech as a direct product of the environment, in which class-like distinctions are certainly implied for those who end up with the standard variety. For the folk, then, class, standard, and style are complexly cross-cutting issues, and we now turn to this complexity more specifically.

3.3 Style, slang, register, and taboo

3.3.1 Styles and style-shifting

Since many respondents feel that knowledge of another variety is rather easily acquired, it follows that the folk believe that many speakers control several varieties. One would expect, therefore, some attention to notions of selection of style or appropriate uses of language. It is clear that some respondents know the techniques of variety-shifting very well:

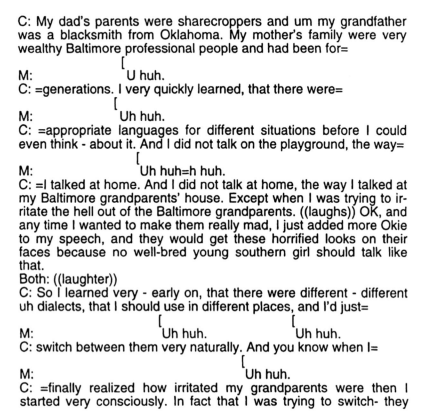

C: My dad's parents were sharecroppers and um my grandfather was a blacksmith from Oklahoma. My mother's family were very wealthy Baltimore professional people and had been for=
                       [
M: U huh.
C: =generations. I very quickly learned, that there were=
                       [
M: Uh huh.
C: =appropriate languages for different situations before I could even think - about it. And I did not talk on the playground, the way=
                       [
M: Uh huh=h huh.
C: =I talked at home. And I did not talk at home, the way I talked at my Baltimore grandparents' house. Except when I was trying to irritate the hell out of the Baltimore grandparents. ((laughs)) OK, and any time I wanted to make them really mad, I just added more Okie to my speech, and they would get these horrified looks on their faces because no well-bred young southern girl should talk like that.
Both: ((laughter))
C: So I learned very - early on, that there were different - different uh dialects, that I should use in different places, and I'd just=
                       [[
M: Uh huh.   Uh huh.
C: switch between them very naturally. And you know when I=
                                       [
M: Uh huh.
C: =finally realized how irritated my grandparents were then I started very consciously. In fact that I was trying to switch- they

tried to smother us and my brother and I always tried to (   ). You
know, oh boy we don't have to put up with all this fake garbage.
And um we'd sing country and western songs. ((sings in a=
[
M: Uh huh.
C: =heavily South Midland accented "country and western" style))
"I heard a wreck on the highway:? ((laughs)) But I didn't hear=
                                      [
M: ((laughs))
C: =nobody pray:." And so we'd sing that. - Roy Acuff's got them
every time. (#49)

C is obviously aware of the status- and geographically-oriented
prejudices held by her proper Baltimore relatives which cause them
to be so horrified when she sings country and western ("cowboy")
songs or speaks with a South Midland variety (here called "Okie"
from a caricature of poor and often displaced Oklahoma residents).
Note, too, her claim that an overt awareness develops, apparently
when she is quite young, of the language shifting she previously did
automatically.

Several respondents report on this manipulation of language for
effect, a device which has come to be known in sociolinguistics as
"metaphoric shift," that is, language choice which redefines a situation rather than adjusts itself to it:

> The language switch ... relates to particular kinds of topics or subject
> matters rather than to change in social situation. Characteristically, the
> situations in question allow for the enactment of two or more relation-
> ships among the same set of individuals. The choice of ... [language vari-
> ety] alludes to these relationships and thus generates meanings which are
> quite similar to those conveyed by the alternation between *ty* and *vy* ...
> ["familiar" and "polite" forms of the Russian second person singular pro-
> noun, respectively]. We will use the term *metaphorical switching*
> [emphasis in the original] for this phenomenon. (Blom and Gumperz
> 1972:425)

Metaphoric switching may be accomplished by extremely simple
linguistic features:

M: What do they call their grandmother?
J: "Grandma"? Or when they want to make her mad they call her
"grammy." ((laughs)) She doesn't like to be called "grammy."
M: What do they call you.
J: "Mom"? "Ma."
M: Do they ever call you "mama"?
J: No.
M: Or "mother"?

J: No it's only "mother:" "mother:" that's when they're up to something. When they're trying to con me into into doing something it's
"mother." (#41)

Situational shifting, however, is also well-known to our respondents.
In the following interchange, D is afraid that V will not understand
the fieldworker's use of "dialect" to refer to everyday usage, so he
steps in and begins a more detailed account of situational shifting
within the African-American community.

C: You have different dialect? I mean-
D:No - no, see there's a street- there's a street talk- let me- let me=
    [
C: No? (   )
D: =explain to V what y- w- what you're talking about. Dialect like=
                                            [
C: Uh huh.
D: =you know like street- street talk is different than the talk we=
                          [
V: Um.
                             [
C: Uh huh.
D: =use normally like if you're in a classroom, then you put on your
best English.
V: Oh=
D: =Ok. Uh when we- when we talk (.hhh) among the saints ((i.e.,
their co-religionists)) we don't use the street talk neither do we use
a very proper form of English - you see - so, uh what's our every-=
                            [
V: [[Yeah.
R: [[Uh huh.
                             [
C: Yeah, that's good. ((laughs))
D: =everyday talk he's talking about well, then what do you use
when he talks about dialect he's talking about (.hhh) what do you
use like around the house. Just for your normal conversational
English.
C: Uh huh. Yeah - that's a good explanation. When you go to a=
     [
D: ((very quietly)) OK.
C: =formal place just like uh we go to the church meeting?
V: Uh huh.
C: We don't speak uh:: - our dialect. We-
V: You speak more looser when you're at home than - at -yeah.
                                         [
C: Yeah y- yeah
you- when you are at home, with your friends y- you always=
                          [
V: We speak more privately in our ho-

C: =talk in a loose way, a- and uh more natural natural way. But=
                       [[
V: Uh huh.   Yeah.
C: =in ki-- kind of a: sort of a uh formal situation - a formal - setting
you use you know use m- a more formal language right.
D: Yes.=
V: =Yeah. (#51)

Although the fieldworker may end this exchange with too much of his own information, it is clearly the respondents who distinguish among varieties which are appropriate to "street," "home," "classroom," and "church."

Some respondents clearly distinguish between situational and metaphorical switching:

D: You talk to maybe the hourly employee one way yet you talk to your supervisor another way and you talk to your co-workers in a different way.
M: Right.
D: I mean depending on who you're talking to and what situation you're in you may change your whole: tone your whole way of - you know.
M: Uh huh are there any levels at which you know you're deliberately like talking down to people for example- well maybe you know what I mean.
D: The only time I know I- well generally I don't talk down to anybody. You know that's just not in my nature. We treat each other- - but as far as um the level of management to worker?
M: Uh huh.
D: Given a situation where somebody is not willing to talk to you adult to adult. Then yes I would tend to put them in their place by talking down in a certain tone.
M: OK.
D: But other than that I try to be above board and talk adult-to-adult unless they force me into the other mode. (#52)

The linguistic distinctions D makes when talking to "hourly workers," "supervisors," and "co-workers" are all clearly defined by situational characteristics (which, of course, includes the participants in the situation and their identities and relationships to the speaker). When some speakers refuse to have an "adult-to-adult" talk, however, D may metaphorically switch to a "certain tone" which will "put them in their place."

Since prescription is the foundation of much folk linguistic belief, however, it is not surprising that a preference for the standard variety dominates. S (in #54) always admires the choice of "careful" and "correct" speech, and respondents such as F and L (in #31) are aware of "improper grammar" all around them in the casual speech of Detroit. They mention multiple negation, third-person indicative marker loss (i.e., *he/she/it go*), and the most frequently cited folk shibboleth – *ain't*.

For the folk, however, the entire story of variety choice is not simply an uncritical preference for the textbook standard. The appropriateness of standard English to some situations is noted by G (#1), the same respondent cited above who was careful to note that people from some backgrounds who learned a standard variety at school had to be careful not to use it at home, lest their usage be taken as a criticism of their "elders."

> G: The idea in America is not that you necessarily talk quote properly, (.hhh) but the idea that you communicate and feel at ease. - Now if you're a SPEAKer, and you're going to get up in front of PEOple and speak, then they expect you to- to speak - properly, or at least what is considered proper English. But if=
> 　　　　　　　　　　　　　　　　　　　　　[
> K: 　　　　　　　　　　　　　　　　　　Or if you're=
> G: =you're having a conversa- ye- or in college, they expect you=
> 　　　　　　　　　　　　　　　　　　　　　　[
> K: =in college, 　　　　　　　　　　　In college and=
> 　　　　[
> ?: 　　(　　　　　)
> G: =to write wel- writ- yeah written is always supposed to be-
> 　　　　　　　　　　　　　　　　　　　　　[　　　　　[
> K: =you're writing a PAper- 　　　　　　　Yes. 　　They- they
> a- a- anytime you- you write, uh the- our language, i- it's=
> 　　　　　　　　　　　　[　　　　　　　　　　　　[
> H: 　　　　　　　　　　(　　　　　) 　　Uh huh.
> K: =expected that you USE the formal language. Yes.
> [　　　　　　　　　[　　　　　　　　　　[
> H: Yeah. 　　　　Formal (form). 　　　　Oh OK.
> 　　　　　　　　　　　　　　　　　　　　[
> G: 　　　　　　　　　　　　　　　　　Yes. Which is
> called formal language. Right. It'll drive you crazy.
> 　　　　　　　　　　　　　[
> H: 　　　　　　　　Oh formal. (#1)

Although G begins with a "democratic" prelude, it is clear that he has identified a number of situations ("speaker," "college") where the standard is essential, and it is clear that the need to use a standard variety in such situations is no laughing matter:

> K: Yeah like I was talking to E or something about the other day - about G? - When - what did he say on the radio?
> A: GB?
> K: Yeah I did not think it was that bad but-
> 　　　　　　　　　　　　　　　　　　[

E: "Me and A."
K: Yeah that's what he said.
A: Oh yeah "Me and A."
K: Yeah.
E: "Me and A."
A: "We are ticket takers here," that's what he said. - Oh yeah, we were raising funds and asking people to pay their own way, yeah, "Me and A we are the ticket takers here."
K: Wh- what happened. She was telling me that some people called or?
A: Yes:. I came in the next morning - well, first of all I came home and E said G used some really improper grammar several times.
All: ((laugh))
A: And I said yeah I know he did and I probably did too.=I don't know. But she said no I don't think=you were OK, but I think he said several things. - Yeah he tends to do that when he gets under the gun.
K: Uh huh.
A: But anyway I came in to work the next morning, and EA the development director - the first thing he said was - uh one of you guys last night, - were saying some things like "Me and G" or "Me and A." And I said well I think it was G=because my wife mentioned something about G saying that.
K: Uh huh.
A: He said well we had a listener call in who said that they shouldn't be talking like that. Your announcers should talk better than that. - Oh - but that - this is the thing they actually had somebody call in - I forgot about this - they called in that night - a listener made a pledge or not. I do not remember but made this comment about - rather upset about that announcer that is using such poor grammar. And so G read this on the air - said something.
                                          [
E: That same night?
A: That same night.
K: What did
          [
A: See this - it says - I guess it was a different time. G- G was on the air and he had said again something that was grammatically incorrect=fairly obviously incorrect. And a listener called in and complained, and G said - the volunteer over the phone wrote it down and G was reading it, he said, "Well this comment says we need to use better grammar or something like that. Well I guess I better learn to talk good."
K: ((laughs))
A: You know it is like - it is like it is the most off - the smile behind his voice=you could see it through the speaker you know. It is like "I AM MAking A JOKE OF THIS." You know but this woman or man or whoever it was - I think it was a woman did not find any humor in it and she called back and said "I think that was incorrect too. I think you should have said 'speak well' or 'talk well.' But I do not think 'talk good' is correct grammar." (#20)

G and A are announcers for a classical-music station, and G's accusative subject ("me and A") is obviously disapproved of by a listener who calls in to complain. When he makes a joke of it on the air with the English usage shibboleth "good" for "well," his continued flirtation with nonstandard is not only noticed but disapproved of by the same caller (who is rather obviously more concerned with his use of the standard than with support for the radio station).

We are, however, less concerned with the notion of the appropriateness of the formal variety to such status-ridden situations. We will focus on what G (in #1, cited above) describes as "the idea in America" – "not that you necessarily talk quote properly ... but ... that you communicate and feel at ease." As both qualitative and quantitative studies of the perception of geographical variation have shown, there is a strong sense among many speakers of American English that a "comfortable," "normal," "appropriate" variety exists, one which is standard enough but not too standard or "posh." It is clear that in the classical radio station example given above, our respondents find the "fussiness" of the caller amusing. Since we have already shown the extensive popular confusion of upper status with formality, this urge to display more "democratic" speech norms is not surprising. Although there is a sense that this "comfortable" English is not "proper" or "correct," there is also a sense that it is not nonstandard or, as the following shows, certainly not "slang."

H: OK. So you know uh sometimes uh - what we learn from books,
- it's I mean it's a:: big difference from - the - we use in the (   )
                                                                     [
D: Oh   yeah
what y- right, what you're learning in the book is different than what people actually use. Yeah because Americans use um: the=
[
H: Yeah.
D: =same word in different ways: and they also come up with slangs: slang or idiom - idiom statements and - makes a makes it=
      [
H: Oh.
D: =hard to learn ((laughs)) I can imagine.
                                      [
H: Ok uh: so you use uh slang a lot or idiom. ((pause)) You mean you say that-
                                      [
G: Probably more than we're aware of, I- I mean I don't think I use slang, but probably a lot of what I- u- do=
                                      [
H: You don't.
G: =use is not proper English or-
                          [

H: Oh you mean not the very formal
English - ( ) uh I mean you call casual way of saying (   )=
       [[
G: Right.   Yeah - more=
       [[
D: Right.   Casual=
G: =casual. (#7)

Although G admits that what she does is not "proper," she is quick to contradict the notion that it is "slang," and both she and D immediately agree with the fieldworker's suggestion that it is "casual." Of course, some respondents note that certain situations absolutely demand more casual forms and reject any alternatives:

SH: I couldn't call my mom "mother."
M: You couldn't?
SH: Too formal. No:, it's too formal. We're too close. (#17)

Address terms (or nicknames and jargon, discussed below) do not, however, raise the specter of incorrectness. In fact, as suggested at the beginning of this section, they are prime candidates for "metaphoric switching," for they carry no prescriptive burden. For some respondents, however, in spite of the dominance of prescription in these interviews, casual or nonstandard forms are sometimes the only real alternative:

B: For "I am no:t." we don't have standard contractions for "I am not." "Ain't" is the only thing we got.
D: (   ) Even if you don't need a contraction but - "amn't," "am not," "amn't I," like- let me see. People don't say that. People say "ain't I," or they say "aren't I?" which is wrong.
B: Yes. That's grammatically incorrect to say- to say "aren't I."
D: You might say "Aren't you going?" That you can ask. "Aren't you coming with us?"
Z: "Aren't you coming with us?"
D: Yes, that's OK. Because you can say "You are coming with us." Or "Aren't you coming with us." But then if you just say "I am coming," I mean, you can't say "Aren't I coming," I mean people do- people do in order not to get black marks by their name. But, rea:lly real English would be "Aren't I- Ain't I coming too?" Because that's more real than "Aren't I."=Because you don't say "Are I coming," you say "I am coming." So: the alternative for "Ain't I coming" is: "Am I not coming," but that is rather stupid for: spoken English. (#19)

D recognizes that actual usage is different from the prescribed standard, so much so that use of the prescribed form in spoken English sounds "stupid." This point of view, taken, as we have seen, by a majority of folk respondents, agrees with the sociolinguist's notion that there are more popular or effective distinctions than that of simply the nonstandard and the standard – there is also a "superstandard":

> Standard American English, in the *informal* [emphasis in the original] sense, or in the informal standard form of any language, must be distinguished not only from substandard forms but also from superstandard forms. There is general agreement about what forms of a language are preferred above others within a language community, even when the preferred forms are not used. It is typical for people to be slightly schizophrenic about their use of language. They acknowledge that some aspects of their use of language are not "correct": they can tell you what the "correct" form is, but they never actually adopt it. At an emotional level, these admittedly correct forms are rejected by some speakers because they are *too* [emphasis in the original] correct. These speakers do not adopt such forms and at unguarded moments will even make negative value judgments about speakers who use them, not because these forms are "bad English" or because the speakers who use them are considered uneducated, but because the forms are "too snooty" and the speakers "too high-falutin'." Of course, the same speakers may smugly reject other vocabulary, grammatical constructions, and pronunciations as "poor English" and tend to consider people who use them as uneducated or stupid. Both the superstandard and substandard forms can be considered "nonstandard" (although elsewhere we reserve this term for what we are now calling "substandard"); that is, they are not the standards by which the speaker actually regulates his speech – they are not effective standards. Everything in between substandard and superstandard represents the effective informal standard to which the individual's speech actually conforms. (Wolfram and Fasold 1974:19)

What Wolfram and Fasold have suspected from their casual observations of comment and usage are specifically borne out in our respondents' interviews and in earlier quantitative studies of folk dialectology (2.1).

S, who has perhaps heard more about linguistics directly than any of the other respondents (since he is a TESOL teacher), continues this theme by also suggesting that there are some forms which hardly have any utility at all (at least in spoken English), due to what he characterizes as their excessive politeness. Even he, however, calls the casual form "not correct":

X: "Who do you speak with" or "Whom, with whom do you speak."
S: "With whom do you speak" is correct.
X: How about "Who do you speak with"?

S: It's not correct, but it's familiar. - It's used.
                        [
X: What do you mean by "familiar."
S: It's something that Americans say every day. It's something that
we say so much, that we're used to saying, we don't think about it.
When someone's on the phone, they hang up the phone and you
say "Who were you speaking with." It's just something we under-
stand - automatically. That's all. He means to ask me is this? So I
say I was speaking with this person.
                        [
X: So when do you speak "whom," do
you speak with "whom." What kind of situation do you speak in=
                        [
S: Because (   )-
X: =this way.
S: Ah. Ah hah. For me, - I never use it.
X: Oh, I see. - Why.
             [   ]
S: Because-
S: Because I'm never in a sit- - situations where I'm dealing with -
anyone with whom I need to be that polite.
X: So that's a very polite way.
                    [
S: Very. (#10)

As the reader has doubtless noticed, S uses the very form which he
claims to have no need for (in a position where it is nearly obligatory
for standard speakers – immediately after a preposition). There is absolutely no evidence from his tone and from the following conversation that S is pulling the fieldworker's leg. If this is a natural performance (and we think it is), then it is certainly a very good example of the mismatch between report (or "belief") and performance –
the subject of much of our discussion in Chapter 1. This suggests that
overt awareness of the features which make up the "informal standard" in contrast to the "superstandard" to which Wolfram and Fasold refer may be less than perfect. There are good reasons for that,
some already outlined in Chapter 1, and we elaborate briefly here on
the most likely source of the mismatch between S's claims and his
performance.

S's estimation of his performance errs in the casual rather than
formal direction, exactly the same sort of bad estimations which
Trudgill (1972) found in a study of "over-" and "under-reporters" –
those who estimate a more frequent use of prestige forms than they
actually use (over-reporters, typically women) and those who estimate a more frequent use of nonprestige forms than they actually use
(under-reporters, typically men). The "covert prestige" of the casual

is apparently what attracts S to it. We will have more to say about gender and the choice of overt and covert norms in 3.4.

This "covert prestige" (the appeal of nonprestige linguistic norms) which Trudgill associates with males is clearly relevant to style-shifting beyond the domain of gender-controlled activities. The same respondent provides a survey of how students might choose more or less formal varieties both to make various impressions on the teacher and to maintain certain relations with their peers:

S: I think in American culture, - ((clears throat)) whether we realize it or not, each person, when we go into a different kind of situation, - we change our attitudes, and we change our=
                           [
X: Uh huh.
S: =speech, - to adjust to the new situation. For example, if a: - a student - is in your class. - And you maybe call on the student to=
                                [
X: Uh huh.
S: =to talk about - their homework. They are going to maybe be a:=
                                  [
X: Uh huh.
S: little more polite, they're going to be a little bit nervous, and=
                    [
X: Uh huh.
S: =they're going to USE - uh maybe different words.=Maybe more polite words. Maybe speak in a little different style, and then when, after class they talk with their friends, maybe after class they get together, and they go (with) their friends to the uh - to the restaurant.
X: What's the- what's uh - What's the different (style). (   ) Can=
                  [
S: To buy a-
C: =you describe, more specific- (because) I don't know, I use the exactly the same WORDS, no matter WHO I'm talking to.
                                  [
S: Right.
S: I think part of it is when when students talk to teachers, they're very vague. - They they use words uh - they - they use - I c- I can't give you examples of the exact words, but they use words so that=
                                              [
X: Uh huh.
S: =you can try to, on the one hand impress the teacher. But=
                                                [
X: Uh huh.
S: =on the other hand you don't want to get too close. So you're thinking of the social situation, a little bit. You're thinking of -=
                                    [
X: Uh huh.

S: =some people - some students say "Well the teacher is my friend. ((clears throat)) And I- I'm going to speak to them like a=
    [
X: Uh huh.
S: =friend." And then you try to be good buddies. But other=
                  [
X: Uh huh.
S: =students say "Well, the teacher - is this person who - telling me about something. The person who's giving me the grade."
        [
X: Um:.
X: Uh huh.
S: (And)- so there's a just a little bit of nervousness, - and they're=
  [[
X: So   ((laughs))
S: =trying to think "What can I say, that will sound good to the=
                 [
X: Uh huh.
S: = teacher.
X: Oh.
S: So I think that there are those two points of view. One is saying "Well, the teacher's my friend." And the other is, "Well the teacher=
         [
X: Uh huh.
S: =is someone that I have to impress."
X: So how do you impress your teacher. What kind of a- is there a - some uh (typical)
         [
S: Well little little things. I don't know. I mean I, (   )
                                      [
X: Oh how
how, tell me, how do YOU, if you want to impr- like I am your=
                    [
S: For example-
X: =teacher and you want to impress me.
        [
S: OK, If I'm your- If you're my teacher, - - well, I think (I'll) certainly uh using slang? - is is something that would indicate=
                [
X: OH!
S: = - friendship. Forexample= if uh the word- if you used the word "ain't,"
X: "Ain't"?
S: "Ain't." "Ain't" means "is not."
X: And how to spell.
    [
S: It's a- it's a slang form. ((spelling)) a - i - n - t.
X: Uh huh. ((spelling)) a - i - n - t. Oh "ain't." Oh I see.
S: "Ain't."
X: Uh huh. "I ain't."
S: Yeah. "I ain't going." - If someone- if a student in a class uses=

X: [
                         Hm. "I ain't going."
S: = - uh: the word "ain't," then he's not concerned too much about impressing the teacher. - Because - usually - uh - in a social- in a=
                        [
X: Oh: I see.
S: =formal situation, you don't use "ain't."
X: What do you use.
S: "Is not." - "Isn't," - or "am not."
             [
X: So - that's the - that;s the very - formal - language. ( )
S: Right
X: (   ) So if you use "ain't," it's like a kind of a way that you want to impress the teacher.
                [
S: Right. Right, it's- but then again some students (   ) - because they don't want to seem too close to the teacher, they=
                                            [
X: Uh huh.
S: =purposely use - b- bad language. So that they can (say) and=
          [[
X: "Ain't."   Oh:.
S: = - seem normal. With the rest of the students. Because if you=
                        [
X: Uh huh.
S: =stick out too much, if you seem too smart, or if you seem too=
                    [[
X: Uh huh.   Uh huh.
S: =polite, then other people will say "Ah, this guy's trying to=
          [
X: Uh huh.
S: =impress the teacher." So I think there's a lot of things that go on. (#10)

Although there is some confusion in this conversation about whether overt or covert norms are being used to "impress," the conclusions are clear. There is more than a double-bind in the use of "polite" and "slang" forms in complex social situations (e.g., classrooms). Students may believe that the role relationships between teacher and student are such that a more formal variety is in order, or they may believe that a more casual one is appropriate. Either solution, however, may annoy peers. Too casual an approach to the teacher may cause one to be labeled a brown-noser or apple-polisher; excessive formal use in the classroom, however, may earn one the reputation of show-off or even traitor. It is not a new observation that classroom norms of behavior (language included) are often at variance with "street" norms. It is, in fact, a distinction which some sociolinguists (and others) have found to be at the very root of educational failure in the United States, particularly in those communities where general cultural values appear to be most at odds with those of the educational community (e.g., Labov 1982).

Whatever the solution to this classroom puzzle, it is clear that for S language is an extremely important instrument in the social work of "fitting in." And for many of our respondents, fitting in simply means adjusting one's speech to match that of one's interlocutors.

```
M:                                    Yeah but I think it's
true of - a- anybody, if you're uh with people - that- speak a=
                          [
S:                        Uh huh.
M: =certain way then pretty soon you're speaking that way. (#15)
```

We have already discussed the folk notions of the rapid (almost "infectious") acquisition of regional varieties and the distaste the folk have for nonstandard speakers who fail to use the standard. From such comments as M's (and from S's perhaps more specific notion in #10 that "we change our speech," "whether we realize it or not"), it is clear that rapid, unconscious accommodation to other speech norms is a common folk belief. In sociolinguistics (or, more precisely, in the social psychology of language), speech accommodation theory has an established history, articulated earliest by Giles (1973) and Giles and Powesland (1975) and elaborated on in a more general sociolinguistic setting by Bell (1984) and in a revised social psychological framework in Giles, Copeland, and Copeland (1991). Giles acknowledges the relationship of accommodation theory to the earlier notion of "response matching," apparently introduced by Argyle (1969), specifically in relation to speech. In all versions of the theory, one finds experiments and observations which confirm the notion that interlocutors (so long as they admire one another) draw closer to one another in speech characteristics, including those of delivery (e.g., pauses, rate of speech) as well as those of style (e.g., slang, specialized lexicon) and even of specific syntactic and phonetic shapes. It is clear that our respondents have embraced the theory. One respondent relates speech accommodation directly to practices in his own field.

```
B: Wha- what I try to do- ((very rapidly)) (   ) psychotherapy, one
thing I do, - which I- which I thought I found myself being able=
       [
Z:     Uh huh.
B: = to do, - is I try to talk like the person who's talking to me.
Z: I see.
```

B: And then there's a- there's a- there's a school of thought, -
which um promotes that. - Like what I do is I do what you call
"pacing." - I'm talking to a person. I will try to simulate their=
    [
Z: Pacing.
B: posture, their- their body posture.
Z: Oh: (   )
    [
B: If they have their leg crossed, I will cross my leg. If they're
like this, I will do that, if they're like that, I do that. I they're sm- if- I
try to - uh - mirror their facial expression, the position of their head,
the pace of their voice, - Imitate. Yeah, but do it subtly.=
      [   ]
Z: Like imitate them, in some way.
B: =Like like their their their voice, uh if they are talking, the=
      [
Z: (   )
B: =speed of their voice, volume, uh even tone. - You know just=
          [
Z: Uh huh.
B: =all these little nuances, as much as possible. And usually peo-
ple don- don't know don't don't don't aren't aware that you're DO-
ing that.
Z: Because you do that so suddenly, and uh- - I mean-
              [
B: Yeah. And (sort of)- (sort of)
just - do it kind of just sort of smoothly. Just sort of do it.
Z: Uh huh.
B: Uh matter of factly, and uh - it really seem- it's w- what the pur-
pose is to get peo- someone to be much more receptive. And
you('ll) feel more comfortable. (Building) trust. And it seems to
work. I think it worked.
Z: (Is tha-) (   ) - (And that's what I) told you that about=
     [
B: I I I think I think it works.
Z: =imitating ME (   )
        [
B: Well I don't do it very- you know I- I- do it I mea-
I've done it for years. So I do a lot of it very automatically. - But I=
[
Z: Unconscious?
B: =don't do it much, I don't do it very much when I'm talking to
people out in a different kind of situation.
        [
Z: Outside. You try to not to I mean you're not -
B: If you and I were sitting down, and I could see your whole body,
from head to foot, like we were sitting in (some) chairs, (there=
             [
Z: Uh huh.
B: =wasn't a) table, and you weren't holding a baby, I'd more=
           [

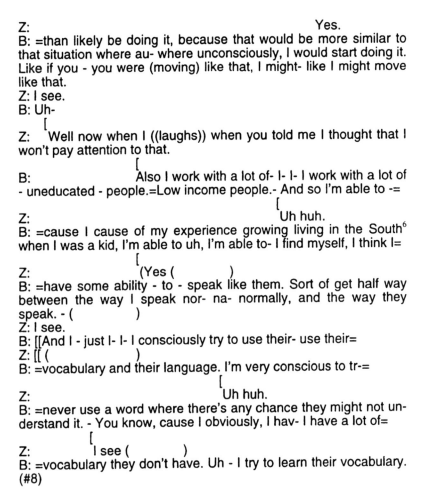

```
Z:                                                              Yes.
B: =than likely be doing it, because that would be more similar to
that situation where au- where unconsciously, I would start doing it.
Like if you - you were (moving) like that, I might- like I might move
like that.
Z: I see.
B: Uh-
         [
Z:         Well now when I ((laughs)) when you told me I thought that I
won't pay attention to that.
                           [
B:                         Also I work with a lot of- I- I- I work with a lot of
- uneducated - people.=Low income people.- And so I'm able to -=
                                                            [
Z:                                                          Uh huh.
B: =cause I cause of my experience growing living in the South⁶
when I was a kid, I'm able to uh, I'm able to- I find myself, I think I=
              [
Z:            (Yes (            )
B: =have some ability - to - speak like them. Sort of get half way
between the way I speak nor- na- normally, and the way they
speak. - (            )
Z: I see.
B: [[And I - just I- I- I consciously try to use their- use their=
Z: [[ (            )
B: =vocabulary and their language. I'm very conscious to tr-=
                                     [
Z:                                    Uh huh.
B: =never use a word where there's any chance they might not un-
derstand it. - You know, cause I obviously, I hav- I have a lot of=
        [
Z:        I see (            )
B: =vocabulary they don't have. Uh - I try to learn their vocabulary.
(#8)
```

Indeed, therapeutic settings have provided examples of accommodation beyond speech. Such features as the increasingly similar pos-
tures of the therapist and client during the progress of a session have
been recorded (e.g., Kendon 1970). B is sensitive, however, to the
possibility of overaccommodation, and he notes as the conversation
continues that he "carefully" uses "expressions." This, too, corresponds to work in accommodation theory in which those who accommodate too much are not admired as much by evaluators as those
who make only minimal adjustments to their speech in the direction
of the listener's norm (e.g., Canadians' phonological accommodation
to British English as reported in Giles and Smith 1979). Giles and
Powesland describe the negative potential for "detected" accommodation quite strongly:

> Accommodation ... seems to depend for its effectiveness upon its *not* [emphasis in the original] being recognized as such by the receiver. Such "covert" accommodation, of which the speaker himself may have little or no consciousness, would probably include changes in speech rate, pauses, grammatical complexity, accent etc. made by way of convergence towards the speech characteristics of the receiver. Detection by the listener of accommodation in this category would possibly tend to discredit the speaker. In the case of accent convergence, for example, the listener might feel that he was being mimicked or patronized and this would not enhance the approval of the speaker. (1975:169-70)

In spite of the folk awareness of casual standards, adjustments of language to fit the situation, and long-term personal adaptation to surrounding norms, there is still evidence in all these citations and many others that we could give that the folk identify a "right" and a "wrong" – an internal property of the language itself. When ethnicity and social status do not explain the inability to use a standard variety, the folk are, of course, confronted with the difficulty of explaining why it is that some speakers fail to acquire and/or use it. A solution, however, appears. In contrast to the belief in the rapid and easy learning of varieties through exposure, there is also a folk belief that adjustment to language norms may be difficult to accomplish if "bad habits" have been established.

> Z: What do you think about that "ain't."
> K: Oh it's improper. It should be stopped. When children come home and talk that way I think they should be corrected. Because it's so easy- I know I don't speak as correctly as I did when I was a child at home. Because you get into bad habits, and that's- The trouble is when they become ingrained and speech patterns, say- And it's much harder to change how you speak once you are an adult. (#22)

Right after this, the fieldworker is able to "browbeat" K into admitting that there might be some appropriate uses of nonstandard, but, in the long run, she is unsympathetic since use of it will lead to behavioral patterns which are hard to overcome:

> Z: I have a friend- She is an English teacher, and even she said to her it's completely fine that people use "ain't." And even she feels better. But in school, as a teacher, she is not allowed to do that. I don't know.
> K: I think, it's how you use it. You can use it- use it in a slangy way so it's- you know, when people speak phrases and sort of put quote marks about it. That- - they're saying it they know it's not correct but they are saying it in a context which they are talking about.
> Z: Oh, I see. So, it means that you need to distinguish.

K: Sometimes. But, I just think, it's so easy to get into bad speech patterns, and why- why encourage it, by letting yourself speak incorrectly. (#22)

We shall return to the theme of patterns of good language behavior in our section on folk views of language education (4.2).

In conclusion, our respondents see stylistic selection as switching between one variety and another. They do not conceive of style as a continuous dimension – the "stylistic continuum" of the sociolinguist (e.g., Labov 1972a) – in which speakers move up and down a scale of formality. For these folk, then, stylistic shifting is more like diglossia (Ferguson 1959) or even bilingual code-switching, in which a more abrupt shift between distinct varieties is the rule. One respondent draws this parallel specifically in her account of "private" and "school" varieties:

K: In a sense it's ((i.e., "home" speech)) informal, in a sense it's uh
no- a better word is uh - private - language. It's (.hhh) it's a b- uh=
                          [
?:   ((whispers)) (Slang.)
                             [
H: Private.
K: =uh (.hhh) what am I trying to think (.hhh) the word is private
and it's also uh - ruled by - not just in the school, it's ruled by -
proper learning.
G: Yeah the rules and regulations of the English language,=
                       [
K: Of - of the standard English,=
G: =they're - in textbooks.
K: =is in a textbook. And - w:e take a lot of that with us, and some=
              [
G: Uh huh.
K: =of us when we go home, have private language that we kind
of- that we like- it would be like if you were bilingual, if you spoke=
[
H: You: use.
K: =two languages, (.hhh) and you- and you went to school=
                  [
H: Uh huh.
K: =here in America, you would learn English. Because that's=
                               [
H: Uh huh.
K: =the language that's spoken and taught an- and you have to
learn to READ. (.hhh) And let's say you go HOME and you speak=
       [
H: Uh huh.
K: =Spanish. You - speak English and you speak Spanish, well=
      [

H: Another language, OK.
K: =sometimes you (.hhh) melt these two languages together and
they kind of get mixed up. And so when you're with your friends
that speak Spanish and English, you're going to speak this this=
          [
H: Uh huh.
K: =kind of strange - blending. Of the language, (.hhh) and then - =
                    [
U: ((yells))
                    [[
H: Strange. Yeah.
K: =when you get in the classroom, and you get to school, with=
                                        [
H: Uh huh.
K: =the rest of the students who speak it,=then you're going to
speak the standard English, you're going to speak that language
that (.hhh) is expected - for you to be able to learn by. (#36a)

This "melting" or "blending" process explains the use of a less
than pure variety at home. Home (or "private") language is, nevertheless, viewed as distinct from school (or "standard") language, and,
we would argue, so are all the varieties discussed by our respondents.

3.3.2 Slang

We turn now to the question of an important alternative to standard
usage – the choice of "slang." The whispered word "Slang" cited
immediately above probably refers to anything which is not standard,
and that is a very common use for many of our respondents, particularly African-Americans. We approach the data here, however, from
a more "linguistic" view of slang – the fact that it is not only nonstandard (perhaps) but also racy, lively, vivid, current, hip, cool, and
in-group.[7] The popular quality and the status-conferring aspects of
slang are clearly known to our respondents, and, in the following, the
media are identified as playing an important role in its use.

C: I think people are going to use it regardless of whether anybody
c(h)onsiders it good or bad. Many think that language is always=
                    [
Z: Yes.
C: =changing. And one thing that's really different now, is that uh=
                                                [
Z: Uh huh.
C: =we have a - slang gets picked up by the media and exploited,
so that (.hhh) - um - a word which - meant something: say in Black
culture, (.hhh) becomes a sort of hyped word used by the media.=

```
       [
Z:      Uh huh.
C: =And (then) the word that everybody uses. You know, the=
       [
Z:      Uh huh.
C: =president uses or whatever.  ((laughs)) To be cool. ((laughs))
(#21)
```

Although C is aware that slang may begin as a solidarity or in-group phenomenon ("Black culture"), she also believes that popular culture distributes it widely. That African-American culture is the source of much United States slang is a common belief:

```
H: I heard th- that teenagers they use - they speak different - from -
adults or something?
A: We speak slang. We use slang, some of our words. We have -
words that we - use like expressions and things like that. Like uh -
uh "man." We say "man" a lot.
H: Well "man" it seems uh I mean uh Black people say "man." But
y- you also use "man"?
A:[[Yeah. We use "man" too. (.hhh) It's just- it's just uh- it's kind of=
K:[[Yes.
                           [
H:                          Ah interesting.
------------------------------------------------------------------
A: Yeah, it's kind of like- it's part of the competition to be=
[
U: ((talking))
A: =accepted, sort of like.
H: Oh- uh- what I noticed only Black people u- say it. Th- that's
their symbol, I mean. Their language uh uh specific (         ).
                                              [
K:                                             That's Black English.
H: Black English, yeah. "Man." But you also u- I mean-
                     [
K:                    Yeah, you c- ((laughs))
A: Yeah we picked it up. We picked it up from - the Black people.=
                        [                 [
H:                       (        )         Oh.
A: =Yeah. We use it.
        [
G:       O- one thing about Americans is we're not afraid to steal.
All: ((laugh))
------------------------------------------------------------------
H: Interesting y- "man" (          ) ((laughs)). - So- no- oh so
you pick up from Black people is it mean - from your classmates
they are - Black - (        )
                  [
G:                 Huh uh.
H: Oh no?
```

[
A: No.
G: It just spreads by word of mouth. Cause it's not a matter of just=
                                                        [
A: Yeah we just
G: =because s-someone is Black in one culture that it stays within
it. (.hhh) If it's overheard by teenagers something that can spread
faster than you and I can get on the telephone and spread it
probably. But so i- it's a kind of thing that's just passed on. It's=
                    [
H: ((laughs))
G: =passed on by the media, by television, by radio, and so - =
                                                        [
A: Uh huh.

G: =you'll find that children listen to - any race - that's a uh actor=
                                                    [
H: Oh.
G: =or actress uh uh disk jockey, uh star, on the - television or=
                                                [
U: ((talking))
G: =whatever. (.hhh) And they pick up the- they- they pick up the
language, they pick up uh the expressions, (.hhh) and - somehow.
they create some of their own slang. (#36a)

Here several folk beliefs about slang creation and transmission come
together. These respondents also believe that the media play a role in
disseminating Black expressions which become a part of teenage
slang, for they are quick to deny that it is a result of face-to-face interaction. (A does not have Black classmates.) Race, however, is not
as important as the "star" status of the contributor, and they note the
rapid (almost miraculous!) dissemination strategies which teenage
culture has at its disposal for the spread of new slang. They, too, are
even more explicitly concerned with the status-conferring aspects of
slang (" ... it's part of the competition to be accepted ...").

For these respondents and others, it is, of course, teenagers who
are the focal group for slang creation and use. G and his family believe this, and he believes that slang (and other aspects of teenage
behavior) are cut off at age twenty-one or twenty-two:

H: Uh- when you are young, you also h-have your own- you use
slang, right.
        [
K: Oh yes, we sure did.

                            [
H: But- it's still the same, they use?
A: It changes.
        [

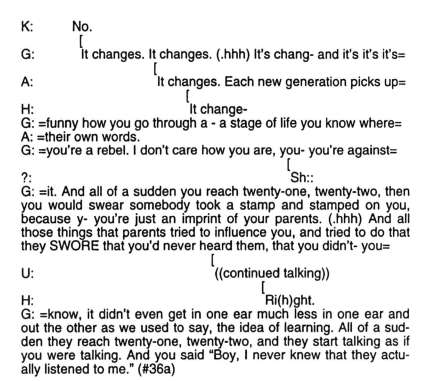

K:　　No.

G:　　It changes. It changes. (.hhh) It's chang- and it's it's it's=

A:　　　　　　It changes. Each new generation picks up=

H:　　　　　　　　It change-

G: =funny how you go through a - a stage of life you know where=

A: =their own words.

G: =you're a rebel. I don't care how you are, you- you're against=

?:　　　　　　　　　　Sh::

G: =it. And all of a sudden you reach twenty-one, twenty-two, then you would swear somebody took a stamp and stamped on you, because y- you're just an imprint of your parents. (.hhh) And all those things that parents tried to influence you, and tried to do that they SWORE that you'd never heard them, that you didn't- you=

U:　　　　　　　　　　((continued talking))

H:　　　　　　　　　　Ri(h)ght.

G: =know, it didn't even get in one ear much less in one ear and out the other as we used to say, the idea of learning. All of a sudden they reach twenty-one, twenty-two, and they start talking as if you were talking. And you said "Boy, I never knew that they actually listened to me." (#36a)

Although the respondents probably put too much faith in the absolute originality of the slang of each generation, in sociolinguistic terms, G is clearly a believer in "age-grading": the notion that certain language use characteristics are appropriate to certain age groups in the society (Hockett 1950). At twenty-one (or twenty-two), childish ways are given up and "adult" language use replaces slang. In fact, sociolinguists have noticed that this age-grading pattern is true not only of slang but of nonstandard use in general. When younger people enter their "work-force" years, there is a tendency for nonstandard and nonprestigious forms (at all linguistic levels) to decrease. The following commentary, although specifically directed towards the alternation between alveolar and velar nasals in the variable (*-ing*), is meant to be more general:

> Why is it that the highest scores [i.e., the most nonstandard] are found for the youngest and the oldest speakers, while it is the middle-aged speakers who have the lowest scores? We can probably account for this by supposing that for younger speakers the most important social pressures come from the peer group, and that linguistically they are more strongly influenced by their friends than by anybody else. Influence from the standard language is relatively weak. Then, as speakers get older and begin

working, they move into wider and less cohesive social networks ..., and are more influenced by mainstream societal values and, perhaps, by the need to impress, succeed, and make social and economic progress. They are, consequently, more influenced by the standard language. For older retired people, on the other hand, social pressures are again less, success has already been achieved (or not, as the case may be), and social networks may again be narrower. (Chambers and Trudgill 1980:92)

In the following, however, a respondent is not so sure that one's teenage slang is completely given up:

Z: Do you think that teenagers uh speak uh differently. - I mean not standard.
 [
K: (   ) I don't have that much contact with te(h)enagers these days. But - teenagers generally - have a slang that I think influences one for the rest of one's life, - that's probably a pretty=
                                              [
Z: Yeh. Heh.
K: =easy way to - a
Z: Did you have ( ) such a vocabulary?
K: Oh yeah. I ( ) Definitely.
        [
Z: What happened=do you still use it?
K: Probably sometimes when I'm when - if I'm not thinking about=
                                   [
Z: .   (   )
K: =it, and someone could go "aHA!, I know exactly when that person went to high school." (   ) Early seventies slang. (   )
        [[
Z: (Oh really?)   Hm::.
Actually what's does slang mean, in general. I mean - bad=
                                                    [
K: Slang
Z: =English, bad grammar, or - How would you define (it).
                                                        [
K: I wouldn't define slang as bad grammar. I'd just call that bad grammar. - But slang is - - a- - very - um: - - It's a a different way of - instead of saying it in plain English. (   ) It would be best to find an example of it.

K: I think it's unavoidable and- in a lot of ways. - And we're going to (g-) find some creeping into your language. (.hhh) And m- much more so at certain times.=Because it's sort of a - ((lip smack)) a - tribal - way of speaking, it's - it- binds you to your group, at the time that you speak and maybe somebody else doesn't understand it, what you mean by that.
Z: I see. What do you think uh whether - uh: - what's- middle age people? have their own slang? or - some vocabulary that they use.

K: [
                                                                     I think
- the slang - i- is more what they used when they were teenagers
or young young. And they probably keep some of that - =
[
Z: Oh I see.
K: =throughout the rest of their life. But - I think I think as people
get older they get more concerned with speaking - more correctly.
(#18)

Although K agrees with the interpretation given by Chambers and
Trudgill above which suggests that more standard usage is required
of older people, she also recognizes the lasting imprint of one's own
generation of slang. She also differentiates slang from "bad grammar," a distinction most linguists would certainly make (e.g., Dumas
and Lighter 1978). Like many of our other respondents, K is quite
specific about the group solidarity function of slang ("a- tribal – way
of speaking"), and she also suggests that some of that solidarity
function is realized by the fact that outsiders may fail to understand,
a fairly common remark about in-group language in general in these
interviews:

H: I mean do you have your own slang.
                                    [
G: Oh, oh I see, no not nearly as much,
adults don't, no. Because teenagers- I think teenagers like to=
[
H: Oh no?
G: =have this feeling of being (.hhh) separated and different an-
and like exclusive, so they have a language that only they understand, so they can sort of (.hhh) separate themselves and- and -
adults don't so much you know look to their peers for=
                   [
H: OK.
G: =support and for (.hhh) um - um for approval, so they don't you
know try to set themselves off with the slang that only they understand. (#7)

And, according to our respondents, woe to the older speaker who
would like to partake in the younger generation's in-group linguistic
behavior. One respondent even suggests that a speaker who would
attempt such a shift might end up being "nerdy."

K: I- I re- remember when *I* was in junior high and high school,
some OL:D person, meaning someone over - eighteen, tried to=
[
Z: Uh huh.

K: =speak like you did. (.hhh) They were just being - I can- I'm=

                                                     [

Z: ((laughs))

K: =sure there's a slang word for that, you know "nerdy," - something like that. That they were trying to do something to fit in=

[

Z: ((laughs))

K: =when the only way you could fit in is to be that age. (#18)

Adolescent and post-adolescent years, however, also introduce speakers to the language of special interests, another likely source of slang according to the folk:

M: I think that until maybe I was in high school: I spoke pretty much as I was taught to speak or what I'd picked up in my family, but - as I reached high school and I was exposed to, you know, the culture of adolescence and especially in Detroit, there were certain - I don't know, subcultures that you might be exposed to- like interests in automobiles and fast cars, you know. And so - I was, of course, interested in those things and started to use - hot rod kind of slang. (#13)

Although older speakers do not use as much slang, they have their own special languages, and some respondents suggest that those varieties have the same etiology and function as teenager talk:

G: But you know speaking about slang with adults I guess there is some, but the slang is more so in work, groups, (.hhh) because - well I'm a computer programmer and I speak a l- - yes (.hhh) and=

                                                    [   ]

H: Oh you're a compu-=

G: =I speak a lot of slang that D doesn't understand because he's=

H: =oh.

                                                              [

D: That's true

G: =not a programmer.

       [

D: (   ) that's true.

H: And you mean that only for you or-=

G: =It's for a work group, there's work related slang.=

H: =I feel much uh- according to what I learned- i- i- it seems=

                           [

G: Much (   )

H: =that's a jargon.

G: Yeah jargon.

         [

D: Yeah jargon. Yeah.

              [

H: It's a jargon you know.

D: Right.
H: Yeah. Like uh you use some in terminology, (   ).
    [[
G: Right   Well right like I'll say
oh: "He's in the read-only mode," which means you know he- he's
only spitting things out or and he's not- (.hhh) you can't tell him
anything.
H: Oh OK. And a- this is only for your group your computer group.
                                                   [
G: Right I- I- yeah- in=
                                               [
H: Uh- uh-
G: =the computer community there's a lot of jargon that outsiders=
                               [
H: Commun-
G: =wouldn't know (.hhh).
H: Oh I think this is jargon right yeah, uh
                                         [
G: Well it's the same thing to me,
but I guess it is jargon really.
H: OK. So if the person can understand you: then you- you can:
know "Oh he must be a- uh work in the ((laughs)) compu- computer: something. Cause he knows what I'm saying" huh.
                          [
G: Yeah he must work with computers.
G: Uh huh. (.hhh) Also if you know a lot of the jargon then that sort
of makes you maybe a little superior because you could (.hhh) like
- you can say things that somebody else wouldn't understan:d an-
and they feel foolish because they don't understand you and you
can you know "I'm a little more superior cause I know more computer jargon than you do." Yeah.
[
D: OK.
   [[
H: Really. (   )   And uh is this a g- is this good or=
                                                  [
D: Huh.
H: =bad I mean.
G: Well: it's hard to say, I just think it's used for you know for different things. I mean it's- OK it's used for verbal shorthand, because a
lot of it are acronyms and things that convey (.hhh) information that
everybody understands more quickly, (.hhh) uh: also: it's because
in a lot of cases there just isn't really you know w- the English to
describe it isn't evolved quickly enough as the computer industry
has so it's just keeping it's describing things that isn't found in normal you know outside of the computer whatever, (.hhh) and I think
too people use it to elevate themselves - and to=
                                      [
D: Yeah -=
G: =(.hhh)
D: =te- technical jargon.

> G: Uh huh:, and to exclude people, like if you're talking with com-
> puter people and you can kind of exclude the other people be-
> cause they won't understand you. (#7)

In fact, G ends up discussing technical language (or "jargon") which
we will also do in the next section, but it is not clear that she originally meant to. Perhaps she meant to distinguish jargon from what
might be called "jargon slang." Her example seems to indicate this.
"Read only" is a term which refers to a computer disk which cannot
be written to, and she cites a metaphorically extended use of this, describing a person who cannot be argued with or convinced of anything. In general, perhaps she is trying to note that adult slang is
more likely to be derived from technical language than from the
popular culture sources cited above for teenage slang.

3.3.3 Register

Whatever her original intent, G is swayed by the fieldworker's (and
D's) insistence on labeling what she is talking about as "jargon," and
she turns to a more general discussion of technical talk. Although she
defends it (since it is both economical and fills gaps in the language),
she admits it may be used to isolate the user group and make its
members feel "superior," particularly when outsiders cannot understand. In some cases, such exclusion is simply taken as a matter of
fact, perhaps only a recognition of the technicality of the field:

> H: For example you listen to doctors talking. And half of it you=
>   [
> S: Uh huh.
> H: =can't understand because you don't know the terms. (#5)

In fact, several respondents report on specialized language as if it
were an inevitable result of specialization itself:

> D: We have jargon in school.
> Z: Yes.
> D: We talk about
>   [
> Z: What is jargon?
> D: Jargon is talk about- profession. Like it's educational jargon.
> B: Specialized vocabulary.
> D: Yeah.
> Z: Do you have that in your field? - Jargon,
> B: I assume it's in every field. (#19)

But technical talk or jargon is often thought of badly. One of the fieldworkers has left one of her theoretical linguistics books lying about, and some of her respondents have had a chance to look at it.

M: Remember when I said- and so J looked at it too, (.hhh) and I was just anxious to see if it was just my - interpretation of the - poor - writing I thought. Bu-
H: Poor writing on the part of its author.
M: That's what I mean.
H: Uh huh.
J: Well it's hard to understand.
((pause))
H: Well. - Very few - uh specialists, Speciall- uh especially in tech-nical fields, write clearly, lucidly, and compellingly so that the=
               [
S: Uh huh.
H: =layman who is NOT in that s- special field, can clearly=
                                   [
S: Uh huh.
H: =understand what they're trying to convey. Very few are able to do that. Most of them write like this guy. ((taps book)) They HIDE their meaning in a lot of - arcane language that uh - that's fine for somebody that's in the field, but for somebody that's not in the=
                      [
S: Uh huh.
H: =field, i- like wading through mud. And that's typical.
                               [
M: As a teacher I think that's
so
H: It's poor. It's absolutely poor communication. That's=
          [
?:   (   )
                                     [
M: Yeah that's it.=
H: =communication.
M: =Poor communication is what it is.

M: But the funny thing is this is an English class an English writer, and English - I mean - so he should have some
               [
H: This guy's pro- this guy's probably - he's probably a a ph- philosopher or something like that.
[
S: He's a very famous - linguistics - linguist.
                         [
H: Uh huh.
M: Uh huh.
H: Uh.
S: [[Uh very very famous.

H: [[Yeah well he just- he's lost himself in the arcane language of his field, see. (#5)

Although J in the above offers a slight defense, suggesting that the material might be hard to understand, M and H cannot see why the author cannot give up the "arcane" language of linguistics to allow the nonspecialist access to the material.

At first one might assume that any folk distaste for specialist register (or "jargon") is no more sophisticated than the usual uninformed railing against any language which fails to match one's personal preferences, as in the writings of such self-appointed pundits as Edwin Newman (e.g., 1974) or the more insidiously elitist and racist John Simon (e.g., 1982). But the folk view is more sophisticated and parallels recent concerns in linguistics. While the oldest tradition in linguistics simply regards specialist language as another descriptive area to be catalogued (e.g., Preston 1973), the post-Watergate era awakened in the linguistically more sophisticated an urge to speak out against convoluted or purposefully misleading language (e.g., Postman 1976, Rank 1974). Following "deconstructionist" models in literary criticism and philosophy, some have examined specialist language for the values (or lack thereof) it may reflect (e.g., Fairclough 1989), but more linguistically oriented work has been done in the same area (e.g., Bolinger 1980). More recently, such obfuscating language has become a target for linguists who work in legal contexts (e.g., Shuy 1990), but the descriptive tradition of the study of highly-specified registers has expanded from interest in the lexicon of such varieties to the investigation of their interactional or discourse practices (e.g., Drew and Heritage 1992). Needless to say, the folk tradition uncovered here is rather more like the tradition in "critical" linguistics.

3.3.4 Taboo

The final stylistic or registral topic which engaged a few of our respondents concerns the use of taboo language. One respondent checks to see if the tape is still running after a friend who has interrupted the recording session leaves. He then admits to the fact that his performance has been different during the taped interview:

DH: Is this thing running.
M: Yep.

DH: I was going to say cause - I am talking different, I don't- I tend
to swear more than (this).=
SH: =Yeah (   ) talking ((laughs))

M: [
                             Do you- do you (p-)
M: At the party the other night.

M: [
                             So do you find yourself talking like
differently, - in front of her: or just in front of people you- people=

DH: [
                               ((clears throat))

SH: [
                                 (   ) not in front of me.
M: =you don't kn(h)ow. ((laughs))

DH: [
                               People I don't know I don't - cause I-
t- it's a bad habit. I fluently swear when I speak.

SH: [
                                   ((laughs)) Fluently
swear. (#42)

DH is not only uncomfortable using taboo forms on tape but also
limits his use to situations when he is with people with whom he is
familiar, suggesting that, like slang, taboo is used for solidarity or in-
group marking. But our respondents do not believe that taboo language is inappropriate only for those who are less well-known or for
tape-recorded interviews. Gender, for example, is important. DH (in
#42) doesn't like the fact that he heard his mother say *fuck* once,
particularly since he has been careful in his use of taboo forms
around her. In fact, gender appears to be a more important factor than
age, since D also reports that his father criticized him for using taboo
forms around his sister, even though she was older. We refer more
specifically to gender and taboo in the next section.

Later in the same conversation, DH flirts briefly with the notion
that there is some regional distribution to the frequency of swearing,
but, in the end, is not so sure. We suspect that what he almost admits
to is not unlike the regional stereotypes of the New York City area
explored above in several places in Chapter 2.

DH: And I get that from my dad's family. Ugh.
M: Yeah I- I remember when I was uh - (   )

DH: [
                               Cause like my aunt J and
stuff it was like- she's from uh - "da" Bronx? I mean to hear her=

M: [
                                     The
Bronx?

DH: =talk - yeah this ((imitates high-pitched growling noise)) and she just starts rattling and - and I really love her but she swears a lot.
SH: You think it's (   )
                       [
DH: They all do.
M: So are you trying to say that easterners heh swear more?
DH: Sure. Well I don't know. (#42)

On the other hand, recall that in our discussion of Southern speech features, S (in #56) associates "colorful" language (including taboo) with that region.

All of interview #48a is a lengthy discussion of slang and taboo in United States youth culture, and we cannot give it the full treatment it deserves here.[8] The participants, all young males, are especially sensitive to the "positive" uses of slang and taboo forms. R notes, for example, that anything positive could be called *hellish*, in contrast with what he calls the "bible" sense of the term. "A sandwich that is five feet long filled to the max, that's a hellish sandwich." "If a girl's got buttocks like this big, she is hellish." For this respondent, then, slang and taboo are not only positive in some minimal lexical sense, they are also more expressive of feelings or emotions:

M: I like swearing a lot. Swearing is just, I don't know, just you can express yourself a lot more. They say it's a bad way to express yourself, using slang words, they say a sort of cop out, but not really. It's just more or less your feeling. Like you know, "fuck you," uh you know, "Let's get fucked up" means two different things. Getting fucked up with drink. Yes, getting fucked up, wasted.
A: When you have a party, "Let's fuck up with drinking"?
M: No, "Let's GET fucked up." When you get fucked up, you're wasted, plowed. And then, you know, that's in a good way a sense of saying it. (#48a)

This same speaker, in spite of his appreciation of taboo, is aware that it cannot be used in all situations:

A: Have you had any experiences you felt awkward to use slangs on some occasions?
              [
M: Sometimes. - Yeah, like in front of, like slang in front of your parents, you know, like I do now since I'm older you know, I obviously got myself into the swing of swearing around my dad. But a - like you're in front of little kids, you try not to swear. You know, try to refrain, hold yourself back, you know you ought to. But, uh, - like uh, you know anybody who you're good friends with, I mean,

are bound to swear, you know. You know just like general talk when you're BS-ing with the guys you know. BS is bull shitting, SHOOTing the SHIT. OK. Ah I just don't know, there's just a time and a place for everything. You know it, I mean you get reactions if it's wrong.

But you know, to me when I'm talking to someone a lot older, if they don't swear, I'm not going to swear. But if they do, you know, I'll swear, even now a lot of times I do when I'm in front of older people. You know it's like I don't really care, you know if they base their opinion of you just because of how you talk you know if you swear. But if you go around just like being belligerent about it you know confronting people and just saying, driving around in the car and going "Hey, fuck you," you know out of your window. You know, it's not nice (   ). I don't know. I like to swear. Everybody likes to swear. Some people won't though. Some people try really hard NOT to swear. (#48a)

M restricts swearing, then, out of delicacy to some social situations ("little kids," "older people," although with the latter he appears to feel freer to use taboo forms), and he brags that he does not care if people form their opinions of him based on the way he talks. M does not use taboo belligerently in public for no good reason, but all his restrictions are in fact a result of holding back what he sees as a "natural" urge to use taboo – "Everybody likes to swear."

M also finds that some taboo items cause different reactions in him than in others. He finds he has an odd reaction to some uses of taboo forms by his father:

M: Like my dad knows every word I know, you know. And I've heard him call a person a "cock sucker." You know it's sort of odd. You know it's not like I think dad wouldn't ever swear, but you know it's like uh it used to be hard for me to picture my dad you know just saying something really you know in a sense not like calling someone a "fucker" or something like that but a more descriptive swear word you know like "cock sucker" or - what else, there's I don't know there's a way to be DIRTier you might say like I mean. - There's a word you use a around people that you know just you know ( ) you can use, say easier around someone else that accepted it because you around you you know you're just fucking around. (#48a)

M is surprised that his father will use more "descriptive" obscenity, a reaction which is perhaps common to many teenagers as they find that much of what they considered their private world is, in fact, shared by a larger (and older) segment of the society than they imagined. Once again, the "non-serious" character of taboo among friends is cited by M when he notes that taboo language is much easier to use among people who know that "you're just fucking around."

For some of our other respondents, however, taboo language use is confirming evidence that the language is in a deteriorating state, although the following conversation reveals not only that belief but a host of other personal reactions to the use of taboo forms:

J: But when we were children, we didn't say "damn," "damn it," or=
        [
S: Uh huh.
J: =any of this- or OH: ((spelling)) "s-h-i-t."
        [
M: (   )
M: ((laughs))
S: So do you think that the language is deteriorating.=
J: =Yes! Uh- my answer is yes.
S: ((laughs))
        [
M: Listen to TV and that'll tell you?
S: Yes, I heard people say "shit," "bullshit" - all the time.
                                [
M: Uh huh. Uh huh. Uh huh.
                            [[
J: Yeah. Yeah. Uh huh. You
never, never would have heard that on TV, (.hhh) (   )
    [
S: "God damn."
            [[
M: Uh huh.   Uh huh.
M: Or listen to some of your athletes, uh th- y- they just I mean it's
just one rotten word after the other.
                            [
J: Yeah.
S: Uh huh. But in your time, when you were students, - well when=
                                            [
J: Never.
S: =you w:ere young,
                [
M: Uh huh.
J: I would never have s- I didn't say "shit" until I had five kids.
All: ((laugh))
J: And then that covered the only word I knew.
All: ((laugh))
J: And then I had a difficult time with i- I was- an- it was difficult for
me, (.hhh) and even to this day if I say that to H, - wh- he says - =
    [
S: Uh huh.

J: ="That's not ladylike" or something like that. "Watch your language." See it's offends him. (.hhh) He isn't offended if HE says
anything he WANTS, (.hhh) but if I say something like that, why
then it's uh unladylike.
S: How about th- those young people today, if they say words like
that. - Well, uh perhaps you- your son and your - daughter-in-law -
they - they speak words like that. How do they feel among=
                                                         [
J: Well, you=
S: =themselves.
J: =don't find- I don't find it in any of my daughters or daughter-in-
laws.
S: They - think
              [
J: They don't talk like that.
S: Oh no? They don't?
           [
J: No- not in my presence, at least. I'm sure I can't imag-
ine - JI talking like that or JA or - any of them.=
   [
S: Uh huh.
S: =No?
     [
M: I got some of them. I got a couple that can really use it.
((laughs))
S: ((laughs))
M: I mean J(h) ca(h) rea(h)lly spiel it off.
J: But you know there was a time there - was it- it was the 60's or=
                [
M: She used to talk like that they were say like in a=
J: = - early 70's when they first started using (.hhh) the word=
M: =drunken (   ) sailor.
J: =((spelling)) f-u-c-k, which today still offends me terribly, (.hhh)
but- what they- - the students and the - young people of the 60's,
were trying to tell us it's just a word. The problem is our reACtion to
that word. It's just we were grown up with that word being - a bad
word that nobody said. So they were trying to break the establish-
ment of (.hhh) saying "Hey, it's only a word. Why do you get so
hung up on a word. It's not necessarily a deed, (.hhh) or a=
                                          [
S: (   )
J: =cruelty or somebody or it's really not harmful. It's just a word."
But- when you come from the background that M and I come from,
you don't USE that kind of language Ever ever Ever.
S: Huh.
J: To this day I-
M: The funniest thing I ever heard in my life and I'll never forget it
was J say (.hhh) "Well I've really, I've arrived. I'm really something
cause now I can say the- ((spelling)) f-u-c-k"=
J: =That was YOU: that said that. It was M. She said "Doesn't=
   [

M: ((laughs)) Was it? Oh it wa(h)sn't me. ((laughs))
J: =bother me anymore, I've come to a point where I can say (.hhh) ((spelling)) f-u-c-k."
All: ((laugh))
S: Why do you say- - why was it- - oh- - why do you say the=
      [
J: M was at our apartment, I w- I remember all of it.
                                        [
M: OK, I was putting the blame on=
S: =letters, not the - pronunciation.
        [
M: =you.   Yeah because it really was still not easy to say=
                                          [
J: Because you can't=
M: =((laughs))
J: =say it. I mean it's just chokes you can't say that word.
S: Oh.
M: Well- well you can now but-
      [
J: When I went- when - yeah but I- don't ever hear you=
                                                  [
M: (   )
J: =saying that. You don't talk like that M, you wouldn't say it in=
                                        [
M: Oh I don't know.
J: =the privacy of your - home.
J: You don't talk like that.
          [
M: Oh I can talk pretty bad ((laughs))
                                      [
J: Well you don't around
me anyway. I r- when I was a child, we'd go down the=
          [
M: (   )
J: =alley to go to school and that word was written over a- all the
garages.=We never knew what it meant.
M: (   )
J: I mean I didn't know what it meant for years and years and
years.
S: Uh huh.
((pause))
J: [[You know - but we still didn't like the word. I don't know why - =
S: [[And you are not- you were not curious.
                                        [
M: Uh huh.
J: =that was a- in our minds, from birth ((laughs)) That was a bad=
                                          [
S: Uh huh.
J: =word.
M: See now there's no word that you can use that's ba- that's
strong any more, because everything's gotten so commonplace,

because you used it, it was - an EMphasis. If you were really mad
then you, you know, you could say ((stage whispers)) "SHIT."
J: Yeah.
    [
S: Uh huh.
       [
M: And now it's gotten so that, now what do you say.=
                                     [
J: That's th-=
M: =((laughs))
J: =the "shit" now it's just a little - tap on the finger, (   )
         [[[
M: Huh yeah.   Uh huh.   Yeah.
                                   [
S: (   )
M: Uh huh. Yeah. Or "damn" and "hell," I mean that's just nothing.=
               [[[
J: But it-   Yeah.   Oh yeah.
M: =Everybody says that. So
                    [
J: Yeah. Uh- you never took the Lord's=
                  [
S: Yes.
J: =name in vain. You never (.hhh) you know nothing upsets me
like somebody saying "Je:sus Christ." Jus- my whole: body just
shakes.
S: Oh really? Now?
J: Yeah now. - And H does that. He knows that I- I'm offended by
that, and uh (.hhh) I- I told him at the store, I said "When I'm in this
store I don't want any of you guys talking like that because - it upsets me, I don't want to hear that kind of language and neither=
                                                [
S: Uh: huh.
J: =do the customers. - So if you want to talk like that, go home." - I
wo- I just won't permit it. When I'm there I'm sure they say (   )
 but I can't stand it. (#15)

M and J agree that times are changing (J didn't say *shit* until she had
five children!) and that words which were once emotive or emphatic
are now so commonplace that they have lost their force, a very common folk belief. J, however, is somewhat sympathetic to the 60's and
70's honesty in pointing out that obscenities were just words and not
deeds, but she notes that her own upbringing prevents her from ut-
tering or even tolerating some herself.

Like linguists, these respondents recognize that their reactions to
taboo are reactions to words, not concepts (e.g., Trudgill 1983:30).
Both J and M note that they knew that *fuck* was a "bad" word long
before they knew its meaning. That does not weaken, however, the

strength of their responses; they are even physical. They puzzle the fieldworker by spelling rather than pronouncing examples, and J notes that trying to say *fuck* "just chokes you" and that, when she hears a religious taboo, "her whole body just shakes."

Although J is more temperate in her approach to the "demythologizing" of taboo, M is more enamored of its covert prestige, however critical she may be of it. J insists that her daughters and daughter-in-laws do not use such language (at least not in her presence), but M reports that she has "a couple that can really use it," and her laughter when she reports that "J(h) ca(h) rea(h)lly spiel it off" shows that she takes a pride in this ability. In an odd case of forgetting, M claims that J revealed once that she was now a modern person since she could freely use *fuck*, but we discover that it was actually M who made the announcement, and M admits to this with no argument, saying that she was perhaps "putting the blame on you." Finally, when J insists that she and M are not taboo language users, M is not so sure and brags that "I can talk pretty bad," following her claim with a laughter which shows her enjoyment of the covert prestige this claim affords her.

We defer discussion of taboo and gender to the next section, although it is worth noting here that J clearly avoids the fieldworker's questions about her son and daughter-in-law, responding only by claiming that she does not know of taboo language use by her daughters and daughter-in-laws. Additionally, she specifically notes that H rebukes her for "unladylike" speech although "He isn't offended if HE says anything he WANTS."

3.4 Gender

While the interaction between speaker sex and language is not discussed by as many respondents as some of the other social factors already examined, the respondents who do discuss it provide a number of viewpoints. The folk wrestle with some of the same issues as linguists who work on sex roles and language; in fact, the two main areas discussed by our respondents were 1. whether or not women use more standard language than men, and 2. whether women's speech is powerless. In addition, a smaller number of respondents mentioned the notion that women's speech was more "relationship-oriented" while men's is more individualistic. Several respondents suggested that women seem to swear less than men, although this is obviously tied to the first (and even, perhaps, to the second) of the main topics just mentioned. Finally, there was some discussion regarding certain gender-specific lexical items.

3.4.1 Sex and standard English

The area most discussed by the folk regarding language and gender involved women's use of "Standard English," in particular, their not using "improper" English. As we have already shown, notions of improper English for the folk often overlap those of slang (3.3.2), and slang is a notion closely tied to folk linguistic conservatism – it is innovative, opposed to historically "proper" or "correct" English. Folk discussions about whether women use slang or not correspond, therefore, to linguists' discussions of whether or not women use more standard language than men, a position which, even for linguists, seems to imply linguistic conservatism (e.g., Trudgill 1983). Of course, linguists are aware of cases in which women do not use more standard forms than men (e.g., Milroy 1980, Nichols 1983, Bortoni-Ricardo 1985) and offer interpretations other than those of linguistic conservatism when they do (e.g., Eckert 1989, Labov 1990). In the following case, a fieldworker (Z) makes the standard language claim to a respondent (B), who agrees immediately and offers the "slang" interpretation:

> Z: There is a belief that women are- are the greatest users of standard (1.0) language - more prestigious. And men, for mascularity purposes- you know, they like to use more slang, nonstandard language.
> B: Women are less likely to use slang. It's an interesting idea. Makes sense. From my own personal - when I think about that, that's probably true. I would agree with that. (#19)

More often in our discussions, when not prompted, as in the above, there was a greater tendency for respondents to attribute *nonstandard* English (again, often in the form of slang or taboo) to men than to directly attribute *standard* English to women.

Social status is also very obviously connected to gender and standard language use. In the following, C explains how she deals with men's language in her professional role:

> C: One of the things that helps me get through a real masculine atmosphere is it's not a very natural style for me to swear.
> M: Uh huh

C: To really swear. And so the decision I made was to not try to- is not to try to match them word for word. Um not to try to be one of the boys but to maintain my distance through the dress and the vocabulary. And so I keep the wall built by using a different vocabulary in- when I'm around uh if you want to call it a working class situation.
M: Right.
C: There's clearly a class difference.

C: I can help them get better relationships going with blue- blue collar men by maintaining my own upper class (0.5) vocabulary. I can't bridge the gap so I don't even try to attempt it because I think an attempt would lose their respect=
M: =they won't- because their expectations of you um are-
C: that I am in upper class management and whatever.
                                     [
M: Right.
C: So I don't (0.5) I don't try to destroy a masculine boundary.
(#49)

It is apparent from this discussion that the respondent, while stressing the class difference between herself and her clients, is also clearly associating the "working class" vocabulary with masculinity and frames her comments about class distinctions within a discussion of gender. Like C, several respondents hold to the notion that swearing is a habit associated with the "working class," indirectly forging another link between women's and upper status speech.

C's characterization of male speech is not only class related but draws on the specific caricature of taboo or "swearing." Several respondents expressed the notion that swearing is "unladylike" behavior, but that for a man, it is more acceptable. One respondent comments that it is especially painful to hear his mother swear:

DH: My mom one day got mad and she said the f-word and I said DON'T do this? She goes well you use you say it and I try to and especially especially around my mom I don't like using that word.
(#42)

Although we shall not pursue it further here, we will take it that taboo language has the same nonstandard folk status that slang does. Numerous citations in the previous section should make that clear. Some interpretations of the female reticence to taboo (particularly sexual taboo) find that it victimizes women (e.g., Johnson and Fine 1980), but we did not encounter those more powerful psychological interpretations among our respondents.

Perhaps the most extreme case of linking female speech with overtly prestigious speech and male with the covertly prestigious variety is found in a conversation quoted in full in 2.2.2. Respondent K tells of two children who moved from Great Britain in their early teens. The girl (who was older) retained her British accent, while the boy within six months "had completely lost his accent COMPLETELY" (#18). K speculates that the boy wanted to "fit in," but the girl may have felt that her accent was "exotic." Sociolinguists, we suggest, would say that the boy responds to the covert prestige of an American accent, while the girl responds to the overt prestige of the British one.

Ideas similar to these of the folk are found in many earlier sociolinguistic discussions of language and gender, usually suggesting the same two trends – 1. women use more standard or conservative language (e.g., Labov 1972a, Trudgill 1983), and 2. men respond to the covert prestige of "working class" norms (e.g., Trudgill 1972). More recently, however, some researchers (e.g., Cameron and Coates 1988, Eckert 1989) have pointed out that there has been a tendency for sociolinguists to take men's speech as the "norm" and then to write of women's speech as if it were some form of "hypercorrection." In fact, the claim that women are more standard and conservative in their speech (and the correlate that men are therefore more nonstandard and innovative) may simply not be a valid one. Researchers have suggested that this finding may have been due in part to experimental design (Bell 1984), biases of the researcher (Cameron and Coates 1988), problems with the notion of "conservatism" (Cameron and Coates 1988), and the problem of applying a concept such as "gender" to a group of people when it may not actually be a defining category (Eckert 1989).

Like this more recent research, a few of our respondents were not ready to buy into the popular notion of women's more standard speech:

> K: Looking back when I was in high school and junior high - when you are more apt to use slang, it seemed to me that girls used that as much as the boys. And I don't really know about now. I think when we get a little older, we probably try not to use slang. (#22)

The folk debate among themselves their reasons for the putative conservatism of women's speech, and their debate parallels those found in language and gender research. We have already suggested that many folk and some sociolinguists regard nonstandard speech as "masculine." Like linguists, however, our respondents provide other reasons for these gender differences. In no place is this clearer than in the following conversation, a continuation of the one above among B, a white psychologist, his wife D, and the fieldworker Z:

> B: I think men are given more freedom (1.0) in a lot of ways than women. Maybe that's just one (1.0) example of that- that men have more choices to- (1.0) to talk the way they want to. If men prefer to use slang compared to standard language maybe they have:- It's more socially acceptable. (1.0) You know, cultures: historically are worried about women not being prim and proper. You know women can't be promiscuous. It's okay for men to be. Well the way not to be promiscuous or immoral or not virtuous is to be very limited in what you do.
> --
> B: I think language is a part of that. That men - so therefore women are given less freedom. Because if women are given a freedom they are going to - They are not going to control their sex- their- their sex drive. Do you think that makes sense?
> Z: Yes, it does.
> B: I think in general men have- are given more freedom than women, and that's just an example that they have more freedom to speak what they want to speak.
> --
> B: You see I like black speech. Black idioms. And I use them. D doesn't.
> ((Discussion of what black idioms are, including "slap me five" and "give me some skin."))
> B: D doesn't talk that way.
> Z: You should ask her why.
> D: Because I'm not with black people as much.
> B: No, because you're a woman. That's what we we're talking about.
> D: (sarcastically?) That's right. It's because I'm a woman.
> B: My interpretation is women are generally granted less freedom. And freedom of choice of- choice- of idiom=
> Z: =Do you feel that way?
> D: Yes. Yes.
> Z: That's interesting. I didn't think about that.
> (3.0)
> D: Yes I agree.
> Z: What do you agree.
> D: That women aren't allowed the same kind of freedom as men.
> (#19)

This discussion is quoted at length because it illustrates quite nicely the parallels between folk reasoning and those of earlier researchers on gender and language. The latter concluded that women were more conservative because they gain status through language use, perhaps particularly so since they are less able to gain status in other ways. Additionally, it was held that since women are expected to behave more "correctly," they do so. Finally, it was claimed that women generally are more likely to have greater contact with children than men, and thus must be more careful with the language that they use – although this care was seen as a nurturing response to the child's need for a standard language model rather than as one in which a caretaker should avoid "rough" or taboo language (Trudgill 1983). These ideas are quite similar to B's – men have the freedom to act the way they would like, and women are more constrained. (B's main reason for that constraint appears to focus on sexual activity, but we will not pursue that suggestion further; it is a well-known popular stereotype.)

D, on the other hand, begins by expressing the viewpoint that she doesn't use nonstandard forms because she doesn't come into contact with speakers who use those forms – a notion paralleled in the sociolinguistic literature by "network theory" (e.g., Milroy 1980, 1987; Thomas 1988). Recent gender researchers have noted that network theory has the ability to explain more satisfactorily than previously-mentioned theories just which gender will be more conservative. Like D, they believe that in order to speak like a social group, one needs to be in contact with members of it. Network theorists contend that when women come into contact with speakers of other dialects (shown most dramatically in cases of high male unemployment and simultaneous entry of women into the workforce), they are just as likely to be as innovative as men in the same situation (e.g. Milroy 1989). When B insists that it is D's femininity and not her contacts that cause her to not use slang, however, she concedes.

Other gender researchers (e.g., Nichols 1984) have suggested that, along with network contacts, the situation women and men are characteristically in has an effect on the language they use. This is also expressed by our respondents – one woman replies to the field-worker's suggestion that women use a "more prestigious dialect" as follows:

> C: It probably depends on the certain situation they run into.
> (#21)

C, in other words, is unwilling to merely accept that women are more "correct"; she suggests, as several recent researchers in language and gender do, that the situation women (and men) are in helps to determine which speech style they will use.

It is tempting to suggest that, just as most of the early researchers who found that women were more conservative were male, so too it was our male respondents who were most likely to accept the idea that women were more conservative. This parallelism suggests that much more work needs to be done by sociolinguists in this particular area to make sure researchers are moving beyond popular instincts and accurately interpreting the complex relationships between gender and standard language use.

3.4.2 Powerlessness

Since Robin Lakoff's *Language and woman's place* came out in 1975, a second notion that is much debated in work on language and gender is the notion that women's speech is "powerless." The so-called Lakoff Hypothesis states that certain forms that are (she claims) most often found in women's speech are inherently "weak" or "powerless," and this situation directly results from the fact that women are conditioned to believe that assertiveness and authority are masculine characteristics.

On the surface, it appeared that many of our respondents may have believed this as well. There were, for instance, those who described women's speech as, for instance, "apologetic." More often, however, respondents were apt to mention the powerlessness of women as stemming from an "internal characteristic" or from the fact that men "demand respect" merely by virtue of their being men. This is closer to the view expressed by researchers like O'Barr and Atkins (1980), which holds that women are not powerless *because* of their speech, but, because they are powerless, they use a powerless speech style.

Like more recent work in gender-oriented conversation analysis, however, the folk do not derive only negative interpretations from this condition. Respondent C expresses the following:

> C: What I'm arguing is that a lot of the reason that women are more facile with language and adapt more quickly to situations is that their powerlessness makes them more attuned to subtle um (0.5) feedback from the power person. Male um- and therefore they're more adept. (#50)

In short, C equates being powerless with another ability that both the folk and language researchers presume women to have – the ability to "connect" with others. Other respondents mentioned this as well:

C: I think they differ in the way they- I think women are more concerned with relationships and therefore: women might tend to say
"we" or "us" when the men might say "I." That kind of thing I noticed. (#21)

This idea is perhaps most associated with Tannen (e.g., 1989, 1990),
who claims that it is distinctly "female" to be concerned with relationships, while it is distinctly "male" to be more concerned with individual achievements. The fact that this is a common folk belief
may explain the popularity of her books among nonlinguists. It is
important to recall that we do not limit the sources (or venues) of
folk belief to so-called "traditional" or "oral" cultures (see Preface).
It is interesting that Tannen tries very hard to keep any notion of
power and powerlessness separate from her notions of report and
rapport (men's vs. women's styles, respectively), while the folk
clearly see the connection between the two.

Another theory regarding the presumed powerlessness of
women's speech is that, quite simply, it is *not* powerless. It is different from men's speech styles (e.g., Johnson 1980, Cameron, McAlinden & O'Leary 1988), but because men possess a disproportionate
amount of the overt power in our society (and others), their speech is
perceived as "powerful." There is, however, nothing *inherently* powerless about women's characteristic speech style. Some of the very
features researchers (and our respondents) attribute to women – tag
questions, raising intonation, asking for confirmation, etc... – are just
different, but not necessarily powerless. For example, Cameron,
McAlinden and O'Leary's (1988) discussion of tag questions shows
that a parent's saying to a child "You broke this window, didn't
you?" is certainly not made less powerful by the presence of the tag.
Deeper investigation of what some of our respondents said about
women's speech, suggests that they may also take this position. Respondent C continues her above statement as follows:

C: I'm trying to think of the word that says that when you're powerless you use a lot of non-verbal techniques to get your way anyway...it's the one that says the powerless person controls the
situation anyway. It's some kind of manipulative behavior it's the
word for the- where the seemingly powerless person manipulates
and controls the the situation um but in a non-confrontive way.

C: Anyway I think that because women and Blacks have traditionally been in this role that they are much more attuned to, the ways
to use language and all these other non-confrontive things in difficult situations. Uh that it's part of their technique to overcome their

powerlessness. Yeah they use all the linguistic rules and linguistic behaviors to control the situation.

C: And because of this powerlessness they have learned all these situational rules on how to behave and how to talk in certain situations to get their way (1.0) covertly. (#50)

C is expressing the viewpoint that although *women* are powerless, their characteristic speech style *affords* them power! Women (and African-Americans), according to C, are able to get things accomplished, rather than always acquiescing to the desires of the more powerful, by using this speech style.

In fact, a number of female respondents stated that they themselves used stereotypical female characteristics in order to get their way. One said that she acts submissive (i.e. powerless) towards her coworker "to let him be the boss in his mind" (#52), but she feels that this way she gets things done the way she wants them done, and he is happy as well. She also states she may be submissive to an older man "just to appease him." In both these cases, however, she feels that she in fact is the powerful one – she is getting accomplished what she would like to accomplish. Another respondent states "I often added a little Southern drawl to my voice because particularly with older men who saw me as just a pretty young thing anyway, it was a very good tool to disarm them" (#49). "And I generally get their vote anyway," she adds later.

In these cases, the women feel that they are in fact powerful – the power is just a different type from the one our society usually recognizes. It is unfortunate that this type of power is associated with "manipulation" or even "underhandedness" while male power is often associated with such positive characteristics as "plain talk." Note, by the way, that these gender-associated roles are exactly reversed in typical men's and women's speech in Malagasay culture (e.g., Keenan 1976). Finally, it is interesting to note that, although C in #50 (cited above) reveals the ability of the powerless to accomplish goals using "women's" speech styles, she later states that when women *do* achieve overtly powerful positions,

C: they have to talk like conquerors.
M: (laughs) they have to talk like conquerors.
C: It's true. One of the things I very consciously do not do in a conference situation is make a statement and then ask anyone if they agree with it. Nor do I preface any statement with "well I don't know but it seems to me"...I do not in any way hedge or couch my opinions when I present them. In fact I work very hard not to denigrate my opinions myself.

M: Okay okay.
C: And that's what I mean by learning to talk like a conqueror.
(#50)

In other words, when C finds herself in a characteristically male role – that of being in power – she feels she needs to work very hard at assuming a different speech style. Apparently, then, there is power in so-called "women's" speech styles, but only for those who "appear" to be powerless. There is obviously no power in this same speech style for those who have already attained overt power, and the implication of the above is clearly that its use by a person of power would be seen as "weakness."

In spite of these more subtle folk interpretations, a few respondents came close to expressing the "pure" powerlessness of women's speech:

C: I think women will often: maybe will express: sort of: in a less confident way. For example, someone that I worked with used to always say "if you don't mind?" and that kind of thing that I don't think men would say. I don't- I don't know, maybe they would. But it seems to me kind of apologetic. "I don't want to make you do=
　　　[
Z:　　　I don't remember hearing-
C: =anything," but, "I'm afraid not." (Laughs)
Z: So they are telling kind of- I don't know=
C: =They want to tell you what to do in a nice way. They want to be nice. (1.0) I think women are more concerned with having people like them. (#21)

C begins by expressing the fact that women are "less confident" and "apologetic," but then goes on to express the belief that women are concerned with being liked, perhaps similar to the idea of "connecting" with someone, but more negatively expressed.

In general we find that our respondents are aware of the relative powerlessness of women in our society but do not attribute that powerlessness to women's speech styles. In some cases, women's speech styles were seen as enabling women to get things accomplished, but women's desires to "connect with" others were also often linked to their powerlessness.

3.4.3 Other factors

The remainder of what was discussed regarding language and gender involved certain words that were not appropriate to say in front of men or women. Most common was the notion that one should not swear around women, particularly older women. In #42, quoted above, DH says he tries not to swear around his mother, then adds:

> DH: and then uh even my dad gets on me when I say it in front of my sister. (42)

A number of female respondents also mentioned that they didn't like people to swear around them, either. It represents to our respondents, as mentioned above, "lower class" or uneducated speech, and, although males are allowed to swear, they should not do so in front of women.

The remaining folk discussions included prohibitions of certain words to either of the genders: "hairdo" in reference to males (#1) – because it is a word for *women's* hairstyles; "mature" in reference to females (#23) – because, the respondent explains, a woman doesn't appreciate references to her age. Both of these were in response to a nonnative fieldworker asking about the lexical item in question and suggests, again, the considerable ability of those perceived as culturally naive in acquiring detailed explanations of the folk perception of cultural practices.

Our respondents discussed many of the same areas concerning gender that language researchers discuss – often reaching the same conclusions. In our opinion, this makes assertions that scholarly discussions about women and language are "introspective, anecdotal" in nature – e.g., Cameron and Coates (1988) concerning conclusions reached by previous researchers on women and the standard and Cameron, McAlinden & O'Leary (1988) concerning the "Lakoff Hypothesis" – all the more interesting. In emerging areas of research, it would be surprising not to find folk belief, categories, and even modes of interpretation among researchers themselves. As we pointed out in Chapter 1, we do not automatically assign folk belief any status for scientific accuracy. It may be right; it may be all wrong. Here, however, we are perhaps impressed more than in any other section by the importance of knowing folk belief to check on its possible influence in (mis)guiding scientific investigation. On the other hand, even if that scientific utility did not exist, we continue to believe that knowledge of linguistic folk belief stands on its own by virtue of its importance in providing an understanding of what we believe about one another.

Chapter 4: Language acquisition and applied linguistics

4.1 First language acquisition

4.1.1 Introduction

Unlike many "technical" issues of language, that of how children become proficient in the language that is spoken around them is one that the folk do not feel needs be relegated to "experts." The several respondents who discussed this issue all had children of their own who had acquired or were in the process of acquiring language, and they were quite willing to voice their opinions on this topic, even, at times, offering unsolicited views. Often a fieldworker could generate considerable discussion by asking something as simple as whether or not the respondent's child was talking yet or what the child's first word had been. In some cases, however, the fieldworker (most often nonnative fieldworkers – see 1.2) were much more direct. In #31, for instance, C (the fieldworker) asked F how he taught his child to speak, a question whose presupposition was not denied and which resulted in a rich discussion of various techniques – intonation, volume of parents' voices, repetition, and the use of picture books. As we shall see, however, it is not the majority folk opinion that parents "teach" their children to speak at all.

Since, in general, our respondents did not find it particularly remarkable that children acquire a language, they were more likely to discuss who had the most influence on the language that the child would eventually speak and how that influence was manifested. Additionally, and as might be expected from what we have seen generally concerning the role of prescription, they were concerned with whether or not the child acquired "proper" English and the implications the "quality" of the language had for the child. There was some interest in certain types of impairments that their children or others' children had and some mention of the nature and role of baby talk that adults use to children and the nature of the "talk" that babies use themselves. Finally, a few respondents discussed several other facets of language acquisition, including commonplaces from child-rearing folk belief and gender differences.

Comparing the folk view of child language acquisition to the linguist's view is a complicated task, however, perhaps because no other area divides the field of linguistics itself like that of child language acquisition. It may even be fair to say that many linguists' conceptions of what is basic to language systems are revealed in how they view the process of first language acquisition. The major division seems to be one between formalist (also called "nativist" or "adaptionist") theories and functional (also called "empirical" or "constructionist") theories. In short, "nature" versus "nurture." Van Valin points out that

> [a] major area of contrast between formalist and functionalist approaches to both language and language acquisition concerns their conception or definition of language. Different linguistic theories have different views of the nature of human language, and the basic orientation of the study of language acquisition from a theoretical perspective follows directly from the perspective of language that underlies it, since that conception defines what the child acquires. (1991:8)

Although it oversimplifies the debate, formalist theory suggests that the structure of human language is biologically programmed, predetermined by the "wiring" of an innate language acquisition device ('LAD') common to all humans. Since infants are born with such a device, language acquisition is a matter of "activating" it, a role which adult language input plays. Formalists believe, however, that such input is "impoverished" (e.g., Pinker 1994) and that children *must* therefore have access to the innate "Universal Grammar" to fill in the gaps. The work done in this area owes much to Chomsky's generative grammar, which has served as its foundation (e.g., Chomsky 1959 and elsewhere, Pinker 1994, Braine 1994). Statements such as the following are typical from this side of the debate:

> The hypothesis that underlies this chapter is that universal grammar (UG) will eventually explain *all* [emphasis ours] of the significant structural and semantic aspects of child grammar. The role of pragmatics and cognition, though intimately connected to language, will be seen to be external to the grammatical heart of language. (Roeper 1988:35)

The functionalist (or empiricist) position, on the other hand, holds that much of the structure of human language is a product of the functions that language serves in society; i.e., social interaction and communication needs, in addition to or even rather than an innate device (e.g., Bates and MacWhinney 1982, 1987). Many functionalists believe that acquisition arises out of a need the child has to fulfill certain functions and that adult input has a much larger role than formalists would allow. They question the "impoverished" view of that input and believe that children are, in fact, exposed to a wider variety of language structure than the formalists suppose; hence, they see no need to posit anything similar to an innate, universal grammar.

On the other hand, some who might be called functionalists simply believe that the innate or cognitive abilities which "drive" language acquisition are not language specific. Among functionalists, however, there is no overarching theory such as the generative (alternatively "transformational" or "generative-transformational," "government-binding" or "GB," or, most recently, "minimalist") approach that serves as a basis for functionalist work; it has been informed by various linguistic approaches as well as by research in psychology, sociology, and language socialization (e.g., Van Valin 1991, Schieffelin and Ochs 1986, Slobin 1982 and elsewhere, Snow and Ferguson 1977).

A fundamental question for linguists, then, is whether there is a specialized device in the human brain that predetermines the structure of language (i.e., the formalist/nativist position), so that children acquire language by "activating" various parameters of this device, or whether the structure of human language is determined by more general cognitive devices and/or by the social and communicative functions that it serves.

This decades-long division in linguistic approaches to first language acquisition is, however, hardly reflected in folk belief at all. It is perhaps not too surprising that the folk did not engage in any discussion as to whether language is innate or learned behavior, nor did they discuss other topics that are central to even more general accounts of language acquisition (e.g., the order in which morphemes, words, and syntactic rules are acquired; the various stages that children pass through – except to state when a child used "words" versus "sentences"; or children's phonological development – except as it applied to dialect acquisition and impairments).

The majority of folk interests lie in what could be characterized as sociofunctional areas of language acquisition and, as such, are more easily comparable with functionalist scientific positions, as we shall show below. These general topics are of interest to the scientific approaches taken to language socialization (e.g., Schieffelin and Ochs 1986, Schieffelin 1990), communicative competence (e.g., Harding 1984; Bates, Bretherton, Beeghly-Smith, and McNew 1982), discourse analysis (e.g., Ervin-Tripp and Mitchell-Kernan 1977, McTear 1985), and sociolinguistics (e.g., Romaine 1984, Andersen 1990). Since so many of these approaches to child language acquisition share a concern about the relation of "patterns of care-

giver/child communication to family and societal values,"
(Schieffelin and Ochs 1986:164), we believe it is a worthwhile en-
deavor to examine these care-givers' beliefs. We begin, however,
with what little folk comment there was on more formal matters.

4.1.2 Acquisition proper

4.1.2.1 The forces influencing the first-language learner. In general,
our respondents believe that children learn language simply because
they are exposed to it. Children "model" or "copy" the language that
they hear spoken by the people around them. Several respondents
used just these terms in their discussion:

> C: Could you - tell me something about that [i.e., how your children
> acquired language?]
> D: Well, I guess uh uh the boys uh uh pretty much picked up lan-
> guage by uh copying what uh they've seen us do.
> C: Umhum.
> ((Pause))
> D: Uh. ((pause)) (hhh) I guess uh most of their - way they - put
> words together to form sentences, early- early on was uh - how uh
> - they: remembered us doing that.=Sometimes uh they did this in a
> way that was kind of a- amusing because they would they would
> bring - bring their own uh - ideas, and then try and stick them into a
> sentence like we did, and it would come up with some really uh
> wild things. (#32)

This "copying" that D and the other respondents mention, however, seems fundamentally different from behaviorist (e.g., Skinner
1957) notions of language acquisition, in which children simply repeat
what they have had explicitly modeled for them. Our respondents' notions of "copying" appear to be similar to more modern notions of acquisition: a child receives input from the adult and, based on that input,
is then able to create new utterances that he or she has never heard
before. Although this respondent characterizes his children's "ideas"
as novel (or at least non-adult), he seems convinced that the
"sentences" (i.e., the structural patterns) are completely provided by
the adult model. If children simply repeated adult input, there would be
no opportunity for them to "come up with ... wild things."

In addition, nearly every respondent who commented on first
language acquisition at all used the phrase "pick it (i.e., language)
up" at least once in their discussions. There is an implication in "pick
up" that the process is a natural, perhaps even effortless one. In a
discussion regarding what one respondent (C) feels is an overemphasis in the United States on "teaching children things" that they would

pick up on their own, she states that "unless you're in a home where there really is a lot of disturbance or there's you know the people either don't talk to each other, or they (.hhh) you know they watch TV," the "normal situation" is that "children just pick it up" (#21).

In keeping with this notion of naturalness, although most of our respondents emphasize the importance of *exposure* to the language (if people don't talk around the child, there will be a problem), they also generally indicate no need for instruction on the parents' part. One child respondent expressed this general sentiment best: "We didn't get taught; we just learned how" (#28). Almost all of the respondents, then, asserted that teaching was unnecessary (*except* in reference to "correct grammar," see below). At first glance this might appear to be at variance with what Roger Brown (1977:12-13) has reported as adults' "unimpressive" attempts to teach language. He reports that in personal communication with Dr. David Rigler, a researcher at the Los Angeles Children's Hospital who worked with Genie (the now-famous case involving a child who was not exposed to language until her early teens), Rigler stated that other adults who came into contact with Genie ('nurses, aides, patients, doctors, visitors') made several "unimpressive" and "unrewarding" attempts at teaching her language and, further, that these attempts consisted solely of "attempts to solicit vocabulary," such as asking "what color?" or "how many?" or "what's this?" Brown states that these attempts "suggest the quite limited notions activated in the amateur by an explicit intention to teach language" (Brown 1977:13). It should be noted, however, that these adults were dealing with a fourteen-year old child and that they were well aware that this was not a normal case. If adults had been asked to "teach" language to a young child, they would surely have responded differently, perhaps even balking at the very notion of "teaching."

In spite of the general agreement that children learn easily and rapidly on their own, there were a few respondents who felt that a more aggressive approach to child language acquisition was necessary. One respondent in particular had an entire regimen worked out. When the fieldworker asked "How do you teach uh J – speak English?," the respondent demonstrates, using a picture book with the alphabet:

F: I have him read books with me. We read - we read books and ((recorder noise)) like uh - like this one book - is very good. It's a - it's a book that that we like to read, he likes to read with with me.
C: Uh.
    [

F: It's called uh "Mother Goose ABC, in a in a Pumpkin Shell."=
            [
C: Uh huh.
F: =And like when we turn to the first page, I'll ask him what the
object is on the page. ((asking the child)) J, what is that?
J: Apple. ((pronounced as if it were "elbow"))
F: [[That's an apple. All right, see he's only he's only a month=
                                              [
C: [[Uh.   Uh huh.
F: =and I mean a year and - nine months and he can say=
                          [
C: Uh huh.
F: ="apple."(#31)

Next the father asks the child "What's this J?" (referring to the letter
"A"), and the child is uncooperative. The child coughs, and F explains that J is "too sick to – to do it right now." F continues:

F: When he does speak, - I'll ask him- I'll ask him to say "D::"=
                        [
C: Uh huh.
                        [
J: ((babbling))
F: =and - then if he doesn't s- - if he says it, then I'll say "D" even
louder and maybe more emphasized, say ((very loud)) "D::," that
way - then when he when he says it, then he gets=
   [
C: Uh huh.
F: =more - the feeling of it, "D." Like, he can say "DOGgie."=
                                     [
C: Hm.
F: =Right. Say "doggie."
J: Doggie.
F: And where's the door::.
J: Doo:::r.
       [
C: (The door) ((laughs))
                     [
F: (T)here's the doo:r.
C: ((laughs))
F: Where's the "e::."
J: "e:."
F: "e::."
((pause))
F: Look it. There's a "g::::." Can you say "g::."
J: "g::."
   [
C: "g:."
F: Yeah. Good boy.
            [

J: (Door.)
F: That's a "h." For a hen that lays the e:ggs.
C: ((laughs))
   [
F: See the eggs. And then - and then just uh: - reading, like=
                [
C: Uh huh.
F: =that, helps him. (#31)

Though this may at first seem like the very tactics that Brown suggested that "amateurs" employ, there are differences. F realizes that
simply asking the questions is not enough and that a louder voice and
repetition are important as well. Additionally, this odd reliance on
written language during the spoken language acquisition process mir-
rors what Heath (1983) found among her respondents. European-
Americans often served as "language teachers" to their children, focusing, particularly on "literacy"; African-American parents did not,
although, in the African-American community Heath studied, this
latter fact was not a reflection of adult illiteracy.

While most of the respondents in our survey did not feel that it
was necessary to take such drastic steps to instruct their child, a few
did, in fact, mention that there was a difference between the talk that
they employ when addressing children and that used to address other
adults. One respondent explained why this was necessary:

B: You want her to accept you,
Z: Uh huh.
B: And see you as an attractive person. ((pause)) Mm you=
                                     [
Z: But do I (   )-

B: =experiment with different a- approaches, and see what she's
going to respond positively to.
Z: But I am wondering why I really use that, baby talk, because
probably she noticed that I speak - to somebody else differ- in dif-
ferent way, different intonation using (   )
                                  [
B: It's probably - genetic.
Z: Yeah. May be.
          [
B: It's proba-=I think it's probably a genetic program - to=
                                          [
Z: Hmm.
B: = - talk baby talk to a baby, - engage them that way, get=
                       [
Z: Uh huh.

B: =them to - connect with you, and then, you use that - connec-
tion, the- that that - that bond.
Z: Uh huh.
B: It's crea- created by that, to then lead them into - more ad-
vanced le- speech.
Z: That's interesting.
B: That make sense? (#19)

B has in fact echoed the beliefs of several of those working in child
language (and recall that he is a psychologist himself). Brown (1977)
discusses several similar reasons that adults use baby talk, concluding that "communication is the most important single determinant of
tuning" (11) and that, as our folk linguist states, a parent will do
whatever is necessary to communicate with the child. Note, however,
that B clearly sees a learning advantage for the child as well, since
such modification will "lead them into – more advanced ... speech."
Although "baby talk" has been a major topic of discussion in language acquisition research, this is one of only a few references in our
data, and the topic was initiated by the fieldworker.

Perhaps one reason the folk are suspicious of baby talk is that they
so strongly believe, as many of our recorded conversations show, that
they serve as models for their children and that children will do what
they have heard their parents do. There were only a few respondents
who believe that children perhaps take a limited but somewhat more
active role in acquiring language. In the following discussion, the
fieldworker Z has just asked the respondent B about whether he feels
that children "mimic" their parents. B answers that he is not sure what
she means by "mimic" but that he feels that children use "modeling";
when Z asks what he means by this, he continues:

B: Children copying ((pause)) ((very fast)) Is that what you mean.
Copying - the behavior - of - others, of adults.
    [
Z: Oh I mean the-
Z: Uh huh. Maybe that would be it. That's- copying uh par- you
know either parents or some uh ((pause)) you know ((Pause))=
    [[
B: Yeah.   Yeah.
Z: =person. (   ) if he's (   )
                      [
B: I think that's the most - powerful - w- uh
form of- that learning takes, - in children.
Z: Modeling?
B: Yeah. Or copying, or like uh learning by example?
                       [
Z: Copying (   )

Z: Uh huh.
((pause))
B: Seeing what other people are doing, and do the same. (#19)

B, then, believes that what a child is exposed to will be what the child learns, but as we shall see later on, even he believes that children play a somewhat more active part in "selecting" their input data, but this appears to be in relation to sociocultural rather than "pure" acquisition facts.

None of the respondents, then, suggests anything similar to the formalist's "autonomous language acquisition device" (e.g., Chomsky 1959). Although several used such words as "instinctive" and "innate," a closer look at the actual discussions where these items occurred suggests that the definitions are strikingly different from the formalist's:

S: The child who hears correct English, correct tenses, and correct grammar at home, without working at it, can usually get an A, whereas a child that hears incorrect really has to struggle for it. I-they can learn it, but it's not innate. It isn't something they just always knew. It's a struggle. (#54)

We assume from this that those children who do hear "correct English" have "correct tenses" and "correct grammar" innately. In other words, S is not using the term "innate" to suggest that *language itself* is innate; rather she suggests that *proper* language will not be innate if one is not exposed to it. This sort of "innateness" obviously refers to acquired behavior and the readiness or "automaticity" of it for later occasions; it is clearly not the innateness of a LAD. (The obviously social sense of this use of innateness is discussed below; the term "instinctive" was used in a similar learned behavioral sense.) There is nothing, of course, in formal theories of language acquisition to suggest that nonstandard dialects inhibit activation of the LAD, nor is there any reference to standard dialects being closer to the universal grammar than formal theories posit as innate. In fact, some theorists suggest that nonstandards (or pidgins and creoles) better reflect natural or universal tendencies (e.g., Kroch 1978, Bickerton 1981).

4.1.2.2 The stages of acquisition. Few parents discussed the preverbal stage, but those who did felt that children could in fact understand what adults said to them and that it was "amazing" how much they could understand (K #18). One respondent felt that early verbalization was not just "babbling," but that "in his (i.e., the child's) own mind he is saying something" (A #20). In her research, Miller (1988) has discovered this as well: parents (mothers in particular) "ascribe communicative function to infants' early vocalizations, and ... this is an area in which greater work is needed" (127).

Research in other cultures shows a considerable folk belief in the "private" language of children. Hymes (1974) notes that, for example, Chinook and Ashanti children are thought to possess a first language which is significantly different from adult language. This language may be shared with other infants, or, as in the Chinook case, with spirits. In the Ashanti case, for example, infants are not allowed in the room where a woman is giving birth, for the infant may communicate with the unborn child in this shared language and, warning it of the tough life ahead, cause a hard delivery due to the unborn's unwillingness to emerge (97-8). More closely related to the viewpoints collected here, however, different cultures take quite different positions on the role of caregivers as "teachers" in the first language acquisition process. Among the Kaluli, caregivers assume the specific role of language teachers (Schieffelin 1979), while in Western Samoa (Ochs 1982), caregivers do not see themselves as active language teachers at all. An anthology is devoted to studies in this framework (Schieffelin and Ochs 1986), and Romaine (1984) provides a review of earlier studies of various cultural attitudes to children's speech and first language learning (164).

Children's early attempts at talk were characterized in our data in terms of whether or not a child was using words yet, or "phrases" (though one respondent reported "one-syllable" and "two-syllable" stages, F #31). Discussions often concerned what the child's first word or first phrase had been (and often baby books were consulted). Our folk respondents do not in general, however, seem to pay much attention to length of utterance (as acquisitionists have, for example, in elaborating the MLU – mean length of utterance – as a standard measure of a child's language development, e.g., Brown 1973). From a more interactionist perspective, there seems to be no suggestion whatsoever in our data that folk respondents have any awareness of the early "verticality" of syntactic development, even in the one-word stages – e.g., Scollon (1979), who uses the notion of "verticality" to show that very young children's conversations, even those of one-word per child, can be made into more complex sentences if stretched out "horizontally." In short, there is no evidence here that our respondents looked at these "milestones" of syntactic development even remotely in the same way that linguists have.

4.1.3 Language socialization

4.1.3.1 The general concerns. In this section we go on to discuss the principal concerns of the folk as they discussed the sources of child language. We first consider in a little more detail the work of those scholars who have addressed the area of language acquisition termed "language socialization."

Fisher (1970) defines linguistic socialization as follows: "the learning of the use of language in such a way as to maintain and appropriately and aggressively change one's position as a member of society" (107-108). Schieffelin and Ochs (1986), in a review article concerning language socialization, add the following:

> Fisher (1970) relates patterns of caregiver-child communication to family structures and societal values. Gleason and Weintraub (1978) in their discussion of input language and the acquisition of communicative competence consider input in terms of its role in instructing children in specific cultural and societal information, including appropriate uses of language. ... They refer to this use of language as the "language of socialization." Further, this function of parental language is depicted as emerging subsequent to the "language-teaching" function of input. (164)

It appears, then, that there is a direct link between what linguists working in a sociocultural framework have found and what our folk linguists believe. The folk are concerned for the most part with the acquisition of *proper* language (not the acquisition of *any language*); their concern, therefore, is one of *socialization* rather than *acquisition*. In other words, children are acquiring societal values as they acquire language. The fact that respondents juxtapose discussions of "good" and "bad" English to those of language acquisition *in almost every case* is evidence for that. The bulk of the following discussion, then, focuses on how, according to the folk, good language is acquired and bad language avoided.

K: So like when you- when you were teaching and stuff too, di- did you have to - did the teachers ever - like did you have to make sure that you spoke English correctly or - were there any uh
E: I just always did.
K: ((laughing) You always did. How did that come about, E?
E: I don't know. I think - I think that my mother and father always spoke very correctly.
K: Uh huh.
E: And and they're both very - smart people. And - and we=
                                                 [
K: Uh huh.
E: =were just raised - to- to speak - ((clears throat)) well. (#20)

From what we have already seen of the dominance of prescriptive notions in folk accounts, it is not surprising to see the association of "good language" and "intelligence" in this account of the setting which was crucial for this respondent's acquisition of the standard. That she was "raised to speak well," however, does not contradict the notions provided above that one simply "picks up" language. Apparently the model her parents provided was sufficient. In fact, if a child hears "correct grammar," there is no choice:

> D: But he was real pleased - with the fact that B [D's son] spoke -
> quote unquote proper English.=
> K: =Uh huh.=
> D: =OK. Uh: - but that again, is - another one of my things.=
> K: =Uh huh.=
> D: =Well plus the fact that's what B heard, - when he was=
>   [
> K: Uh huh.
> D: =growing up, so he didn't really have a whole lot of choice.
>   [
> K: Uh huh. (#12)

One might argue that since "correct English" is, according to this respondent, "one of my things," little B might have been treated to some behaviorally-oriented training (i.e., punishment and reward), but the principal fact here for early acquisition (not whatever evil influence B's peers might have had later on him which might have led to corrective "training") is that the invariably correct English input he had gave him no "choice" about what form to acquire. The following respondent's remark has already been quoted, but it bears repeating here:

> S: The child who hears correct English, correct tenses, and correct
> grammar at home, without working at it, can usually get an A,
> whereas a child that hears incorrect really has to struggle for it. I-
> they can learn it, but it's not innate. It isn't something they just al-
> ways knew. It's a struggle. (#54)

Since proper English is what is valued by the larger society which our respondents belong to, passing on this form of the language is, therefore, a passing on of societal values. More than a few respondents attributed "bad language" to parental or family influence:

> SH: It's like D's family they all talk funny I think.
> DH: My family?
> SH: Uh huh. Like we D we had a big problem about one word that
> he said.

M: Oh yeah?
DH: What word was that.
SH: The word "iDEa." Er you used to say "iDEAL"=whenever he would be saying something he'd say "I have an ideal." I'd be like DH it's "I have an idea." And that used to dri:ve me: nuts. (#42)

Although it may not directly bear on socialization, we cannot ignore the relationship between "good language" and "intelligence" (raised explicitly by E in #20, quoted above). That the notion that exposure to "good grammar" leads to intelligence is a highly attractive one to the folk should not be surprising. We need only review what happened to Bernstein's *elaborated* and *restricted codes* in the hands of educators in the 1970's. Simply put, Bernstein's idea was that one needs to use a code (i.e., language) that is more *elaborate* when speaking with outsiders, a form of use which is unnecessary for intimates. The code that is used for intimates is "restricted," in that it may not contain, for instance, the complex referential tracking system of the elaborated code (e.g., Bernstein 1971). Educators used these codes – perhaps due to the unfortunate labels – to claim that middle class children, who appeared to display a greater use of the elaborated code, had a distinct advantage over inner city children. (e.g., Bereiter and Engelmann 1966). In other words, a child who grows up in a home where improper English is spoken (i.e., one where a *restricted* code is used) will have a hard time in the educational system *just because* the child has not been given the proper tools – a conclusion similar to S's "not innate" (#54) cited above. There was, however, little other discussion of this sensitive topic, perhaps the result of its very sensitivity.

On the sociocultural front, however, there were respondents – in most cases, teachers who had dealt with speakers of AAVE or counselors who counseled such students – who were able to recognize that there was a *function* for so-called "improper" language. Recall that G (in #36a, cited in 3.2) is very much concerned that children do not use school language at home lest they be thought of as "uppity" or "looking down on their elders." After he makes that point, G goes on to explain that school English might be found in some homes but not in others.

G: That's not true in ALL families, because what you're being exposed to right now are those that DO go on to college. Those that DO put in for professionals. (.hhh) But not everybody goes to college. Not everybody goes into professional fields. (.hhh) You have everything from mechanics to (.hhh) uh factory workers, to all kinds of people.

K: Ditch diggers.
H: Don't you f(   ) - - So if in you mean uh - uh students use=
                [   ]
G: Which is good money.
H: =the another - uh English. I mean - not the proper English=
                               [
K: Proper English.
H: =in home at home, (.hhh) and uh use proper English. Then=
                                  [
G: In other=
H: =it's proper E- Eng-
G: =words in the home it's not unusual to have some of the English
which is spoken to actually be improper English.
H: But where you see the- wher- uh b- because they learn a lot at
schoo:l
G: (.hhh) Because when they went through and actually learned
from THEIR parents, they learned improper English - by word of
mouth. (.hhh) And you learn more from those=
   [
H: Uh huh.
G: =around you than than you learn from the teacher who is trying
to teach you.
H: Uh huh.
  [
G: And what happens is is that you ARE a product of your envi-
ronment.. (.hhh) And the environment is not - proper English.
Proper English is textbook English. (.hhh) It is proper English in
cert[h]ain homes, (.hhh) in certain uh once you s-=
                            [
H: Uh huh.
G: =start getting into the professions, (.hhh) once you start=
                                  [
H: Uh huh.
G: =getting into those fields which take college degrees, (.hhh)
then you are expected - to speak with proper English.=
                          [
H: Yes.
G: =But in the other homes of factory workers and all that, they
could, or they could not. (.hhh) *It really depends on what they've
learned from their parents and what they've passed on.* ((emphasis
ours)) (#36a)

From a linguistic point of view, G has realized several important
things. There is a good reason for children to learn "improper" English – it is "passed on" from their parents. Unlike E (#20, cited just
above), G does not appear to equate good language with intelligence,
for he suggests that the parents who model improper English are not
necessarily lacking in intellect (although he does seem to feel that
they may be lacking in ambition, and, at least from this perspective,

he joins the large number of majority culture folk respondents who continue to be puzzled by the existence of nonstandards). In spite of that puzzlement, and, perhaps most importantly, he asserts that *this language is valued in their society.* G recognizes that the values of these children's parents are being transmitted to the children and, further, that there is nothing wrong with these values. (In fact, he suggests later in the same discussion that these lower-status people end up making more money than the people who have college degrees.)

It is interesting to note, however, that even in cases like the one just cited, nearly all our respondents personally claimed that they (and their parents) spoke "proper" English. Our respondents seemed to be eager to assure us that they were passing on correct language to their offspring.

Although comments on specific features of bad language were rare, those most often commented on were sociolinguistic stereotypes. One respondent, for instance, notes the following: "Where if you hear 'ain'ts' and all these things, just- - and double negatives, – it's really hard for children in school. I think it almost it takes takes them another year to catch up on on speaking English" (S #54). *Ain't* and multiple negation were, in fact, the stereotypes mentioned most often by our respondents. Although the details were slim, the concerns were great, and we turn now to the question of "what's a caretaker to do?"

4.1.3.2 Modeling and correction. As we suggested earlier, B, for example, believes that the child's model is not simply whatever is around; he suggests some active selection process may be taking place:

> B: I think children have - a sense of - who they want to be like. If they- even if it's not conscious, even on very little children, when they see other people, and if they want ((pause)) what that other person has, or want to be like that person because they they feel that person has certain power, or control, over over something that they don't have.
> Z: Uh huh.
> B: Oh little kids want to be o- kids little kids always want to be older, 'cause they feel they have more strength and power, -=
> [
> Z: Uh huh.
> B: =and (I don't know) they can do- you know and freedom and everything. - So they'll yeah they'll they'll try to copy. (#19)

In other words, B suggests that it is not necessarily the behavior of the parent that is "copied." In fact, he states that his younger daughter sometimes copies "step by step by step" the behavior of his older son – "repeats his words, repeats his actions" (#19). Although this conversation does not deny the role of copying, it suggests that the child learner is somehow active in selecting who (if not exactly what) will be copied and that the selection process is determined by the child's grasp of the most efficient sociocultural outcomes. It is, of course, just such "freedom of selection" which makes many parents fear that "bad language" will be copied, and, while our respondents had no doubt of parental influence on a child's language, many of them were also aware of the role a child's peers play as well. These respondents suggested that, early in life, a child would be most influenced by the language of a parent or parents but that later the child, spending more time with older siblings or schoolmates, would be influenced by peers. One respondent in particular felt that peers must have a particularly significant effect:

> K: I think you you speak where you - you are growing up. You probably (would) be modified by your how your parents speak.
> [
> Z: (   )
> Z: Yes. Uh huh.
> K: And uh
> Z: So, you you mean (it seems like though) the surroundings - would be - more influential? Yeah.
>   [[
> K: (Greater.)   Yes. I think so.
> Z: Uh huh.
> K: Otherwise I would be speaking with a Norwegian accent.
> Z: Yeah, that's all (   ) but you see that you were - for such a=
>   [[
> K: ((laughs))   Yes.
> Z: =short time.
> K: Oh no no. I mean from my parents. My parents both speak=
>   [
> Z: Oh, I see!
> K: =with a - my m- my father with quite a heavy accent.
>   [[
> Z: accent   Uh huh. (#18)

K's proof that peers have a greater influence on language is that she did not acquire the "accent" of her parents, although it is important to note that in this case the parents are not native speakers of the language of the speech community in which the child found herself. We deal directly with folk views of childhood bilingualism (and, in fact, with the beliefs of the parents of this respondent) in 4.2.4.

At the phonological level, K's view is consistent with linguists' views on the influence of peers. Payne (1980), for instance, showed that virtually all of the children in her study who moved into a new dialect region were likely to acquire a number of features from that new dialect (although not all of them).[1] She stresses that, although models "based upon the parent-child relationship" are valuable, "they have not dealt with the broader social context of language learning" (143).

Most respondents felt that the essential component in helping a child acquire language was to speak "correctly" or "properly" around the child, but some went further to suggest that correction and the insistence on proper speech were important activities. "An:d but it's the parents I think who set the tone as far as insistence on proper grammar and speech" (K, #22). This same respondent stated that children should be corrected if they make grammatical errors because "it's much harder to change how you speak once you are an adult," a claim which seems to contradict at least some of the notions of "easy variety acquisition" encountered in the discussion of ethnic and regional varieties above but clearly corresponds to the notion that early-acquired "habits" produce the easy, "innate" ability for later use.

For an African-American respondent (V in #51, cited in 3.1.1), this task is even more difficult. She is an AAVE speaker herself (which she refers to as "slang language"), but she does not allow her daughter to use this variety, even at home. For this respondent, some of the impetus for "proper" language use comes from the environment, but, in this case, that environment does not include the family, and overt instruction (actually prohibition) is required. In an interesting reversal of this situation, a European-American respondent (B in #19) demonstrates his efforts to teach his child African-American behavior patterns, including his idea of some nonlinguistic aspects of that behavior (e.g., "giving skin"); this conversation is cited extensively in 3.1.1.

On the other hand, since the folk also believe that first language acquisition is such a "natural" process, not all respondents agreed that correction was appropriate. Some few felt that correcting a child's speech was not helpful because "They do seem to learn on their own" (C #21), and one felt that correcting a child was "dangerous" since children speak according to their developmental level (B #19), although it is important to note that B is a psychologist. All these comments, however, seemed to have more to do with acquisition proper than with the acquisition of "good English." We have already dealt with many of the concerns of models of regional, slang, taboo, and other linguistic behavior on the older child learner in Chapters 2 and 3.

The general consensus of the folk appears to be that parents are largely responsible for a child's "grammar," that peers are responsible (perhaps surprisingly) for the phonological system (see K's statements from #18 cited above, for example), and that both parents and peers share responsibility for lexicon (particularly "bad words," the main focus of many discussions). Teachers and others of "those who are trying to teach you" (D, #36a) were seen by the folk to have the least impact on the eventual language that a child will speak, their role being relegated simply to that of teaching "big words" (S, #54). Surprisingly, the folk do not see the teachers' duty as that of teaching syntax because "good grammar" (i.e., "proper" syntax) is learned long before a child enters school and, perhaps, cannot be taught. As we have already seen in discussions of different dialects (2.2) and AAVE (3.1.1), however, the folk feel that mastery of another variety is a simple matter, and they resent or at least are puzzled by the persistence of nonstandards. Since phonological systems are learned from either the parents (in the earlier years) or the peers (in later years), in this area again the teacher does not play a significant role. A few of the respondents mentioned television as an influence on their child's language, but its role was often seen as that of yet another place for children to learn "bad words" and could, therefore, be considered a more important factor in language socialization than early acquisition. This specific folk belief interestingly corresponds with recent linguistic evidence from the children of deaf parents, who apparently did not acquire spoken English, even though they were exposed to considerable television (Ervin-Tripp 1987).

In conclusion, there is considerable difficulty in disentangling folk views of "good" models from those of "necessary" ones, a confusion which further reflects the pervasiveness of folk concern for prescription.

4.1.4 Varia

Folk linguists had a difficult time characterizing the nature of speech problems of their children or of other children they had heard. Most of the concern was with phonology, and respondents stated ideas similar to the following: "words didn't come out of his mouth right" or that a child "needs to learn to form the letters with his mouth."

(#28). (The typical folk association of sounds and letters, see 5.1 below, was obviously in evidence here.) Similar to the folk, the professional focus on acquisition difficulty is often also on the delayed development of phonological systems (e.g., Weeks 1974).

A few of our respondents attributed acquisitional delay to "slow" people (K #53 and E #55) or to those who were "backwards"; one respondent noted that a particular child's delay was a result of the fact that "that part of the brain is not developed" (K # 53), although there is no evidence that this respondent, despite the fact that she is a teacher of emotionally challenged children, had any information about language localization theories in general or about any specific dysfunction of this particular child's brain. However, most respondents attributed a delay not to a lack of intellect, but perhaps to a lack of muscle control (evidenced in the need to "learn to form letters with his mouth") (unidentified child, #28) or the natural variation found in children's overall development. As the older brother of the child respondent quoted above ('We didn't get teached, we just learned.') explained to the fieldworker in the discussion concerning his younger brother's impairment: "He's just a little late in learning how" (unidentified child respondent in #28). Some respondents cited hearing impairments as the cause of language impairments (K #37).

One respondent suggested that her child actually heard the parents say the words incorrectly:

> D: The teacher told her how to say the word and she learned? how to say it. But she could not get those th's ((pronounced as "tee-aitches")) together unless she really thought about it so I and so then she said "You know how to say it [tʌrməs]?" And it was like she was teaching us like we weren't saying it right either that was what she was meaning. We had been saying it wrong all the time too, so she was telling us how to say it. (#46)

To these parents, then, the problem did not lie in faulty intellectual development but perhaps with the fact that the child wasn't paying careful attention to adult speech. (There was one respondent who felt impairments were due to the linguistic experiences of past lives [E #55]; however, this was a unique opinion, and no linguists who concur have yet been found.)

Parents felt that speech classes offered by the public schools were worthwhile. Respondent D quoted above (#46) felt that her child's speech class was the only place she talked correctly: "You know as long as she wasn't in class she didn't need to speak correctly" (D, # 46). Her mother believed that eventually she learned to extend correct speech beyond the realm of the class. Most respondents with children with speech impediments took it for granted that the children needed these courses.

There were additional topics touched on by only a few respondents. One respondent who discussed the gender differences in language noted that his girl "picked up" language more quickly than his boys. According to him, she was "innately more talkative," and the boys "didn't use the language a lot" (D #32). Earlier language development in girls is an observation which has been made by a number of acquisition researchers (e.g., O'Brien and Nagle 1987) and by anthropologically oriented sociolinguists who find the etiology of differences in women's and men's language strategies in the uses put to language in children's largely monosex play groups. In general, these researchers stress the greater importance of language in girl's groups (e.g., Maltz and Borker 1982). This discussion was, however, the result of the fieldworker asking a direct question to the respondent about gender differences in acquisition, and, unfortunately, it was not pursued by other fieldworkers in their sessions. (See 3.4 for more on gender and language differences.)

Finally, one set of respondents discussed several myths that they had heard regarding language acquisition, such as "if you cut a child's hair before they are one year old they will have a lisp" (SR # 40). It is interesting to note, however, that this myth and the one concerning past lives concern *impairments* rather than normal development; this seems to suggest again that, in the eyes of the folk, normal development is nothing very exciting; it is *abnormal* development that requires help from the realm of the supernatural or experts.

4.2 Language and education

It is not surprising to find that the folk comment frequently on educational linguistics. It is irrelevant to our purposes here that perhaps the great majority of the folk (and probably a considerable number of linguists) see little or no connection between scientific language study and educational efforts, particularly those referred to, at least in the elementary school grades, as the "language arts." In fact, however, linguists in the United States and Canada have a long record of interest in educational matters, particularly in three areas. 1. Psycholinguists (and to a lesser extent phonologists) have been interested in the acquisition of reading skills (e.g., Fries, 1962, Gunderson 1970, Wardhaugh 1969). 2. Dialectologists and sociolinguists have been interested in the difficulties minority children face in language-oriented school requirements (e.g., Labov 1969a). 3. Ethnographers and anthropological linguists have been concerned with the more general uses of language which characterize home, school, and community (e.g., Cazden, John, and Hymes 1972). The analysis of classroom discourse might be added to this last concern, but the impetus for such study developed principally in England (e.g., Sinclair and Coulthard 1975), although it has now been taken up by some US researchers (e.g., Mehan 1982). Also more characteristic of work done in England than in the United States and Canada, linguists have taken a direct interest in language arts programs, in some cases preparing actual course materials and syllabi (e.g., Doughty, Pearce, and Thornton 1971).[2] Although titles such as "Educational linguistics" (e.g., Stubbs 1986) are, therefore, more common in linguistics in Great Britain than on this side of the Atlantic, there is still a very lively professional interest (and contribution to teacher education) in this area in the United States and Canada, and surveys of "applied linguistics" (e.g., Allen and Linn 1982, Reed 1971, Wardhaugh and Brown 1976) reveal that that has been the case for some time.[3] A survey of the relatively new journal entitled "Linguistics and Education" shows, for example, a majority of US contributions and concerns.

Many past studies have catalogued media comment, particularly "pundit" discussions of spelling, literacy, usage, and language norms in general, including claims that the schools have failed in these areas. Although not all of the following explicitly comment on educational linguistics, all are excellent surveys of popular culture and/or literary expressions of just such matters as often form the core of public concerns over language in the schools: Bailey 1991, Bolinger 1980, Drake 1977, Finegan 1980. All these, of course, are substantially different from the ethnographic, conversational examination carried out here. We have already detailed in Chapter 1 some of the philosophical underpinnings of folk prescriptivism, and we have already seen its manifestations in concerns of variety, particularly in Chapters 2 and 3. There is no doubt that these very concerns influence folk concerns about language education as well.

4.2.1 Spelling, reading, and writing

Declining public literacy is often held up in the media as the prime example of the failure of current educational practices; it is no wonder, then, that the folk are particularly inclined to comment in this area. Their concerns, however, are not only the result of what they

may perceive as recent failures. The US public has always held universal literacy (and, peculiarly enough, good spelling) in very high
regard (and has, for a long time, as well, believed the language in
general to be in serious decline). It is, after all, the United States
which has a "national spelling bee," and there is an oddly immoral
(as well as dysfunctional) taint attached to those who spell poorly.
(Who of us has not heard, at one time or another, that poor spelling is
an "insult" to our readers?) The history of such attitudes (as well as
their current status) is reviewed, although not always with a specific
focus on the relation of such belief to educational practices, in Bailey
1991, Drake 1977, Finegan 1980, and Greenbaum 1985.

It is not accidental that reading, writing, and spelling are joined
in this section; they are, for the folk, all pretty much reflexes of the
same ability. The folk faith that spelling (or a knowledge of the
"sound values" of the "letters") is the key to reading, however, is not
reflected in psycholinguistic work on reading. Linguistically oriented
approaches to reading distinguish between the "sounding out" of
letters (often called "decoding") and reading which results in the in-
take of information, suggesting that overemphasis on the former does
not lead to either initial or eventual success as a reader. The folk are
more optimistic about the efficacy of "spelling" along the general
front of literacy.

The folk suggest that a serious impediment to literacy is the
"crazy" English spelling system, a folk fact so commonly held that it
seems hardly worth documenting here (but we do so anyway):

```
K:  You should not feel that way. Even our- even our OWN=
         [
H:      Oh really.
K: =children, - when they're learning to READ, have that=
         [
H:      Oh really.
              [                                    [
A:             Heheh.                                Heh.

                                          [
W:                                         O(h)h.
                                                  [
H:                                                 Uh huh.
K: =problem, with our language. They have serious=
              [
A:            Yeah.
              [
H:            Oh really.
                                       [
W:                                      Oh.
```

K: =PROblems with understanding, (.hhh) you know there's so=

           [

H: Oh.

K: =many - inconsistencies in our language. That even our=

           [

W: Uh huh.

                         [

H: Uh-

K: =children when we're teaching them to read, they SPEAK- =

                [

?:   (   )

                             [

H: Uh huh.

K: =linguistically they pick up the language very easily because they HEAR it, (.hhh) but you start showing them the=

      [

W: Uh huh.

K: =written word and they go "Oh (.hhh), what is this?" - "What=

                        [

All: ((laugh))

K: =IS this, Chinese," see.

All: ((laugh))

K: ((mock simplification)) "We teach you new language." ((laughs)) But- yes, that's- see that's wha- I'm working with first graders and they're learning to read, and many of them struggle very hard with the inconsistencies of the language to=

                        [

H: Oh.

                      [

W: Uh huh.

K: =be able to understand in written f- - form. - So it's you=

                [

H: O:K, so:-

K: =know, is it- - Yeah. That's fine. (#1)

First, with "You should not feel that way," K tries to reassure H (the fieldworker, a non-native speaker of English, whose first language is Mandarin) that her family's inability to understand him in the section which has just preceded is not at all unusual. (He has said the phrase "blood type" several times, but his listeners could not understand it. One respondent helpfully offers "bra type" as an interpretation, doubtless reflecting the /r/-like pronunciation of the /l/, the [ɑ]-like pronunciation of the [ʌ], and the deleted or weakly articulated /d/ [particularly before /t/], all features predictable from H's native language). It is, however, the nature of K's reassurance which is interesting. She tells the fieldworker that native speakers also have such troubles. Her rationale is, as we suggested above, the inconsistencies of the English spelling system. K goes so far as to suggest that teaching English-speaking children to read is like teaching them another language (and even indulges in a little mock-simplification performance to drive that point home – "We teach you new language"). The children are so surprised by English spelling, K suggests, that they think it might as well be Chinese, a common folk caricature of a "difficult" language. This typical folk view of the inconsistencies of English spelling is perhaps particularly interesting since K is preparing to be an elementary school teacher.

Inconsistent or not, correct spelling in the United States seems to have moral, intellectual, and educational overtones. D's discussion of her feelings about spelling and her hopes for her son's performance in that area is not at all atypical:

> D: But that was an expectation from the time we were in elementary school. We had a spelling test every Friday. The goal was to get one-hundred percent. And (0.2) that was a personal goal=to be able to spell the word. I am a person who likes to write and likes to read so words are important to me, and it may well be that it may just have been important enough to me so that I knew how to spell them. I found it (0.3) oh OK. I find it very disconcerting to date to be reading something that somebody has written and find misspelled words in it, or for people to not know the difference between the two words "principal" "principle." One means one and one means the other=that sort of thing. So for - I realize that is my own personal thing and that is one of the reasons I eased up on B [her elementary school age child, who, in D's opinion, has started spelling tests much too late in his school career] so much, OK, to give him a while to get used to certain things. He has never had spelling tests before, and a lot of people say to me my child is good at math, my child is good at computers=he does not have to be able to spell.
> K: Right.
> D: WRONG. You still have to write papers to demonstrate your knowledge, OK. It is like I told B, if you hand in a paper in a course, I do not care if it is a science project, and the first thing the teacher sees is you can not spell, you are automatically going to lose points on the paper. There is no way around it. If I were marking the paper and there was a misspelling I would begin to deduct points (0.2) psychologically for words or things you misspelled even if the paper is fine. Then what I am probably going to have to do is go back and read your paper again. I will be mad because I had to read it twice to get the content, when if you had spelled the things correctly I could have read the content the first time. So: (0.3) and so we have a mode of expression in this country that does not entail putting words on paper. As far as I am concerned the written words and the proper spelling of words is important. (   ) I was talking to a school psychologist, - an Ann Arbor school psy-

chologist the other day, and she was saying her daughter is like a junior, - a sophomore, junior in high school who does not spell very well. And this is a woman who grew up down the street from me, and I said I (0.3) "well B has to know how to spell," and she said "well my daughter is really good in math," and she is good at this and she is good at that, "so if she was not a speller, she just was not a speller." I tend to agree with the neurologist who said that if a person can read, they can not spell, then they are lazy. Because spelling is rote. Now it is true you can be a math person and have difficulty with the English language. For every rule there are twenty exceptions. So it is real difficult sometimes to learn, but you just accept the fact that it is a necessary part of life, and you go on and you learn it. (#12)

When the fieldworker offers a back-channel (with "right"), D is emphatic in her rejection of those sentiments which suggest that children's deficiencies might be made up for by their abilities in other areas. For her, good work in other areas can be overwhelmed by deficiencies in spelling. Additionally, she believes that the "bad" reaction poor spelling causes may be subtle since she claims that she would "psychologically" deduct points from a paper with such errors.

D further emphasizes the unreasonableness (but insidiousness) of the position that spelling is unimportant by noting that even "a woman who grew up down the street from me" holds it. Since B previously attended a private school (which D was very fond of), but now attends the public school system for which this woman works, D may be expressing her disapproval of educational theories which inform that system, symbolized by her neighbor.

It is also important, we believe, to note that D is African-American and, no doubt, quite reasonably extends her experience of and/or belief in societal racism into language. It is a commonplace among African-Americans, for example, that, although "good" language use by African-Americans will not remove racist attitudes, it will give those who hold them one less excuse for applying them in such areas as employment and education. D's personal linguistic history (already elaborated somewhat in our discussion of AAVE in Chapter 3) would seem to support this interpretation. Whatever the underlying causes, D, like K, believes that English spelling must simply be memorized and that its rules are so full of exceptions that scientific minds, in particular, will find it an odious task, but one, according to D, quite necessary. This mismatch between "science" and "language" is, in fact, a folk concept met in several other places. It is perhaps most directly stated by J (in #11) who notes, quite simply, that "in math you have to be more precise than with words."

The linguistic view is quite different, whether from an older, structuralist approach (based on the quantitative evidence of grapheme-phoneme correspondences, e.g., Hanna and Hanna 1966), in which the degree of "regularity" in English spelling is found to be quite high, or from newer, generative approaches in which the spelling of English words is found to be "optimal": "There is, incidentally, nothing particularly surprising about the fact that conventional orthography is ... a near optimal system for the lexical representation of English words" (Chomsky and Halle 1968:49).

Although surely not related to scientific studies of grapheme-phoneme correspondence (and certainly not to generative notions), a folk faith in sound-letter correspondence lies behind the competing tradition in folk belief, which stresses the utility of relating sounds to spelling by "sounding out" or "phonics." A fieldworker (M) asks parents if they notice any difference in the language development of their two children:

> SR: I did notice one thing though that uh my (1.5) uh I was trying to think which one it was my daughter learned by phonics.
> M: yeah?
> SR: And my son didn't.
> M: Uh huh.
> SR: Uh how to read and pronounce words and I find that she's a better speller and better - can read better than what he did.
>   [
> M: Really?
> M: Uh huh my mom used to argue against that.
> SR: Well I-
> M: No basis whatsoever but she used to complain a lot.
> SR: I think that's one of the best things to learn, in fact they're still using that in school now, cause my granddaughter is learning that right now, and she's sounding out words and learning how to um
> M: How old are they? How old was your daughter when she- I'm trying to think when phonics came in.
>   [
> SR: Well my daughter was um she? started kindergarten when she was still four but she turned five in November, so it=
>   [
> M: Uh huh.
> SR: =was (1.0) so it was that time period, so she's twenty-five now, so it would have been twenty years ago.
> M: I think that's when it got real big as far as when I know
>   [
> SR: Now now see I? I learned how to uh read by phonics.
> M: Oh you did?
> SR: Yeah. When I was in-
>   [[

```
SH:                    I don't know what I did
                   [[
M:                     You must have done that here.
```
SR: Oh yeah. It it's been in the school system for a long: time. Well uh it went out for a long time, but uh I find that you are a BETter speller and a BETter reader if you learn by that as far as I'm concerned. I feel that uh that's the only way to teach.
SH: I don't know what I learned on. I don't really know.
M: Is this phonics one, I'm trying, was it the thing where you actually-
```
     [
SR: You sound out words. (#17)
```

SR, then, not only has faith that words are spelled as they sound but that learning to read on this basis enhances reading skills in general, the process referred to in more recent psycholinguistically oriented approaches to reading instruction (see above) as "decoding," not one which, it is now assumed, is particularly beneficial to the acquisition of rapid reading comprehension skills. For the folk, however, spelling seems to be the key to reading, and, perhaps because it is seen as that "gateway" to literacy, it holds such importance in United States folk linguistics. Only a few respondents are suspicious of an overemphasis on spelling. J, however, (in #11) believes that such pickiness in Catholic schools "stifles creativity," although she admits herself to a "knack" for spelling and, like so many of our other respondents, is annoyed at misspellings.

The beneficial effect of spelling on writing, however, is not so universally admired, perhaps, in part, a recognition of the rote manner in which spelling skills are acquired by many. One mother notes that her daughter is not "exceptional" in language arts and adds the following:

J: K's [her daughter] biggest problem is she doesn't - she can spell perfect on her spelling test,=
```
     [
M:      Uh huh.
```
M: = Uh huh.=
J: =But when she writes it in a sentence she spells it wrong.
M: Hm:. Uh huh.
J: It's using her spelling in her written work she has a problem with. And I think it's because she gets in a hurry. (#41)

It was rare, however, for the folk to comment negatively on the relationship between the "detailed" skill of spelling and any influence it might have on skills such as reading and writing which require greater "fluency." In general, the folk simply perceive spelling as a prerequisite to literacy, and most remember their own "language arts" programs as an admixture of instructional targets:

> M: In elementary school they stress:ed - you know, the spelling? and the grammar:, and the sentence structure:, (and) things like that. I don't remember we did too much composition.=A little bit. By the time we were in seventh and eighth grade, we were encouraged - you know, to be reading a lot of books. (#13)

One respondent, however, remembers earlier instruction in effective writing and is grateful for it.

> H: I was thinking about the other day,=very few people made me think, and I remember them very fondly. Yeah. The teacher I had as a junior in high school who really taught us how to write well. One I had in graduate school who gave me a B+ on a paper because (   ) - he wanted more, and I thought=
>   [   ]
> S: Five minutes R ((child's name)).
> H: ==that's great. Very few people asked that of me.
> K: How did he decide to write well. What did your teacher do to help you write well.
> H: I am not exactly sure what she did,=she (0.2) she just - she had us (0.5) I was trying to think about that the other day. I (0.3) did not feel like I was (0.5) coerced into anything. She just somehow got us to learn good writing habits, listening to each other's work, and (0.2) teaching us how not to overstate things,=to write clearly, concisely, and I got so many comments on that in college, you know people who would try to write, (0.3) what they thought was wonderful papers, and professors would think that they were flowery, and I got lots of comments on how tersely I could say things, and I had learned that from her. I do not know how she did it. (#3)

In general, however, the folk commented very little on general language arts matters or on instruction in such more advanced linguistic matters as composition.[4] When they did, as H notes just above, they did not seem to remember what specific instructional devices were used. H (in #5), however, notes that students learned to write well since they were directed to read and use as models well-written "classics."

4.2.2 *Grammar and standard language*

4.2.2.1 Explicit instruction. Although the folk may feel that schools are one of the last lines of defense against deteriorating language standards, we have already seen in our survey of folk belief about first language acquisition that children who come to school without a standard variety as a result of their early learning experiences may already be "lost." Additionally, even those who prize standard varieties seem to believe that explicit grammar instruction does little or no good. H (in #5) is a typical example of a respondent in whom these several tendencies may be seen. On the one hand, he believes that language "structure changes to adapt to the common usage" and that "if it's used enough, it becomes correct," a view which might be applauded by linguistically-oriented students of usage. On the other, however, he notes that a sentence he heard at a nearby swimming pool ('We ain't got no more towels') is "really terrible." Of explicit grammar instruction in school, he reports that he "cheated" his way through it and learned nothing. D (#12), who, as we have seen above, is very much concerned with her son's acquisition, use, and maintenance of the standard (including even correct spelling) shares this view of the uselessness of overt grammar instruction:

> D: I could remember thinking this is torture ((diagramming sentences)). I do not have to like this kind of stuff, but they should have been tarred and feathered and driven out of town because it really was not any good reason to do it that they had us do it. (#12)

In spite of these unfond memories, there is a reluctance to approve of "modern" approaches to language arts, which appear to do away with grammar instruction altogether:

> S: ( ) Which one? I di- I don't know. We haven't learned grammar in like- three years, we've just been studying books.=
>   [
> G: Uh huh.
> S: =Two years now. - That's- that's-
>   [[
> D: ((laughs))   Maybe they ought to go back to grammar.
>   [
> H: ((laughs))
> S: Yeah we have the- we have the occasional grammar in=
>   [
> All: ((laugh))
> S: =English but once hi- once you hi:t the ninth grade, I'm in tenth, so, yeah, for th- for the last - year and a half now, (.hhh)=
>   [

```
W:                                              (    )

S: =we haven't been studying grammar at all, we've- just been s-
(.hhh) learning literary-
                        [
D:                      It's a weakness of the Ann Arbor School System,=
                                                        [
S:                                                      Yeah:
D: =traditionally they - have done it that way. Because what=
                                                    [
S:                                                 Yeah, what they do=
D: =you have is most people going on to college.
S: =is- they assume that after seven years of having grammar
pumped into you, you know it well enough, and you've got it all -
memorized, and you don't need it, and if you just- it'll just come
naturally to you. (.hhh) And so they concentrate on learning litera-
ture, (.hhh) you know, s- r-reading and studying like - u- famous lit-
erary works. - And stuff like that, (.hhh) so=
                    [
H:                  Uh huh.
S: =you tend to forget it ((laughs)). (#23)
```

D's son (S) believes you "tend to forget" all your earlier grammar instruction, but D is concerned that the failure to teach it is a
"weakness" of the local system. His explanation of that weakness
appears to bear on the fact that some children come to school with a
standard grammar already placed there by their home environment
while others show up in need. D notes that in Ann Arbor "what you
have is most people going on to college." At first this might seem to
justify only the emphasis on "literary" topics (presumably most useful for the college bound), but we believe D's rationale is a bit more
subtle. An ignoring of grammar would be fine if only those college-
bound students were involved, for, presumably, they have the standard provided from their home and neighborhood experiences. D, we
believe, expresses concern for those students who require grammar
instruction in the schools, that is, for those whose pre-school experiences have not equipped them with a knowledge of "good grammar."
This concern, of course, brings us back to a reconsideration of prescription and language standards, this time with a focus on the role of
education.

4.2.2.2 Upholding the standard. As we have seen in a number of
places in our discussion of first language socialization above, although the schools may have no effective program to teach standard
English to those who come to them without it, the schools are expected to carry out their work in that variety. Some respondents,

however, report that the schools do provide explicit instruction in "formal" English:

A: Yeah, we learn formal English in school, and then when=
                                    [
H: In school.
A: =we home, (.hhh) yeah. We ge- we get home sometimes we don't use it - exactly. (#36a)

H, the fieldworker, is interested in knowing what a student might learn at school and use differently at home. G, A's father, a European-American teacher in an African-American school, responds as follows:

G: A- an example would be. The easiest one are the verbs, the action words, (.hhh) to- to say som- such as uh - uh "Dad has=
                                                              [
H: Uh huh.
G: =gone to work." - Instead of say- instead of saying "Dad has=
                 [
H: "Dad has gone."
G: =gone," you'd say "Dad has went to work." You don't say=
                                                          [
K: "Went."
G: ="went" with the word "has," you say "gone." (.hhh) Because "went" is past, and "gone" is a past tense, but it's a past=
        [
H: Uh huh.
G: =participle if they use "has," "have," or "had" or (.hhh) present - participle or whatever. (.hhh) But its the idea that it's used with a special helping verb, and it has a special verb - that you use. (.hhh) It's a irregular verb. (.hhh) (#36a)

G gives no indication, however, how he might (or how he understands other teachers might) "instill" this usage in those who do not come to school with it already in place. We have seen above that G is concerned that students who learn "correct" forms at school do not go back to their home or street environments and appear "uppity." Perhaps he has little actual fear of this, for he appears to believe that the standard or formal variety which is taught is principally for written English:

G: Well, see, what you do is, you=
                          [
K: Right.

> G: =go to school, yeah. You go to school, and you learn what's
> called proper English. (.hhh) And this is your writt(h)en English.
> And it's also what's considered proper. But once you take that=
>   [
> H: Uh huh.
> G: =back home, everybody's home is a little different. (#36a)

We shall see, however, that G is adamant about the use of "standard"
English as a model for schools, particularly when faced with the option of AAVE.

Some of our respondents, however, are more concerned about the
emotional effect of demanding unrealistic or untaught standards:

> D: I am furious with those teachers who say "Don't use 'aint.'" I am
> furious with them.=I think it's cruel to children. It's like saying
> (   ) There's enough that kids get and (   ) (not allow them to
> use in school). And then you tell kids that their basic speech is bad.
> You know, and you don't even give them a reasonable substitu:te,
> for most of the time. (#19)

D (and her husband B) go on to have a discussion about why teachers (and schools in general) demand standard language:

> B: If you said to one of those teachers D, "Why:". "Why is it not OK
> for these children to use the word 'aint.'"
> D: Because we have a responsibility of teaching them how to use
> the standard English so that they can get GOOD JOBS.
> Z: I see.
> B: You see, that's a bunch of bull. Because you don't have to use
> the (finest) (   ) English to get a good job.
> D: I know.
> B: That's not reality. It's - it's a lie.
> D: But the teachers beLIEVE IT.
> Z: That is a lie.
> D: Yes.=No, they believe it's true. They don't believe that is a lie. I
> mean the teachers believe what they say it's is true. Teachers be-
> lieve that if the children use the word "ain't" (0.2) that they won't get
> a good job.=And of course, (0.1) it's crazy anyway because a lot of
> the kids aren't saying "ain't."
> Z: You see, if the teachers would teach the kids to say "ain't" an:d, I
> think that they would be bad- badly respected.=
> D: =Exactly.=
> Z: =Toward parents.
> D: Oh yeah. The parents would be furious. "You are letting my child
> say 'ain't' in school?"
> B: The reason why- the very reason then is why they teach- why
> they don't say "ain't" is so, that then parents don't criticize them.
> D: Right.

B: And complain to the school. That's the reason. That's the true answer. That's the honest answer.

Z: Maybe parents? And maybe a little society,

D: Well, that's what society is, that the part of a society that directly hits teachers is parents. (#19)

D and B apparently believe that the school's (teachers') insistence on standard English is a direct reflection of conservative societal (parents') values. They also believe, as we have already seen in G's remarks on class and language education, that standard English is no requirement for a good job, but, unlike G, they apparently believe that it need not play such a central role in the schools.

In general, linguists recognize the following positions on the teaching of standard English and the treatment of nonstandard varieties:

> 1. the *eradicationist* or *replacive* position attempts to wipe out students' nonstandard varieties and provide them with a standard one (presumably for all situations);
> 2. the *additive* or *bidialectal* approach recognizes the societal need for and linguistic fullness of nonstandards and seeks to provide nonstandard speaking students with an alternative variety for those situations in which it is appropriate;
> 3. the *dialect rights* position recognizes the linguistic fullness and social needs, as in (2) above, but contends that the decision to acquire alternative varieties should be left up to individuals (Wolfram 1991: 213-14.)

B and D appear to come pretty close to the "dialect rights" position, but they are alone among our respondents in taking this point of view. The majority opinion of our respondents, however, does not appear to be represented in these three alternatives. Most of our respondents seem to hold to a modified (or even grudging) bidialectal approach, one which recognizes the social need for nonstandards but one which does not extend to them any linguistic status. In spite of his recognition of the need for nonstandards outside of school, G is quite explicit about what is "correct":

G: And so somebody got it in their head that what was actually SPOken should be the correct English. (.hhh) And then through the idea of saying well it's racist not to teach it and started pushing it, (.hhh) they tried to push that as an (deliberately) actual correct way to speak. ((pause)) And thank God for most of us it died. It didn't work. Because it IS improper to say. The=
                                                [
H: Yes.

G: =children themselves - all of us at time may say the improper endings. We may say it. (.hhh) But we recognize it is somebody says to us "Is it correct," you say "No," you know, "This is the correct way (to) speak." (.hhh) But- to sit and TEACH it incorrectly I don't think is right. Cause you DO say "I have gone," You do not say "I have went." (#1)

There is perhaps no better expression of what in Chapter 1 we referred to as the "abstract" or "platonic" folk belief in the standard than this. G appears to believe that all speakers of English somehow recognize the "incorrectness" of nonstandards. Although he is specifically referring to AAVE here (which we shall investigate in the educational setting in more detail in the next section), it is clear that he does not believe that it is the only source of "incorrectness," since he explicitly states that "all of us at time may say the improper endings." Apparently, all one need do is confront any speaker with a request for the standard or nonstandard character of a construction and that speaker will intuitively ('innately'?) know the difference between "correct" and "improper" forms.

G's position, then, and we believe it is a majority position among the folk, is a modified "bidialectal" position. On the one hand, he believes that a standard variety (perhaps principally for writing, as shown above) should be taught in the schools, and, unlike the "dialect rights" position, he nowhere suggests that this might be an option for students or a matter of discussion in the larger school community. On the other hand, he obviously does not believe that the utilitarian, nonstandard varieties of the speech community itself deserve linguistic respect. They are "incorrect" and "improper," and, interestingly, everybody knows it.

This should not be a surprising state of affairs. As we have shown in Chapter 1, there is a double consciousness regarding language in the US. There is a great deal of linguistic insecurity which defers to a historical (perhaps eventually British-based) standard, felt by some to be even a "hyperstandard," good only for writing and fancy occasions. In its proper (educational) environment, this variety is OK; outside it, it is "uppity" or "condescending." It is, however, the historically, abstractly "correct" form of the language. Nonstandards are the democratic side of this coin. They represent family and community solidarity, but, as US national linguistic insecurity would have it, they are just plain "wrong."

4.2.3 AAVE (African-American vernacular English) in language education

Although we have used them to display a more general attitude, G's comments cited just above are specifically connected to what he characterizes as a proposal to "teach" AAVE in the public schools. G observes that this proposal, in his opinion, failed: "Thank God for most of us it died." Many of our respondents may be more sensitive to the AAVE and public education issue since Ann Arbor was the site of the famous "Black English" trial, in which a suit was brought against the Ann Arbor Michigan School Board on behalf of African-American children at the Martin Luther King Junior Elementary School. Briefly, the upshot of that trial was that Judge Charles W. Joiner of the federal court which heard the case decided in favor of the plaintiffs. He noted that it was "not rational" for the Ann Arbor School Board to fail to provide teachers with the training and information necessary for them to understand that AAVE was the "home and community language of many black [sic] students" and that knowledge of the existence and structure of that language should play a role in the education (particularly as regards reading standard English) of these children (Martin Luther King Junior Elementary School Children et al. v. Ann Arbor School District Board, 473 F. Supp. at 1385 [1979], quoted in Bailey 1983).

Chambers (1983) points out that the misunderstandings of this case brought on by the media were considerable. They " ... gave the impression that the judge had ordered that children be taught in Black English" (xi). We would maintain, however, that the folk impression of the plans to use information about AAVE in public school settings was based on the understanding that AAVE was to be *taught* in public schools. G claims he was specifically instructed to do so:

G: And this idea of BLACK English, - which was- to us was=
          [   ]
H: You mean like - "ain't"?
G: =improper English. It- I went through a period for a while in=
          [
H: Uh huh.
G: =school where they came around and told us that (.hhh) it was up to us=cause I teach Black students. That we were supposed to be teaching what was called quote Black English.
H: Quote Black English.
     [
G: An:d - w- we were lucky that in the city of I-----, the uh - most of the parents, did not want their children taught quote Black English, because they knew they had to compete in society with

what was called quote regular English. (.hhh) And so it died very quickly. But that wasn't true in Detroit and a few of the other cities, they- they want the idea (#1)

Even B, a psychologist who paid considerable attention to the Ann Arbor case, at first slips when he characterizes the event for a non-native fieldworker:

B: There is- there is a very publicized case in Ann Arbor.=About-for the Black English case-,=whether or not the Ann Arbor Public Schools teach- (0.4) should, recognize Black English as a legiti-mate form of English. (#8)

It is not surprising that public opinion was confused. Starks (1983) notes that the media presented interpretations of the Ann Arbor deci-sion which " ... ranged from expecting Black English to be taught in school, to forcing the use of a dual language system, to teaching teachers to speak Black English" (99). Many African-American me-dia pundits joined in their damnation of the decision, some seeing it as a further indication of racist attitudes towards African-American children:

What black children need is an end to this malarkey that tells them they can fail to learn grammar, fail to develop vocabularies, ignore syntax and embrace the mumbo-jumbo of ignorance – and dismiss it in the name of "black pride." (Rowan 1979:36)

Our European-American respondents also believe that even accep-tance of AAVE in the schools is an abrogation of responsibility:

D: It's just like when they came up with that business about Black English that time in the Ann Arbor schools, and that these kids should be allowed to (0.2) You were young but one time they had this thing going on with Black English, and these children should not be condemned for using what is foul - language to the rest of the world. I mean (0.1) again that's unfair to this CHILD because you condemn them to a second class life because of their lan-guage. (#59)

As we shall see below, D is consistent in this belief and extends it to bilingual education. Her characterization of AAVE as "foul-language" reflects, perhaps, the misunderstanding that AAVE is principally a lexical matter.

    One might have thought that a younger generation would have been exposed to a more "linguistically oriented" view of the role of

AAVE in the schools, but T, an undergraduate who, as she says, has
" ... been learning in school about the Black English," has the same
folk understanding as G, an experienced teacher.

> T: When they're around each other and they can- do speak that
> way, they fall into that pattern. Uh C's old roommate? her friends
> that were in music school, and one was from Jamaica, a- and this
> other girl's from down South, and they spoke perfect English, but
> when they were around their Black friends, you couldn't even un-
> derstand them. So, yeah, that's more like a cultural- and don't mind
> that, but I think to teach Black English in a school isn't right be-
> cause it's the structure, it's not the English language anymore. (#9)

Apparently, even recent (i.e., late 1980's) education classes have not
been able to define what most linguists and educators have in mind
for the role of AAVE in the schools. At least one respondent was
enthusiastic about the results of the Ann Arbor decision, and she
provides a detailed commentary about the relationship of the problem to class as well as ethnicity. This is, by the way, the same European-American respondent cited in Chapter 2 who has an Oklahoma
upbringing and used to use her "Okie" speech to annoy her Baltimore relatives.

> C: Tell me about it. It was Ann Arbor that started the whole thing.
> M: Yes I know. Could you give me a little narrative of that?
> C: Oh sure. Green Road. The kids from Green Road, some of the
> kids who lived in subsidized housing over on the northwest side
> were going to a school that was plunk in the middle of a very uh
> (2.5) Not the richest neighborhood in Ann Arbor. But one of the
> better off neighborhoods in Ann Arbor.
> M: Uh huh.
> C: An:d again. I think the people involved confused social class
> snobbishness with racial snobbishness, although I suspect those
> are inextricably intertwined in many cases.
> M: Uh huh.
> C: Um and their kids were being told how stupid they were for us-
> ing a dialect, the Black dialect.
> M: Uh huh, their kids were being told by=
> C: =white teachers.
> M: Educators.
> C: Yeah. Right. Because (0.5) what you had was two social
> classes.
> M: Uh huh.
> C: Which happened also to split along racial lines.
> M: Right.
> C: Okay?
> M: OK. Uh huh.

C: Um. (0.5) And the- I suspect it was the social attitudes of the
teachers that caused them to denigrate the behavior and=
      [[
M: Uh huh.   Uh huh.
C: =speech patterns of the lower? class kids. But because it
couldn't, it's totally imbedded in racial distinctions as well and racial
consciousness was very high.
M: Uh huh.
C: The Black parents took the defensive and said, "Hey you can't
do this to our kids."
M: Uh huh.
C: And that was the point at which everybody suddenly discovered
that Black English actually is a very structured dialect of its own.
That it has grammatical patterns.
M: Uh huh.
C: That is has- that they weren't just speaking (bad). It has a his-
tory? and it has a grammar and a structure that most white=
                                                    [
M: Uh huh.
C: =PEOple had never understood that you had to learn a gram-
mar in order to speak Black English. They were just=
                                             [
M: Uh huh.
C: =misusing English. They had learned a whole different gram-
matical structure, and I think what that case did was=
                   [[
M: Uh huh.   Uh huh.
C: =enlighten a lot people about English dialects, who had always
believed that Americans spoke ENGlish, period. OK?=
                                                [
M: Uh huh.
C: =And um and I that's what that case did. I mean it was a social
economic fight. But the point that was being fastened upon was a
grammatical one. Um and it was a very=
                  [
M: Uh huh.
C: =enlightening one to ninety-nine percent of the people of the
world. You see? A linguistic one. And it was part of the you know
Black you know respect Blacks for who they are and what they are,
you know? Quit running them down just because=
               [
M: Uh huh.
C: =they're Black. Um again I say it was a social thing that got=
                   [
M: Uh huh.
pinned on racial stuff, um because I don't think anybody would
have realized if- if all the poor Black kids had been little white
cracker kids from Alabama. You can just establish I don't think=
                                      [
M: Uh huh.

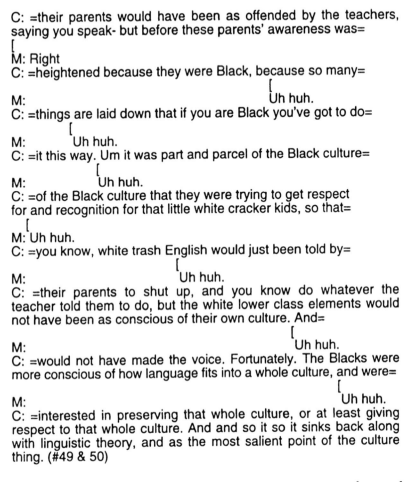

C: =their parents would have been as offended by the teachers, saying you speak- but before these parents' awareness was=
[
M: Right
C: =heightened because they were Black, because so many=
                                                    [
M: Uh huh.
C: =things are laid down that if you are Black you've got to do=
          [
M: Uh huh.
C: =it this way. Um it was part and parcel of the Black culture=
                [
M: Uh huh.
C: =of the Black culture that they were trying to get respect for and recognition for that little white cracker kids, so that=
  [
M: Uh huh.
C: =you know, white trash English would just been told by=
                                            [
M: Uh huh.
C: =their parents to shut up, and you know do whatever the teacher told them to do, but the white lower class elements would not have been as conscious of their own culture. And=
                                                        [
M: Uh huh.
C: =would not have made the voice. Fortunately. The Blacks were more conscious of how language fits into a whole culture, and were=
                                                      [
M: Uh huh.
C: =interested in preserving that whole culture, or at least giving respect to that whole culture. And and so it so it sinks back along with linguistic theory, and as the most salient point of the culture thing. (#49 & 50)

C's theory is that African-American parents, aware and proud of their own cultural (and even linguistic) heritage protested the treatment of their children. By doing so, she believes they have provided a service to all nonstandard speakers by making the general population more aware of the structured nature of all dialects. She interestingly speculates that this would not have come about if there had not been the racial quality to the difficulty. Poor white children's parents, she contends, would have simply told their children to do whatever the schools demanded and, presumably, suffered the school's denigration of their language and cultural heritage. Although C is not a linguist and has had no formal linguistic training, she surely represents the informed sort of public linguists might hope for, but, perhaps surprisingly, she is also a believer that nonstandards have no place in public education:

M: So what is your opinion about (0.5) how should Black (0.5) English be used in school
C: Black English has NO place in the schools.
M: OK. But it does have- but it has you said-
C: Just like white cracker dialect has no place.
M: But where does it have a place then.
C: Hey at home. Just like the Jewish kids learned a lot of Yiddish at home, but it is not appropriate for the teacher to=
    [
     Uh huh.
C: =teach in Yiddish at school. Just like it's perfectly OK for=
                      [
M: Uh huh.
C: =me to use all kinds of Oklahoma Okie slang when I'm=
                                       [
M: Uh huh.
C: =around my Okie friends. But it has no place in a formal=
                      [
M: Uh huh.
C: =setting. (1.0) Black English has no place in schools. (#49 & 50)

Although she grasps the linguistic complexity of other varieties, C does not believe that they might be used as transitional or "helping" devices in achieving whatever language arts goals the schools have. In short, she obviously believes in a doctrine of "appropriateness," but she does not extend that belief to the use of those nonstandards for any purpose in the schools themselves. Hers, then, is even another position, distinct from the three that linguists have described and from G's. For her, bidialectalism is the goal, and, unlike G, it includes respect for the fullness of the grammatical systems of nonstandards, but those nonstandards play no role whatsoever in the school curriculum. For her, obviously, the victory of the Ann Arbor decision was one related to information about nonstandard varieties and attitudes towards them (and their speakers) but not one which suggested an educational utility for them. Apparently C, and those who share her opinion, believe that children will sort out which varieties belong where and that the schools' only business is to provide them with the standard.

Perhaps in this case it is not as appropriate to compare the folk opinion to that of linguists as it might be to compare it to that of educationists. Many of them, although they are sympathetic to the fact that racism has brought the situation about, are extremely negative about the symbolism African American behavior of any sort brings to the educational setting. Ogbu (1988) believes that there is a "counterculture" which is created by means of clothing, language, and other modes of behavior which both set minority students apart from others and challenge the school's authority. Stanlaw and Peshkin (1988) also identify AAVE as a symbol of minority students' separatism. On the other hand, Cummins (1990) says that a failure to incorporate community standards of behavior (perhaps predominantly those of language) into the school setting directly results in minority students' failures.

Without appeal to professional educators' opinions, however, folk attitudes to AAVE in general (3.1.1) predict folk attitudes towards AAVE in the public schools and, by extension, attitudes towards any nonstandards in the schools. What we have found, however, is that the list of positions on the uses of nonstandards in the schools as outlined by linguists does not reflect some of the strongest opinions held by the folk. That, we believe, is the result of doing applied linguistics without talking to those on whom it is to be applied. Folk linguistics is one sure corrective to that omission.

4.2.4 Bilingual education

In 4.3 below we shall see that many of our respondents have negative attitudes towards bi- and multilingualism in the US, although there is a grudging respect for those who learn other languages. Here we concern ourselves briefly with the specific question of bilingual education.[5] For most of our respondents, the position concerning other languages in the schools is the same as their attitude towards nonstandards:

> D: Y- You jus- I just can't believe that anybody - when they start on this business. - I mean when foreign people come to the country, I think that when the foreign kid from - Japan arrives, I think we should have a time, and someone to help him adjust, but I think the ultimate goal should be for that kid to ((very slowly and deliberately) learn English, if he's going to stay here.
> N: Uh huh.
> D: It's just - the same thing like all these people coming from Mexico and this kind of stuff? I- I just think that the ultimate goal should be for them - for these children - to have to learn to speak English.
> --
> D: ... when you listen to the stuff about all the stuff that we should have for - bilingual students and should we really be making the poor Mexicans out in wherever it is learn English and - YES if they're going to be part of this country.
> N: Uh-huh.
> D: I think you're just creating another subculture.
> N: Yeah.

D: =That is always going to be a down-trodden subculture. To me if
you take this little Mexican kid who's come over with his family and
- you structure it so that he really doesn't have to learn English, you
forever condemn that child to a second-class living. I think you take
something away from him. You=
                    [
N: Uh huh.
D: =OWE that kid - something, and what- part of what you owe him
is forcing him to learn, and become assimilated into the=
                              [
N: Uh huh.
D: =English world.
N: He's not going to get a job at IBM and- (   )
                                          [
D: No he isn't. You for-
ever condemn that kid to a second-class life if you structure his
education, so that he can get by without speaking good English.
(#59)

What many folk believe about legal decisions concerning bilingual
education and the appropriateness of such programs in public schools
is pretty well summarized in the following:

J: If you're going to be in the United States you got to teach- you
got to speak English.
S: Uh huh.
J: You know and there's a lot of flack about teaching Spanish in the
uh in the schools in in uh California and in Texas and they had to-
they had to go to the Supreme Court? And the Supreme Court said
they have to be taught in their own language.
S: Uh huh.
   [
J: Well you know but then if that person wants to - uh really go
places in the United States you've got to have a good hand- handle
on English. You've got to be able to be able to speak=
                              [
S: Uh huh.
J: =English because uh - if you just want to speak Spanish in your
own little uh area, i- in your community, fine. Teach=
              [
S: Uh huh.
J: =them in Spanish then- but then (.hhh) they c- it's very difficult
for them to move out of that into the main stream [not pronounced
as a compound] (.hhh) So they should be taught English and- but
not take their Spanish away from their culture and everything by
(.hhh) uh switching them completely to English. (#15)

It is worth noting that this "milder" folk opinion concerning home
culture comes from a respondent with a Canadian background. In

fact, bilingual education was a very infrequent topic in these conversations, and D (in # 59) was certainly the most outspoken commenter. Related topics will be touched on in 4.3 below.

What we find in general, then, in relation to language education are (1) a general folk belief in the importance of spelling (based on sound correspondence) as an indispensable aid to progress in literacy in general, and, perhaps not unrelated (2) a not very surprising extension of folk concerns for correctness, placing on schools the principal responsibility for preparing students in the use of "formal" and "correct" language and carrying with that responsibility a denial of any role for nonstandards whatsoever.

4.3 Second language acquisition

We begin with the more linguistically oriented features of second language acquisition and move to socially related concerns for both acquisition and use.

4.3.1 Structure

In our work so far, we have found no better illustration of the need for empirical data from folk linguistics than what must surely be for many the surprising level of concern the folk have for linguistic structure in language learning. Linguists and language teachers who intuit what folk linguistic concerns might be would probably rate this item very low,[6] but it was frequently mentioned by our respondents, and they covered a variety of linguistic levels. We begin by citing the phonological:

4.3.1.1 Phonology

> M: I thought German was supposed to be one of the harder languages to learn. I don't know if it's because they gurgle when they talk or (   ) you know. Yeah that's got to be hard it's like you're trying to clear your throat - while you're=
>   [
>   ((laughs))
> M: =speaking. I mean that would really be hard for me.
> N: Yeah well if you
>   [
> T: ((laughs)) (   )

> [
> M: Huh?
> T: I said you do it all the time.
> M: ((talks while clearing throat)). Let me clear all this phlegm out of
> my throat. (#9)

French nasals and French "flat" intonation are also singled out as particularly difficult phonological phenomena (A #36).

The folk confusion of sounds and spelling is as much a part of second- as it is of first-language education.

> G: ((Talking about English)) And the pronunciations differ from
> word to word.
> [
> ?:Ah
> H: Yeah yes yes. And-
>   [
> G: Spanish is so much easier because the
> pronunciation's very (.hhh) very uh much uniform throughout.=
>   [
> H: Oh really?
> G: =It's the same in- i- if you learn a few simple rules of pronuncia-
> tion, you can read almost anything. (#7)

SLA researchers have only rather recently returned to more careful work in phonology, and it is interesting to note that two of the features mentioned in the above quotations (velar or other back fricatives and nonassimilated vowel nasality) figure prominently in both current and older research programs. First, since English lacks both of these features (assuming that we should not classify English [h] as a fricative), approaches to second language phonology which emphasize difficulties which arise as a result of the contrast between the learner's native system (L1) and the target language (L2) might be noted as the theoretical parallels to these folk comments. That is, the folk "notice" L2 areas of contrast. The research focus on the difference in systems was earliest put forth as a "contrastive analysis hypothesis," one which suggested that a ranking of the degree of difference would predict the errors which language learners from a particular L1 would make in the acquisition of a specific L2. The following is representative of the strongest version of this hypothesis:

> We assume that the student who comes in contact with a foreign language
> will find some features of it quite easy and others extremely difficult.
> Those elements that are similar to his native language will be easy for him
> and those elements that are different will be difficult. (Lado 1957:2)

Such an apparently common-sense approach seems a likely candidate to emerge in folk comment. One of our respondents makes the specific claim that related languages are easier to learn (T #9).

On the other hand, this hypothesis was found to fail in its predictive ability. Errors occurred when they were not supposed to (where the two languages were similar) and did not occur when they were supposed to (where the two languages were dissimilar). Attempts to repair the hypothesis from a theoretical perspective focused on the possible influence of linguistic universals.[7] That is, learners might not be exclusively under the influence of patterns and habits which might be "transferred" from L1; they might also have access to one form or another of universal categories of linguistic "markedness" or "naturalness." Although the search for universals in language has taken several forms, we must be satisfied here by noting the empirical tradition (e.g., Greenberg 1966) and the rationalist (e.g., Cook 1988:53-4). Although the distinction between the two research traditions is important to linguists, for the folk, the upshot of both will be the same. Some linguistic forms are more difficult, more unusual, more "marked" than others. Such forms occur less frequently in the languages of the world, are late developments in first language acquisition, and, according to some researchers (e.g., Eckman 1987), help account for otherwise unexplainable difficulty (and ease) in particular SLA situations which are not covered by the "plain" version of the contrastive analysis hypothesis.

All such universalist claims suggest (either overtly or implicitly) that second language learners have some sort of (obviously tacit) access to linguistic universals.[8] If, for example, an area of L2 turns out to be less difficult than one might have thought (since it is different from L1), it may be that it is an "unmarked" (simpler, more natural) construction on some sort of universal scale. Perhaps, then, our folk linguists above are not (or not only) referring to the fact that English lacks velar fricatives and nonassimilated nasal vowels; perhaps they are accessing the universal information that these are relatively marked features in human language in general.

It is difficult to see how one might tease this theoretical distinction out in a folk setting. Perhaps in overt folk reckoning, sounds which are not a part of their L1 are simply "strange," and contrastive and universalist approaches to phonology collapse. There is evidence from learners' performance, however, (as well as in overt comment) that they consider the language learning task to be one which will require them to learn "maximally different" (or "strange") items (in contrast to the forms of the language they already know). This belief is so powerful, apparently, that learners actually avoid some forms which are similar in the native and target languages, apparently from the disbelief that the two systems could share such items (e.g., Jordans 1977).

4.3.1.2 Morphology. According to the same respondent who observed that Spanish pronunciation is easy due to its "uniformity," Spanish verbal morphology is simpler than English as well:

> G: The verb forms are standard throughout, and - English is not
> standard, the verb forms aren't standard, like "would," where=
>   [
> H: Yeah, uh huh.
> G: =does THAT come from, (#7)

One possible interpretation of this surprising folk notion is that G's study of Spanish has given her an analytic knowledge of the language (which she perhaps does not have for English), and she may equate her overt knowledge of facts about Spanish with regularity in the language itself. In fact, of course, Spanish verbal morphology is considerably more complex than English, both from the point of view of the range or variety of its regular forms (i. e., what G calls "standard," presumably the ordinary conjugations of the *-ir*, *-er*, and *-ar* verbs) and its considerable number of partially or completely irregular forms.

On the other hand, without better information about G's ability level in Spanish, we cannot reject another interpretation. Perhaps G knows only the regular forms of Spanish and, like both first and second language learners, extends ('analogizes') the regular patterns everywhere.[9] It is very likely that limited fluency in a language can lead to the belief that it is peculiarly regular or even limited in its resources, no doubt one of the sources of such belief about so-called "primitive" languages. One of the authors once had an interesting discussion with a native speaker of Spanish (of surprisingly advanced English-speaking ability) who noted that Spanish was a highly sophisticated and diversified language since it contained so many synonyms and that English was, from her point of view, incredibly restricted. She cited the example of English "big," the only word available in English to indicate greater size.

4.3.1.3 Syntax. Higher levels of structure are also dealt with, and, in that territory too, some respondents clearly have well-developed notions of contrastive analysis:

D: I've studied uh French, and I know (.hhh) and I know that the STRUCture sentence structure changes (.hhh) uh between languages, and that's one of the, that's one of the things that translators have (.hhh) have to do is you know - (to make-) uh: to underst- to take the structure and underst- and understand exactly what's being said and then put it in the (.hhh) uh in the in the context of the language. And this- people that (.hhh) uh that that take uh - uh - uh take a- another language, they realize that this - this is typically what happens. Whi- uh "s'il=

                    [

C: Uh huh.

D: = vous plait," "if you please." We don't go around saying, (.hhh) oh uh "pa- pass the potatoes, if you please." (We don't=

                              [

C: Uh huh.

D: =do that,   ). We say "pass the potatoes, please." (.hhh) So=

                                     [

C: ((laughs))

D: = - this, you know bu- w- when we go from from English to Chinese, I'd probably try and bring my English structure to your Chinese language and then it will not work. ((laughs)) And that's what you do when you come to English, you try and=

                    [

C: ((laughs))

D: =bring your good Chinese to our good English language and - you'd have a lot of - bumping heads. (#32)

4.3.1.4 Idiom and communicative competence. Although D begins this observation by talking about "structure," his example clearly covers idiom and conventional expressions as well. This leads us to observe that the folk see contrastive structure at even higher levels, those of pragmatics and communicative competence, areas which have attracted considerable recent attention in the SLA literature (e.g., Kasper and Blum-Kulka 1993). For example, the following folk account characterizes the "come and see me sometime" leave-taking of American English which caused a Chinese student to get a cool reception when she actually followed up on it:

A: It's the way you say good-bye.
H: It's a way (of) say good-bye?
A: Yeah, sometimes what is necessarily SAID, is not - what is actually meant. (#36a)

That "what is said" is not "what is meant" clearly indicates a folk awareness of indirectness or "speaker meaning" as opposed to "sentence meaning" (Levinson 1983:17) and, apparently, an awareness that those indirectnesses differ from language to language.

4.3.1.5 Degree of difficulty. Another more linguistically oriented topic mentioned is the degree of difficulty of various languages. One respondent (D #23) reports that he has been told that German is easier to learn than French because it is more "systematic." A respondent who went to college hoping for a career in translation ranks Spanish – French – Latin as increasingly difficult [D #46], but another finds French easier than Spanish [A #36a]). One respondent claims that English is by far the most difficult since it is a result of a "mish-mash" of languages and seems to have only exceptions rather than rules. In fact, that same respondent notes that English is so illogically spelled that engineers, who have logical minds in her opinion, are among the worst spellers of it (K #22).

Linguists and SLA researchers have not recently dealt with overall degree of difficulty, perhaps, in part, as a result of the deterioration of the strong version of the contrastive analysis hypothesis outlined above. Empirical work on progress in a variety of second languages has been done, however, and Cleveland, Mangone, and Adams (1960) shows no difference in the amount of time required to achieve minimal fluency (i.e., sufficient for routine travel needs) in the Romance and Germanic languages. (Slavic and Finno-Ugric languages required greater time to achieve similar proficiency, and other non-Indo European varieties [e.g., Arabic, Korean, Thai, Chinese] required even more.) In spite of this finding, any person familiar with United States university undergraduate folk belief can testify to the fact that the notion that Spanish is "easier" than German is widespread.

4.3.1.6 Comprehension. Comprehension is rarely singled out as a difficult factor, but some respondents note that language varieties (i.e., dialects) in the second language may cause problems (e.g., H and S #3, A #36b). Eisenstein and Berkowitz (1981) and Eisenstein and Verdi (1985) have studied the degree to which learners of English as a second language can understand various social dialects of spoken American English. Their results show that middle-class learners found the standard more intelligible but that working class learners found nonstandard and standard varieties equally intelligible, with the exception of AAVE, which learners from both social status backgrounds found difficult. Oddly enough, SLA researchers do not appear to have paid attention to the degree to which regional varieties of a language are more or less intelligible to a learner, although that is precisely the focus of the folk comments we encountered. There are several studies of the intelligibility of non-native speaker varieties (e.g., Berkowitz 1979) and a large number of studies of attitudes towards non-native accents (summarized in Eisenstein 1983), but these were not the focus of the folk commentary we recorded.

Rapid or allegro speech was also cited as a bar to comprehension, and, at least in one interview, is caricatured by the rapid repetition of nonsense syllables (e.g., M #9). In a survey of studies which check the degree to which modified input by the native speaker enhances non-native speaker comprehension, Parker and Chaudron (1987) show that in four studies in which rate of speech was slowed, comprehension was enhanced for the non-native speaker, although it should be noted that various other simplification strategies accompanied all of these studies in which rate change was a factor.

4.3.2 Other conditions for learning and use

After linguistic structure in general, the second most-often mentioned condition influencing second languages is frequency of use:

> T: It's just like anything else. You use it or lose it. Um at the time there was not anybody that I could talk to on a regular basis. Okay. (#6)

> SH: Yeah see if you don't use those languages, especially a tough language? you will lose it. I don't care what anybody says, your brain will just not hold a whole different language if you do not USE it all the time. (#17)

There is little doubt in the professional literature that limited use leads to attrition (e.g., Lambert and Freed 1982).

This second concern is probably related to a third: that natural (or natural-like) situations promote language learning and retention, and this concern seems to carry the corollary for the folk that classroom learning does not result in communicative ability:

> T: So therefore - I knew the book way=the textbook way how to speak it, but actual conversation okay was in high school okay, but once I got to college it was null and void. Impossible. (#6)

In fact, a number of SLA studies show little difference between instructed and "naturalistic" learners (e.g., Krashen, Sferlazza, Feldman, and Fathman 1976; Felix 1981). The following is typical of conclusions reached in such research:

> ... foreign language learning under classroom conditions seems to partially follow the same set of natural processes that characterize other types of language acquisition. ... there seems to be a universal and common set of principles which are flexible enough and adaptable to the large number of conditions under which language learning may take place. (Felix 1981:109)

If classroom and naturalistic learners are moving along in the same way, there would appear to be little support for the folk faith in the latter mode. On the other hand, more recent research suggests that naturalistic learners may have a small edge. Pica (1983), for example, suggests that classroom learners often err more in oversupplying morphological marking (e.g., "He liv*ed* in London now") and in generalizing regular to irregular forms (e.g., "He buy*ed* a car yesterday"). Since such forms (perhaps particularly the latter) are caricaturistically noticeable, they may exaggerate for learners the degree to which classroom learners are at a disadvantage. Perhaps more to the point, Pica (1983) also notes that classroom instruction has a tendency to inhibit the use of forms which are ungrammatical in L2, *even if the forms are communicatively efficient.* In this case, learners might note the greater general fluency available to naturalistic learners, even if grammatical precision is less than the classroom learner's.

Completely contrary to the folk claim, however, is considerable recent research which, although it notes that processes in naturalistic and classroom acquisition are similar, suggests that the rate of L2 acquisition by classroom learners is enhanced (Long 1983). Since folk observations are less likely to be longitudinally made, it is perhaps not surprising that this finding has little folk representation. Nevertheless, one particularly successful adult multilingual noted that classroom study of the structure of a language was an optimum prerequisite to gaining fluency in a natural setting (D #44),[10] and G (in #36b) comments briefly about the effective use of L2 conversation in modern foreign language classrooms (although he admits that he took Latin in High School specifically so he would not have to speak in a foreign language).

There are, however, sociolinguistic as well as psycholinguistic concerns connected with this "naturalness" issue. Tarone and Swain (1995), for example, note that learners (particularly younger learners in immersion programs) feel they simply do not get "real" language from their classroom exposure. They are not equipped with the language of their age group, for example, and, therefore, are not ready to argue, discuss, express emotion, and the like. Perhaps this registral failure is at the root of some folk belief about the inefficiency or "unnaturalness" of classroom learning (or is, at least, a partial explanation for the folk admiration of "natural" learning).

Finally, both naturalness and frequency of use may be related to a final concern – exclusivity. Several respondents felt that one needs to hear the language being learned exclusively if it is to be learned well:

> H: I never did well in German. The centers were kind of like- they had three centers I think in Germany. They were based a lot on speaking level ability and mine was the lowest. And because I had an English roommate - an English speaking roommate, she would never really (   ) much German. So I could understand general conversation and get around okay but I never was fluent at all. Which was too bad. (#3)

Exclusivity is an especially sensitive factor for children who face schooling in another language:

> K: My parents are Norwegian. And they didn't speak Norwegian at home. My mother had been here less than two years when I was born. And they had really kooky idea- (   ). They just believed that we would have a lot of problems learning- at school, if we had spoken only Norwegian at home.(#18)

We have already observed the influence of such folk belief on language education programs in the United States, particularly bilingual education, in 4.2.4. It is perhaps enough to note here that few SLA researchers or students of bilingualism in general have found any support for the fear that, unless one uses a language exclusively, it will not be learned well, a conclusion dating back, at least, to early anecdotal records of childhood bilingualism (e.g. Leopold 1939-49) and to empirical work by Peal and Lambert (1962) and many following studies.

It may be surprising to teachers that techniques and methods of language teaching engage the folk so little. One respondent speculates on the preference for native speaker teachers at beginning or advanced levels (S #3), and another wonders if sleep teaching will work (T #9).

In general, the folk believe that languages are tricky, at every level of structure, but that frequent use, natural settings, and exclusive use of one language may overcome the difficulty.

4.3.3 Results

In addition to the conditions for language learning, the folk are concerned with the results, and one concern is with the linguistic form of
the product itself.

4.3.3.1 Prescription and style. An interesting belief, which appears
several times, is that non-native speakers are actually better users of
the language than native speakers along several dimensions. The
following comment is made to a Chinese fieldworker:

> G: (.hhh) Well - yeah. The difference really is, is if you speak Eng-
> lish, actually speak proper English, (.hhh) you are probably speak-
> ing it better than we. - I know that sounds strange. (#1)

This is undoubtedly related to the notion that non-natives speak more
formally. As pointed out in Chapter 1 and, more specifically, in 3.2
and 3.3.1 above, the confusion of style with status (and
"correctness") is a folk commonplace. One respondent comments on
a mutual acquaintance from Switzerland:

> D: Yeah he's very - v- ver- more formal I think in his- in his=
>   [
> H: Yeah.
> D: =English, more formal in his speech. (#7)

Among SLA researchers, Tarone (e.g., 1988) has been particularly
concerned with stylistic variation. She notes that early learners of a
second language may be "*monoregistral.*" (Tarone 1983). That is,
they may shift stylistically only according to the amount of time
available for processing or, perhaps more accurately, for focusing on
linguistic form, but, as yet, they do not have stylistic differentiation
which carries social symbolism available to them. There is little
doubt that such monoregistral behavior (particularly if it is the result
of classroom instruction) is of a more formal variety. We have already noted that some researchers have suggested (e.g., Tarone and
Swain 1995) that input from and interaction in classroom settings result in an extremely limited proficiency, often one not geared to the
expressive and interactional needs of a learner. Additionally, and
more to the point of advanced learners, Preston (1981, 1989c) suggests that non-native speakers may, in fact, use more formal varieties
as a result of sensing that less formal behavior by non-natives is not
well-received by native speakers.

4.3.3.2 Accent. A number of respondents noted that accent was the principal difficulty in understanding non-native speech, and several mentioned groups which they found especially difficult to understand (e.g., Koreans [S #54]). Although there are a number of interesting studies of native speaker abilities to understand non-native speaker varieties (surveyed in Eisenstein 1983), the specific elements of non-native speech which promote misunderstanding are not yet well understood.

4.3.4 Social factors

In their discussion of language learning, these respondents were particularly concerned with a number of social as well as linguistic matters. The responsibility of individuals to speak the languages of their environment was particularly strongly expressed and reveals a deep folk disparity between the regret for the loss of language abilities in succeeding generations on the one hand and the emphasis on accommodation on the other. For many this need for accommodation is very explicit:

D: I mean I- I think that language is the one- the one thing that uni-
fies the country.
N: Uh huh.
D: I mean we have different religions, we have different - ethnic
backgrounds, we have - teRIFfic different socio-economic standards, and - different - lifestyles from one part=
                                     [
N: Uh huh.
D: =of the country to the other. I mean - uh what's a lifestyle and a
way of living to somebody that lives in - Birmingham Alabama is
certainly almost foreign to someone in Boston=
                                 [[
N: ((sniffs))   Uh huh.
D: Massachusetts or Seattle, but - the one unifying thing in the
country is the language, and - and to suggest that we want to start
a bilingual language uh country is -
N: I don't know, I oh I think-
              [
D: I mean I think it is that people are just crazy. - I
mean if you look at history, countries that have bilingual - things
are countries that have problems because=
N: =Uh huh. ((sniffs) Well yeah, that's definitely true.

D: I- I can't see setting it up so that they can - because I I I mean -
You're talking to a person that couldn't learn a foreign lang(h)uage
for her li(h)fe depor- depended on it, (.hhh) but I really think that if

you're going to go to another country to live that that's just something you should accept and they should have to do.

D: I can't see that we should have to - have bilingual things on -
driving? I mean what is the point in giving someone - a- a- a
driver's test - in Spanish, - and say Oh swell they can read, they
can have this driver's license because they can read in Spanish,
and they get on the road and all the signs are in English?
N: ((laughs))
D: I- I mean that's kind of=
N: =(uh) it doesn't - mesh.
D: It- it just doesn't uh - I don't know, to me that's really that's really
something. I can't worry about their rights. Their rights are that they
should learn. (# 59)

Although there are a number of themes in this typical observation,
we will point out only those parallels to professional views of national unity on the one hand and assimilation on the other. First,
unity.

> The political and social situation created by linguistic diversity ranges
> from the harmony of Switzerland ... to India, where the entire political
> fabric is torn with linguistic conflict. Although both represent extremes,
> *there is usually at least some conflict and dissent within multilingual na-*
> *tions.* (Lieberson 1970 [1981:1], emphasis ours)

Although there is no doubt that the folk fear of national bilingualism
in the United States is exaggerated (both in the likelihood of its occurrence and the disruptive effect it might have), there are, as can be
seen in Lieberson's remarks, professional opinions which parallel the
folk ones. In general, however, the opinion of professional linguists
suggests that language is an unlikely force against national unity in
the United States and in many other areas as well (e.g., Larmouth
1987).

The strong folk notion that individuals "need" English, both to be
assimilated into United States culture and to provide themselves with
the benefits of the society, is, in fact, an expression which appears to
have two focuses. First, it is a reaction against bilingual education
and the assumption that children who are being taught in their native
languages are not learning English language skills. Second, perhaps
more generally, there appears to be a historical sense of both fairness
and need. Extensive bilingual services were not provided, the folk
often suggest (e.g., Hakuta 1986:213), for their non-English speaking
ancestors, yet these same ancestors "made it."

In fact, the United States has a long and healthy bilingual tradition, marred only, perhaps, by bans on the use of German during and right after World War I (Kloss 1977). Nevertheless, recent times have seen an increase in linguistic chauvinism and xenophobia, and folk expressions such as those cited above clearly parallel attempts at so-called "English Only" or "Official English" legislation. An excellent survey, including historical background, of the popular, legislative, and professional discussion of such matters is given in Crawford (1992).

It is as nearly universally held, however, that Americans fail in their responsibilities to learn other languages:

> J: I would LOVE to be able to speak another language. I- I think
> that that's one of the bad things about Americans, that we (.hhh) go
> into other countries and we expect everybody else to be able to
> talk to us - but we don't - think it's necessary for - it's=
>   [
> S: To ((laughing)) speak English.
> J: =really very arrogant I think. (#15)

Professional and public attention are often dramatically drawn to the need for more United States citizens to know foreign languages. The National Defense Education Act of 1958, for example, linked knowledge of foreign languages and cultures to national defense in the coldest days of the Cold War, and high school enrollments in foreign languages increased from 16.4 percent in 1958 to 26.4 percent in 1965, and even larger gains were made in undergraduate and graduate university foreign language study (Kant 1969, 1970). Nevertheless, our respondents feel that the United States does not have the "tradition" of language learning.

> J: But uh- other countries are way ahead of us in that. You know=
>   [
> S: So-
> J: =like uh Jose from Chile he could speak five languages.
> S: Who?
> J: Oh that- that - yeah. He could speak Spanish, he spe- spoke=
>   [
> S: Chile person - Aw
> J: =uh Portuguese, he spoke - French, he spoke English, and uh a
> little German.
> S: But where did she- did he learn all these - in Chile
>   [
> J: In Chile   -   He didn't learn it here.
> Sure. Of course Chile has a big Ger- uh German=
>   [

```
?:                                  (          )
J: =population there (.hhh) and uh if they want to - study overseas
they've got to be able to speak the language. And=
                                    [
S:                                  Uh huh.
J: =that's what they do. They go to France s- to study or go to
(.hhh) (hhh) uh Germany or to Great Britain - you know or to the
United States. (# 15)
```

Finally, though less important, the instrumental consequences of language learning are mentioned.

```
J:        Well you know the Japanese come over here and they-
they've got wonderful engi- engineers. They- they come and they
learn they study they come here and they can speak English as
well as any one of us.  They don't come over here=
                       [
S:                     Um:
J: =speaking Japanese to us.
S: ((laughs)) That's right.
J: Yeah. I mean uh that's because they want to get ahead, (.hhh)
and if they're meeting with people (.hhh) that they're going to sell
their commodities to or whatever they want to be able to speak
good English. Because uh - because we don't understand Japan-
Japanese. (# 15)
```

In some cases the instrumental gains are even more baldly stated:

```
M: You know if s- a person was smart, we'd s- academically and
thinking of their future, - any kind of person that could - grasp a
language, to- boy could they ever make the money, couldn't they:?
(# 15)
```

In general, the folk seem more concerned with social outcomes than with linguistic ones. Linguistically, they are tolerant, even admiring of non-native speech (although several note pronunciation or "foreign accent" as a particularly difficult area). Socially, however, although individual bilingualism is usually seen as a plus, the folk are suspicious of societal bilingualism or of plans which might result in it.

4.3.5 The learner

Finally, there are folk opinions of learner characteristics, and motivation and talent vie for most frequent mention in this area. Without proper motivation, learning is doomed:

M: ... but I think the trouble is that the kids get turned off because
they - they need to learn conversational language more than they=
                 [
S: Uh huh.
M: =do. Unless they're going to be some- I mean if they could - =
   [
S: ( )
 [
J: Yeah.
M: =knew what they were going to go into I=
        [
J: I agree.
M: =I suppose maybe they know- need to know the grammar=
                [
S: Uh huh.
M: =and all this declaring[11] and all this (.hhh)- because mostly if
they could learn to speak it-=
J: =There'd just be a kind of a s- just a second - second=
             [
M: Uh huh.
J: =language tha- that you- they picked up. (# 15)

It is clear that this notion of motivational loss is connected to the folk
notion that less natural learning takes place in classrooms, a belief already discussed. Professionals have long recognized the powerful
force of motivation for language learning success and have been
concerned with means of identifying, classifying, and fostering it
(e.g., Gardner and Lambert 1972).

For the folk, some social demands are seen as powerful motivations:

K: ... there are children around here who've been here for a year
or two, and they sound like they were - they were born in America.
An:d it's something to do, I think with fitting in, too. They really want
to uh fit in. (#18)

This folk notion of "fitting in" is felt to be a very powerful force in
language acquisition (even in the acquisition of alternative dialects).
At one time, professional opinion also suggested that the motivation
to be like or identify with another linguistic group was especially
effective (Gardner and Lambert 1972). This motivation was called
integrative, and was contrasted with the *instrumental* or more
"practical" motivation one might have in second language acquisition. Subsequent research, however, suggested that many instrumental learners also achieved considerable proficiency, and Gardner and
Lambert subsequently revised their original definitions:

It seems that in settings where there is an urgency about mastering a second language – as in the Philippines and in North America for members
of linguistic minority groups – the instrumental approach to language
study is extremely effective. (1972:141)

And some feel that the American situation itself may be responsible for poor motivation:

> Z: Do you think that people don't have interest? or desire?
> K: We don't need to. It's such a large country and we don't- Most people don't need to. They don't come into contact with other languages (#22).

Motivated or not, however, many respondents feel that some have a talent for language learning:

> H: It is just something that comes more easily to me.
> K: Why - why
>   [
> H: I never worked at it. I do not know. People just have different gifts and that is something that was easy for me. (#3)

And there may be different gifts for different linguistic levels. R was apparently a successful Spanish student, but she never learned to roll (presumably her "r"s) and remembers to this day a nun who modeled the sound for her:

> M: It never rolled off my tongue. I never really even though I=
>   [[
> J: Yeah.   Yeah.
> M: =Spanish, (.hhh) it came easily to me. I mean I could=
>   [
> J: Yeah.
> M: =never get my tongue to roll:. To sound right. Yeah. You=
>   [
> S: Uh huh
>   [
> J: To sound right. Yeah. Uh=
> M: =know, and you had to roll:, I can remember the nun,=
> J: =huh. (I remember that.)
> M: ((imitates nun?)). Never forget it.
>   [
> S: ((laughs))
>   [
> J: Heh yeah. Yeah. (#15)

One respondent seems to relate musical with language learning talent since he notes his "tone deafness" along with his poor language learning skills (G #36b). Our most engaging explanation of why some have it and some don't, however, came from a respondent who believes in reincarnation. Those who have spoken a language in an earlier life will obviously have an easier time picking it up the second time around (E #55).

Professionals have also studied individual differences in language learning and considerable time has been spent in devising tests of "aptitude," the best-known of which is probably the "MLAT" (Modern Language Aptitude Test) (Carroll and Sapon 1959). It is interesting that this test (although not all such measures) does not place motivation or general verbal intelligence within the framework of "aptitude" (Larsen-Freeman and Long 1991:168-9). More recent research suggests that all normal human beings can master second languages but that some academically oriented aspects of SLA (e.g., reading, overt knowledge of the grammar, advanced vocabulary) may be correlated with intelligence or general education (Neufeld 1978, Collier 1989). Only one of our respondents felt that intelligence is important in language learning (M #9) – an interesting contrast to the large number of respondents who associated intelligence and standard English usage.

There is no doubt, however, that the characteristic most intriguing to both professionals and the folk is that of age. All the respondents who mention age believe that younger learners are more adept, perhaps particularly in achieving good pronunciation, but various remarks show that our respondents believe that younger people are more adept at acquiring second languages at every linguistic level, including even the adaptability of life style necessary to the acquisition of different rules of cultural behavior (or what linguists might call "communicative competence"). Once when a linguistically sophisticated fieldworker let slip the "technical" information that some scholars feel that language learning after puberty is difficult, a respondent was quick to exclaim: "I'm not lazy guys I'm past eleven" (M #9).

Professional accounts of the advantages of age are more diverse (and complex). Larsen-Freeman and Long (1991:163-4) outline the following explanations:

1. Children have the advantage in that they are less inhibited and less likely to have and encounter negative attitudes towards other languages.

2. Children and adults learn second languages very differently; adults can think abstractly (e.g., Piaget 1929), and this provides them with advantages in, for example, problem-solving activities while the young child still has his or her internal, "language acquisition device" (LAD) available.

3. Children have the advantage of having "modified L2 input" (i.e., simplified structure) and greater amounts of L2 input.

4. Children's brains are more "plastic," and, after puberty, are likely to become more inflexible and have an adverse effect on SLA.

Although Larsen-Freeman and Long (1991) show how each of these research conclusions may be flawed (165-66), they still come down solidly on the folk side – children are superior language learners:

> ... children ultimately win out not just quantitatively but qualitatively: only child starters seem capable of attaining native-like SL abilities, The evidence here is clearest for phonology but also exists for accent recognition, listening comprehension and syntax, with suggestively similar tentative findings for collocation, discourse and pragmatics (1991:166).

In conclusion, the folk hold strongly to talent and motivation as important learner characteristics for success, and they give younger learners the edge.

In all such technical areas, it might be easy to ridicule what a Bloomfield dinner table conversation would doubtless label "stankos" about language learning, but these data are not all that strange and, more importantly, not all that distant from professional opinion. Most importantly, they are the beliefs and the products of reasoning about such questions based on folk knowledge and folk ways of bringing resources to bear. Only those who hold to the radical opinion that overt knowledge never has anything to do with ways of acquiring and employing a second language would regard this information as trivial. What people believe about how they learn, how difficult the target of their learning is, what special talents they have (or lack) for learning, what social outcomes await them, and the host of other matters that only an empirically designed folk-linguistic investigation can lay bare are surely important matters for applied linguistics. Teacher trainers, national and local curriculum developers, materials developers, and classroom practitioners will surely fare better with some knowledge of the speech community's own understanding of the second language learning process.

Chapter 5: General and descriptive linguistics

In this chapter we examine general and descriptive linguistic notions from a folk linguistic point of view, reminding the reader that we continue to define the folk only as those not professionally involved in formal linguistic study. The fact that the folk are not so involved, however, does not mean that they are uninterested in these more "technical" areas or that their ideas are insignificant. In fact, the folk are fascinated with language structure and function, and they are more than willing to offer their opinions and theories.

We choose to focus, however, on two main themes: folk responses to "problem" sentences and an extended conversation about the passive. Our principal reason for not giving a fuller treatment to many other categories (e.g., phonology, lexical semantics) is that these topics are, in keeping with the major classificatory notions of folk linguistic belief, a necessary part of other sections of this book. That is, the folk rarely discuss phonology qua phonology, but they reveal beliefs about the phonological concerns in their discussions of dialects and varieties, reading and educational linguistics, second and first language acquisition, and so on. That is not a surprising contextualization, for it places language structure as a presupposed background to more "fronted" folk linguistic concerns (e.g., correctness). We review here, nevertheless, a few subtopics which can be extracted from these conversations.

5.1 Phonology

At the phonological level (aside from a concern for sound-letter correspondences, discussed in Chapter 4.2.1), the folk seem to reflect both the "ease of articulation" and "perceptual separation" professional positions (e.g., Ladefoged 1975), although both would seem to be encoded into their doctrine of correctness. "Ease of articulation" is often equated with "laziness," and optimal "perceptual separation" would appear to be a presupposition about the quality of the "standard." For example, the loss of g in -ing endings is a common folk preoccupation, and the tendency to do it is attributed to "laziness." A (in #4) is eager to note that "we" (presumably the respondents present, perhaps even local people in general) pronounce the *g*. R (in #51), however, attributes "laziness" specifically to "Blacks" who, she says, " ... don't put the endings – on their words." This phenomenon is not, however, exclusively tied to ethnicity in our data. J (in #38) suggests that the loss of *r* in *car* (in his characterization of Massachusetts speech) is "quicker" and "easier," alternatives which he offers to another respondent's characterizations of the pronunciation as a "lazy thing."

In general, the folk appear to believe that pronouncing the standard variety requires more "effort," a theory not unlike that of Kroch (1978) who notes that the "elite" dialect

> ... characteristically resists normal processes of phonetic conditioning (both articulatory and perceptual) that the speech of non-elite strata regularly undergo. (18)

In #28, for example, D notes that in English "you have to move your tongue a lot" to say *l*. This notion of effort appears to be related to some comments which reflect what must be for American English a "hyperstandard." In #5, for example, H admits that he pronounces "letter" with a flap but suggests that he means to use an aspirated stop when he notes that " ... actually I mean to pronounce the 't' ((laughs))," and his laughter would appear to reveal the linguistic insecurity which has been awakened by this "confession." Among the same group of respondents, however, A (in #4), who has earlier insisted that he "says the 'g'" in "hunting," also insists that he uses an aspirated *t* in *water*. When the other respondents laugh, however, he admits "I figured that might get a laugh," suggesting that his hypercorrect performance claim is not a reflection of his usual behavior.

Although we generally agree with Labov's observation (in Hoenigswald 1966) that specific terminology for phonological matters is lacking in the Anglo-American tradition, we hold to our claim in 1.1.1.1 that "awareness" of phonological matters surfaces in folk comment in a variety of interesting ways. It is not at all our experience, as we have shown in many places, especially in 2.2.4, that the folk have no overt recognition and/or imitative abilities of even rather low-level phonological features, a contention of Labov, citing work by Ash:

> The subjects [in a test survey of individuals who were asked to disguise their voices] modified tempo, voice quality, and intonation, but none modified the segmental features specific to their geographical dialect.(1994:111).

Of course, people asked to "disguise" their voices may not pick on a suitable role to elicit performance imitations which they are particularly good at. Preston 1992, for example, showed that European-Americans imitating AAVE did, in fact, make such segmental modifications while African-American respondents made only the vocal quality, tempo, and such other adjustments as Labov suggests in their performance when they were asked to "talk like a white person." On the other hand, African-American respondents have a rich repertoire of African-American speech types (e.g., Kochman 1972). Wolfram and Schilling-Estes (1994) have shown that residents of the off-shore islands of North Carolina systematically shift segmental features when they imitate more "local" or more "old-fashioned" examples of regional speech. We conclude, therefore, that a great deal of folk linguistic evidence, even at the systematic phonological level, could play an important role in matters of language variation and change. We are still such a good distance from providing more than tentative answers to the "actuation problem" (e.g., Weinreich, Labov, and Herzog 1968:102) that, no matter how trivial (or "socially" oriented) tentative solutions may seem, it would, in our opinion, be a mistake to ignore them.

That does not mean that we disagree at all with the concept of "change from below" in the sense in which it refers to sound change below the conscious level (e.g., Labov 1972a). It is the case, however, that folk linguistic data may provide interesting perspectives even on such unconscious speech community changes. The Northern Cities Shift (e.g., Labov 1991) is a classic example of change from below in this sense, and, in general, residents of those areas where it is taking place (or has taken place) have no awareness of its progress (or attribute one aspect of it or even its occurrence in a small set of lexical items to a usually prejudiced-against social group, both denying personal use and ignoring the rest of the shift). The following discussion, however, reveals an interesting folk realization of what must surely be a part of this general vowel movement.

H: I always uh hear uh: people here say [kʰɔfi]. - but I- we always say [kʰɑfi]. Is any different?
                   [
?:   [kʰɑfi].
R: I don't think so. It's p(h) probably the way we pronounce it here.
                                [
?:   [kʰɑ]
K: ['kʰɑfe] no [kʰɑ'fe]. It would be German, but I think i- it would,
    [
R: [kʰɑfi]

H: [
                                                             [kʰafi] is
German?
K: [kʰɑˈfe] is German, yeah, but [kʰɔfi], I think that's English
wherever you go
[
J: Uh huh. Maybe.
H: I mean in German they: [kʰafi]?
K: [kʰɑˈfe].
H: [kʰafi], Uh::: ((sing-song, "surprised" agreement intonation))
That's very interesting.
                          [
K: "k" (   ) a ver- hard hard [ˈkʰafe]
                                                       [
H: [kʰafi].
H: [kʰæfi].
K: [kʰɑˈfe].
H: Interesting. You know. Why in English then [kʰɔfi].
K: [kʰɑˈfe].
J: (Why don't) you say [kʰafi].
R: [kʰafi].
H: Oh you don't say the same [kʰafi]?
((They discuss the pronunciation of "coffee" and "tea" in Chinese
and other European languages)) (#2)

The fieldworker observes (whether truthfully or simply to open discussion on this matter) that he has heard [kʰɔfi] in US English, but
"we" (presumably Chinese who have learned English in Taiwan) say
[kʰafi]. Although there are interesting contributions from the other
nonnative speaker (K, a Swiss French speaker, who is also concerned
with the lexical stress pattern and the quality of the initial consonant), it is clear that at least R simply believes that the lower and
fronter vowel is "the way we pronounce it here." H (feigns?) surprise
when both J and R do not use the [kʰɔfi] form in their performances
at the end of this section. It is reasonable to assume that for both R
and J [ɔ] has moved forward to (at least) [a], which, itself, has
moved on towards [æ]. They do not, however, comment at all on the
possibility of this being a part of any systematic change and, as is
often the case in folk comment on phonology, focus on the pronunciation of the item in question.

Of course, when phonological matters are caricatures or stereotypes, then there is a fairly full folk awareness, and we have commented already on a number of these in Chapter 2. Michigan respondents (particularly those with Canadian backgrounds or those who
live closest to the border) are aware not only of the characteristic *eh*
(i.e., [ey]) tag but also of Canadian raising. Several respondents imitate and many comment on Southern monophthongization (e.g., *tired*

and *oil* in #41), and we have noted in 4.2.1 the folk awareness of the Asian languages /r/~/l/ difficulties in the fieldworker's problems with *blood* in #1.

There is almost no need to comment further on the folk confusion of spelling and sound, treated more fully in 4.2.1, but it is worth noting that the folk may be annoyed with the language when the sounds and spellings do not match, although their rules are often interestingly inconsistent. G in #29, for example, rebukes the fieldworker for the [ɑ] pronunciation of *wainscot* (correcting it to [o]), apparently unannoyed with the fact that the spelling is not a good clue. When the fieldworker suggests that he was especially confused with the creation of verb forms (*wainscoted*), however, the respondent rebukes him again, noting that he should have known that the pronunciation was [o] because there was only one *t* in *wainscoted*, an interesting presupposition, which suggests that one ought to know how to spell an item before risking a pronunciation of it. G, however, is a linguistically secure speaker, who, when the fieldworker first worries about the alternative pronunciation, declares "All you need is me. I'm the dictionary." (The conservative American Heritage Dictionary, by the way, allows spellings with both one and two *t*'s in *wainscot(t)ed* and allows three pronunciations, the two contested ones and a third with a schwa.) In general, however, the opinion that there is a bad mismatch between English sounds and spelling is believed by most of our respondents.

M: Yeah. Well, you know, the English language I think is (1.0) I don't know who started it if it (0.2) I always thought when kids were trying to learn words like (0.5) you have two words that are SAID identical. But SPELLED DIFferently, "principal" and "principle."
N: Uh huh.
M: Bouquet [boke] and [buke]. You know "bow," "bough." I mean all these words that are the same. I think we've got the hardest language to learn.
N: Well yes.
M: For someone coming in.
       [
N: Uh huh.
M: You know, and like "POlish" and "polish." You know. I mean they're they're spelled the same and yet they're two different words. (#9)

Although M begins with examples which are homophones but not homographs, she switches to items which have alternative pronunciations (unless she distinguishes two senses ["bunch of flowers" and "odor"] for her two pronunciations) and, finally, to items which are

homographs but not homophones (*Polish* [polIʃ] versus *polish*
[palIʃ]. Although it is not clear that she understands all these distinctions, it is clear that she thinks the system is a mess. She goes on
in the same conversation to complain that it is especially difficult to
spell in English after one has learned a foreign language, establishing
even further, we suspect, the claim that English sounds and spelling
are a poor match, but we have strayed too far from the concerns of
this section.

Although there is some concern with suprasegmental facts (as in
K's admonishing of H just above for his failure to stress German
Kaffe correctly), in general there are only a few overt comments, and
those appear to be regionally and/or socially distinctive (e.g., the
pronunciation of *Monroe* with stress on the first or second syllable
cited in 2.2.4 and a brief discussion in #5 of stress placement on
Caribbean which interestingly concludes that stress on the penulti-
mate is "posher" than that on the antepenultimate). Recall, however,
that a respondent in #38 distinguishes intonation patterns in different
regions of the US by referring to talk which is "up and down" versus
"sideways," the latter doubtless referring to "monotonous" or less
varied contours. The respondents in #36b also refer to English as
"musical," and those in #5 find Caribbean English "song-like." Further work in the folk perception of such matters might prove productive, both in the search for overt comment and imitation.

5.2 Lexicon

In 1.1.2 we have shown the primacy of the "word" as the folk linguistic object par excellence, and discussions of word meanings (see
our treatment of *gift* versus *present* in that section) are common. A
few others are worth mentioning here (as well as the perhaps too obvious fact that folk lexical semantics is a rich field). The folk also see
words as "classifiable," that is, belonging to certain groupings, and
these will, as well, be briefly illustrated, but, as we shall see, those
classifications, perhaps not surprisingly, also bear heavily on social
rather than strictly linguistic characteristics.

In #57, two young European-American respondents (B and S)
both claim they want to avoid "maturity." The Chinese fieldworker X
(and her husband T) are a little puzzled by this claim, and they ask
why. S explains that he associates "maturity" with "limitation" and
"closed-mindedness." The fieldworker goes for the dictionary, while
her husband says, to the contrary, that he associates "maturity" with

the ability to find out how to do things more easily but at the same time to do them "wisely" and "correctly." He especially associates "maturity" with the ability to choose among options. After the fieldworker reads the dictionary definition (which seems to focus on the development of plants), S feels that his definition is bolstered and notes that "maturity" is the period right before "decadence" or "decay." The fieldworker agrees that there may also be some young people in China who do not want to grow up, but S goes on to indicate that he may in part agree with T's definition, indicating that he approves of the sense of "maturity" in which it refers to a willingness to accept adult-like responsibilities.

T suggests that all this may be the result of a misunderstanding of the word, but S holds to a more relativistic definition strategy, suggesting that each speaker may have a slightly different interpretation of the word. He notes that this is especially true of such items as "maturity" because they are "value-laden." B tries to clarify the discussion by saying that he would rather express the degree to which he and S agree with T by "not wanting to be immature," revealing an obvious connotative if not denotative distinction between a form and its negative (see Langendoen and Bever 1973). T, however, cannot understand how B can want to be "not immature" but not want to be "mature" at the same time.

Like our analysis of *gift* and *present* above, the respondents' contextualization (in this case having to do with such specifics as personal stereotypes of life-style) is the "real" key to definitions. The nonnative speaker's suggestion that there is a misunderstanding of the "real" meaning of a word is rejected, for native speakers seem to hold to the need for rich (even personal) connotative values, although, as we have seen, they may be browbeaten by linguistic insecurity into admitting that their own meanings are not the "real" ones. Many respondents are happy to provide "non-dictionary" distinctions between words, distinctions which they obviously regard as real. G in #29, for example, says that a "diary" consists of only "notes," while a "journal" is "reflective" and "book-like." In #1, the fieldworker notes his embarrassment in using *hairdo* to describe a man's hair; he was told by native speakers that *haircut* refers to men and *hairdo* to women, exclusively.

In only a few cases do respondents run into a richer dictionary explanation than their personal experiences suggest. The respondents in #5, for example, are confused by all the definitions of *shall* and *will* in the dictionary; they admit they do not make these distinctions but also suggest that they probably should. B would probably point out that such items are not "value-laden," but, rather obviously, their usage, from a "correctness" point of view is.

The potential for fine semantic distinctions between and among words appears to be a generally held folk concept. Why would two words persist if there were not practical differences between them (in spite of what the dictionary might say or be imagined to say)? In #1, for example, there is an extended discussion of the difference between a *shake* and a *malt* and a bemoaning of the fact that in modern fast-food environments this distinction is ignored. ("It doesn't matter, whichever. Cause you're going to get the same thing no matter what you say.") Of course, the folk know that real synonyms exist, but, in every case, they seem to attribute them to region (e.g., *pop* versus *coke* in #23), formality (*mom* versus *mother* in #30), or some other classificatory factor which justifies the existence of two labels for the same thing.

Some respondents, however, recognize lexical items with *no* meaning. R (in #48a), for example, cites *cool*, *shit*, and *fuck* as items which have no meaning. He explains that each is " .. just another word you put in there to put more emphasis. Emphasis is more – making it more colorful." Apparently a number of respondents believe that slang and obscenity perform such "meaningless" tasks. Similarly, what most linguists might see as "discourse markers" (e.g., Schiffrin 1987), including such items as "well," "like," and "you know," are also regarded as meaningless, or, worse, "dumb" and "bad habits" as the respondents in #5 agree.

The folk also regard some words as perhaps meaningful but "nonwords" since they are not cataloged in any recognized word repository. D in #35, for example, "justifies" his definition of *turkey* as "loser" by noting it is "in the dictionary." It is difficult to tell if G (in #1) identifies a "pre-slang" state (in which such items are not yet in the dictionary) or is unhappy with new dictionaries in which such items are tolerated: "I remember when I went through school the word 'ain't.' you know, was nonexistent in the dictionary. (.hhh) Now we put in 'ain't' as slang, and it's said in certain places."

As we have shown in 3.3, there is considerable folk interest in "slang." The respondents in #51, for example, discuss AAVE and "suburban" new and slang words and note that African-Americans may be particularly adept at making up new items. They list and gloss *chappie*, *yo*, *geek*, *gopher*, *gump*, *psych*, *nerd*, *dork*, *cinderella*, *wimp*, *epic*, *doofer*, and *faking* in a very short space. The same respondents are aware of the process of semantic reversal in slang, and they describe for the fieldworker (in #23) the item *bad*. It is important to note, however, that this extensive glossing is done for a nonnative fieldworker. In #18, the respondent not only glosses but indicates the generational provenience of such slang items as *rap* and *groovy* for another nonnative fieldworker, and yet another nonnative fieldworker is told in #1 that *yummy* (referring to tasty food) is said only by children. That same nonnative fieldworker has both slang (e.g., *bad* and *chill out*), metaphoric (*green* in the sense "inexperienced"), and culturally specific items (e.g., *hick*) glossed for him by the respondents, and the respondents in #10 define what could be characterized as a close-knit semantic field of culturally specific words (*yuppie, hipster, beatnik,* and *preppy*) for a Chinese fieldworker and her husband, but perhaps we make too much of this glossing of slang and/or culturally specific words. Many of the respondents simply find themselves in an "expert" position when they gloss words in general for the nonnative fieldworkers, as these same respondents do in #56 for the item *nudge*. We believe the details of these glosses, however, might provide another rich source of folk linguistic investigation, providing detailed insight into the working operations of how the folk believe words "mean."

Although several of our respondents are aware of language change, those changes appear to be for the worse (a "loss of standards") or simply the importation of new slang and technical vocabulary. In the area of lexicon, however, there is also a more general sense of the history of the language itself. In #15, the respondents note that "classy" and "prestigious" words in English often come from French (e.g., *svelte* and *per se* [sic]), and the respondents in #4 also note that French words have been extensively borrowed into English. The respondents in #10, however, claim that "small words" are the real core of the English vocabulary.

For quite a while we believed that there was a folk understanding of pidgin/creole language concerns, but *pidgin* turned out to be confused with "Pig Latin" by the respondents in #15, leading, by the way, to their complete rejection of the dictionary definition of *pidgin*.

Although we have given lexicon short shrift here, we believe that a more concerted collection and interpretation effort could be very rewarding in the search for folk understandings of language. We regret, in fact, that we do not have the space to treat some of these discussions of lexicon in a more extended way. Even if there were room, however, we lack the analytic models for genres outside "narrative" and "argument" necessary to treat such interactions. We turn now, however, to items which intrigue linguists more than they do the folk.

5.3 Syntax

5.3.1 Folk grammaticality

There is comment on sentence-level phenomena here and there in these conversations, particularly in discussions of nonprestige varieties, but the principal tactic we used in order to elicit grammaticality judgments was the presentation of thirty sentences taken from current work in syntax. These sentences are listed at the end of this section and are simply referred to by number (e.g., "7") in the following discussion to avoid confusion with conversation numbers (e.g., #7).

In an attempt to provide a realistic setting for these sentences, it was our original intent that the nonnative fieldworkers would present them as examples of their own writing which had been criticized by a professor. The respondents were to have provided expert (native-speaker) correction, and the site and manner of those corrections (plus attendant explanations) would have constituted our data. The fieldworkers, however, presented these samples under various guises, sometimes simply telling the respondents that they were asked by their professor to submit them for judgment, making no pretense that they were sentences actually produced. More often, however, the fieldworkers tried to disguise the sentences as ones which had been actually used. One fieldworker went so far as to use as many of them as she could in a piece of connected text; unfortunately it consisted only of these sample sentences, and the disjunctiveness of that at first frustrated the respondents and then caused them to doubt that the fieldworker had actually produced such an awful piece. In spite of the variety of presentations, respondent consideration of these sentences provided data which allowed us to gain some insight into folk belief about the grammar of the language.

At first, however, it will be necessary to determine if the respondents have considered the actual sentences on our list. In some cases they may simply have filtered the potential ungrammaticality out. Recall that in Chapter 1 we established that even students of linguistics who are trying to be meticulously accurate in transcribing dialogue often hear sentences on the basis of what their processors predict they should hear rather than on the basis of a simple copy of the actual data. For instance, several respondents heard 5 (Who did you give a picture of to?) as "Who did you give a picture to?" and either responded that the sentence was correct or referred to the fact that it ended with a preposition, overlooking altogether the problem which interested linguists originally. Variances in judgments could also occur as a result of the sentences' being read aloud rather than shown to the respondents. Many respondents had trouble with 8 (Who do you think that won left?) because it was read to them, and they misinterpreted *won* as *one*, causing them to either delete *that one* altogether (a massive reinterpretation even with the misunderstood form) or to interpret *left* as transitive. When the respondents in #15 were able to look at the fieldworker's paper after wrestling with these interpretations of *left* for several minutes, however, they resolved the issue by changing *that won* to *the winner*, and offered "Who do you think the winner left?," but since they had interpreted *left* as intransitive, they go on to produce the entirely different "Why do you think the winner left?" That they and other respondents are not bothered by the eventual semantic change such revisions cause is dealt with below.

An expected feature of folk syntax is the respondents' inability to characterize the causes of ungrammaticality they recognize. Respondents dismiss sentences as unacceptable and offer better versions, but they do not isolate or describe the errors. In #7, for example, G explains in great detail the changes that need to be made in 6 (John is probable to win): "Not 'is' but 'will'"; "No 'to'"; "'probably' with a '-ly' on the end," but she does not explain why these changes are necessary, despite the fieldworker's request for her to do so.

On the other hand, when respondents attempt to explain their corrections, they are often forced to reformulate their proposed rules due to their lack of generality. Although such attempts often frustrate the respondents, leading them to conclude that rule-making is impossible, the diversity of these explanations reveals sensitivity to a considerable variety of considerations which folk linguists use in their deliberation on structure. In nearly all of their various corrections of 26 (It was apparent yesterday John left), the respondents in #7 have, perhaps unconsciously, moved *yesterday* to the end. In their continuing discussion of the sentence, G notes that "... and the 'yesterday' would be at the end, written or spoken." The fieldworker responds to this by stating that time words in initial position are normal in Chinese. D rephrases this as a rule: "... you start the sentence – the sentence with the time first and then – the action," and G states the opposite for English: "No it's always the a- uh time is at the end." D agrees, but they both immediately realize that sentences can begin with time elements. Nevertheless, G suggests that initial placement is not as "natural" and that "It sounds awkward if you put it at the beginning for some reason." She also weakens what she has previously characterized as "always" to "usually" or "often." The fieldworker then suggests that his own usage is incorrect because he

says such things as "Today I want to go to visit uh something: (   )."
G interrupts him, suggesting that his usage in such cases is not incorrect since he has "a lot of things to say." She then goes on to formulate an exception to the time placement rule, one apparently based on
focus and end weight; "I guess it's sort of like where you want to put
the emphasis." She notes that a long list followed by a time word
would normally put undue emphasis on the time word itself and that,
in such cases, it ought to come first, "... to get that out of the way.
Because then you've got a whole bunch of other things to say."

Their reasoning on the placement of temporal words seems to
have moved along the following path: First, a simple structural-
positional formulation was proffered (time words come at the end);
second, exceptions were allowed but noted as marked (time words
may occur at the beginning but do not sound natural there); third,
justifications permitting exceptions which do sound natural were offered (if the predicate is long, the time word should come at the beginning of the sentence).

How do these respondents come to the conclusion that the temporal initial position is not usual but more natural if the predicate is full
of other information? Although they do not state it explicitly, they
are responding to functionalist or information structure properties of
sentence formation. Adverb preposing removes the adverbial element
from the asserted status of the predicate:

    a. What are you doing tomorrow?
    b. *I'm leaving tomorrow.
    c. Tomorrow I'm leaving.[1]

With ordinary stress and intonation, b. is an unacceptable answer to
a. since it asserts *tomorrow* unnecessarily (e.g., Creider 1979:7-8).
(Note that b. is good and c. no good as answers to *When are you
leaving?*, a question which does not place *tomorrow* into the information structure of the conversation.) It is reasonable to assume that
if a relatively more specific discourse context is required to make a
syntactic structure seem acceptable, then folk linguists will, especially at first glance, assume that such structures are abnormal. When
G suggests that long predicates cause time words to move to the beginning, she is responding to the reasonable assumption that a long
predicate would be the new, asserted information. "Tomorrow I'm
going to go to the bank, go shopping, visit my sister, and eat lunch
with a friend" is surely a likely answer to some such question as a.
above and not to one such as "When are you going to go to the bank,
go shopping," etc... . If *tomorrow* and the long predicate are both

new information, the time element would surely be less likely to bear the focus or center of attention, justifying its placement in the initial or topicalized position.

We are satisfied with these discourse-sensitive solutions to syntactic problems, but the folk appear to be unhappy with the fact that exceptions to simple positional formulations of syntactic structure exist and that pragmatic and extra-sentential reasoning must be brought to bear. After her explanation of the heavy predicate exception, G observes that "It kind of depends on the context, really." Her *kind of* and *really* hedges suggest that folk linguists do not regard such explanations as scientific or rigorous.

The determined effort by D and G to formulate a consistent rule for time placement is unusual, particularly since it does not involve the restatement of any prescriptive rules. Most respondents readily admit to not being able to describe a structured system, and they make no apology for it. In fact, as we will show more fully below, they often discredit the system that they were taught in grammar classes, asserting that no native speakers really follow it (or follow it only in certain instances). In fact, they believe the system is incomplete, for it describes only schoolroom or formal varieties. For many of them, however, this incompleteness is not strange; that is simply the state of affairs one would expect, for they do not regard language use as rule-governed behavior (although that does not at all deny their belief in the ideal, abstract "language" discussed in Chapter 1).

In place of explicit or systematic accounts, the respondents' concern is more often only with whether a given sentence sounds natural or not, and many are not so conscientious as D and G in providing justifications based on context or other considerations for these assessments. This concern for naturalness combined with the ever-present one for prescription makes many respondents identify some sentences as correct but never used. In #15, for example, the respondents have been discussing "There swims a frog in my tub"[2] quite a while when M notes that a sentence can be both "grammatical" and "clumsy" at the same time and that this sentence, despite the fact that it is grammatical, is "wrong." Such remarks about naturalness are often characterized by the respondents as feelings. When S is asked about "I have read often these books," he says that it's not good because of the "feeling," although it may be "correct grammar" (#10).

The converse of this also obtained: sentences may be ungrammatical but natural. For instance, when S was asked about 30 ("Which concert did you sleep during?") he replied:

S: OK. We're talking about the difference between what is grammatically correct and what sounds - is stylistically believed appropriate. (#10)

Apparently S applies the prescriptive rule which forbids placing prepositions at the end of sentences but, at the same time, finds 30 quite natural. We shall examine this specific relationship between prescription and grammaticality judgments in greater detail below.

We turn our attention now, however, to those sentences found unacceptable or strange. Respondents most often said that a sentence felt wrong if they had difficulty getting at the semantics of it: "It's hard for me to put it onto good English if I don't know what it means." This is not a surprising source of such feelings if one assumes, as we do, that communicative appropriateness and efficiency dominate in folk accounts. Luckily, many respondents suggested alternatives to the sentences they found unacceptable or strange, giving us a better opportunity to speculate about the specific source of the difficulty.

Ambiguous sample sentences rank high among those with difficult semantics which often provoked these feelings of unnaturalness. In #7 G says that 26 ("It was apparent yesterday John left") is grammatical but that the idea is "funny." She explains that if it were changed to "Apparently Joan [sic] left yesterday," "different information" would be transmitted, and then the idea would not be as strange, although she says "I don't know why though." G is reacting to the ambiguous scope of *yesterday* in the original and the unambiguous scope it has in her correction, but she is apparently not capable of explaining the difference between the two on that basis.

G responds to a semantic difficulty imposed by ambiguity by removing the complicating embedded clause, but in #18 K changes the unambiguous but complex embedding of 23 ("The book that reading would be fun was too expensive") to simple coordinated main clauses: "I saw a book that I would like to read but it was too expensive." In addition to doing away with the syntactic source of the semantic complexity, K's revision also does away with the indefiniteness of the subject of *read*. Such additional but minor modifications, not true to the semantics of the original, do not seem to bother many respondents.

There are many examples of even greater semantic alteration, most of which apparently result from the respondents' inability to realize the interpretation of the sample intended by the linguists who devised them. Recall that the respondents in #15 have altered 8 ("Who do you think that won left?") to "Why do you think the winner left?" One of the respondents justifies this correction by noting that the sentence they offer is "the only sense that can be made out of it." When the fieldworker in #7 asks about 27 ("Jack remembers who said who left"), G says that "if that's really what you want to say, then you said it correctly," but in providing an acceptable interpretation she physically inserts quotation marks: "Jack remembers who said 'Who left?,'" effectively reducing one sentential embedding by making it a simple NP object (a quotation) and severely altering the interpretation. (Even after her correction she adds that "the idea is still funny.") Several respondents corrected 12 ("Whom did your interest in surprise?") to "Who(m) are you interested in surprising?," altering the category of the word *interest* and significantly changing the interpretation. Nominalization rather than embedding is the syntactic cause of the difficulty which is simplified here. Finally, 19 ("I wonder who lost the newspaper without reading?") was often taken to mean that the speaker didn't read the paper; in #48a, for example, the respondent says it's really two sentences: "I wonder who lost the newspaper," and "I didn't get a chance to read it."

Respondents also altered semantically complex sentences by deletion. In several cases 5 ("Who did you give a picture of to?") is simplified to "Who did you give a picture to?" and the pronoun in 3 ("The man who John saw him left") is deleted. Both involve what appear to be for the folk linguist only minor deletions, in spite of the massive semantic change imposed on the first. There were, however, many cases of deletion of even larger elements. 27 ("Jack remembers who said who left") was often revised to "Jack remembers who left." and in #15 M says that the deleted clause "didn't matter anyway." On the other hand, M in #48a makes the same correction and is aware of the semantic loss imposed by his change. He is unable, however, to come up with a structure capable of encoding all the information: "I don't know a sentence for it."

At first the analytic process of constructing simpler clauses from complex material would appear to be the most straightforward folk strategy for revision, but many respondents either in justifying the deletion of material in the sample sentences or in some other context emphasized that the shorter a sentence is, the more natural it sounds. In #32, D says of 5 ("Who did you give a picture of to?") "That-that's a lot lot of words there that you could economize the words." In #5, J notes that "The fewer words you use to explain something, the better it is." The focus on communicative efficiency is so great that deletions which impose considerable semantic change are overlooked or ignored. Since these sample sentences are often presented out of context, they impose a considerable information load on the hearer. The natural tendency is to allow multiple bits of information in structural units only when considerable background and/or anaphoric information is available. Since none is there, the respondents quite naturally want to reduce the information content in each unit (e.g., Grimes 1975:277-8). In some cases they are semantically responsible and reduce the load by producing (usually) coordinated, simpler clauses but in others they simply do away with information in the simplification process.

Communicative efficiency is not, however, the only factor involved in folk prejudice against long sentences. As we have shown in Chapter 3, there is a considerable folk association between length on the one hand and formality and status on the other. This association is so strong that one respondent paints himself into a corner by mistakenly concluding before actually counting that a formal expression is longer than an informal one. In a conversation about the who/whom distinction, the fieldworker asks S to compare "Who do you speak with?" to "With whom are you speaking?"

> S: It also takes a long- It's also uh harder to say.
> X: What- what happens, you know-
> S: "Who're you speaking with," think about it. "Who are you speaking with." Right? Right. "Who are you speaking with," five words. "With whom are you speaking," "Wi-" uh: "Who are you speaking with." It's awkward to say "whom" - "with whom." "Who=
>   [
> X: So it's a- it's concerned about the the
> S: =are you speaking with." It's easier. (#10)

S goes on to say that this type of "awkward" language is used in "polite" settings, but that "polite" and "natural" speech are two different things, a sentiment expressed by many respondents. The fact that formal or polite speech is often negatively valued by these respondents, who refer to it as "overly formal," "pretentious," or "snobbish," has already been discussed in several places in Chapter 2.

Such conversations often led to a discussion of the prescriptivist edicts which many respondents claimed they were forced to learn in school but which only upper class or pretentious people follow. Perhaps the most common example of a prescriptive rule referred to by respondents is that against ending sentences with prepositions. Although they cite the rule, the respondents say that such sentences are "good colloquial English," and that Americans use them all the time:

D: And if you say "To whom does this picture belong," everybody sort of laughs at you. And you feel like you're trying to be real pompous. And hardly anybody ever talks that way, except for teachers that are trying to teach kids not to end sentences with prepositions.
Z: Do you talk without preposition endings?
D: On rare occasions. And then I'm sort of embarrassed. But I did it just because I'm just a goody-goody and I learned my lessons so: well when I was a student. (#19)

The only two sentences accepted by all the respondents contained a violation of this very rule: 30 ("Which concert did you sleep during?") and, after deleting *of* (see above), 5 ("Who did you give a picture to?"). To sum up, the general consensus is that such rules are for the upper class, English teachers, the overly formal, and the pompous. Small wonder that sample sentences which appear to obey such constraints are regarded as unnatural.

There were other constructions which triggered prescriptivist memories in our folk linguists; the second most mentioned rule was the *who/whom* distinction. Almost every respondent who discussed this, however, claimed that the distinction "is something many Americans don't worry about," and in #5, H says that if he hears someone say *whom*, he thinks "Who's getting so formal around here?" Only D (in #19), in correcting 3 ("The man who John saw him left"), replaces *who* with *whom*, and when the fieldworker repeats the sentence back to her using *who*, she stresses that the correct word would be *whom*.

Some few prescriptivist rules were more strongly upheld by respondents, one of whom likened their being broken to an "out of tune violin." In #16, R says that one must use "the right verbs with the right nouns and the right tense." Failure to observe person-number agreement rules in English have long been singled out by sociolinguists as highly stigmatized (e.g., Wolfram and Fasold 1974:81), although the notice of this feature (as of others discussed below) is specifically related to ethnolinguistic minorities, who constitute a special case in the folk regard for prescription. Some other respondents noted that using an adverb form for verb modification was important, suggesting that the schoolroom proscription of, e.g., "speak incorrect," has had some lasting influence. Even these stereotypes and a few others are regarded by the respondents as learned, and their memories of school grammar are not positive. They were taught "sentence analysis" ("What was it called, 'parsing'?") in schools, and they are not so sure as a group that it has done them any good. In general, mention of these caricaturistic rules took place in conversations which focused on social and stylistic rather than on grammatical matters or were triggered by the sample sentences and not directly associated with judgment of them.

Other than avoiding these few shibboleths, there appears to be only one venue for strict attention to prescriptive rules: writing or some forms of spoken public media. One respondent remembers being deeply embarrassed by a listener's calling in to note that he had said "Me and Alan" (presumably in subject position) on the radio. Sentences labeled noncolloquial were said to occur "in written form." In #7, during the discussion of 26 ("It was apparent yesterday John left") D disallows this sentence except for written English. He uses medium as a proper contextual setting after he has explained from a more functional perspective why the sentence sounded odd in the first place: "It sounds like an exclamation or a statement of fact." He apparently finds these uses more likely in writing, although that is an admittedly odd assessment of "exclamation" unless of course he simply means by that something strongly asserted. Another respondent even suggests that this construction would be found in poetry but nowhere else. The folk are aware of there being a standard or proper grammar, but their contention is that it is found in books and on the airwaves and that they themselves do not use it, at least not in everyday speech.

The folk are unwilling to compromise prescriptivist rules even in everyday speech, however, for some social groups. They believe that the use of proscribed forms by ethnolinguistic minorities is not natural and colloquial but an indication of ignorance and/or recalcitrance. There is perhaps no better example than this of our contention that shifting points of view in folk linguistics may produce apparently contradictory results. The two most common constructions disapproved of in these data are *ain't* and multiple negation, but in the cases where these violations are criticized the conversation was specifically about nonstandard varieties, most typically AAVE. These same constructions are noted as natural or informal when the discussion did not focus on ethnolinguistic minorities. A similar disapproval for young persons' or student usage arose. In the context of social disapproval, then, colloquial or nonstandard speech is universally disapproved; in the context of grammaticality judgment, however, when no ethnolinguistic labels were attached, even the same constructions are not stigmatized.

Once these prescriptivist attitudes are overcome (and that is a great deal easier for folk linguists than we expected), their primary goal is the assignment of a reasonable interpretation to, but not description of these "misshapen," often disembodied, sentences. Since this retrieval (and production) of meaning is unconscious and mechanical, even our most grammatically sophisticated respondents, perhaps ones who have previously thought more about the sorts of things which engage linguists, summarize attitudes which any professional would agree with:

> G: I don't think we know much about- I don't think we analyze our grammar or our speech very much, so we really aren't even used to thinking about how we speak.
> D: It's kind of neat though.
> S: It just comes naturally. (#23)

Although they admit to a passing interest (D's "neat") and although it is possible and interesting to engage them in speculation about such matters, the folk normally defer structured accounts or authoritative pronouncements to experts – the dictionary (consulted in three separate interviews), the English teacher, and the "ling-goo-istic person." Unfortunately, the structural paucity and social irrelevance of prescriptive grammars have left them with the idea that a human language is not a rule-governed or describable system (hence, not open to scientific investigation) and that those concerned with grammar are interested only in evaluated rather than general language behavior.

When engaged in talk about language, even at the structural level, however, the folk often reach the same conclusions as theoreticians.[3] Although they feel no need to explain their doing so, the respondents in #15 substitute *likely* for *probable* in 5 ("John is probable to win"), introducing the very same lexical item which figures in the contrasting example transformationalists and their offspring have trotted out for years to show this verb categorization distinction.

As we hope to have shown, however, many folk more interestingly resolve issues in these sentences by appealing to the context, to the stress or intonation, or to other features often associated with functional and pragmatic concerns (what the respondents so often refer to as "naturalness") which many sentence-level grammarians often ignore or dismiss as trivial. Such matters are not trivial to the folk in their search for sense, and linguists might do well to consult these strategies more directly among language users. Such folk reflection may provide keys to wider and more effective scientific as well as folk understandings.

Although some provoked little comment or revision, we summarize here, after each of the sample sentences, the principal folk reaction and its relation (if any) to the theoretical point illustrated in the sentence.[4] Since a large list of sentences was presented and since many respondents did not consider each, we consider this part of our investigation only a preliminary study in the employment of questionable sentences in context presented to nonspecialists as actually occurring ones, a technique which we still believe holds promise for more finely-tuned investigations of folk grammar.

Sentences presented to the respondents (with selected illustrative comments and corrections):

1. I have read often these books.
" ... often can't go there; sounds unnatural"

2. All some men left the room.
"'all' and 'some' can't occur together"

3. The man who John saw him left.
" ... don't need 'him'"

4. I wonder who they think that if the president appoints him everyone will be happy it is.
Several respondents didn't "want to use all the words."

5. Who did you give a picture of to?
" ... delete 'of'"

6. John is probable to win.
" ... use 'likely' or use 'will probably'"

7. They seem to elect each other would be hard.
"It would be hard to elect each other."
"It would be hard if both people elected each other because then there would be no winner."

8. Who do you think that won left?
The sentence is "messed up."
One respondent " ... can't figure out which 'won' or which 'left.'"

9. They know how each other to solve the problem.
"They know how each other solved the problem."
"They each know how to solve the problem."

10. Jack was called a criminal as often as Bill called an angel.
Most respondents noted no error here.

11. I forgot who lost which newspaper without reading.
One respondent wanted to change *forgot* to *forget.*

12. Whom did your interest in surprise?
"Who are you interested in surprising?"

13. This is the sort of book that no one who has read would give to his mother.
One respondent noted that one " ... can't get to the meaning."

14. He is the man whom everyone who meets the woman who marries admires.
No respondents commented on this sentence.

15. Someone who John expected to be successful though believing to be incompetent was in my office.
One respondent made the following elaborate correction: "Someone who John expected to be successful was in my office, but I found out he was incompetent" and then added "So I didn't hire him."

16. A book from which I copied without buying was gone from the bookstore.
Some respondents found this correct; some found it "unnatural."

17. Mary is pretty to tell people to look at.
One respondent noted it " ... doesn't make sense" and another offered the following correction: "Mary is too pretty to look at."

18. The man who he thought that if Mary marries him, then everyone will be happy is too old for her.
Several respondents offered an interpretation but could not give a correction.

19. I wonder who lost the newspaper without reading?
One respondent suggested a change to "the unread newspaper" or recommended making two sentences out of this.

20. He is the man who everyone who meets is sorry.
One respondent made the correction "Everyone who meets this man is sorry" but went on to suggest that it was still wrong.

21. Jones was the influential professor that John went to college to impress.
No respondent found an error here.

22. Who did they wonder whether to consider intelligent?
No corrections.

23. The book that reading would be fun was too expensive.
No corrections.

24. Who did you see that picture of?
Some respondents recommended changing *that* to *a*, but most found it correct.

25. Jack is the boy of whom pictures are on the table.
"The pictures on the table are of my boy John."

26. It was apparent yesterday John left.
No corrections.

27. Jack remembers who said who left.
No corrections.

28. Jack remembers which students Bill said that left.
One respondent notes the sentence is "messed up," even after making the correction "John remembers which student that Bill said had left."

29. Bill believes, but Jack doesn't, Sally is intelligent.
No corrections.

30. Which concert did you sleep during?
No corrections.

5.3.2 *The passive*

The passive construction in English and other languages has always been problematic for linguists (and others as well – educators, writers, editors). Is the passive used more prominently for focusing the theme (Givón 1979:186) or defocusing the agent (Shibatani 1985)? Is it essentially a "weak" construction to be avoided (e.g., Curme 1947 and most prescriptively oriented grammars and handbooks), or does its very markedness make it "strong" (e.g., Davison 1984)? Is it used predominantly in writing (Chafe 1982), or is it the genre of the text that determines whether the passive construction will be used (Biber 1986)? Does the construction reflect empathy (Kuno 1980), or is it one used for deceit (Bolinger 1980) or politeness (Brown and Levinson 1987)?

The text examined in detail (from conversation #23) for this discussion of the passive is reproduced below. The respondents were white, upper middle class residents of southeastern Michigan: a computer programmer (G), a social worker (D), and a high school sophomore (S [D's son]); the fieldworker was a Taiwanese linguistics graduate student. Incidentally, this analysis provides further evidence of our earlier contention that nonnative fieldworkers make an especially interesting contribution to this investigation in general. More detailed information about the fieldworker and respondents is available in the Appendix.

The data quoted here are taken from the fieldworker's second tape-recorded interview with these respondents and occurred towards the end of that ninety-minute recorded session.

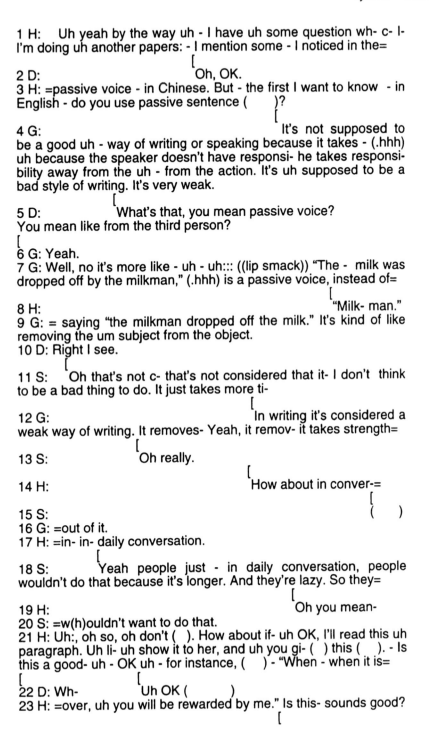

1 H: Uh yeah by the way uh - I have uh some question wh- c- l-
I'm doing uh another papers: - I mention some - I noticed in the=
                                    [
2 D: Oh, OK.
3 H: =passive voice - in Chinese. But - the first I want to know - in
English - do you use passive sentence (   )?
                                              [
4 G: It's not supposed to
be a good uh - way of writing or speaking because it takes - (.hhh)
uh because the speaker doesn't have responsi- he takes responsibility away from the uh - from the action. It's uh supposed to be a
bad style of writing. It's very weak.
                          [
5 D: What's that, you mean passive voice?
You mean like from the third person?
[
6 G: Yeah.
7 G: Well, no it's more like - uh - uh::: ((lip smack)) "The - milk was
dropped off by the milkman," (.hhh) is a passive voice, instead of=
                                                      [
8 H: "Milk- man."
9 G: = saying "the milkman dropped off the milk." It's kind of like
removing the um subject from the object.
10 D: Right I see.
           [
11 S: Oh that's not c- that's not considered that it- I don't think
to be a bad thing to do. It just takes more ti-
                              [
12 G: In writing it's considered a
weak way of writing. It removes- Yeah, it remov- it takes strength=
                   [
13 S: Oh really.
                   [
14 H: How about in conver-=
                                            [
15 S: (   )
16 G: =out of it.
17 H: =in- in- daily conversation.
         [
18 S: Yeah people just - in daily conversation, people
wouldn't do that because it's longer. And they're lazy. So they=
                                        [
19 H: Oh you mean-
20 S: =w(h)ouldn't want to do that.
21 H: Uh:, oh so, oh don't (   ). How about if- uh OK, I'll read this uh
paragraph. Uh li- uh show it to her, and uh you gi- (   ) this (   ). - Is
this a good- uh - OK uh - for instance, (   ) - "When - when it is=
[[
22 D: Wh-   Uh OK (   )
23 H: =over, uh you will be rewarded by me." Is this- sounds good?
                              [

24 G: That's passive voice.
25 H: Yeah, a- and in- in this case is this sounds good or sounds
bad.
26 D: (.hhh) Uh: we wouldn't say it that way, we would say uh - "I
will reward you when it's over."
27 H: So you-
              [
28 G: That's the active voice.
29 D: [[Right.
30 S: [[Yeah.
31 H: [[Yeah- so you w- will use active voice-=
32 D: =Or "When it's over I'll reward you." Yeah. (   )
              [
33 S: Yeah.

34 H: [
                                                          You won't
say "You will be rewarded by me."
35 G: [[No.
36 S: [[Probably not. An- you know people will do that occasionally,
- but it'd be an accident.
[
37 G: They do that in writing more than - in speaking.
38 S: Yeah, it'd be more of an accident if somebody said that.=
                                         [
39 H: (   )?
40 S: =And they'd- they'd you know it means the same thing, but
they probably wouldn't mean to say that, i-
((pause))
41 H: So in: uh conversation y- you -
                                         [
42 S: Use the active voice.
                                         [
43 G: Tend to use the active voice.=
44 H: =You don't use - passive voice at all. Uh use active voice?
                                         [
45 D: R:ight.
46 D: Right.
47 S: Yeah.
48 H: Uh huh. - ((quietly)) Oh this seems the same choice. - But in
writing you use.
49 S: [[Uh-
50 G: [[It's not good, actually - people (.hhh) it's- I don't know it- it's
a weak way of writing, but some people fall into the habit, because
it seems to uh - ((lip smack)) it's- I don't know, i- i- you don't have
to express a real strong opinion with it sort of thing.
51 D: That's true.
52 S: ((laughs)) Politicians.
              [
53 D: (   )
54 D: Yes. Politicians use that.
              [

55 G: (   )

                   [

56 S: Politicians use that a lot. Because y- - they=

                           [

57 ?:   ((sneeze))

                                  [

58 D: (   )

59 S: =don't say why. ((laughs))

     [

60 W: (   )

                       [

61 D: That's right.

                     [

62 G: Right.

((pause))

63 G: Anyways it's really discouraged in writing, but a lot of people seem to do it. Speaking, people don't.

                   [

64 S: I haven't seen a lot of it in=

                     [

65 H: Oh really?

66 S: =writing.=

67 H: =How abou- "Tell me the truth, wh- what was done by you."=

        [[

68 G: Right.   And they talk about in=

69 H: =Can you - (   ).

70 G: =writing class a lot.

     [

71 S: I do it. I do that. I (   ) when uh- when I'm trying to fill up=

                   [

72 D: Oh OK your- oh this is the sentence=

73 S: =space.

74 G: Oh really. ((laughs))

75 S: Yeah. When I'm trying to fill up (   ) space,

76 D: =right here. "Tell me the tru- - t- tell t- tell me the truth what=

                     [

77 G: ((laughs))

78 D: =was"-

79 H: Yeah- OK - "Tell me the truth, what was done by you last night."

80 G: That's passive again.

81 H: Yes. And the- I mean, sounds good or sounds bad, and it's=

              [

82 S: (   )

83 H: =natural or not.

84 D: You might just say- you might just say "What did you do=

                 [

85 H: "For you."

86 D: =last night."

87 S: They'd say like "He's not- tell me the truth. What did you=

     [

88 D: (   )
                        [
89 W: Oh. (   )
90 S: =do last night."
91 H: (   ) You don't say: I mean you won't say "What was done
by- What was done by you last night."
                        [
92 S: No.

((Deleted part of the conversation which is a discussion of the form
of "done" and the lack of formal grammar instruction in the
schools.))

93 H: Oh uh so you don't use that huh? - Huh?
94 All: ((laugh))
                    [
95 D: OK, try another one.
                            [
96 H: Ho-
97 H: Oh, how about- uh OK. (Just a minute.) Uh- for instance uh
the - parent uh - two people are speaking. Or maybe two students
they are classmates or something. - OK. "You can't do this or you
will be punished by teacher."
((pause))
98 G: Well: you might say that.
99 D: Yeah, that would be OK.=
100 H: =This will be sound OK right?
101 D: That would be OK.
                        [
102 G: I mean they all sound OK, but they sound kind of=
                                    [
103 S: It might. - Yeah
104 G: =w- wordy.
105 S: Yeah.
106 H: Oh w- oh you uh I mean uh you we don't necessary to use=
                                                        [
107 W: Oh:.
108 H: =a l- long word (   ).
                        [
109 S: That's probably another thing that'd be considered
upper class, is talking passive li(h)ke.
((pause))
110 G: I wonder- - maybe (.hhh) it's- it's just weak.
111 D: Uh- why don't you make a study of it and write us a paper=
                    [
112 G: (   )
                                [
113 H: (   )
114 D: =S. - That'd be interesting.
                    [
115 G: Yeah. (   ). (.hhh) Uh in Chinese, is that a- a form - =

116 S: [
            Yeah. ((laughs))
117 G: =that's typical?
118 H: Th- this is the: - my purpose of this paper is to uh - examine the Chinese passive voice. Because in Chinese - sometimes if uh for instance, - uh in English you say "You will be rewarded by me." This is uh: - good sentence right? Good, right?
[
119 G: Uh huh.

                                        [
120 D: Uh huh.
121 G: ((tentatively)) That's fine,
                                    [
122 H: Fine. - This sou- sounds good.
                                        [
123 S: (Fine), yeah.
                                            [
124 D: That sou- sounds fine.
125 H: Sounds good, right.
126 D: Right.
127 H: But if in Chinese you say uh - the same sentence, we say, - oh ((Chinese sentence spoken very rapidly)) This in Chinese. I think uh: a Chinese- i- uh- we listen- must be- I mea- sounds odd.
128 D: Right.
129 H: It's not very natural, it's huh:, uh w- why- I think we won't=
                                                    [
130 S: Yeah.
131 H: =say that, you know. But English you say ai- although you maybe in conversation you don't use it often, but still sounds good.
132 D: Right.
            [
133 S: Yeah.
            [
134 G: It sounds OK:
                            [
135 H: Sounds OK, yeah.
136 S: It s- it sounds kind of odd, but not much.
137 H: Odd. Oh still sounds odd?
138 S: A little bit.
139 G: Yeah, it sounds a little - odd.
                        [
140 H: Oh, maybe this sentence- I (   )
                        [
141 S: A little odd.
                                        [
142 W: ((laughs))
                                            [
143 S: If- if
you weren't- if you weren't listening carefully, you probably=
            [
144 D: (   )

145 S: =wouldn't notice it. - You know, if yo- if you're kind of half
paying attention, t- to somebody, (.hhh) you probably wouldn't=

            [
146 G: Uh huh.

                          [
147 W: (   )
148 S: =notice it, but if you were like listening intently you'd probably notice it and think it was a little bit odd.
149 H: Oh, OK. (   ) I mean, when if- th- if so, i- that's the same
as Chinese. But "You will be punished by parents or some- by
mother or something-" that's good. Right?
150 D: Yeah. That's fine.
151 G: It's all: - it- it's all about the same, I think that it's not quite
as direct, but (.hhh) people would hear it and they certainly would
understand it, and it sounds - a little odd, but not very, and it's certainly acceptable. ((quietly)) Or: you know understandable=

                              [
152 ?:   (   )
153 G: =and all.
154 H: We- how do you- OK, how do you - express this sentence.
You want to say uh, "You will be pu- punished by:

                                       [
155 G: Well maybe it's=

                                     [
156 S: Say that=
157 G: =where you want to put the emphasis, "If- if you don't be=
158 S: ="Your mom will punish you."
159 G: =good, you will be punished by ME," y(h)ou know, that=

                                      [
160 H: Oh you'll=
161 G: =sort of thing.
162 H: = be punished by ME.
163 S: [[Or you could say "I will punish you." Uh- y- you could say=

                                     [
164 G: [[Right, (   )   Y- you could.
165 S: =that, so-

            [
166 D: Or "Y- your- your parents'll punish you, if you don't
behave." - Or, "If you don't behave, your parents'll punish you."
((pause))
167 G: I s- I've seen a lot of - writing though in a- in a workshop,
writing workshops they try to discourage the passive voice, because they say it's a real problem.

       [
168 S: Yeah.
169 S: (.hhh) Yeah, well-

                   [
170 D: Well maybe that's just the opinion- of=

                                 [
171 S: Sa- same=

                                       [

172 G: U of=
173 D: =whoever's teaching it.
174 S: =with- same with th- same with the - English - dialects,=
175 G: =M's people, yeah.
176 S: =there's - very little of a standardized English grammar.
There is, but it's not really used. (.hhh) Because English is - pretty
much a complex language when it comes to the grammar.
177 G: Uh huh. There's a lot of different ways to say the same=
                                                          [
178 H: But - English=
179 G: =thing that are acceptable.
180 H: =is - not an easy language.
181 D: No. Cause there's w- w- w- what G just said, there's a lot of
different ways - to say the same thing.
              [
182 H: Lot of different ways.
183 H: Yeah.
184 D: [[You know.
185 W: [[Uh huh.
186 H: (.hhh) Oh:
187 ?: Ssssssh.
          [
188 D: ((laughs))
189 H: Ye- y- you know- uh thank you very much, because I don't
know: - English passive voice - I mean - what it- how about-
                                        [
190 W: Uh huh.
                                            [
191 S: It's- it's acceptable,
but you wouldn't use it in everyday talking.
192 D: Yeah, you don't use passive voice in everyday talking.=
                                            [
193 H: But maybe in a: - in- in-
194 D: =Maybe in writing - sometimes, yeah.
                          [
195 H: Writing or something-
                              [
196 S: Yeah.

((Short discussion of H's use of these data for both discourse
analysis and sociolinguistics courses which he is enrolled in.))

197 H: ... I want to know: - some uh - if the passive voice you use
in day uh day conversation, odd or not. Or no.
                    [[
198 D: Right.   Right. No. Our opinion=
                                            [
199 H: Oh.
200 D: =would be no, we don't.
201 G: Huh uh. No we don't. I don't think we know much about- I=
          [

202 D: Well-
                            [
203 S: No, not that much.
204 G: =don't think we analyze our grammar or our speech very=
                                                        [
205 ?:   (   )
206 G: =much, so we really aren't even used to thinking about how
we speak.
207 D: (.hhh) I don't know, it's kind of neat though.
208 H: [[(   )
209 S: [[It just comes naturally. We do- yeah.
                            [
210 H: Yeah maybe you- if I say some
passive voice you will be uh uh ((clicks)) sounds odd or -
                                                [
211 D: Yeah, we'd have
to think about what- what- what is that, and then figure out=
                                        [
212 H: ((laughs))
213 G: =what you're doing.
            [
214 W: ((laughs))
            [
215 D: Figure out. Cause we have- we have not had=
                                        [
216 S: Yeah.
217 D: =that class.
All: ((laugh)) (#23)

The fieldworker's initial approach to the topic

3 H: ...I want to know - in English - do you use passive sentence[5]

causes G to respond immediately, overlapping his question (so that
the last word or words cannot be heard):

4 G: It's not supposed to be a good uh - way of writing or speaking[6]

From the rapidity and strength of her response, it is evident that she
has strong, negative feelings about the passive. Later we learn that
she has attended several writing workshops, and her distaste for the
passive may spring, at least in part, from these. In fact, several of G's
remarks about the passive pertain directly to writing:

4 G: It's uh supposed to be a bad style of writing. It's very weak.
12 G: In writing it's considered a weak way of writing.
50 G: It's a weak way of writing, but some people fall into the
         habit,
63 G: Anyways it's really discouraged in writing,

And even more telling:

> 68,70 G: ...they talk about in writing classes a lot.

Perhaps the prescriptivist ideas that pervade most writing classes are responsible for this disdain for the passive. (For example, Curme's 1947 English grammar states that "the present literary passive is the weakest part of our language... .") S, however, a current high school student who ought to be strongly subjected to such prescriptivist norms,[7] disagrees.

> 11 S: ...that's not considered that it - I don't think to be a bad thing to do.

He apparently finds the passive acceptable even in writing, speculating that it's not used that frequently because it "just takes more ti-" [time].

> 18 S: ...people wouldn't do that because it's longer. And they're lazy.

In other words, the passive may even be the ideal, but it isn't used due to laziness. S undoubtedly has the full passive (with an agent by-phrase) in mind when he suggests that its length causes it to be avoided due to laziness (a notion he has suggested earlier in connection with pronunciation and social status (3.2)). His later suggestion that the passive is rare in writing is accurate, for the full passive is far less frequent than the agentless form (Biber 1986).

Perhaps agentless passives are not even being considered at this point. The examples provided by both the interviewer (23 H "You will be rewarded by me") and the respondents (7 G "The milk was dropped off by the milkman") contain agents. In fact, in this conversation in general, natural occurrences of agentless passives ("it's used...," "it's discouraged...," and so on) are commonly used with no self-consciousness, in spite of the fact that the passive construction is the focus. Furthermore, as our later analysis of functions will show, G certainly has agentless passives in mind at a crucial point in the discussion. We shall show below that this failure to distinguish between the two forms is the source of an apparent disagreement between G and S concerning appropriateness for the use of the passive.

The length of the full passive form is surely what S has in mind when he explains one of its functions, at least in his own writing:

71,73 S: I do that. I ( ) when uh - when I'm trying to fill up space.

This function of the passive, however, is not one that the other respondents agree to – in fact, it is treated with humor. The more serious functions they mention correspond to some of the ideas found in linguistic theory as early as Jespersen (1924):

    a. The active subject is unknown or cannot easily be stated.
    b. The active subject is self-evident from the context.
    c. There may be a special reason (tact or delicacy of sentiment) for not mentioning the active subject.
    d. Even if the active subject is indicated the passive turn is preferred if one takes naturally a greater interest in the passive than the active subject.
    e. The passive turn may facilitate the connection of one sentence with another.

G makes use of an idea missing from Jespersen's account – the prototypical notion of the "active subject" (agent):

4 G: ... it takes - (.hhh) uh because the speaker doesn't have responsi- he takes responsibility away from the uh - from the action.

For G, then, the agent subject is, at least at first, most typically ego (Givón 1984:107). When G says that the speaker is not responsible for the action, of course, she means the speaker as most typical agent subject. It will be important, at least in this text, to distinguish between speaker as sayer of sentence and as prototypically agent subject. On the other hand, it seems clear that G's characterization carries over to less prototypically agent subjects. In the above, she moves away from an interpretation of agent as ego since her syntactic construction is mixed between "doesn't have" (ego) and "takes ... away" (non-ego). G has shifted from speaker as agent to speaker as sayer.

When G first regards the prototypical agent subject as ego, then Jespersen's b) function is highlighted, for ego is the most usual given agent subject. But G's shift suggests that for her the principal function of the passive is Jespersen's third, although the notion of "tact" or "delicacy" is represented by that of "responsibility" in her version. G's belief that the passive construction is "weak" is, therefore, not simply a writing seminar proscription of its use, for she clearly connects it to the function "avoid assigning responsibility."

When G relates this responsibility to "strength" (e.g., 50 G), that makes S think of political discourse, almost certainly through its connection to the idea "fail to take a strong stand." He explains why politicians use the passive by referring to their failure to assign responsibility.

> 56,59 S: Politicians use that a lot. Because y- - they don't say why. ((laughs))

There is also an apparent contrast between what Bolinger (1980) and these respondents believe about passives. Bolinger claims that politicians state strong opinions and "facts" but that the passive allows them not to have to attribute these "facts" to anyone. G says that a strong opinion is not expressed by the passive exactly because it fails to attribute a source. As shown above, G associates "strength" with "responsibility"; therefore, G believes that "facts" are "weakly expressed" when they are not attributed. In the course of the interview, G follows exactly that pattern; at the beginning of the discussion of the passive, she says

> 63 G: ...it's really discouraged in writing,

using the passive to express an opinion. Later, in order to strengthen her claim, G switches to the active:[9]

> 167 G: ...in a workshop, writing workshops they try to discourage the passive voice, because they say it's a real problem.

She apparently feels that she needs to attribute this idea to a credible source in order to strengthen her argument (since S holds the contradictory notion that the passive is acceptable, perhaps even preferred, at least in writing).

These opposing positions of S and G, however, can be partly accounted for by noting that they are not systematically distinguishing between the full and short forms of the passive. Although G (and the other participants) focus on the full form of the passive at first (perhaps always in discussions of its form), it is the agentless passive which is highlighted in G's discussion of its function; S's laziness contention, on the other hand, highlights the full passive.

G's notion of lack of strength, dependent on a failure to take responsibility (i.e., attribute), is similar to what Shibatani (1985) calls "agent defocusing." Shibatani's assertion that agent defocusing is the primary function of the passive (as opposed to topicalization) appears to be the principal characterization given in this folk-linguistic account as well. G, like Shibatani, sees the passive as "centered around the agent," not as "a process by which a non-agent is promoted into the role of main topic" (Givón 1979:186).

In fact, even when G mentions that the passive can be used for emphasis, her focus is still the agent:

> 155, 157, 159 G: Well maybe it's where you want to put the emphasis, "If- if you don't be good you will be punished by ME," y(h)ou know, that sort of thing.

Perhaps G is tempted to search for re-emphasis or other meanings in the passive because the construction is marked, a notion expressed in Davison (1984). But G's conclusion that the passive might focus on the agent is exactly contrary to Davison's idea, which suggests that the markedness of the passive leads one to focus on the topicalized subject.

S understands that emphasis on the agent by the passive would be strange, for his response to G is:

> 163,165 S: Or you could say "I will punish you." Uh- y- you could say that,

Although G's comments on the passive throughout agree with Shibatani's agent defocusing argument and S appears to agree with her in the concern with attribution, it is not safe to conclude from these few remarks that there is no folk linguistic concern with the topicalized non-agent. Perhaps other respondents or other approaches to the topic with similar respondents would highlight that aspect of the construction, but here concern for the agent has predominated.

Considerations of meaning and function may even influence the way the form of the passive is talked about. Although G and S appear to know how to construct passives, D at first seems not to share this knowledge.

> 5 D: ...passive voice? You mean like from the third person?

This may be easy to dismiss as grammatically naive, but more careful consideration suggests that D's mention of "third person" may be similar to G's later emphasis on the agent defocusing function. Utterances in the third person assign responsibility to persons not only removed from the speaker but from others present at the time of speaking, and a third person subject is as far removed from the prototypically agent first person subject as possible (short of agent removal entirely).

D's lack of accurate structural information causes G to offer an example of a passive ("The milk was dropped off by the milkman") and describe it:

7,9 G: It's kind of like removing the uh subject from the object.

At first glance, perhaps due to the choice of *from*, this could be interpreted as a partial transformational approach to the passive – the subject is created by removing it from the object position. Another possibility exists, however, one connected to G's concern with the agent in nearly everything else she has said about the passive. In spite of her use of *from*, perhaps a better paraphrase might be something like the subject is removed and put over in an object position. G has attended writing workshops and seminars, and she is used to using "subject" and "object" when she talks about grammar, but that doesn't necessarily mean that she knows exact definitions. She may in fact mean to the right of the verb, or object of preposition, or even deleted agent when she says "object." The fact that she hesitates ("uh") suggests that she has not fully formalized the grammatical relations she wants to describe. The interpretation that emphasizes her concern with the agent is, if not preferred, plausible.

Another formal notion discussed by the respondents was the fairly straightforward idea of equivalency. Each stresses that passive sentences mean the same thing as their active counterparts, and several times during the conversation they actually construct active forms of passives and vice versa. For instance, when the fieldworker asks for paraphrases of "You will be punished by your parents," S suggests:

156, 158 S: ... "Your mom will punish you."

And even D, who at first does not seem to understand the mechanics of the construction, comes up with:[10]

166 D: ... "your parents will punish you, if you don't behave." Or, "If you don't behave, your parents will punish you."

There is certainly nothing linguistically remarkable about this association, since it is one of the most basic assumptions made about this construction.

The most important folk linguistic notion about distribution in this conversation is found in the disagreement between G and S concerning the occurrence of passives in speech versus writing. G feels that the passive is frequent in writing (inappropriately, since it is "weak") but "sounds odd" in speech. On the contrary, S thinks that the fieldworker's passive examples "sound fine," even though he believes that most people are too lazy to use them. When G says that "a lot of people seem to" use the passive in writing, S disagrees, although he has already admitted that he makes use of it in writing to "fill up space." A clue to the resolution of this is given by S:

191 S: ...it's acceptable, but you wouldn't use it in everyday talking.

S's use of "everyday" suggests that it is not speech versus writing, but a stylistic dimension which determines the various constructions that are opted for. Biber (1986) shows that the passive is used just as frequently in formal genres of speaking as it is in formal genres of writing, and it is used just as infrequently in "everyday" varieties of both mediums. S's reference to "everyday talking" implies that in non-everyday talking (formal) the passive might be used. It fails to surface in everyday talk, according to S, because we are too lazy to construct it in those situations. So, for S, the passive occurs when a writer or a speaker wants to "fill up space." We know already from the discussion in Chapter 3 that S directly associates length with both higher social status and more formal varieties. Since the respondents believe that the passive is "longer," there is no doubt, then, that S regards it as more appropriate to more formal expression.

G's principal concern is not with the fact that she finds the passive a little strange in speech but with its inappropriateness in writing. For her, then, the passive has no suitable venue; its frequency in writing is in bad writing, and it "sounds odd" in speech. G would undoubtedly be surprised at Biber's finding the passive a frequent construction in both formal speech and writing, a position much closer to S's, and it is almost certainly the case that G does not consider "informal writing" at all; perhaps it is not even a viable folk notion.

G's explanation of why the passive sounds odd in speech triggers S's specific association of upper-class and/or formal speech with greater length.

102, 104 G: I mean they all sound OK, but they sound kind of w-wordy.

S, who has earlier observed that "big words" are upper class, now concludes that lengthier syntactic expressions may be fancier:

109 S: That's probably another thing that'd be considered upper class, is talking passive li(h)ke.

This supports S's belief that the passive is used in formal settings (presumably those settings that the "upper class" find themselves in), but it does not correspond to a notion expressed by both S and G at the very beginning of this discussion of the passive.

36, 40 S: People will do that occasionally, but it'd be an accident ... it means the same thing, but they probably wouldn't mean to say that,

It is odd that S believes a speaker might lapse into the passive since his later arguments focus on its length and formality. Most folk notions of speech accidents go in the opposite direction. But S has an opinion about the overt awareness of grammar which explains, at least, why constructions may go unnoticed, an opinion which many linguists would share:

143, 145 S: ...if you weren't listening carefully, you probably wouldn't notice it. - You know, if yo- if you're kind of half paying attention,

Since the ordinary language user's focus is on message, not form, S's claim that much goes unnoticed in ordinary conversation is not controversial.

It is less odd that G believes the passive might sneak in since she associates it with bad writing.

50 G: ... It's a weak way of writing, but some people fall into the habit,

Since G believes the passive "sounds odd," the bad "habit" developed in writing is, specifically, a writing habit, not one carried over from speech. This corresponds with the composition teacher's commonplace that much of what is bad about inexperienced writing comes from a writer's imagination of what good writing ought to be rather than from the importation of speech habits into writing. Formal writing and prescription remain dominant concerns for G.

G's focus on good language behavior, S's on social class and formality, D's frequent role as conversational mediator, and the consideration of passives with and without agents lead to conflicting but overlapping perspectives. Although these shifting perspectives may help account for some diversity in the respondents' claims, they do not convincingly explain all the contradictions. Perhaps some of the remaining ones are a result of the fieldworker's strategies.

Although this conversation is relatively short, the fieldworker has succeeded (or failed, if it is an error to make the respondents attend to things they normally ignore) in awakening consideration of form. Although he asks from time to time if the respondents can "say" or "use" the construction or if it "sounds right," his questions are relatively context-free. Like any linguist, the fieldworker is used to making and getting grammaticality judgments on sentences. Even though his aim is to discover usage characteristics of the form, his method of investigation is still that of the theoretician – "Is this OK?" (e.g., 81 H, 100 H, 118 H). This approach, of course, leaves it up to the respondents to invent the contextual concerns which they find relevant. As suggested above, they are varied – prescription, class, speech versus writing, and so on, but such context-free presentation of sentences which are not proscripted for judgment is an odd pastime for nonlinguists.

G appears to be the first to play the linguist's game when H asks for a judgment on a passive (at 97 H):

    98 G: Well: you might say that.
    99 D: Yeah, that would be OK.=
    100 H: =This will be sound OK right?
    101 D: That would be OK.
                    [
    102, 104 G: I mean they all sound OK, but they sound kind of w-
    wordy.

Although one might argue that the fieldworker sets a minimal context, his attempt to do so is surely limited to semantic prototypes (students, teacher, punish) not to any larger network of contextual facts related to age, status, gender, genre, and so on or to even more complex discourse settings that might be relevant. After H's request, there is a telling pause; G finally agrees, but hedges: "Well" is long, and "might say" is an indication that something is amiss. Apparently D misses this hedging, for his "would be" is assertive, not tentative. G goes on to indicate her misgivings about the status of such sentences when she tries to re-explain her position, which she may suspect D and H have misunderstood, with "I mean," a discourse marker noted in other studies as serving just this function (Schiffrin 1987).

A little later, the fieldworker persists in seeking judgments about the passive, and G again appears to respond to its grammatical status, although her hedging continues to show that other notions are at work.

118 H: ... "You will be rewarded by me."
This is uh: - good sentence right? Good, right?
[
119 G: Uh huh.
                             [
120 D: Uh huh.
121 G: ((tentatively)) That's fine,
                               [
122 H: Fine. - This sou- sounds good.

G's first *uh huh* simply signals reception or understanding (back-channeling), not agreement that the sample sentence is correct or usual. In contrast, although D's first *uh huh* is positioned so that it might be such a back-channel, it is more likely an agreement that the sample is "good." Although G's "that's fine" is an unambiguous response to the status of the sentence in question, it triggers unqualified agreement among the respondents again. G's tentativeness, however, signals that she has not completely gone over to the grammarian's game; the sentence is fine as a structure, but she obviously has reservations about its use.

When all this grammatical focus is left behind and the fieldworker seeks a summary, D returns to his earliest observation, a purely usage-based observation:

197 H: ... I want to know: - some uh - if the passive voice you use in day uh day conversation, odd or not. Or no.
                               [[
198 D: Right.   Right. No. Our opinion=
                                                  [
199 H: Oh.
200 D: =would be no, we don't.

G's summary is more tentative, and reflects her emerging ability to deal with form:

151 G: It's all: - it- it's all about the same, I think that it's not quite as direct, but (.hhh) people would hear it and they certainly would understand it, and it sounds - a little odd, but not very, and it's certainly acceptable. ((quietly)) Or: you know understandable=
                                              [
152 ?:   (   )
153 G: =and all.

G is having trouble finding the right words to express the fact that passives are well-formed ("acceptable," "understandable"), but she has clearly come to distinguish between the structure of passives as structures and the uses of passives in context. Perhaps she realizes that "acceptable" might be taken to refer to the prescriptivist issue and substitutes "understandable" as a value-free label for structural integrity.

In conclusion, although there are apparent inconsistencies which arise from shifting points of view, some even generated by the fieldworker's approach, the respondents dealt with four major areas of concern: 1. Desirability: G, who is most concerned with prescription, finds the passive undesirable, weak (a word which she uses more than twenty times to describe the construction); S, on the other hand, finds it prescriptively appropriate, even a signal of formal, high class behavior. 2. Function: Much of the discussion stresses how the passive construction affects the agent, as opposed to the non-agent, although fewer formal linguistic accounts highlight this function. At other levels of functional concern, there is an almost caricaturistic concern with the passive's use by politicians, but it is more clearly related to the idea of avoiding responsibility (one of the principal senses of G's "weak") than to any extensive discussion of the rhetorical employment of structure. 3. Form: Although the conversation wavers between consideration of passives with and without agents, there is, as might be expected, little attention given to form itself. G's description of "removing the subject from the object" is confusing, and attention to the formal acceptability of the construction is probably more a reflex of the fieldworker's concern than the natural folk expression. 4. Distribution: Although the fieldworker appears to focus on speech, the respondents, particularly G, are most concerned with the appropriateness of the construction to formal writing. S, however, appears to arrive at a stylistic split between formal and informal by assuming the passive is longer (therefore higher class and more formal). The respondents' wavering in dealing with the passive as construction versus the passive in use is almost certainly one of the causes of difficulties in determining distribution.

As we have already shown, folk notions of grammar have implications for linguists and ethnographers. For our respondents, consideration of grammatical structure is not an unapproachable mystery, and even those whose business it is to theorize might pay attention to, for example, the fact that these folk linguists find the passive to be agent oriented. In many cases, there is a consistency in their folk representations (as there is in most folk taxonomizing), and where inconsistencies arise, they are often due to a shift in point of view (e.g., the respondents tentatively accept passives as viable structures, but then reject them in various specific contexts or roles). Perhaps the greatest inconsistencies are imposed by the linguist's desire for formal considerations, but we cannot know in advance what levels of form and/or function are available to the folk until we inquire. Moreover, we may not want to limit our inquiry to items which have already been focused on in the speech community. Elicitation and analysis of the process of reasoning about language in discoursal settings may be more valuable than the elicitation of static, prepackaged folk belief. This is consistent with more recent approaches to folklore study in general, in which process rather than items are the focus (e.g., Toelken 1979) and also more consistent with interactive forms of discourse analysis (e.g., "conversation analysis").[11]

Chapter 6: The last words

6.1 Metalanguage 1

We hope to have shown in the preceding chapters that, in the world outside of linguistics, people who are not professional students of language nevertheless talk about it. Such overt knowledge of and comment about language by nonlinguists is the subject matter of *folk linguistics*. It is language about language, and it is just as much a metalanguage as the linguist's.

In this concluding section we refer to such overt comment about language as *Metalanguage 1*. Like the linguist's metalanguage, such folk metalanguage is conscious. That is, it is not directed to a phenomenon which a speaker is unaware of, but to one which he or she has focused on in some way. Schmidt (1993:36-37) summarizes Bowers' (1984) account of the conscious awareness of information as that which "...is processed to the level of short-term memory and selectively attended to."

This consciousness requirement would appear to cause severe difficulty in the search for the nonlinguists' representation of some linguistic facts because language use itself is largely automatic (and therefore unconscious) behavior.

> An automatic process is characterized by the following properties. It occurs (a) without intention (and is therefore unavoidable), (b) without giving rise to any conscious awareness, and (c) without producing interference with other ongoing mental activities. (Flores d'Arcais 1988:117)

One might argue, however, that there are, on the one hand, many occurrences of deliberate (or even contrived) language use which are the result of conscious planning (or "monitoring") and that, on the other, there is the possibility of introspection which would allow for retrieval of linguistic material, however efficiently (and unconsciously) it is usually realized. Under these monitoring or introspective conditions, ordinary speakers ought to be able to provide linguistic commentary. Commentary about what? At first glance, language seems pretty simple; there are only three parts to it:

> Broadly speaking, three things determine the form of a message's expression: (1) The content the speaker wishes to convey, (2) the effect the speaker wishes to produce in his or her auditors, and (3) the forms permitted by the language being spoken. (Garrett 1988:70)

One may certainly give a fully conscious report about what content they intended to convey (or what they believe someone else intended to convey to them). One may even report on what effect they intended to produce in the hearer or what effect a speaker apparently intended to produce in them (ranging all the way from the blandly illocutionary – *I was asking a question* – to the complexity of per-locution – *I was trying to impress them with how responsible I was*). When we ask nonlinguists to reflect on Garrett's third characteristic of message expression (*the forms permitted by the language*), how-ever, we run into trouble (as we obviously did in Chapter 5). Réca-nati (1991 [1989]) states explicitly that the levels of language below what is *said* and *communicated* (his terms for what we might call the "literal" and "conversational" meanings) are not available to con-sciousness:

> In the case of sentence meaning [i.e., the result of semantic but not prag-matic processes], abstractness and cognitive depth go hand in hand with a further property, that of conscious unavailability. Of sentence meaning we can assume only tacit (unconscious) knowledge on the part of the speaker who utters the sentence. To be sure, users of language claim to have in-tuitions concerning what the sentences in their language mean; but these intuitions are not about their purported objects – linguistic meanings. They do not bear on the linguistic meanings of sentences, which are very abstract and unaccesible to consciousness, but on what would be said or communicated were it uttered in a standard or easily accessible context (106).

This inaccessibility is not just due to the fact that the production and reception of such forms is automatic and therefore unconscious. It is because there is, at least from one point of view, simply nothing there to report on.

> [I]t does not make much sense to say that a model "uses" the passive rule because the rule does not really exist. What does exist is a system of con-straints and principles. To use this kind of system all that the computa-tional model must do is operate according to these constraints. (Berwick and Weinberg 1986:198)

Most modern scientific approaches share this view. Constructions which exhibit linguistic well-formedness emerge from the interaction of very general principles, but these principles are not obvious in the constructions they authorize. For example, passive constructions, discussed in great detail by one group of folk respondents in Chapter 5, exist in many languages because of the incidence (or "cooperation") of a number of underlying linguistic principles, none of which, in itself, has anything to do with passives (or could be construed as a "passive rule"). These parts of the linguistic system belong to what Jackendoff (1997) has called the "computational mind" and, as such, are outside consciousness. What we are conscious of is the *result* of computations rather than the computations themselves.[1]

One might argue, therefore, that folk linguists are interested in only the "superficial" results of deeper operations. That is, a passive construction has a patient-as-subject (*The house*), a specific verb form (*was burned down*) and an (optional) agent-as-object-of-preposition (*by the arsonist*), and all that (identified with whatever folk terminology might be used to express it) is available to conscious representation by nonspecialists. In fact, our Chapter 1 discussion of Silverstein's (1981) categories focused on the likelihood that such semanto-syntactic (and pragmatic) forms might be available to folk awareness. Perhaps such levels are available to folk respondents, but they are not the usual things people discuss (even when asked to focus on particular constructions). Recall, from Chapter 5, that, when asked about the passive, the first facts G mentioned were those of proscription and rhetorical effect.

> G: It's not supposed to be a good uh - way of writing or speaking because it takes - (.hhh) uh because the speaker doesn't have re-sponsi- he [sic] takes responsibility away from the uh - from the action. It's uh supposed to be a bad style of writing. It's very weak.

One may suggest, as we have above, that G's *...takes responsibility away from...the action...* is an indication of her knowledge of a structural element of the passive (the "demotion" – or even deletion – of agent), but it is also possible that it is nothing more than an echo of a proscription from writing classes she has taken (which she mentions explicitly in a later segment of this same conversation). No matter what detail(s) she has in mind about the structure of passives, it seems fairly clear that her motivation for noticing them at all (i.e., the source of her metalinguistic comment on passives) comes from some sort of stylistic *rule* which suggests that passives are "weak."

In other words, even the functional correlates of form are not usually noticed by nonspecialists unless some other factor brings them into focus. One may argue, we believe, that the automatic processes outlined above have the effect of allowing communicators to focus on messages rather than on form. This is clearly the idea Sibata has in mind when he notes that "...the average language user is so involved with communicating that he [sic] is usually not conscious of the words he [sic] uses." (1971:375). It remains, therefore, to be seen what sorts of social and/or psychological incidents divert speakers and hearers from their conscious attention to message and cause them to focus on form. We believe there are essentially two.

Many such notices which we have recorded in this book are pretty obviously contrastive. That is, some speakers have rules which are different from those of their interlocutors, and the latter notice the different performance which arises from the application of these rules; this notice may be the source of folk linguistic comment. Sibata also notes the likelihood of this sort of overt awareness: "It appears to be natural for forms which differ from those which one usually uses to attract one's attention" (1971:374). Let us call this the "internal" factor which motivates nonspecialist comment on language.

In Chapter 1 we referred to the fact that folk awareness of language may, in addition to having a cline of *availability*, range along a continuum of *detail*, from the *specific* to the *global*. To believe otherwise would cause us to conclude that people who lack information about internal combustion engines are not aware of trucks bearing down on them. We shall also claim these global sorts of folk linguistic comments may be internally motivated ones, for they seem to be based on the respondent's awareness of a difference between his or her language use and that of some others, however unspecified the details of the difference may be.

G's comments on the passive, however, and many other details outlined in the preceding chapters suggest that a second major social-psychological factor which motivates the folk notice of language has its origins in institutionalized or conventionalized regulations. We shall refer to such factors as "external" ones, and anyone who has been to school, listened to "language pundits," or read books on how to speak or write "better" has certainly absorbed much of this information, and some of it has even filtered into oral tradition. For example, there is little doubt that the reportedly many calls to CBS after the initial appearance of Harry Reasoner and Barbara Walters as co-anchors of the evening news some years ago were motivated by the perception that Reasoner's closing line was "incorrect": *Good night from Barbara and me*. Perhaps the origins of this particular folk belief about correct language are based in school-years' proscriptions of such constructions as *Bill and me want to go out*, but knowledge of the proscription of "X and object pronoun" (regardless of the grammatical slot the coordinate structure fills) is widespread in US English. *Whom* occupies a similar position as a result of what must have begun as institutionalized instruction. Now, the more complex a construction, the more likely *whom* is to appear – again, regardless of case (e.g., *I don't know whom he said called*).

These two conditions, then, which might be paraphrased as the *You ain't from around here, are you?* and the *He don't talk so good, does he?* motivations for language notice seem to cover the territory fairly well. We note, as well, that the two obviously overlap when speakers from some areas (e.g., Michigan, as shown in Chapter 2) believe that their own language most closely corresponds to an institutional norm, allowing them the *Since you ain't from around here, you obviously don't talk so good* perspective. We also note, of course, that members of prejudiced-against groups may exhibit a *Since I am from around here, I obviously don't talk so good* mentality, the classic case of "linguistic insecurity."

Although we have focused more on overt commentary about language by the folk, we have occasionally drawn attention to other ways of expressing *Metalanguage 1* belief. We would claim, for example, that all "performance" speech (including even the most fleeting "imitation" of another's linguistic characteristics) requires a momentary focus on and hence reference to language itself, referring, perhaps, to a previously shared conversation if not a well-known cultural "script." When one "embeds" an imitation of a group or individual in an anecdote (or even in ordinary conversation), there is a dependence on the listener's recognition of the *Metalanguage 1* script (or "common knowledge") which lies behind (and therefore need not be explicitly mentioned in) the performance. Needless to say, identities and associated stereotypes are also awakened by such performances. Coupland (1998), for example, shows how a US television audience depends on clues of various performance voices by a television comedy series character (Sgt. Bilko) to detect the character's deception of others. Rampton (1995) shows how the performance of the voices of various ethnic groups is used by those who perform to establish an awareness in others of the performer's "life style" choices.

Notice, by the way, that an interesting problem remains in determining the *Metalanguage 1* status of the responses to many social psychological studies of language, particularly those "classic" experiments which submit regionally or ethnically different voice samples to respondents for evaluation, often by means of their placing the voices on a continuum of such paired opposites as "fast – slow" – the so-called "matched guise" model employing the "semantic differential" (e.g., Lambert et al. 1960). Some such experiments may use stimulus voices which do not awaken recognition of a caricaturistic sort on the basis of language form, but others may. In the latter case, we would say that covert *Metalanguage 1* forces were at work. For example, many European-Americans regard any occurrence of African-American Vernacular English (AAVE) as a "performance," even though for its native speakers its everyday use is "ordinary" (Preston 1992). In other words, the mere occurrence of some varieties which have been caricatured and stereotyped is enough to count as a "performance" of them and qualifies any use of them whatsoever as a likely trigger of a *Metalanguage 1* response. Language, therefore, among other social factors, may be one of the things which marks certain groups themselves (and their ordinary behavior) as "folk objects" in some cultural settings. It should be clear, therefore, that those surveys of language attitudes which respond to voices which awaken *Metalanguage 1* responses should not be simply compared to similar studies which use voices which do not (or are not likely to) awaken such responses, even though covert reactions to variation may be obtained.

6.2 Metalanguage 2

With these classificatory preliminaries in mind, we should be ready to explain how we "picked apart" the *Metalanguage 1* content of the exemplary discourses of this book. Let us return to an example already cited.

> M: Yeah, ah see that - that's what upsets me. You can see a really - an educated Black person, I mean I- you know I don't care what color a person is. It doesn't matter to me. - And you can under-STAND them and you can TALK to them and - Look at on the news, all the news broadcasters and everything. They're not talking ((lowered pitch)) 'Hey man, ((imitating African-American speech)) hybyayhubyhuby.' You can't understand what they're saying. And - I just don't think there's any excuse for it. It's laziness and probably - maybe it is you know, because they are low class and they don't know how to bring themselves up or they just don't want to.

This is very clearly a discourse which has language (the unintelligibility of AAVE and the irresponsibility of those who speak it) as its topic. M's notice of AAVE is very clearly motivated by both the conditions outlined above: AAVE is different from her own variety (the internal reason) and it is clearly not a "prized" or "correct" variety (the external reason). M also employs a "performance" to focus the listener's attention on the fact that AAVE is indeed unintelligible by providing a string of nonsense syllables, presumably an imitation of the "acoustic effect" AAVE has on M, but surely one she expects will "ring true" to her listener.

Doubtless all that is true, but for those who seek a revealing excursion into M's folk philosophy of language, it is perhaps pretty "blandly descriptive." Above we have only reported on M's *Metalanguage 1* commentary, but we believe there is more to it than that, and we have had to dig out M's (and perhaps most) folk belief about language from resources other than just the overt content of *Metalanguage 1* commentary.

For us, the richest territory to mine for folk belief about language has been the presuppositions which lie behind much *Metalanguage 1* use. They are, we believe, sorts of unasserted beliefs which members of speech communities share. We will call such shared folk knowledge about language *Metalanguage 2*, although we are aware that such underlying beliefs do not literally constitute a "language" or even a specific kind of language use. Linguists and philosophers alike agree that presuppositions form the backbone of mutual understanding among conversational participants.

> Presuppositions are what is taken by the speaker to be the *common ground* of the participants in the conversation, which is treated as their *common knowledge* or *mutual knowledge*. (Stalnaker 1978:320, emphasis in the original)

It should go without saying that the deeper the sense of community or shared culture among participants, the more likely that enormous amounts of presupposed (and therefore usually unstated) beliefs will play an important role.[2]

Perhaps reference back to the "research triangle" (Figure 1.4) will clarify the distinctions we are trying to make here. The c corner of the triangle (the "folk linguistic" corner) shows the connection to the beliefs and organizing principles which underlie nonlinguist (*Metalinguistic 1*) commentary. Although the data from the b corner are acquired from "covert" responses to language samples and the ones from c are overt commentary, both have *Metalinguistic 2* beliefs (represented at b' and c') in their background. Of course, data from the c corner have been the concern of this book, and we hope to have exposed their underlying beliefs and organizing principles in much of our discussion of them.

Such deeply-rooted folk beliefs about language as those represented in *Metalanguage 2* may also be thought of as forming a *cultural model*, and there is no doubt among culture theorists that they correspond closely to what we have characterized as underlying pre-suppositions.

> A cultural model is a cognitive schema that is intersubjectively shared by a social group. ... One result of intersubjective sharing is that interpretations made about the world on the basis of the folk model are treated as if they were obvious facts of the world. ... A second consequence of the intersubjective nature of folk models is that a great deal of information related to the folk model need not be made explicit. (D'Andrade 1987:112-13)

Oddly enough, this most important of the investigations of meta-language, the determination of the underlying folk theory (or theories) of language, has not received very much attention except in anthropological investigations, usually of cultures rather distant from modern industrial and technologically oriented ones (see the list of anthropologically-oriented studies of folk linguistics given in Chapter 1). That is too bad for two reasons. First, we ought to know the folk theories of language of all societies, not just for scientific completeness but also to avoid any accusations that scholars believe that folk notions abound only among cultures different from their own (usually industrial-technological ones where so little of this work has been done). Second, however, when work is done across cultures, the discussion is often contrastive. That is, readers are expected to be familiar with patterns of behavior and belief in their own culture (or to recognize them easily), and these are often the jumping-off spot in a scholarly characterization of behavior and belief in a less familiar setting. (Of course, we do not mean that the other culture's behaviors and beliefs are not "taken on their own terms" or have the meanings of the more familiar culture imposed on them. It is simply an anthropological convenience to provide a contrastive setting for many such discussions.) Unfortunately, a contrastive discussion cannot occur unless the knowledge of linguistic folk belief is rich on both sides. Some anthropologists seem to have studied their target culture very well but assumed (without investigation) the details of their own.

Rumsey (1992) is an example of such work, and we believe that he is nearly correct about the western languages (including English) which he contrasts with Ungarinyin (an aboriginal language in northwestern Australia). Roughly, his argument is as follows: English contrasts direct (*She said "I'm going to Osaka"*) and indirect (*She said she was going to Osaka*) reported speech. In Ungarinyin there is no indirect reported speech, and Rumsey concludes that a Western ideology of language – that language and use are not one and the same – is not viable for speakers of Ungarinyin. Westerners, he contends, believe that language items (vocabulary, for example) have an out-of-context existence which is somehow separate from its use. For speakers of Ungarinyin, language structure and use are inseparable, and language itself does not really exist except in use.

We are pretty sure that language, at least in the US, is indeed regarded as being separate from use, but we suspect it is not as abstract as Rumsey might seem to believe.

For the folk we have studied, language itself is the very real (although admittedly ideal) fact which dominates language use. (So far, Rumsey would appear to be right; the Ungarinyin apparently do not have this Platonic form lurking behind their usage.) For the folk, however, the only possible usage which derives from this ideal is "good" language, the forms enfranchised by the ideal itself (as we tried to represent graphically in Figure 1.2). All other forms for them are deviations from what a language ought to be. In short, only language which derives its shape from the ideal is rule-governed; all other use deviates (as indicated by the broken lines in Figure 1.2) and, to the extent to which such deviations do not make use of the rule-governed form as their basis, they are "without rules."

Linguists, on the other hand, believe that a language is a very abstract notion. The label *English* is only a convenient fiction for the varieties which are its constitutive, not derivative, elements. (In Figure 2.1 we have limited detail at this level to dialectal variation, although, of course, other types could be mentioned, e.g., gender, age, ethnicity, even idiolect.)

With this understanding of the folk theory of language in mind, let us return to M, who states very directly why some African-Americans speak a variety which she cannot understand – they are lazy. M may feel this is a little too blunt, for she goes on to excuse this behavior by noting that such speakers are low class and don't know how to escape that situation, although she is also quick to add that it may be that "they just don't want to."

M notes that "an educated Black person" can be understood and can be talked to (after the disclaimer that she does not care what color a person is), but she says she cannot understand other African-Americans (and she gives a little imitation of how they talk, which, except for "Hey, man," does not even consist of words).

Her first important folk claim is, therefore, that she cannot understand some varieties of African-American speech, but isn't this because M and speakers of AAVE do not, as we suggested earlier, share rule systems? Let's look at this more closely.

Remember, M claims that she can't understand speakers of AAVE because they are "lazy." For her, the proof of this lies in the fact that many of them have not made the effort to learn her variety. She says "I don't think there's any excuse for it." What is "it"? Of course, "it" can only be the use of a variety which M cannot understand (at least within a social setting in which she believes she has the right to understand). It might appear at first that she simply believes that speakers cannot be excused for using their native-language rule-system when there is another one around preferred by some.

How can M justify her belief that those who do not acquire another rule system are "lazy"? Isn't such acquisition difficult? In fact, we have already seen one reason why many nonlinguists believe that standard English can be almost effortlessly acquired. As Figure 1.2 suggests, many find the standard variety to be the only embodiment of rule-governed behavior. The idea that nonstandard varieties are also rule-governed is a very strange notion since they are most often described by nonlinguists as "lacking" rules. The relative ease with which speakers who "have no rules" should catch on to a system which "has a grammar" appears to be obvious to speakers like M.

We were wrong then, at first, to suggest that M's underlying belief was that people with different rule systems ought to acquire hers. In fact, her belief is that people who use non-ruled-governed systems should make the minimal effort to acquire an orderly one.

From the linguist's point of view, this is, of course, the most serious misunderstanding. No matter what language system another person has, it is a system. And, equally important, for those who know that rule system, it is just as efficient a device for communication and/or the organization of thought as any other language system, as Labov has shown so convincingly in his article "The Logic of Nonstandard English" (1969b).

There is, in fact, an alternative view of minority speakers which may cause even greater disparagement of them than the "lazy" interpretation we have just seen. In this view, they are plain old recalcitrant because they already know "good English" but simply refuse to use it. Recall the teacher who found that an African-American child was just "misbehaving" when he failed to speak standard English.

J: And I used to teach Black children. And I had a difficult time understanding what they were saying. And I found out later though that they were - it was intentional, because they could speak - like we speak. And they wer- because: I - was having difficulty with this o(h)ne little bo(h)(h)y. He was twe(h)lve. (.hhh) And - I - was supposed to test him, for uh reading problems. And I couldn't understand what he was saying. And so I called uh the teacher next to me was Black. ( ) next to me. (.hhh) So I did go over and get her,

> and I asked if she would help me. (.hhh) And she came in and she-
> - just- said to him, she said 'You straighten up and talk - the right
> way. She's trying to help you.' ((laughs))

You can bet that M would be even madder if she thought that all
those people who were saying "Hey man, hybyayhubyhuby" could
speak better but just refused to do so, but this is clearly what J has
learned from her experience with a stubborn elementary school pupil,
and she has been aided in this interpretation by a Black teacher,
whom she, reasonably, regards as authoritative on the matter.

G, another school teacher who has been often cited in the previous chapters, also voices the opinion that (apparently) *all* speakers
know (somehow) the rules of the standard English.

> G: The children themselves - all of us at time may say the improper
> endings. We may say it. (.hhh) But we recognize it is somebody
> says to us 'Is it correct,' you say 'No,' you know, 'This is the correct
> way (to) speak.' (.hhh) But- to sit and TEACH it incorrectly I don't
> think is right. Cause you DO say 'I have gone,' You do not say 'I
> have went.'

G seems to believe that nonstandard usage is "recognized" by its
speakers. Of course, to the extent that such speakers have been instructed on the details of the contrast between nonstandard and standard grammar or to the extent that they have constructed a contrastive grammatical analysis of their own on the basis of their exposure
to both varieties, G may be in some small part right. But he appears
to mean more than that. He appears to believe that there is some sort
of "innate" recognition that nonstandard constructions are "not
right." Except for slips, then, which he recognizes, "there is no excuse" for the use of nonstandard varieties because we all "know better."

Of course, that is not so. We do not know the rules of a variety
we do not know! For example, if you are not a native speaker of
AAVE, try to imagine a situation in which everything you said or
wrote would be judged and graded by how accurately it conformed to
the rules of AAVE (or "Ebonics" or whatever you choose to call this
variety). After all, you have surely had a lot of exposure to it – from
movies, TV programs, books, and even interpersonal communication. We suspect, however, that most of us would not fare very well,
though some would do better than others. Among those who would
get failing grades are those syndicated columnists in the US (both
Black and white, by the way) who wrote about the 1996-7 Ebonics
controversy, attempting to include examples of the variety. In fact,

they performed miserably in AAVE. Most of their sentences would fall into the category "not valid examples of the variety in question." Their pathetic attempts were perfect illustrations of the pervasive folk belief that AAVE (or any nonstandard variety) consists merely of breaking the rules of standard English (any of its rules, any way one chooses to break them). (Admittedly, they seemed to use some such strategy such as "sprinkle uninflected *be* widely throughout," but that is simply further proof that nonstandard varieties in the minds of the folk are not really rule-governed.)

As Rumsey suggests, however, there is a dichotomy between use and "the language" for westerners, but we believe he fails to see that that is a result of the westerner's faith in the Platonic ideal of the language itself, resulting in a "second-class" status for linguistic facts which can be discovered in "mere usage." We repeat here the most telling example of this in our data. Recall that D, G, and U are all trying to explain to H (the fieldworker, who is not a native speaker of English) what the distinction is between "gift" and "present."

D: Oftentimes a gift is something like you you go to a Tupperware party and they're going to give you a gift, it's- I think it's more=
                                                 [
H: Uh huh.
D: =impersonal, - than a present.
                   [
G: No, there's no difference.
                                 [
D: No? There's real- yeah there's
really no difference.
         [
G: There is no difference.
D: That's true. Maybe the way we use it is though.
U: Maybe we could look it up and see what "gift" means.
                                      [
D: I mean technically
there's no difference. (#28)
((They then look up *gift* and *present* in the dictionary.))

The telling lines here, of course, are those which say that there is "really no difference" ("technically") but that there is a difference "in the way we use it." Linguists (apparently just like the Ungarinyin) understand that the meaning of a word is, in fact, something like the collection of all its uses – all its contextual instantiations. Obviously, for the folk, words have a "real" meaning (separate from use), and the dictionary is a guide (as are teachers and language pundits of one sort or another) to that shadowy but for the folk very real authenticator of all that in language is rule-governed.

6.3 The discourse prospect

While we value the collecting of *Metalanguage 1* comments and attitudinal responses to language, we also believe that such investigations ought to lead to an enriched understanding of the underlying folk beliefs speakers of a language have about the nature of the object itself (what we call *Metalanguage 2*).

From earlier work done on the perception of language variety in the United States (cited extensively in Chapter 2), we have little doubt that the principal folk belief that speakers of US English have is the Platonic one of a rule-governed, "correct" system from which all "good" language use ensues.[3]

We have not, however, subjected every conversation about language quoted in this book to the kind of scrutiny which would allow one to see the full ramifications of this folk model of language (and others) in action, although, by seeking folk linguistic commentary, we believe we have avoided the flaw (or at least incompleteness) of many of the anthropological and ethnographic investigations listed in Chapter 1, which have reasoned back from language use, whether of structure, as in Rumsey, or of performance, as in Sherzer (e.g., 1974, 1983) and others, to the folk model of the speakers.

Although we have tried to discover underlying folk belief from the study of what the folk have said about language, we can envision an even more "linguistically" oriented approach to such an enterprise. One might uncover *Metalanguage 2* beliefs with more principled approaches to the analysis of the content as well as the structure of discourse. That is, we need what was called in Preston 1994 a "content-oriented" discourse analysis. Although numerous advances to discourse from a variety of approaches have been made over the last several decades (many reviewed in Schiffrin 1994), few have attempted to show how structure is "intimately" related to content, including the underlying presuppositions of speakers which must be taken into consideration if a "full" account of the content is to be given.

Even analysts who focus on 'topic' do so to determine how a topic is handled in the structure of a text or discourse, not, usually, to understand how a particular topic is related to the structures in which it appears. In short, most past research has cared about how topics are handled in general but usually not about how a particular topic is realized in text structure. That lack of concern is a disadvantage for many who would like to use the tools of discourse to get at particular instances of talk, for us, obviously, talk about talk itself.

It might seem that an established method for investigating the cross-currents of content and discourse form exists in "critical linguistics," but a closer look at credos of this style of analysis (e.g., Kress 1991) shows that it has a preoccupation with the degree to which social relations (particularly power asymmetry) have an influence on every aspect of language (including, of course, text and discourse structure). There is no doubt that social relations are crucial in the understanding of language in use, but it is not at all clear how that overarching concern spells out a method for the detection of form-content interaction. We suspect, in fact, that the over-riding social concern of that approach has led to a misuse of the linguistic evidence, in spite of its practitioners' claim that " ... CDA [Critical Discourse Analysis] must rely ultimately always on quite precise analyses and descriptions of the materiality of language – on close linguistic descriptions" (Kress 1991:86). Unfortunately, the linguistic analysis in this approach seems always to play second fiddle to presumptions about the influence of power. The following is typical: "We know that different conceptions of a relationship are involved in saying Mary married Bill, or Bill married Mary, or Bill and Mary married, etc." (Kress 1991:91). There is a "sexist reading" of *Bill married Mary* which would, indeed, suggest that the word order revealed something of the "different conception of the relationship." In this case, however, critical linguists overlook the fact that word order with such verbs as "marry" may simply reflect given-new patterns of information in the sentence. The "fundamental relationship" between Bill and Mary is not changed in the following invented data:

(Two of Mary's old friends)
A: Who did Mary end up with?
B: Oh, didn't you know? Mary [or, better, 'she'] married Bill.

(Two of Bill's old friends)
A: Who did Bill end up with?
B: Oh, didn't you know? Bill [or, better, 'he'] married Mary.

Reversing the two (or substituting *Bill and Mary married* [or *Mary and Bill married*]) will produce bad discourses (or ones which require strikingly different interpretations from the "normal" ones).

In short, critical linguistics does not appear to offer a general method or consistent application of techniques which would allow one to move back and forth between the social factors critical linguists seem most interested in and the textual and discourse features which support them.[4]

This is not a problem to be swept under the rug, however; knowledge of a speaker's intentions and the like are fair game in discourse analysis, and pragmatics in general would fail (or be disqualified from scientific inquiry) if such matters could not be used. In fact, it is very likely the case that many of the conclusions critical linguists reach about power asymmetry in discourse are exactly correct, but it is difficult to see how linguistic reasoning, however loosely defined, has been the vehicle for such conclusions. The difference, as we see it, is this: literary critics, social critics, and critical linguists bring knowledge of the world (past and present), likely identities and intentions of individual and group actors, and a host of other interesting social factors to bear on a reading or an interpretation of a text. There is no doubt that such a reading is an important and interesting one,[5] but the leap from that interpretation to the specific linguistic content of that situated text is a dangerous one. How may one know that the use of a passive (or modal, or any linguistic device which has been a part of the encoding of that particular text) is wholly or in part responsible for the interpretation made? While it may be the case that a text has the meaning suggested by such resourceful and knowledgeable analysts, attributing that meaning to specific text elements is a risky business indeed.

What sorts of other investigations, then – ones which could have a bearing on the specific meaning of the text in hand – could one hope to carry out? We believe that at this stage – a sort of infant stage in the study of text and discourse in general and perhaps an almost prenatal one for the study of the relationship between content and form – the best way to proceed is to look for patterns of established textual elements (that is, linguistic forms) which are not behaving normally (although, of course, one may discover that just such patterning is the norm for the special sort of text under investigation). Here is a simple example from our data.

The following is the opening of a conversation in which AAVE is the "topic" (at least in the common-sense definition of "what the conversation was about," a notion perhaps closest to that of "topic framework," Brown and Yule 1983:73-79).

1 C: We uh - linguistics, in this field, uh - from the book I s- I mean,
I saw from the book that - many linguists quite interest in black
English. So could you tell me - a little bit about - your dialect?
2 D: Dialects.
3 C: Heh yeah
4 All: ((laugh))

    [
5 D: Well, uh: - well - see the world's getting smaller. There's=

        [[
6 C: ((laughs)) I- I mea- do you have-
7 D: =not - even among all the ethnic groups we're- we're getting-
getting less and less of dialectual in- inFLUence. (.hhh) Uh I'm-
happen - not to be - from the South, uh: uh u- du- There is a certain
aMOUNT of black English that's (.hhh) spoken. There's a certain -
certain uh: forms and uh certain idioms that uh uh- blacks use
that's indigenous to blacks.

    [   ]
8 C: Could - could you gi- ((clears throat)) give me some.

. . . .((section on AAVE lexical items excluded))

50 R: I don't know=I don't know too much - about black di(h)- -
well, I don't KNOW.
[
51 A: Heheh.
52 D: We don't know THAT much. We don't- see th- to be- to=
            [
53 C: Huh.
54 D: =really KNOW the up - the the uh uh - I guess the the the the
sayings that are now - USED, you have to be out - aMONG uh
people tha- like uh: You would have to be (.hhh) where uh - =

             [[
55 C: Uh huh.   You=
56 D: =you know sports:, you uh you'd be, that would be it- =
          ]   [
57 C: =mean you can't pick up. Uh huh.
58 D: =like if I played basketball: (.hhh) down the street I'd have-
I'd have access to a lot (.hhh) of uh the current language that's
that's going DOWN. (.hhh) Uh: uh I could under(heheh)=
              [ ]
59 R: 'That's going do(h)wn.'
                 [
60 C: ((laughs))
61 D: =differently. Uh then uh - you'd have to uh be- I would have
to be in the black CHURCH. That would be another kind of=
              [
62 C: Uh huh.
63 D: =good place to- (.hhh) to find the current usage. Uh uh and
you'd d- you have to be uh - you kno- involved in a- in a lot of black
activities which (.hhh) I don't, I am NOT basically in. I- - mostly into
uh: uh uh WORK, going to school, church life, (.hhh) that's pretty

much it, and just taking care of my (.hhh) basic family, but I
don't have the - social life as such that-=
   [   ]
64 R: But uh more or less uh
                   [
65 C: Uh huh.
66 D: =that- that- it- that you know gives us access to this=
                                          [
67 R: Access.

68 D: =kind of - kind of language.
              [
69 R: And then again we weren't brought up
70 C: Uh huh.
71 D: To use
      [
72 R: So it's h- it's hard for me to rem- think you know (of) black=
                                               [
73 D: Course=
74 R: =dialect.
75 D: =you did cause your - brothers, your brothers used it quite a
bit.
76 R: Yeah but that's because they w- well usually when they were
with other GUYS. Then they- you know they were in that - and you
know enVIRONment, where they could pick it up and use it, and
they could still do it, but I CAN'T. I can't - you know just - right off
the top of my HEAD: just start talking - black dialect.
                                             [
77 A: I can heheh.
                                  [
78 R: Maybe she can, I don't
know.
79 C: [[Tell me, tell me. Sh- give me just give me some example.
                                               [
80 A: [[( ) ((laughs)) Why.   Well yeah when I-
well I was forced to at first when uh I moved up to Detroit,
because=
[
81 C: Uh huh.
82 A: =they would make fun of the way I talked, because I talked
proper s-, quote unquote. ((laughs))
                     [
83 D: Quote unquote.
                       [
84 C: ((laughs))
                     [
85 R: ((laughs))
                        [
86 A: I wa- ((laughs)) so I was
- just forced to use it.
87 C: Uh huh.

88 A: So-=
89 R: =So say something.
90 A: [[No: I don- I can't really say any NOW, cause I'm not=
91 C: [[Say something yeah.
92 D: [[So (   ) say something.
93 A: =among people who speak, it just comes o(hh)ut.
94 R: Oh yeah. That's another thing. Sometimes - when like=
       [[
95 C: Uh   Uh huh.
96 R: =when we're WITH other blacks we could - do it. ((laughs))
                                           [
97 C: Oh you
can - you can - uh spontaneous - spontaneous - you c- you=
[   ]
98 A: It just comes out.
 [
99 D: Yeah you can bounce it off if you want.
                  [
100 R: You can bounce off each=
101 C: =you just begin to talk, right?
    ]   [
102 R: =spontaneously bounce it off of each other. - Right. (#35)

This is a rich conversation and might be approached from several discourse analytic points of view (and has, for example, in Preston 1993c). We will look at it here only from that of "topic establishment." There are basic misunderstandings at the beginning of this conversation. C, the fieldworker, presupposes that there is a "Black English," that his respondents (who are African-American) are speakers of it, and that it is a "dialect" (all in 1 C). D "disputes" all of this, at first by simply stating "dialects" (in 2 D) with an intonation which clearly suggests that there is something very wrong with C's initial request and then (in 5 and 7 D) by rebutting all of the (relevant) presuppositions in 1 C: 1) It's unlikely that there are any "true" dialects any more (since "the world's getting smaller"); 2) There are perhaps outlandish places (e.g., the South) where there are "true" dialects, but I am not from there, and 3) If a "Black English" exists (presumably in the North), it would not qualify for "true" dialect status since it differs only in terms of its "forms" and "idioms" (apparently, for D, elements insufficient for dialect distinctiveness).

After several more turns, however, D and R have had a chance to redefine for C their understandings of (and personal abilities in) AAVE. During this period in which the participants were unsure of one another's understanding of the topic, normal anaphoric representation of the topic was rare; after the discussants have had a chance to present their views, normal anaphora in reference to the topic began. Table 6.1 shows a complete (ordered) list of mentions of AAVE in the first section of the conversation reported above (Sample #1) and in the second section (Sample #2). Even a cursory (nonstatistical) view will show that there are indeed two very different linguistic means used here to handle the topic of the conversation.

Sample #1		Sample #2	
C1	Black English	D75	it
C1	dialect	R76	it, it, it, Black dialect
D2	dialects	C79	some example
D7	Black English	A86	it
D7	forms and idioms	R89	something
C8	some	A90	any
R50	Black di(h)	C91	something
D54	sayings	D92	something
D58	current language	A93	it
D63	current usage	R96	it
D68	kind of language	A98	it
R72-4	Black dialect	D99	it
		R102	it

Table 6.1: References to AAVE in two sections of the conversation

Only one pronominal (or pro-NP form) appears in Sample #1 ("some"); in Sample #2, however, only one full NP form, "Black dialect," occurs (and one example of the referential phrase "some example"). While AAVE is being negotiated in Sample 1, it is being treated as *newer information*, in spite of the fact that it has already entered into the discourse context.[6]

The relationship between this topic, or, more specifically, its failure to establish itself as an agreed-upon concept in the early stages of this conversation, and the odd use of referential terms in the discourse is straightforward. The patterning of such referential phenomena, choices among discourse markers and even pronouns themselves (e.g., *you* versus *they*), and the uses of a number of other well-established linguistic phenomena allow the content-oriented discourse analyst to make ready but principled connections between the concerns of the text under investigation (the content) and at least some of the forms involved in its linguistic instantiation.

The relationship between topic and anaphoric structure outlined above did not, however, develop simply from a reading of the text and a sudden decision to look at patterns of reference. A full characterization of the conversation from several discoursal perspectives (Preston 1993c) had already taken place. There are, in fact, analytic procedures which characterize the larger organization (and identity) of texts from which the analyst may more safely move in the search for interconnections between low-level elements of linguistic structure and other matters (some perhaps not those strictly of "content"). Labov (1972b), for example, elaborates a theory of personal experience narrative which recognizes the parts *abstract, orientation, complicating action, evaluation, resolution*, and *coda*. (363). He is careful to detail what linguistic elements are usual (in some cases required) for each of these rhetorically-determined segments, and one may confirm even sub-sections of these categorizations by appeals to linguistic elements. Reference is again exemplary. In a personal experience narrative which Labov cites (1972b:358-9), a young man tells of the worst fight he ever had, one with a girl. A study of the pronominal reference in this story shows that the only references to the fight itself occur in the abstract and coda and that two subsections of orientation may be identified. In the first, almost exclusive references to the boy clearly indicate that the function of that orientation section is to provide background information about him and his family (particularly their impoverished situation), which the teller feels is necessary to an understanding (or, better, an appreciation) of the story. In the second, almost exclusive references to the girl show that that orientation section fulfills another function – letting the hearer know just how tough the girl was (not a bad idea if a young man is to perform a believable narrative in which the worst fight he can remember was with a girl!).

In this case, the linguistic details of narratives confirm the rhetorical subdivisions Labov proposes and even allow principled identifications of further content-oriented subdivisions. In general, then, one may be able to account for the use of marked or unusual patterns of linguistic features by associating them with particular content-features of texts themselves – specific orientation sections of narratives, topics yet to be agreed on in argument, and the like.

We agree, therefore, with Blommaert and Vershueren (1998), who, in their investigation of cultural and ethnic diversity (as revealed in public discourse) assert that "language ... [is] a way into ideology" (32). They list "wording patterns and strategies," "local carriers of implicit information" (i.e., lexical and other items which trigger understandings of presuppositions and implications), "global meaning constructs" (i.e., larger patterns of language use such as argumentation and narration), and "interaction patterns" as pragmatic areas likely to bear fruit in the search for the exposure of ideology in discourse. Unfortunately, for our purposes at least, their work has focused on written or relatively planned spoken language; nevertheless, their general approach to content would seem to be very similar to the one we recommend here.[7]

Perhaps a more intensive investigation of discourses about language itself will eventually allow exposure of the cognitive models the folk use in reasoning about language. We will need to look very carefully at many more *Metalanguage 1* conversations before we can hope to go on to these deeper and more revealing levels of *Metalanguage 2*. Language itself is surely as important an area as those Fodor apparently had in mind when he wrote the following:

> Much everyday conceptualization depends on the exploitation of theories and explanatory models in terms of which experience is integrated and understood. Such pre-scientific theories, far from being mere functionless "pictures," play an essential role in determining the sorts of perceptual and inductive expectations we form and the kinds of arguments and explanations we accept. (1981:62)

In short, if we had it to do over again (knowing what we know now after recording and transcribing hours and hours of folk conversations about language, only a small sample of which we have been able to show here), we suppose we might take a more principled discourse-analytic point of view in all our analyses. Perhaps we can be forgiven for not doing so by asking readers to remember that much of the territory we have explored has not even been approached before, particularly not for Western or principally European-oriented societies.

Since we have covered much of the territory of linguistics, any attempt at a concluding summary might frighten readers by making them believe that we intend to go on and on. We admit, in retrospect, however, that that temptation reflects one of our conclusions: we have only scratched the surface of this valuable ethnographic and linguistic resource. We hope we have pointed out along the way the opportunities for expansion and modification of the collection and interpretation techniques used here (and, as always in such work, the possibility of application of these same methods to different groups and/or topics). Historical linguistics, for example, is not extensively treated; our work on syntax was, frankly, narrowly conceived. In fact, the list of whom we might have talked to, how we might have alternatively planned interviews, and what additional devices we might have used for interpretation is a long one, and we hope to get on with it.

At the risk of enormous oversimplification, however, we cannot resist the temptation to make a few final comments. First on the personal and/or social side:

1. Nothing in the collecting or interpretation of data or in the writing of this book has caused us to question the definition of *folk* used here. Everybody is a folk, and the nonspecialist views of topics which touch the lives of all citizens are worth knowing for their bearing on public life in general, on education in particular, and, most specifically, on the regard in which the prejudiced against are held.

2. Although we have transcribed and reported beliefs and comments about language and their users which we do not personally hold, we did not expect to find in any speech community what we believe to be the majority view of any linguists. On the other hand, by extracting and reporting on these views, we have not meant to shame or belittle any of our respondents. In fact, in nearly every case, we find that these discussions reflect stongly-held positions about language and its repercussions in communities. We think it is important for language professionals, especially perhaps those involved in the field known broadly as applied linguistics, to know as much as possible about these folk positions.

On the "substantive" side, we believe the following are worth noting especially:

3. Folk linguistics is radically contextualized. Chapter 5 is our shortest chapter (next to this concluding one), and even there we have had to infer theoretical positions from discussions of language in use. This contextualization extends all the way from sounds to discourse and is an important consideration in approaching any task in this enterprise: collecting or interpreting. Since this is the case, we believe (as we hope to have shown throughout and as we have stressed just above) that the discoursal investigation of folk linguistic matters is indispensable.

4. In spite of its contextualization, folk linguistic opinion (at least for our respondents and we suspect for many in the rest of the US and in many other locales as well) is filtered through an abstract view of "The Language" itself. Real language use is a personal and social phenomenon for our respondents, but lurking behind it is an abstraction, the only construct capable of maintaining the "correct" form of the tongue.

5. Because of 3. and 4., folk opinion about language radically shifts between what is done and what ought to be done, often in a short space of conversation. A failure to recognize these two important bases for opinion will lead to damaging collection techniques

and uninformed interpretation of folk linguistic opinion (or even of folk responses to more traditional attempts to get at belief, e.g., so-called language attitude studies). This fact bolsters, we believe, our contention in 3. that discoursal investigations of these facts are particularly appropriate, although we do not deny the value of quantitative approaches.

Finally, whatever the reader may think of our interpretations, we hope these data themselves add weight to Hymes' contention, which we repeat here:

> If the community's own theory of linguistic repertoire and speech is considered (as it must be in any serious ethnographic account), matters become all the more complex and interesting. (1972:39)

We hope to have provided, at least then, an opening description of this rich territory, recalling here our original justifications, all of which might be rolled into one: Folk linguistics is an integral part of the ethnography of a speech community. Any research (or "action" based on research results) which depends on an understanding of such a community will, therefore, "need" this information as much as any other demographic and/or linguistic characterization of such a community.

Appendix: Fieldworker and respondent identifications and recording data

Tapes, in almost every case sixty-minute cassette recordings, are referred to by number (#) and are so marked in the text; in a few cases, there are video recordings only or audio and video; these are noted. In some cases an interview lasted for more than sixty minutes, and the tapes are numbered consecutively (e.g., #49 & 50), except in one case (#36) in which two such tapes are identified as #36a and #36b." In one case (#48a & b) the 'a' and 'b' labels identify the fact that two different recording sessions (with, in fact, two different sets of respondents) were made on the same tape.

We hope here to show sufficient demographic information to allow those who are interested in such matters to form whatever conclusions they may like about the nature of the folk linguistic data reported in conjunction with the respondents' social status, age, ethnicity, and the like. We believe that, in spite of the essentially nonquantitative, broadly ethnographic approach taken here, these data are representative of the population of the urban and suburban southeastern Michigan speech community and, in many ways, of United States perceptions in general.

We have tried to indicate, so far as possible, the circumstances of the interview, the relationship between the fieldworkers and respondents, and even relationships among respondents across interviews.

The authors would be happy to respond to inquiries concerning further details about these data; we have, however, committed ourselves to respecting the anonymity of our respondents, except for those who allowed their interviews to be videotaped and who signed waivers indicating that they were aware that these videotapes might be widely distributed for academic purposes. All respondents, of course, signed waivers granting permission to use their tape-recorded interview data for academic study and publication.

For further information, contact:

Dennis R. Preston
Department of Linguistics and Germanic, Slavic, Asian and African Languages
Wells Hall
Michigan State University
East Lansing MI 48824-1027
Fax: (517) 432-2736
Phone: (517) 353-0740
e-mail: preston@pilot.msu.edu

or

Nancy Niedzielski
Department of Linguistics, MS-23
P.O. Box 1892
Rice University Houston TX 77251-1892
Fax: (713)527-4718
Phone: (713)527-6010
e-mail: niedz@ruf.rice.edu

Recorded data:

Tape #1 Fieldworker H – Horng-ming Wu, Taiwanese, male, 30, linguistics gradu-
        ate student, W's spouse
Recording date: 11/7/87; recording site: respondents' home; small, semi-rural
        southeastern Michigan community
Respondents:
        G: White, male, 44; Army officer, MS.Ed.; elementary-junior high school
            teacher in predominantly African-American schools in urban
            southeastern Michigan; born urban southeastern Michigan, some
            childhood years in southern Indiana; elementary, secondary, and
            higher education in southeastern Michigan; K's spouse
        K: White, female, 42; B.S., civil service and telephone company worker,
            training for elementary school teaching; born central Michigan,
            higher education in southeastern Michigan; G's spouse (K was
            Wu's classmate in a graduate/undergraduate level History of the
            English Language course at Eastern Michigan University)
        A: White, female, 14; junior high school student; G and K's daughter
        J: White, male, 8; elementary school student; G and K's son
        U: Unidentified younger children of G and K
        W: Taiwanese, female, 26; H's spouse

Tape #2 Fieldworker H – Horng-ming Wu (see #1 above)
Recording date: 11/14/87; recording site: respondents' home; small, southeastern
        Michigan semi-rural community
Respondents:
        R: White, male, 53; high school; formerly policeman, now a grounds-
            keeper; lifelong suburban southeastern Michigan; J's spouse
        J: White, female, 52; B.A., former teacher and social worker; born in
            Canada, elementary school and continuous residence thereafter
            in suburban southeastern Michigan; R's spouse
        K: White (Swiss[French]), male, mid-30's; computer science graduate
            student; R and J's son-in-law

Tape #3 Fieldworker K – Kathleen Keller, white, female, 25; TESOL graduate
           student
Recording date: 11/15/87; recording site: respondents' home in urban southeastern
           Michigan
Respondents:
        H: White, female, 31, B.A., masseuse; schooling through high school in
            Indiana, came to western Michigan for undergraduate studies;
            now lives in urban southeastern Michigan; S's significant other
        S: White, male, 38; B.A., former social worker now salesperson; born and
            early schooling in Minnesota, came to western Michigan for un-
            dergraduate studies; now lives in urban southeastern Michigan;
            H's significant other

Tape #4 Fieldworker S – Mei Shen, Taiwanese, female, 26, linguistics graduate
           student
Recording date: 11/6/87; recording site: respondent J's home in urban southeastern
           Michigan
Respondents:
        M: White, female, 65+, divorced; high school graduate, former store
            clerk, now assists in managing fast-food concern; born and all
            schooling in Ontario; now lives in urban southeastern Michigan;
            A's significant other
        J: White, female, 65+; B.A.; store clerk and owner; born and early
            schooling in Ontario; now lives in urban southeastern Michigan;
            H's (see #5) spouse
        A: White, male, 65+, B.A., retired automobile plant worker; born and
            early schooling in Upper Peninsula of Michigan; M's significant
            other

Tape #5 Fieldworker S – Mei Shen (see #4)
Recording date: 11/13/87; recording site: (see #4)
Respondents:
        M: See #4
        J: See #4
        H: White, male, 68; retired chemist and laboratory owner; born Colorado,
            elementary school California, high school Pennsylvania, some
            college; adult residence in Chicago and western Michigan; urban
            southeastern Michigan since 1962; J's spouse

Tape #6 Fieldworker K – Kathleen Keller (see #3)
Recording date: 11/11/87; recording site: unknown
Respondent:
        T: African-American, female, 28; M.S., parole officer, county employee;
            grew up in small city southern Michigan; urban southeastern
            Michigan resident since 1978

Tape #7 Fieldworker H – Horng-ming Wu (see #1)
Recording date: 11/21/87; recording site: D's home in urban southeastern Michigan
Respondents:
>   G: White, female, 35; B.A., computer programmer; lifelong urban southeastern Michigan resident; D's spouse
>   D: White, male, 38, M.A., social worker; lifelong urban southeastern Michigan resident; G's spouse and S's (see #23) father

Tape #8 Fieldworker Z – Larisa Zlatich, Yugoslavian, white, female, 30, linguistics graduate student
Recording date: 11/22/87; recording site: respondents' university campus apartment in urban southeastern Michigan
Respondents:
>   B: White, male, 40; Ph.D. candidate, psychologist in juvenile facility; born in New York City; elementary school through undergraduate work in Texas; moved to urban southeastern Michigan for graduate studies; D's spouse
>   D: White, female, 42; M.A., elementary school teacher; born and early schooling New Jersey; moved to urban southeastern Michigan for undergraduate studies; B's spouse

Tape #9 Fieldworker N – Nancy Niedzielski, white, female, 23, linguistics graduate student
Recording date: 11/20/87; recording site: respondents' home in suburban southeastern Michigan
Respondents:
>   M: White, female, 44; high school, secretary; lifelong suburban southeastern Michigan resident; T's mother
>   T: White, female, 23; undergraduate art student; lifelong suburban southeastern Michigan resident; M's daughter

Tape #10 Fieldworker X – Zhi-qun Xing, mainland Chinese, female, 28; linguistics graduate student
Recording date: 11/21/87; recording site: unknown
Respondents:
>   S: White, male, 24; English teacher in Japan, TESOL graduate student; born, schooling in New York City; US southern parents; now urban southeastern Michigan resident for graduate studies
>   B: White, male, late 20's?, engineering graduate student, Chicago, urban southeastern Michigan for graduate studies; friend of X's spouse
>   T: Mainland Chinese, male, early 30's, engineering graduate student; X's spouse

Tape #11 Fieldworker J – James Cudney, white, male, 44, technical writer and graduate student in technical writing

Recording date: 11/23/87; recording site: respondent's home in urban southeastern Michigan
Respondent:
>G: White, female, 40; food store owner; born in western New York;
>moved to southeastern Michigan during elementary school years;
>E's (see #55) sister

Tape #12 Fieldworker K – Kathleen Keller (see #3)
Recording date: 11/19/87; recording site: unknown
Respondent:
>D: African-American, female, 38; lawyer; born and schooling in urban
>southeastern Michigan; law school in Indiana; returned to urban
>southeastern Michigan in 1975

Tape #13 Fieldworker Z – Larisa Zlatich (see #8)
Recording date: 11/28/87; recording site: unknown
Respondent:
>M: White, male, 42; some high school, carpenter; lifelong urban south-
>eastern Michigan resident (friend of Z's husband)

Tape #14 Fieldworker N – Nancy Niedzielski (see #9)
Recording date: unknown; recording site: home of La Leche group leader
>Respondents on this tape are not individually noted; they are all members
>of an urban southeastern Michigan La Leche group

Tape #15 Fieldworker S – Mei Shen (see #4)
Recording date: 11/20/87; recording site: J's residence in urban southeastern
Michigan
Respondents:
>M: See #4
>J: See #4

Tape #16 Fieldworker M – Mina Sommerville, white, female, 28; rhetoric and
composition graduate student
Recording date: 11/30/87; recording site: unknown
Respondent:
>R: White, female, 29; Army officer, B.A., lifelong suburban and urban
>southeastern Michigan resident (friend of J, see #41 and C, see
>#49 & 50)

Tape #17 Fieldworker: M – Mina Sommerville (see #16)
Recording date: 11/30/87 (Video only); recording site: unknown
Respondents:
>SR: White, female, 46; university secretary, business college; born and
>early schooling in central Michigan; came to urban southeastern
>Michigan to attend business college after high school; DR's
>spouse (see #39 & 40); SH's friend and co-worker

SH: White, female, 23, university secretary, some college; born in Germany and grew up in Army bases principally in southern US; 10 years in California before moving to small-town southern Michigan in 1980; DH's spouse (see #42); D's daughter (see #44 & 45); SR's friend and co-worker

(Contact with both SR and SH made by M's spouse through professional acquaintance)

Tape #18 Fieldworker Z – Larisa Zlatich (see #8)
Recording date: 12/2/87; recording site: fieldworker's campus apartment in urban southeastern Michigan
Respondent:

K: White, female, 35; B.S.; born in suburban southeastern Michigan; adult residence in Indiana and Connecticut; returned to urban southeastern Michigan in 1987

Tape #19 Fieldworker Z – Larisa Zlatich (see #8)
Recording date: 12/5/1987; recording site: (see #8)
Respondents:

B: See #8
D: See #8

Tape #20 Fieldworker K – Kathleen Keller (see #3)
Recording date: 11/29/87; recording site: respondents' home in urban southeastern Michigan
Respondents:

A: White, male, 29; teacher-broadcasting, B.A.; grew up in North Dakota; moved to western Michigan in 1982 and to urban southeastern Michigan in 1984; E's spouse
E: White, female, 35; college graduate, junior high school teacher, salesperson; grew up in western Michigan and Florida, moved to urban southeastern Michigan in 1984; A's spouse

Tape #21 Fieldworker Z – Larisa Zlatich (see #8)
Recording date: 12/8/1987; recording site: unknown
Respondent:

C: White, female, 38; B.F.A., secretary; grew up in Tennessee and Kentucky; came to urban southeastern Michigan in 1987; friend of B and D (see #8)

Tape #22 Fieldworker: Z – Larisa Zlatich (see #8)
Recording date: 12/14/87; recording site: unknown
Respondent:
K: See #18

Tape #23 Fieldworker: H – Horng-ming Wu (see #1)
Recording date: 12/6/87; recording site: D's home in urban southeastern Michigan

Respondents:
    W: See #1
    D: See #7
    G: See #7
    S: White, male, 15; high school student; D's son; has traveled in southeast
        Asia and speaks some Tagalog

Tape #24 Fieldworker: H – Horng-ming Wu (see #1)
Recording date: 12/13/87; recording site: (see #1)
Respondents:
    K: See #1
(This recording with K and H with several of K's friends is not audible
due to ambient party noise; the participants are not identified)

Tape #25 Fieldworker: H – Horng-ming Wu (see #1)
Respondents:
Recording date: 1/14/88; recording site: (see #2)
    R: See #2
    J: See # 2

Tape #26 Fieldworker: N – Nancy Niedzielski (see #9)
Recording date: 1/20/88; recording site: respondents' home in suburban southeast-
        ern Michigan
Respondents:
    E: White, male, 48; telephone lineman, high school graduate; lifelong
        suburban southeastern Michigan resident; D's spouse
    D: White, female, 42; sales clerk, some college; lifelong suburban south-
        eastern Michigan resident; E's spouse

Tape #27 Fieldworker: N – Nancy Niedzielski (see #9)
Recording date: 1/16/88; recording site: B and D's home in suburban southeastern
        Michigan
Respondents:
    B: White, male, 54; greenhouse owner, high school graduate; lifelong
        suburban southeastern Michigan resident; D's spouse
    D: White, female, 54; teacher's aide, M.A.; grew up in the South; college
        in Bowling Green, Ohio; moved to suburban southeastern
        Michigan after college; B's spouse

Tape #28 Fieldworker: H – Horng-ming Wu (see #1)
Recording date: 12/12/87; recording site: (see #7)
Respondents:
    D: See #7
    G: See #7
    W: See #1
    U: Unidentified younger children of G

Tape #29 Fieldworker: J – James Cudney (see #11)
Recording date: 2/7/88; recording site: unknown
Respondents:
>   G: See #11
>   P: White, female, 27; manages food store for G; educational and residence history unknown

Tape #30 Fieldworker: J – James Cudney (see #11)
Recording date: 2/7/88; recording site: unknown
Respondents:
>   G: See #11
>   C: White, female, 49; medical assistant; residence history unknown

Tape #31   Fieldworker: C – Chi-jen Hwang, Taiwanese, male, 32, linguistics graduate student
Recording date: 1/10/88; recording site: unknown
Respondents:
>   F: White, male, age unknown; educational and employment data unknown; born and grew up in Cleveland, Ohio; moved to urban southeastern Michigan in 1980; L's spouse
>   L: White, female, age unknown; educational and employment data unknown; lived in Canada for 15 years, other residence history unknown; F's spouse
>   J: F and L's infant son

Tape #32 Fieldworker C – Chi-jen Hwang (see #31)
Recording date: 2/7/88; recording site: respondent's home in urban southeastern Michigan
Respondent:
>   D: African-American, male, 40, community college associate engineering degree, now college student, former auto mechanic, now in engineering design, from urban northeastern Ohio, urban southeastern Michigan since 1980; R's spouse; A's father (see #35)

Tape #33 Fieldworker K – Kathleen Keller (see # 3)
Recording date: 2/1/88; recording site: unknown
Respondent:
>   J: African-American, female, 27, manicurist, community college student, beauty school graduate, suburban and urban southeastern Michigan

Tape #34 Fieldworker – Not present, recording arranged by James Cudney (see #11)
Recording date: 1/29/88; recording site: unknown
Respondents:
>   G: See #11

N: White, female, young adult, friend of G's (no further information available)

Tape #35 Fieldworker C – Chi-jen Hwang (see #31)
Recording date: 1/11/88; recording site: (see #32)
Respondents:
    D: See #32
    R: African-American, female, 41, teacher's aide, two years college, from urban northeastern Ohio; eight years in urban southeastern Michigan, D's spouse (see #32); A's mother
    A: African-American, female, 19, community college student, from urban northeastern Ohio; eight years in urban southeastern Michigan, D and R's daughter

Tapes #36a & #36b Fieldworker: H – Horng-ming Wu (see #1)
Recording date: 1/23/88; recording site: see #1
Respondents:
    G: See #1
    K: See #1
    A: See #1
    W: See #1
    J: See #1

Tape #37 Fieldworker: M – Mina Sommerville (see #16)
Recording date: 12/2/87; recording site: unknown
Respondent:
    K: White, female, 34; southern Indiana until age 7; urban southeastern Michigan since (no further information available)

Tape #38 Fieldworker: M – Mina Sommerville (see #16)
Recording date: 1/21/88; recording site: unknown
Respondents:
    J: White, male, early 40's, GM engineering drafting, some college; from northern Michigan, urban southeastern Michigan for the last fifteen years, B's spouse
    B: White, female, late 30's, GM, some college; lifelong urban southeastern Michigan, J's spouse
    (J and B are the fieldworker's neighbors)

Tapes #39 & #40 Fieldworker: M – Mina Sommerville (see #16)
Recording date: 1/2/88; recording site: respondents' home in urban southeastern Michigan
Respondents:
    SR: See #17
    DR: White, male, age 49-50, automotive mechanic, high school, lifelong resident of urban southeastern Michigan, SR's spouse

Tape #41 Fieldworker: M – Mina Sommerville (see #16)
Recording date: 1/28/88; recording site: unknown
Respondent:
   J: White, female, 36, high school, secretary, sales, lifelong urban south-
      eastern Michigan; friend of SR and SH (see #17) and R (see #16)

Tape #42 Fieldworker: M – Mina Sommerville (see #16)
Recording date: 1/31/88; recording site: unknown
Respondents:
   SH: See #17
   DH: White, male, 26, community college student, maintenance, rural
      southern Michigan, now urban southeastern Michigan (SH's
      spouse)

Tape #43 Video-tape version of #42

Tapes #44 & #45 Fieldworker M – Mina Sommerville (see #16)
Recording date: 2/3/88; recording site: unknown
Respondent:
   D: White, male, mid-50's, B.A., retired Army noncom, corporation per-
      sonnel employee; grew up in western New York, urban south-
      eastern Michigan since 1980; SH's father (see #17)

Tape #46 Fieldworker: N – Nancy Niedzielski (see #9)
Recording date: 1/27/88; recording site: respondents' home in suburban southeast-
      ern Michigan
Respondents:
   E: See #26
   D: See #26

Tape #47 Fieldworker: N – Nancy Niedzielski (see #9)
Recording date: 1/28/88; recording site: R's home in suburban southeastern
      Michigan
Respondents:
   R: White, female, 45, housewife, some college, grew up in Upper Penin-
      sula of Michigan, now suburban southeastern Michigan
   V: White, female, 50, B.S., nurse, lifelong suburban southeastern Michi-
      gan
   M: White, female, 50, high school, housewife, lifelong suburban south-
      eastern Michigan

Tape #48 a & b Fieldworker: A – Tadayuki Adachi
a: Recording date: 10/30/87; recording site: off-campus student apartment in urban
      southeastern Michigan
Respondents:
   M: White, male, 22, community college student, lifelong urban southeast-
      ern Michigan

R: White, male, 23, some high school, grew up in suburban southeastern Michigan, now urban southeastern Michigan

N: White, male, 20's, no further information available, friend of M and R

b: Recording date: unknown; recording site: respondents' home in urban southeastern Michigan

Respondents:

J: White, male, age 61, auto plant foreman, grew up in Toledo, Ohio, now urban southeastern Michigan, W's spouse

W: White, female, age and other details unknown, J's spouse

Tapes #49 & #50 Fieldworker: M – Mina Sommerville (see #16)
Recording date: 2/21/88; recording site: unknown
Respondent:

C: White, female, 42, M.A., business communications consultant, grew up in Oklahoma; urban southeastern Michigan for the last 18 years; friend of SR and SH (see #17)

Tape #51 Fieldworker: C – Chi-jen Hwang (see #31)
Recording date: 2/23/88; recording site: (see #32)
Respondents:

D: See #32

R: See #35

V: African-American, female, 31, seeking high school equivalency, unemployed, lifelong southeastern Michigan, friend of D and R

S: African-American, male, 12, elementary school student, born in urban northeastern Ohio, last eight years in urban southeastern Michigan, D and R's son

Tape #52 Fieldworker: M – Mina Sommerville (see #16)
Recording date: 2/25/88; recording site: unknown
Respondent:

D: African-American, female, 37, graduate business degree, auto plant personnel department, lifelong urban southeastern Michigan; friend of T's (see #44 & 45)

Tape #53 Fieldworker: C – Chi-jen Hwang (see #31)
Recording date: 2/24/88; recording site: unknown
Respondent:

K: White, female, late 20's?, graduate student in special education, teacher of emotionally impaired, grew up in suburban southeastern Michigan; now urban southeastern Michigan

Tape #54 Fieldworker: T – Tim Powell, white, male, late 20's, southeastern Michigan, English department graduate student
Recording date: 2/22/88; recording site: unknown

Respondent:

      S: White, female, 68, graduate science degree, chemist, born urban east-
          ern Pennsylvania, elementary through college education in Can-
          ada, urban southeastern Michigan since college graduation

Tape #55 Fieldworker: J – James Cudney (see #11)
Recording date: 3/26/88; recording site: respondent's home in urban southeastern
          Michigan
Respondent:

      E: White, female, 36, suburban western New York until 6th grade, urban
          southeastern Michigan since, G's sister (see #11)

Tapes #56 & #57 Fieldworker: X – Zhi-qun Xing (see #10)
Recording date: 2/7/88; recording site: unknown
Respondents:

      S: See #10
      B: See #10
      T: See #10

Tape #58 There is no #58

Tape #59 Fieldworker: N – Nancy Niedzielski (see #9)
Recording date: 5/24/88; recording site: respondents' home in suburban southeast-
          ern Michigan
Respondents:

      B: See #27
      D: See #27

Notes

Foreword

1. Robert A. Hall, Jr., in his obituary of Bloomfield, reports that it was Bloom-field's custom to collect these "ignorant or stupid remarks about language" (Hall 1950 [1970:552]).
2. Language is not the only cultural area where there might be a mismatch be-tween account and performance. (For a thorough discussion of this issue from several perspectives, see Ryle 1949; Geertz 1966; Harris 1968; Caws 1974; Lave, Stepick, and Sailer 1977; Frake 1977; Holy 1979; Holy and Stuchlik 1981; Clement 1982; Holland and Quinn 1987.) Previous linguistic work has focused on the mismatch between report and performance (e.g., Labov 1966, Trudgill 1972), but that work has been carried out within the framework of a quantitative sociolinguistic paradigm, and the focus, however broad the inter-pretation, has been on the contrast between the respondents' estimate and an actual tallying of their performance on a single feature (e.g., /ŋ/ versus /n/ in such pronunciations as *running* versus *runnin'*). Although Labov specifically states that one of the goals of the sociolinguistic interview is "to obtain a rec-ord of overt attitudes towards language, linguistic features and linguistic stereotypes" (1984:33), very little of his work (e.g., 1966, chapter 13, where the folk linguistics is justifiably largely limited to opinions about New York City English) illustrates such a concern. Haugen 1952 (1969) is an earlier ex-ample of the use of some folk linguistic opinion woven into a sociolinguistic account. Research which has specifically focused on folk linguistics has most often taken place in relatively homogeneous, nontechnological societies and dealt with such larger linguistic genres as ways of talking, often with specific concern for valued or artistic performance (e.g., Gossen 1972, Sherzer 1974, Stross 1974, and many later examples). The few studies which have looked at diverse technological societies have most often taken as their goal a charac-terization of communicative efficiency, patterning, norms, or style (e.g., Wie-mann, Chen, and Giles 1986; Heath 1983 — quantitative and ethnographic approaches respectively).

Chapter 1

1. Linguistics is a little better known nowadays (but see Preston 1984); in 1944 the idea that a mature adult might earn a living studying language (not *lan-guages*) must have been very peculiar.
2. It is, at least from a linguistic point of view, as old as F. Polle's *Wie denkt das Volk über die Sprache?*, Leipzig, 1889.
3. Not only linguists among social and cognitive scientists have held folk belief in low esteem. Levi-Strauss (1953) regarded native models of culture as sim-ply false accounts.

4. Labov is describing nasality as an overlaid general speech phenomenon, not as the phonological distribution of nasals. The characterization of French, Portuguese, or Polish as a "nasal" language by folk respondents might have to do with the latter.
5. These are, in fact, the subjective responses of one of the authors and are perhaps not idiosyncratic. In a popular late-night comedy show, a family of constant complainers (named the Whiners) spoke with excessive nasalization. Folk imitations of big dumb tough types are often excessively denasalized.
6. We ignore the technical distinction between "nasal" and "nasalized"; the folk term "nasal" refers to nasalized speech, not speech produced exclusively through the nasal passages.
7. It is odd that Labov should find the shift in point of view by the folk in the area of phonology uninteresting. He criticizes Grootaers 1959 for rejecting a folk dialectology in which the respondents find dialect boundaries along historical political boundaries rather than currently determined scientific ones. Ferguson and Heath attribute some inconsistency in folk linguistics to "basic ambivalences in American values." They note, for example, the "tension between belief in correctness and pride in being able to speak without authoritarian control" (1981:xxvii).
8. This account is too brief and too nationalistic, but it makes the point that theoretical linguists (of both structuralist and generativist sorts) have not made much use of folk accounts. (That the latter have not considered messy language *use*, inventing the "ideal native speaker hearer" – a creature available only to trained linguist intuitions – is a related issue and is considered later.)
9. This is the first reference to the data collected for this study. See the appendix for a description of the respondents and fieldworkers (always indicated by letter) and the interaction (always indicated by a recording number) from which the citation was taken. Symbols and transcription conventions are provided in the pages just before the preface.
10. "Technically" (versus "loosely") is the focus of a philosophical approach to folk theories of language (Kay 1987).
11. There is no more telling example of the massive influence of stereotypes than Williams, Whitehead, and Miller 1971. In this experiment the voice of a standard English-speaking Anglo child was played while the side-view (to avoid lip-reading) of an Anglo, an African-American, or Mexican-American child was shown. The respondents (teacher education majors in Texas) rated the standard speech as significantly less standard when it was accompanied by the visual image of a minority child. In fact, when the minority children's images were shown with accompanying *nonstandard* performances, there was no significant decrease in the teachers' ratings of their standardness.
12. The vehemence with which some receive news of language specialists' abrogation of their responsibility to describe the abstraction is best exemplified in the flurry of emotion which accompanied the publication of the partly usage-based Webster's III dictionary. There is a good account and analysis of these reactions in Finegan 1980:116-129. Studies of popular culture folk linguistics, by the way, have been done. The majority of contributions to Greenbaum

(1985) discuss such matters, and the Introduction to Ferguson and Heath 1981 reviews several "American myths about language" (see note 7).

13. Milroy and Milroy suggest that the folk "... believe in a *transcendental* norm of correct English" (emphasis added) (1985:38).

14. We know that this characterization of the principal aims of linguistic research will not satisfy all linguists.

15. Of course, the attitudinal history may be even more complex. Michiganders may have prejudices against the merger as a result of contact with African-American speakers, contact with Appalachian and/or Southern immigrants to the local area, or members of the armed services, personal travel to, or family ties with, Appalachian areas, and/or exposure to popular culture caricatures of Appalachians.

16. Recordings were done on Sharp RD-664AV1 cassette recorders; in most cases the built-in microphones of these units were used. Ninety-minute Scotch AVX Studio Master cassette tapes were used with these machines. In a few cases when a multi-person interview had been adequately prepared for, a Tascam Porta Two recorder with four-track unidirectional cassette recording capability was used. Audio-Technica Pro 7 miniature electret condenser low-impedance microphones were used with the Tascam so that up to four individuals could be recorded on separate tracks. Ninety-minute Maxell UDS-II (High Bias) were used with the Tascam recorder. The video tapes were recorded on a Panasonic AG-160 VHS recorder, but the video cassette tapes were not standardized.

Data forms were filled out for each respondent so that we were assured at least basic information about each, although the fieldworkers were asked to prepare short biographies of the major respondents. Every respondent signed a form consenting to the use of their data in publications and presentations, and some signed forms consenting to the similar use of data gathered during videotaped sessions.

We collected sixty audio tapes in all, totaling approximately thirty hours of dialogue. In addition, five video tapes were made. The fieldworkers transcribed the sections of their tapes which contained discussion about language and coded their transcriptions using the fifty categories from Preston 1986b. We checked these transcriptions, added transcriptions of our own and, in some cases, made detailed summaries of the contents.

Chapter 2

1. The work reported on here for Michigan and Indiana was supported by a grant from the National Science Foundation. The respondents were subdivided into relatively well-balanced subgroups based on age, status, and gender, but in the findings reported here, these groups are combined. Data collected from Appalachians and African-Americans in southeastern Michigan were excluded from the general findings reported here; the Indiana respondents were all European-Americans.

2. We are indebted to Michael Montgomery for these maps; they are from respondents from Kentucky, Tennessee, North and South Carolina (the major-

ity), Florida, Louisiana, Georgia, Alabama, Texas, Virginia, and West Virginia. They represent both sexes, a considerable variety of social status and age groups, but only a few African-Americans and no other ethnically distinct groups (e.g., Hispanic).

3. One might justifiably complain that the number of older raters is very small, but a map of the extent of where even one respondent in this age group drew the area is smaller than the fifty percent realization of the under twenty decade.

4. This tendency exists, in fact, for a number of areas and may represent an interesting proclivity for older respondents to isolate a more core-like territory and/or to tolerate more undesignated areas on their maps in general.

5. We are grateful to Ann Pitts for providing these data from Auburn University students.

6. The 7.00–7.99 rating for Washington is a result of many respondents' not distinguishing it from Washington, D.C. In this task the states and areas were presented in an alphabetical list, not on a map.

7. Oddly enough, New Hampshire and Delaware belong to this group in the Michigan responses.

8. The confusion of Washington and Washington, D.C. shows up even in the factor analysis (group #7).

9. Washington, D.C. (and adjoining Maryland) are, in fact, rated in the 7.00–7.99 range.

10. Although the map does not show it, many Indiana raters made so bold as to say that northern Kentucky was "the same."

11. Recall J's (#38) imitation of "tree little boids," cited in 1.1.2.

12. G (and his family), in fact, believe the word *drawl* is *draw*. (They spell it for the fieldworker.) They have a folk etymology which relates this *draw* to the "drawing" out (lengthening) of sounds.

13. These data are taken from fieldwork records from Southern Indiana in Preston's private collection.

14. Interestingly, however, she makes nothing of the [ɛ] to [I] shift before nasals in the first syllable of the same word, and no other respondents comment on this feature which we still believe to be a caricature of Southern speech.

15. Popular culture abounds with references to Southerners gone North; one of the earliest (and most plaintive) is a "country" song of the 1960's entitled "Detroit City," in which the removed Southerner is "... dreaming of them cotton fields at home."

16. "Ypsitucky" speech and attitudes towards it are currently under study by Betsy E. Evans of Michigan State University.

Chapter 3

1. Among nonlinguists, "slang" is a count noun in many varieties which refers to slang items ("He uses a lot of slangs"); in much AAVE use, however, the plural form is in addition often noncount and seems to refer to the entire variety ("He speaks slangs").

2. This is not quite true. B and D (in #8) offer more sophisticated appraisals of the status of AAVE as a linguistic system (although not of its origins), but D has had some linguistics courses, and B is a psychologist who read some Chomsky during his graduate training. Both heard William Labov speak when he was an expert witness for the *King* case, a suit brought against the local public schools in Ann Arbor, Michigan for failing to recognize the distinctiveness of African-American speech (see Chambers 1983). In addition, D (in #12) cites information she has from an ex-spouse who has apparently done some sort of university level research paper on the origins of AAVE. Her report of that research, however, does not touch on a creolist or Africanist perspective at all. She notes that the slaves learned the language of their masters (from necessity, since they were from different linguistic backgrounds) and that the language of African-Americans is, therefore, essentially "Southern."

3. This conversation shows what both the Indiana and Michigan mental maps (Figures 2.10 and 2.11) reveal – that Texas is a separate dialect area, at least not a part of the "South."

4. See Cooke (1972) for an account of "giving skin" and other aspects of African-American nonverbal communication.

5. In fact, in very relaxed environments, most European-Americans have an AAVE "performance" variety (Preston 1992), but that was triggered very little in these interviews. The perception of such performances as "racist" doubtless contributed to the respondents' reluctance.

6. Of course, in keeping with good US stereotypes, B's facility with nonstandard varieties comes from his time spent in the South.

7. No one will be happy with this grab-bag definition of slang. See Dumas and Lighter (1978) for a more serious attempt.

8. A thorough current treatment of such matters can be found in Allan and Burridge (1991).

Chapter 4

1. Research in this area has unfortunately been limited, due to the belief that "the nature of peer language and the effects of peers on language acquisition" is a "performance topic" (Bates 1976). Bates further reports on the limited research that has been done in this area, particularly on 1. the nature of "egocentric" speech that children engage in even if they are seated next to another child or an adult or 2. the language of children of immigrants, who usually learn the language of peers as opposed to adults, although this is largely dependent on sociological factors. She also makes several suggestions for future research, but, as Andersen (1990) points out, her suggestions have yet to be carried out. Chambers (1988) and Wolfram (1974) are exceptions, but they focus on the "assimilation" to new peer groups among older children. Romaine (1984:182-95) reviews peer influences on children's and adolescents' language.

2. The chief exception to this in the United States tradition consists of a number of initial reading series prepared by linguists (Bloomfield and Barnhart 1961, Fries, Wilson, and Rudolf 1966, and Smith and Stratemeyer 1963-67) and a

variety of pedagogical grammars by Paul Roberts, the first rather solidly based in the tradition of American Structuralism (e.g., Roberts 1956) but later ones espousing the then-new transformational-generative movement (e.g., Roberts 1966).

3. This is a brief summary which touches on only some of the earliest educational contributions from professional linguists, and the list provided here is incomplete. So far as we know, there is no general source which surveys professional interest in contributions to this field.

4. In fact, one of the fieldworkers was very much interested in technical writing and engaged a few respondents in discussion on this topic and on writing in general, but this topic strays into rather more specialized areas, and we do not explore them here since they are concerned with folk attitudes to writing itself rather than to the teaching of writing.

5. Hakuta (1986) reports briefly on a student assignment in which folk opinions about bilingual education were sought. The results he cites (213) are very similar to the findings reported here.

6. We admit to caricaturing rather than investigating the folk beliefs language professionals have about the linguistic folk belief of nonprofessionals, but we hope to be granted this one lapse into intuition. Besides, "Language Teacher Folk Belief about the Linguistic Folk Belief of Language Learners" sounds like a great thesis topic.

7. The history of the dissatisfaction with contrastive analysis, the movement to error analysis, and the subsequent use of increasingly sophisticated linguistic mechanisms to explain error sources in SLA is too complex to be given in full here. Interested readers might consult Larsen-Freeman and Long 1991 for an account (and references), particularly Chapters 3, 4, and 7.

8. The focus on universals in SLA, particularly within the framework of current generativist theories of grammar, is not limited to the markedness extension of the contrastive analysis hypothesis. White 1989 is a good example of current work in other areas.

9. It is possible, however, that such overgeneralizations have been exaggerated, perhaps because they are so "glaring" or salient to the listener. In an actual study of learner data, Pica (1983) found no more than one to two percent of such errors.

10. That, of course, is not unlike comments made in earlier studies of "good" language learners (e.g., Rubin 1975, Schmidt 1986).

11. "Declaring" is probably an idiosyncratic folk term for "declension," which, as an earlier part of this conversation shows, actually refers to "conjugation."

Chapter 5

1. It is possible to make c. a good answer to a., but one must put contrastive stress on *tomorrow*, focusing on an item which has been moved to a position usually reserved for topicalized or old information. This contrastively stressed form of c. would be an even more likely answer to some such question as "Are you leaving today?" G is certainly aware of this possibility, for she places contrastive stress on *today* in one of her own sample sentences.

2. This sentence is not one of those suggested to the nonnative fieldworkers for presentation.
3. At other times respondents seem to suffer from the same problem that many linguists have. After looking at about eight of these sentences, M (#15) sighs and then says: "After a while they all just scramble in your mind like."
4. These questionable and ungrammatical sentences were taken from a large number of texts within the GB (government and binding) framework of generative syntax.
5. A native speaker of English certainly would not have been able to pose such a question!
6. Quotations of the conversation here in the discussion contain some ellipsis. The reader is invited to study the full text for more elaborate interactional detail.
7. Later in the conversation, however, D, G, and S observe that a current problem in the local schools is the lack of formal grammar study.
8. Unfortunately these words were unintelligible; however, the discussion was about writers using the passive.
9. Note the awkwardness of a passive which would include the agent "We are discouraged from using the passive by conductors of writing workshops," undoubtedly the result of the most available agent's nonhuman status ("writing workshops").
10. D, who seems to have much less knowledge of descriptive grammar than S and G, agrees with and repeats their comments; it's almost as if he is learning from them, but to continue to play some role in the conversation, he acts as a translator of S and G's remarks for the fieldworker.
11. A treatment of a lengthy "folk linguistic" conversation in a variety of discourse analytic frameworks is the subject of Preston 1993c and Preston 1994.

Chapter 6

1. We do not mean to suggest that native speakers would not detect a sentence which illustrated the "breaking" of one of these underlying principles, but they would certainly conceive of it as an "error" of some other sort than the failure to apply a universal (or perhaps even language specific) linguistic constraint on well-formedness. (See Chapter 5 for a detailed examination of folk responses to such ungrammatical sentences.)
2. Not all presuppositions in a conversation come from the rock-bottom shared cultural knowledge of a speech community or society. Some are revealed (or even negotiated) on the spot and become part of the ongoing presuppositions of a particular conversation.

> Presuppositions can be created or destroyed in the course of a conversation. This change is rule-governed, up to a point. The presuppositions at time t' depend, in a way about which at least some general principles can be laid down, on the presuppositions at an earlier time t and the course of the conversation (and nearby events) between t and t'. (Lewis 1979:339)

By and large, these are not the sorts of more deeply-seated presuppositions (about the nature, structure, function, and use of language) under consideration here.

3. Some of these underlying folk beliefs in the area of attitudes towards "correct" use have been brought to light in previous sociolinguistic studies under the heading "language ideology." Effective recent treatments include Bolinger (1980), Finegan (1980), Milroy and Milroy (1985), Cameron (1995), and Lippi-Green (1997).

4. Like Widdowson (1998), we are personally sympathetic to the political stance of this approach but cannot find in it, as its proponents claim, any considerable dependence on linguistics, however socially sensitive and insightful their analyses might be.

5. For example, there are interesting contributions to the study of discourse content by social psychologists. They are not, however, linguistic analyses, nor do they pretend to be. Potter and Wetherell (1987) is a good example of this young tradition.

6. The details are not important here, but it is interesting to note that the topic avoidance of Sample #1 (with the exception of participant "A") and the normal anaphora of Sample #2 are both participated in by all the participants. The "peculiar" treatment of AAVE as topic is, therefore, conversationally agreed on here. In Preston 1993c a fuller analysis of this 'anaphoric avoidance' is carried out, making use of *referential distance*, *topic persistence*, and *potential interference*, devices introduced by Givón (1983) to provide a quantitative account of 'topicality' in texts.

7. Unlike the social psychological tradition (mentioned in note 5), there are other approaches to discourse which, like critical linguistics, claim to be based in linguistic-style investigation. Van Dijk (1987, 1993) purports to relate racism to discourse structure (and underlying cognitive structure), but linguists will not recognize much of what is there. Again, such work is an interesting reflection by an obviously sensitive and intelligent reader on what people have said about race in conversations (and other sorts of texts), but it uses only infrequently the techniques of linguistically oriented discourse analysis (e.g., the use of Labov's narrative structure outline) or the more established methods of linguistic analysis at any level (e.g., casual references to the specific referents of pronouns).

References

Akinnaso, F. Niyi – Cheryl Seabrook Ajirotutu
    1982   "Performance and ethnic style in job interviews," in: John J. Gumperz (ed.), *Language and social identity.* Cambridge: Cambridge University Press, 119-44.
Akmajian, Adrian – Richard A. Demers – Robert M. Harnish
    1979   *Linguistics: an introduction to language and communication.* Cambridge, MA: MIT Press.
Allan, Keith – Kate Burridge
    1991   *Euphemism and dysphemism: language used as shield and weapon.* Oxford: Oxford University Press.
Allen, Harold B. – Michael Linn (eds)
    1982   *Readings in applied English linguistics* (3rd edition). New York: Knopf.
Andersen, Elaine S.
    1990   *Speaking with style: The sociolinguistic skills of children.* London: Routledge.
Argyle, Michael
    1969   *Social interaction.* London: Methuen.
Bailey, Guy
    1993   "African-American English," in: Dennis R. Preston (ed.), *American dialect research.* Amsterdam/Philadelphia: Benjamins, 287-318.
Bailey, Richard W.
    1983   "Education and the law: The *King* case in Ann Arbor," in: John Chambers, Jr. (ed.), *Black English: Educational equity and the law.* Ann Arbor: Karoma, 1-28.
    1991   *Images of English: a cultural history of the language.* Ann Arbor: University of Michigan Press.
Bates, Elizabeth
    1976   *Language and context: The development of pragmatics.* New York: Academic.
Bates, Elizabeth – Inge Bretherton – M. Beeghly-Smith – S. McNew
    1982   "Social bases of language development: a reassessment," in: H. W. Reese – L. P. Lipsitt (eds), *Advances in child language development and behavior 16.* New York: Academic Press.
Bates, Elizabeth – Brian MacWhinney
    1982   "Functionalist approaches to grammar," in: Eric Wanner – Lila R. Gleitman (eds), *Language acquistion: The state of the art.* Cambridge: Cambridge University Press, 173-218.
    1987   "Competition, variation, and language learning," in: Brian MacWhinney (ed.), *Mechanisms of language acquisition.* Hillsdale, NJ: Erlbaum, 157-94.

Bauman, Richard – Joel Sherzer (eds)
1974   *Explorations in the ethnography of speaking.* Cambridge: Cambridge University Press.

Bell, Allan
1984   "Language style as audience design," *Language in Society* 13:145-204.

Bereiter, Carl – Siegfried Engelmann
1966   *Teaching disadvantaged children in the pre-school.* Englewood Cliffs, NJ: Prentice-Hall.

Berkowitz, D.
1979   "Grammatical intuitions of second language learners: implications for placement tests." Paper presented at the NYS ESOL/BEA Annual Conference, Buffalo, NY.

Bernstein, Basil
1971   *Class, codes, and control,* Vol. I. London: Routledge and Kegan Paul.

Berwick, Robert C. – Amy S. Weinberg
1986   *The grammatical basis of linguistic performance: Language use and acquisition.* Cambridge, MA: MIT Press.

Biber, Douglas.
1986   "Spoken and written textual dimensions in English: resolving the contradictory findings," *Language* 62:384-414.

Bickerton, Derek
1981   *Roots of language.* Ann Arbor, MI: Karoma.

Blom, Jan-Petter – John J. Gumperz
1972   "Social meaning in linguistic structure: code-switching in Norway," in: John J. Gumperz – Dell Hymes (eds), *Directions in sociolinguistics: the ethnography of communication.* New York: Holt, Rinehart and Winston, 407-34.

Blommaert, Jan – Jef Verschueren
1998   *Debating diversity: Analysing the discourse of tolerance.* London: Routledge.

Bloomfield, Leonard
1944   "Secondary and tertiary responses to language," *Language* 20:45-55 (reprinted in: Charles F. Hockett (ed.), 1970: *A Leonard Bloomfield anthology.* Bloomington and London: Indiana University Press, 413-25).

Bloomfield, Leonard – Clarence L. Barnhart
1961   *Let's read.* Detroit: Wayne State University Press.

Bolinger, Dwight
1980   *Language – The loaded weapon.* New York: Longman.

Bortoni-Ricardo, Stella M.
1985   *The urbanization of rural dialect speakers.* Cambridge: Cambridge University Press.

Bowers, K.
1984   "On being unconsciously influenced and motivated," in: K. Bowers
         and D. Meichenbaum (eds), *The unconscious reconsidered.* New
         York: Wiley, 227-72.
Braine, Martin D. S.
1994   "Is nativism sufficient?" *Journal of Child Language* 21,1:9-41,
Brown, Gillian – George Yule
1983   *Discourse analysis.* Cambridge: Cambridge University Press.
Brown, Penelope – Stephen C. Levinson
1987   *Politeness.* Cambridge: Cambridge University Press.
Brown, Roger
1973   *A first language: The early stages.* Cambridge, MA: Harvard Univer-
         sity Press.
1977   "Introduction," in: Catherine Snow – Charles Ferguson (eds), *Talking
         to children: Language input and acquisition.* Cambridge: Cambridge
         University Press, 1-30.
Burton, Frank
1978   *The politics of legitimacy – struggles in a Belfast community*
         (Appendix: Theory and methodology in participant observation).
         London: Routledge.
Cameron, Deborah
1995   *Language hygiene.* London and New York: Routledge.
Cameron, Deborah – Jennifer Coates
1988   "Some problems in the sociolinguistic explanations of sex differ-
         ences," in: Jennifer Coates – Deborah Cameron (eds), *Women in their
         speech communities.* London: Longman, 13-27.
Cameron, Deborah – Fiona McAlinden – Kathy O'Leary
1988   "Lakoff in context: The social and linguistic functions of tag ques-
         tions," in: Jennifer Coates – Deborah Cameron (eds), *Women in their
         speech communities.* London: Longman, 74-94.
Candlin, Christopher – Jonathan H. Leather – Clive J. Bruton
1976   "Doctors in casualty: Applying communicative competence to com-
         ponents of specialist course design," *International Review of Applied
         Linguistics* 14,3:245-72.
Carroll. John B. – Stanley Sapon
1959   *Modern Language Aptitude Test – Form A.* New York: The Psycho-
         logical Corporation.
Carver, Craig
1987   *American regional dialects.* Ann Arbor: University of Michigan
         Press.
Caws, Peter
1974   "Operational, representational, and explanatory models." *American
         Anthropologist* 76(1):1-11.
Cazden, Courtney B. – Vera P. John – Dell Hymes (eds)
1972   *Functions of language in the classroom.* New York: Teachers Col-
         lege Press.

Chafe, Wallace
  1982   "Integration and involvement in speaking, writing, and oral litera-
            ture," in: Deborah Tannen, (ed.), *Spoken and written language: Ex-
            ploring orality and literacy*. Norwood NJ: Ablex.
  1987   "Cognitive constraints on information flow," in: R. Tomlin (ed.), *Co-
            herence and grounding in discourse*. Amsterdam: Benjamins, 21-51.
Chambers, Jack K.
  1988   "Acquisition of phonological variants," in: Alan R. Thomas (ed),
            Methods in dialectology. Clevedon: Multilingual Matters, 650-65.
  1989   "Canadian raising, blocking, fronting, etc.," *American Speech*
            64,1:75-88.
Chambers, Jack K. – Peter Trudgill
  1980   *Dialectology*. Cambridge: Cambridge University Press.
Chambers, John, Jr.
  1983   "Preface," in: John Chambers, Jr. (ed.), *Black English: Educational
            equity and the law*. Ann Arbor, MI: Karoma, ix-xiv.
Chomsky, Noam
  1959   "Review of Verbal Behavior by B. F. Skinner," *Language* 35:26-58.
  1986   *Knowledge of language: Its nature, origin, and use*. New York:
            Praeger.
Chomsky, Noam – Morris Halle
  1968   *The sound pattern of English*. New York: Harper.
Churchill, Lindsey
  1978   *Questioning strategies in sociolinguistics*. Rowley, MA: Newbury
            House.
Clement, D. H.
  1982   "Samoan folk knowledge of mental disorders," in: A. J. Marsella –
            G. White (eds), *Cultural conceptions of mental health and therapy*.
            Dordrecht: D. Reidel, 193-215.
Cleveland, Harlan – Gerald J. Mangone – John C. Adams
  1960   *The overseas Americans*. New York: McGraw-Hill.
Cohen, Gerald
  1969   "How did the English word "just" acquire its different meanings?" in:
            Robert Binnick – Alice Davison – Georgia Green – Jerry L. Morgan
            (eds), *Papers from the fifth regional meeting of the Chicago Linguis-
            tics Society*. Chicago: Department of Linguistics, University of Chi-
            cago, 25-29.
Collier, Virginia P.
  1989   "How long? A synthesis of research on academic achievement in a
            second language," *TESOL Quarterly* 23,3:509-31.
Cook, Vivian J.
  1988   *Chomsky's universal grammar*. Oxford: Blackwell.
Cooke, Benjamin G.
  1972   "Nonverbal communication among Afro-Americans: An initial clas-
            sification," in: Thomas Kochman (ed.), *Rappin' and stylin' out*. Ur-
            bana: University of Illinois Press, 32-64.

Coupland, Nikolas
1998 "Stylized deception: Sociolinguistics, authenticity and the comic rogue," a paper presented to the 3rd Cardiff Round Table on Sociolinguistics ("The Sociolinguistics of Metalanguage"), Gregynog, Wales, June 1-33.

Crawford, James
1992 *Language loyalties: A source book on the Official English controversy.* Chicago and London: University of Chicago Press.

Creider, Chet
1979 "On the explanation of transformations," in: Talmy Givón (ed.), *Syntax and semantics 12: Discourse and syntax.* New York: Academic Press, 3-21.

Cummins, James
1990 "Empowering minority students: A framework for intervention," in: Nitza M. Hidalgo – Caesar L. McDowell – Emilie V. Siddle (eds), Facing racism in education. Cambridge, MA: *Harvard Educational Review*, 50-68.

Curme, George O.
1947 *English grammar.* New York: Barnes & Noble, Inc.

Daan Jo – D. P. Blok
1970 *Von randstad tot landrand. (Bijdragen en Mededelingen der Dialecten Commissie van de Koninklijke Nederlandse Akademie van Wetenschappen te Amsterdam, XXXVII).* Amsterdam: N. V. Noord, Hollandsche Uitgevers Maatschappij.

D'Andrade, Roy
1987 "A folk model of the mind," in: Holland – Quinn, 112-148.

Davison, Alice
1984 "Syntactic markedness and the definition of sentence topic," *Language* 60,4:797-846.

Dillard, J. L.
1972 *Black English.* New York: Vintage Books.

Doughty, Peter – John Pearce – Geoffrey Thornton
1971 *Language in use.* London: Edward Arnold.

Drake, Glendon F.
1977 *The role of prescriptivism in American linguistics, 1820-1970 (Amsterdam Studies in the Theory and History of Linguistic Science III: Studies in the History of Linguistics, Vol. 13).* Amsterdam: Benjamins.

Drew, Paul – John Heritage (eds)
1992 *Talk at work: Interaction in institutional settings.* Cambridge: Cambridge University Press.

Dumas, Bethany K. – Jonathan Lighter
1978 "Is *Slang* a word for linguists?" *American Speech* 53,1:5-17.

Eckert, Penelope
1989 "The whole woman: Sex and gender differences in variation," *Language variation and change* 1:245-267.

Eckman, Fred R.
  1987   "Markedness and the contrastive analysis hypothesis," in: Georgette
            Ioup – Steven H. Weinberger (eds), *Interlanguage phonology: The
            acquisition of a second language sound system.* New York: Newbury
            House, 55-69.
Eisenstein, Miriam
  1983   "Native reactions to non-native speech: A review of empirical stud-
            ies," *Studies in Second Language Acquisition* 5:160-76.
Eisenstein, Miriam – D. Berkowitz
  1981   "The effect of phonological variation on adult learner comprehen-
            sion," *Studies in Second Language Acquisition* 4:75-80.
Eisenstein, Miriam – G. Verdi
  1985   "The intelligibility of social dialects for working-class adult learners
            of English," *Language Learning* 35:287-98.
Ervin-Tripp, Susan.
  1987   "Speech acts and syntactic development. Linked or independent?"
            *Keynote address, 12th Annual Boston University Conference on Lan-
            guage Development.*
Ervin-Tripp, Susan – Claudia Mitchell-Kernan (eds)
  1977   *Child discourse.* New York: Academic.
Fairclough, Norman
  1989   *Language and power.* London and New York: Longman.
Falk, Julia
  1978   *Linguistics and language: A survey of basic concepts and implica-
            tions (Second Edition).* New York: Wiley.
Feagin, Crawford
  1979   *Variation and change in Alabama English.* Washington, D.C.:
            Georgetown University Press.
  1985   "The southern drawl: an acoustic and sociolinguistic analysis." Paper
            presented at the John F. Kennedy Institute of North American Stud-
            ies, Free University, Berlin.
Felix, Sascha
  1981   "The effect of formal instruction on second language acquisition,"
            Language Learning 31,1:87-112.
Ferguson, Charles
  1959   "Diglossia," *Word 15*:325-340.
Ferguson, Charles – Shirley B. Heath (eds)
  1981   *Language in the USA.* Cambridge: Cambridge University Press.
Finegan, Edward
  1980   *Attitudes toward English usage.* New York: Teachers College Press.
Fisher, Pamela M.
  1983   "Interaction: The work women do," in: Barrie Thorne – Cheris
            Kramerae – Nancy Henley (eds), *Language, gender and society.*
            Rowley, MA: Newbury House, 89-101.

Fishman, Joshua L.
1970   "Language socialization: Japan and the United States," in: R. Hill –
        R. Honig (eds), *Families in East and West*. The Hague: Mouton,
        107-119.
Flores d'Arcais, Giovanni B.
1988   "Language perception," in: Newmeyer, 97-123.
Fodor, Jerry A.
1981   *Representations: Philosophical essays on the foundations of cogni-
        tive science*. Brighton: Harvester Press.
Frake, Charles O.
1977   "Playing frames can be dangerous: Some reflections on methodol-
        ogy in cognitive anthropology," *Quarterly Newsletter of the Institute
        for Comparative Human Development* 1,3:1-7.
Fries, Charles C.
1962   *Linguistics and reading*. New York: Holt, Rinehart and Winston.
Fries, Charles C. – Rosemary Green Wilson – Mildred K. Rudolph
1966   *Merrill linguistic readers*. Columbus OH: Charles C. Merrill.
Fromkin, Victoria – Robert Rodman
1983   *An introduction to language (Third Edition)*. New York: Holt, Rine-
        hart & Winston.
Gardner, Robert C. – Wallace E. Lambert
1972   *Attitudes and motivation in second-language learning*. Rowley, MA:
        Newbury House.
Garrett, Merrill F.
1988   "Processes in language production," in: Newmeyer, 69-96.
Geertz, Clifford
1966   "Religion as a cultural system," in: Michael Banton (ed.), *Anthropo-
        logical approaches to the study of religion (A.S.A Monographs 3)*.
        London: Tavistock Publications, 1-46.
Giles, Howard
1973   "Accent mobility: A model and some data," *Anthropological Lin-
        guistics* 15:87-105.
1979   "Ethnicity markers in speech," in: Klaus R. Scherer – Howard Giles
        (eds), *Social markers in speech*. Cambridge: Cambridge University
        Press, 251-90.
Giles, Howard – Justine Coupland – Nikolas Coupland
1991   "Accommodation theory: Communication, context, and conse-
        quence," in: Howard Giles – Justine Coupland – Nikolas Coupland
        (eds), *Contexts of accommodation*. Cambridge: Cambridge Univer-
        sity Press, 1-68.
Giles, Howard – Peter F. Powesland
1975   *Speech style and social evaluation*. London: Academic.
Giles, Howard – Philip M. Smith
1979   "Accommodation theory: Optimal levels of convergence," in: How-
        ard Giles – Robert N. St Clair (eds), *Language and social psychol-
        ogy*. Oxford: Blackwell, 45-65.

Givón, Talmy
  1979   *On understanding grammar.* New York: Academic Press.
  1983   "Topic continuity in discourse: An introduction," in: Talmy Givón
          (ed.), *Topic continuity in discourse: Quantified cross-language stud-
          ies.* Amsterdam: Benjamins, 1-43.
  1984   *Syntax: A functional-typological introduction (Volume I).* Amster-
          dam/Philadelphia: Benjamins.
  1990   *Syntax: A functional-typological introduction (Volume II).* Amster-
          dam/Philadelphia: Benjamins.
Gleason, Jean Berko – Samuel Weintraub
  1978   "Input language and the acquisition of communicative competence,"
          in: Kieth E. Nelson (ed.), *Children's language, Vol. 1.* New York:
          Gardner, 171-222.
Gossen, Gary
  1972   "Chamula genres of verbal behavior," in: Americo Paredes – Richard
          Bauman (eds), *Toward new perspectives in folklore.* Austin: Univer-
          sity of Texas Press, 145-67.
Gould, Peter – Rodney White
  1974   *Mental maps.* Harmondsworth: Penguin.
Greenbaum, Sidney (ed.)
  1985   *The English language today.* Oxford: Pergamon.
Greenberg, Joseph H.(ed.)
  1966   *Universals of language (Second Edition).* Cambridge MA: The MIT
          Press.
Grimes, Joseph E.
  1975   *The thread of discourse.* The Hague: Mouton.
Grootaers, Willem
  1959   "Origin and nature of subjective boundaries of dialects," *Orbis*
          8:355-84.
Gunderson, Doris V. (ed.)
  1970   *Language and reading: an interdisciplinary approach.* Arlington,
          VA: Center for Applied Linguistics.
Hakuta, Kenji
  1986   *Mirror of language: The debate on bilingualism.* New York: Basic
          Books.
Hall, Robert A., Jr.
  1950   "Obituary of Leonard Bloomfield," *Lingua* 2:117-23 (cited from
          Charles F. Hockett (ed.), 1970: *A Leonard Bloomfield anthology.*
          Bloomington and London: Indiana University Press, 547-53).
Hanna, Paul R. – Jean Hanna
  1966   *Phoneme-grapheme correspondences as cues to spelling improve-
          ment.* Washington, D.C.: USOE.
Harding, Carol G.
  1984   "Acting with intention," in: Lynne Feagan – Cathy Garvey – Roberta
          Golinkoff (eds). *The origin and growth of communication.* Norwood
          NJ: Ablex.

Harris, Marvin
1968   *The rise of anthropological theory.* New York: Thomas Y. Crowell.
Haugen, Einer
1952   *The Norwegian language in America* (1969, one-volume edition). Bloomington: Indiana University Press.
Heath, Shirley B.
1983   *Ways with words.* Cambridge: Cambridge University Press.
Hockett, Charles F.
1950   "Age-grading and linguistic continuity," Language 26:449-57.
Hoenigswald, Henry
1966   "A proposal for the study of folk-linguistics," in: William Bright (ed.), *Sociolinguistics.* The Hague: Mouton, 16-26.
Holland, Dorothy – Naomi Quinn (eds)
1987   *Cultural models in language and thought.* Cambridge: Cambridge University Press.
Holy, Ladislaw
1979   "Segmentary lineage structure and its existential status," in: Ladislaw Holy (ed.), *Segmentary lineage systems reconsidered (Queen's University Papers in Social Anthropology 4).* Belfast: Queen's University, 1-22.
Holy, Ladislaw – Milan Stuchlik
1981   *The structure of folk models (A.S.A. Monographs 20).* New York: Academic Press.
Hymes, Dell
1972   "Models of the interaction of language and social life," in: John J. Gumperz – Dell Hymes (eds), *Directions in sociolinguistics: The ethnography of communication.* New York: Holt, Rinehart, and Winston, 35-71.
1974   *Foundations in sociolinguistics: An ethnographic approach.* Philadelphia: University of Pennsylvania Press.
Jackendoff, Ray S.
1997   *Consciousness and the computational mind.* Cambridge, MA: MIT Press.
Jespersen, Otto
1924   *The philosophy of grammar.* London: Allen & Unwin.
Johnson, Fern L. – Marlene G. Fine
1980   "The 'vision' of obscenity: Sex differences in victimizing and victimization," paper given at the Speech Communications Association convention, New York, November.
Johnson, Janet L.
1980   "Questions and role responsibility in four professional meetings," *Anthropological Linguistics* 22:66-76.
Jordans, P.
1977   "Rules, grammatical intuitions, and strategies in foreign language learning," *Interlanguage Studies Bulletin* 2:5-76.

Kant, J. G.
1969   "Foreign language registrations in institutions of higher education, Fall 1968," *Foreign Language Annals* 3:247-304.
1970   "Foreign language offerings and enrollments in public secondary schools, Fall 1968," *Foreign Language Annals* 3:400-58.
Kasper, Gabriele – Shoshana Blum-Kulka (eds)
1993   *Interlanguage pragmatics*. New York: Oxford University Press.
Kay, Paul
1987   "Linguistic competence and folk theories of language: Two English hedges," in: Dorothy Holland – Naomi Quinn (eds), *Cultural models in language and thought*. Cambridge: Cambridge University Press, 67-77.
Keenan, Elinor Ochs
1976   "The universality of conversational postulates," *Language in Society* 5:67-80.
Kendon, Adam
1970   "Movement coordination in social interaction: Some examples described." *Acta Psychologica* 32:101-25.
Kleiner, Brian
1993   "Social class ethos in a northern US city: A quantitative study of politeness behavior, unpublished M.A. thesis. East Lansing: Michigan State University.
Kloss, Heinz
1977   *The American bilingual tradition*. Rowley, MA: Newbury House.
Kochman, Thomas
1972   "Toward an ethnography of black American speech behavior," in: Thomas Kochman (ed.), *Rappin' and stylin' out*. Urbana: University of Illinois Press, 241-64.
Krapp, George P.
1926   "The psychology of dialect writing," *The Bookman* 63:522-7.
Krashen, Stephen – Victoria Sferlazza – Lorna Feldman – Ann K. Fathman
1976   "Adult performance on the SLOPE test: More evidence for a natural sequence in adult second language acquisition," *Language Learning* 26,1:145-51.
Kremer, Ludger
1984   "Die Niederländisch-Deutsch Staatsgrenze als subjektive Dialektgrenze," in: Grenzen en grensproblemen (Een bundel studies nitgegeren door het Nedersaksich Instituut van der R. U. Gronigen ter gelegenheid van zijn 30-jarig bestaan = Nedersaksiche Studies 7, zugleich: Driemaandelijkse Bladen 36), 76-83.
Kress, Gunter
1991   "Critical discourse analysis," in: William Grabe (ed.), *Annual review of applied linguistics* (vol. 11). Cambridge: Cambridge University Press, 84-99.
Kroch, Anthony
1978   "Toward a theory of social dialect variation," *Language in Society* 7:17-36.

Kuno, Susumu
1980   *Functional syntax.* Chicago: University of Chicago Press.
Labov, William
1966   *The social stratification of English in New York City.* Arlington, VA:
        Center for Applied Linguistics.
1969a   *The study of nonstandard English.* Champaign, IL: National Council
        of Teachers of English.
1969b   "The logic of nonstandard English," in: James Alatis (ed.), *George-
        town Monographs on Language and Linguistics* 22:1-44.
1972a   *Sociolinguistic patterns.* Philadelphia: University of Pennsylvania
        Press.
1972b   *Language in the inner city.* Philadelphia: University of Pennsylvania
        Press.
1982   "Competing value systems in the inner-city schools," in: Perry Gil-
        more – Allan Glatthorn (eds), *Children in and out of school.* Wash-
        ington, D.C.: Center for Applied Linguistics, 148-71.
1984   "Field methods of the project on linguistic change and variation," in:
        John Baugh – Joel Sherzer (eds), *Language in use: Readings in so-
        ciolinguistics.* Englewood Cliffs, NJ: Prentice-Hall, 28-53.
1990   "The intersection of sex and social class in the course of linguistic
        change," *Language variation and change* 2,2:205-54.
1991   "The three dialects of English," in: Penelope Eckert (ed.), *New ways
        of analyzing sound change.* New York: Academic, 1-44.
1994   *Principles of linguistic change: Internal factors.* Oxford: Blackwell.
Ladefoged, Peter
1975   *A course in phonetics.* New York: Harcourt Brace Jovanovich.
Lado, Robert
1957   *Linguistics across cultures.* Ann Arbor: University of Michigan
        Press.
Laferriere, Martha
1979   "Ethnicity in phonological variation and change," *Language*
        55,3:603-17.
Lakoff, Robin
1975   *Language and woman's place.* New York: Harper & Row.
Lambert, Richard D. – Barbara F. Freed (eds)
1982   *The loss of language skills.* Rowley, MA: Newbury House.
Lambert, Wallace E. – R. C. Hodgsen – Robert C. Gardner – Samuel Fillenbaum
1960   "Evaluational reaction to spoken language," *Journal of Abnormal
        and Social Psychology* 60:44-51.
Lance, Donald M.
1994   "Variation in American English," in: John S. Kenyon, *American pro-
        nunciation (12th edition, expanded).* Ann Arbor, MI: George Wahr,
        333-56.
Langacker, Robert W.
1973   *Language and its structure: Some fundamental linguistic concepts
        (Second Edition).* New York: Harcourt Brace Jovanovich.

Langendoen, D. Terence – Thomas G. Bever
  1973   "Can a not unhappy person be called a not sad one?" in: Stephen R.
            Anderson – Paul Kiparsky (eds), *A Festschrift for Morris Halle*. New
            York: Holt, Rinehart, and Winston, 392-409.
Larmouth, Donald W
  1987   "Does linguistic heterogeneity erode national unity?" in: Winston A.
            Van Horne (ed.), *Ethnicity and language (Volume VI of the Ethnicity
            and Public Policy series)*. Madison: The University of Wisconsin
            System Institute on Race and Ethnicity, 37-57.
Larsen-Freeman, Diane – Michael H. Long
  1991   *An introduction to second language acquisition research*. London
            and New York: Longman.
Lave, Jean – Alex Stepick – Lee Sailer
  1977   "Extending the scope of formal analysis," *American Ethnologist*
            4,2:321-39.
Leopold, Werner F.
  1939-49   *Speech development of a bilingual child: A linguist's record, 4 vols.*
            Chicago: Evanston.
Levinson, Stephen C.
  1983   *Pragmatics*. Cambridge: Cambridge University Press.
Levi-Strauss, Claude
  1953   "Social structure," in: A. L. Kroeber (ed.), *Anthropology today*. Chi-
            cago: University of Chicago Press.
Lewis, David
  1979   "Scorekeeping in a language game," *Journal of Philosophical Logic*
            8:339-59.
Lieberson, Stanley
  1970 [1981]   "Language and ethnic relations," Chapter 1 of *Language and
            ethnic relations in Canada*. New York: Wiley (quoted from *Lan-
            guage diversity and language contact*, 1-18. Stanford: Stanford Uni-
            versity Press).
Lippi-Green, Rosina
  1997   *English with an accent*. London and New York: Routledge.
Long, Michael H.
  1983   "Does second language instruction make a difference? A review of
            research," *TESOL Quarterly* 17,3:359-82.
Macaulay, Ronald
  1977   *Language, social class, and education*. Edinburgh: Edinburgh Uni-
            versity Press.
McTear, Michael
  1985   *Children's conversation*. Oxford: Blackwell.
Malinowski, Bronislaw
  1923   "The problem of meaning in primitive languages," in: Charles K.
            Ogden – I. A. Richards, *The meaning of meaning*. London: Kegan
            Paul, 451-510.

Maltz, Daniel L. – Ruth A. Borker
  1982   "A cultural approach to male-female miscommunication," in: John J.
          Gumperz (ed.), *Language and social identity*. Cambridge: Cambridge
          University Press, 197-216.
Mehan, Hugh
  1982   "The structure of classroom events and their consequences for stu-
          dent performance," in: Perry Gilmore – Allan A. Glatthorn (eds),
          Children in and out of school: Ethnography and education. Arling-
          ton, VA: Center for Applied Linguistics, 59-87.
Miller, Cynthia
  1988   "Interpretations of infant vocalizations," *First Language* 8:125-42.
Milroy, James – Lesley Milroy
  1985   *Authority in language*. London: Routledge & Kegan Paul.
Milroy, Lesley
  1980   *Language and social networks*. Oxford: Blackwell.
  1987   *Observing and analysing natural language*. Oxford: Blackwell.
  1989   "Gender as a speaker variable: The interesting case of glottalised
          stops in Tyneside," *York Papers in Lingusitics* 13:227-36.
Milroy, Lesley – Paul McClenaghan
  1977   "Stereotyped reactions to four educated accents in Ulster," *Belfast
          Working Papers in Language and Linguistics Vol. 2, September*, 1-11
          (N.B.: items in this publication are numbered spearately).
Montgomery, Michael
  1992   "The etymology of *y'all*," in: Joan H. Hall, Nick Doane, and Dick
          Ringler (eds), *Old English and new: Studies in language and linguis-
          tics in honor of Frederic G. Cassidy*. New York: Garland, 356-69.
Morgan, Marcyliena
  1994   "The African-American speech community: Reality and sociolin-
          guistics," in: Marcyliena Morgan (ed.), *Language and the social con-
          struction of identity in creole situations*. Los Angeles: Center for
          Afro-American Studies Publications, University of California, 121-
          48.
Neufeld, Gerald
  1978   "On the acquisition of prosodic and articulatory features in adult lan-
          guage learning," *Canadian Modern Language Review* 34,2:163-74.
Newman, Edwin
  1974   *Strictly speaking: Will America be the death of English*. Indianapo-
          lis/New York: Bobbs-Merrill.
Newmeyer, Frederick J. (ed.)
  1988   *Linguistics: The Cambridge survey, III. Language: psychological
          and biological aspects*. Cambridge: Cambridge University Press.
Nichols, Patricia
  1983   "Linguistic options and choices for Black women in the rural South,"
          in: Barrie Thorne – Cheris Kramerae – Nancy Henley (eds), *Lan-
          guage, gender, and society*. Rowley, MA: Newbury House, 54-68.

358 *References*

1984　　　"Networks and hierarchies: Language and social stratification," in: Cheris Kramarae – Muriel Shulz – William O'Barr (eds), *Language and power*. London: Sage.

O'Barr, William M.
1982　　　*Linguistic evidence: Language, power, and strategy in the classroom*. New York: Academic Press.

O'Barr, William – Bowman K. Atkins
1980　　　"'Women's language' or 'powerless language'?" in: Sally McConnell-Ginet – Ruth Borker – Nelly Furman (eds), *Women and language in literature and society*. New York: Praeger, 93-110.

O'Brien, Marion – Keith Nagle
1987　　　"Parents' speech to toddlers: The effect of the play context," *Journal of Child Language* 14,2:269-79.

Ochs, Elinor
1982　　　"Talking to children in Western Samoa," *Language in Society* 11:77-105.

Ogbu, John U.
1988　　　"Class stratification, racial stratification, and schooling," in: Lois Weis (ed.), *Class, race and gender in American education*. Albany: State University of New York Press, 163-82.

Parker, K. – Craig Chaudron
1987　　　"The effects of linguistic simplifications and elaborative modifications on L2 comprehension," *UHWPESL (University of Hawaii Working Papers in English as a Second Language)* 6,2:107-33.

Payne, Arvilla
1980　　　"Factors controlling the acquisition of the Philadelphia dialect by out-of-state children," in: William Labov (ed.), *Locating language in time and space*. New York: Academic, 143-78.

Peal, Elizabeth – Wallace Lambert
1962　　　"The relation of bilingualism to intelligence," *Psychological Monographs* 76,546.

Piaget, Jean
1929　　　*The child's conception of the world*. London: Routledge and Kegan Paul.

Pica, Teresa
1983　　　"Adult acquisition of English as a second language under different conditions of exposure," *Language Learning* 33,4:465-97.

Pinker, Steven
1994　　　*The language instinct: How the mind creates language*. New York: William Morrow.

Postman, Neil
1976　　　*Crazy talk, stupid talk*. New York: Delacorte.

Potter, Jonathan – Margaret Wetherell
1987　　　*Discourse and social psychology: Beyond attitudes and behaviour*. London: Sage.

Preston, Dennis R.
1973   *Bituminous coal mining vocabulary of the eastern United States. Publication of the American Dialect Society #59.* University, AL: University of Alabama Press.
1981   "The ethnography of TESOL," *TESOL Quarterly* 15:105-16.
1982a   "Perceptual dialectology: Mental maps of United States dialects from a Hawaiian perspective," *Hawaii Working Papers in Linguistics* 14,2:5-49.
1982b   "'Ritin' fowklower daun 'rong: Folklorists' failures in phonology," *Journal of American Folklore* 95,377:304-26.
1983   "Mowr bad spellun': A reply to Fine," *Journal of American Folklore* 96,381:330-39.
1984   "Linguistics – science's best-kept secret" *Indiana English* 7,3:16-22.
1985   "The Li'l Abner syndrome," *American Speech* 60,4:328-36.
1986a   "Five visions of America," *Language in Society* 15:221-40.
1986b   "The fifty some-odd categories of language variation," *International Journal of the Sociology of Language* 57:9-47.
1989a   "Standard English spoken here: The geographical loci of linguistic norms," in: Ulrich Ammon (ed.), *Status and function of languages and language varieties.* Berlin & New York: Walter de Gruyter, 324-54.
1989b   *Perceptual dialectology.* Dordrecht: Foris.
1989c   *Sociolinguistics and second language acquisition.* Oxford: Blackwell.
1989d   "Folk speech," in: Charles R. Wilson – William Ferris (eds), *Encyclopedia of southern culture.* Chapel Hill: University of North Carolina Press, 768-9.
1992   "Talking black and talking white," in: Joan H. Hall – Nick Doane – Dick Ringler (eds), *Old English and new: Studies in language and linguistics in honor of Frederic G. Cassidy.* New York: Garland, 327-55.
1993a   "The South: the touchstone," A paper presented to the LAVIS (Language Variety in the South) Meeting, Auburn, AL, March.
1993b   "Folk dialectology," in: Dennis R. Preston (ed.), *American Dialect Research (a volume of studies celebrating the 100th anniversary of the American Dialect Society).* Philadelphia and Amsterdam: J. Benjamins, 333-77.
1993c   "The uses of folk linguistics," *International Journal of Applied Linguistics* 3:181-259.
1994   "Content-oriented discourse analysis and folk linguistics," *Language Sciences* 16,2:285-331.
1996   "'Whaddayaknow,' The modes of folk linguistic awareness," *Language Awareness* 5,1:40-74.
To appear *A handbook of perceptual dialectology.* Amsterdam: Benjamins.
Preston, Dennis R. – George Howe
1987   "Computerized studies of mental dialect maps," in: Keith M. Denning – Sharon Inkelas – F. C. McNair-Knox – John R. Rickford

(eds), *Variation in language: NWAV-XV at Stanford.* Stanford,CA: Stanford University, Department of Linguistics, 361-78.

Rampton, Ben
1995   *Crossing: Language and ethnicity among adolescents.* London: Longman.

Rank, Hugh (ed.)
1974   *Language and public policy.* Urbana, IL: National Council of Teachers of English.

Récanati, François
1991 [1989] "The pragmatics of what is said," in: Steven Davis (ed.), *Pragmatics: A reader.* Oxford: Oxford University Press, 97-120. (originally in Mind and Language 4).

Reed, Carroll E. (ed.)
1971   *The learning of language.* New York: Appleton-Century-Crofts.

Rensink, W.
1955   "Dialectindeling naar opgaven van medewerkers," *Amsterdam Dialectbureau Bulletin* 7:20-3.

Roberts, Paul
1956   *Patterns of English.* New York: Harcourt Brace Jovanovich.
1966   *The Roberts English series: A linguistics program.* New York: Harcourt Brace Jovanovich.

Roeper, Thomas
1988   "Grammatical principles of first language acquisition: Theory and evidence," in: Frederick J. Newmeyer (ed.), *Linguistics: The Cambridge Survey, Vol II, Linguistic theory: Extensions and implications.* Cambridge: Cambridge University Press, 35-52.

Romaine, Suzanne
1984   *The language of children and adolescents: The acquisition of communicative competence.* Oxford: Blackwell.

Rowan, Carl T.
1979   "Black English is silly," *Chicago Sun-Times,* July 10, p. 36.

Rubin, Joan
1975   "What the 'good language learner' can teach us," *TESOL Quarterly* 9:41-51.

Rumsey, Alan
1992   "Wording, meaning, and linguistic ideology," *American Anthropologist* 92:346-61.

Ryan, Ellen B.
1979   "Why do low-prestige language varieties persist?" in: Howard Giles – Robert St Clair (eds), *Language and social psychology.* Oxford: Blackwell, 145-57.

Ryan, Ellen B. – Howard Giles
1982   *Attitudes towards language variation.* London: Edward Arnold.

Ryan, Ellen B. – Howard Giles – Richard J. Sebastian
1982   "An integrative perspective for the study of attitudes towards language," in: Ellen B. Ryan – Howard Giles (eds), *Attitudes towards language variation.* London: Edward Arnold, 1-19.

Ryle, Gilbert
1949   *The concept of mind*. London: Hutchinson House.
Schieffelin, Bambi
1979   How Kaluli children learn what to say, what to do, and how to feel:
        An ethnographic study of the development of communicative com-
        petence. Unpublished Ph.D. dissertation, Columbia University.
1990   *The give and take of everyday life: Language socialization of Kaluli*
        children. Cambridge: Cambridge University Press.
Schieffelin, Bambi – Elinor Ochs
1986   "Language socialization," Annual Review of Anthropology 15: 163-
        191.
Schiffrin, Deborah
1984   "Jewish argument as sociability," *Language in Society* 13:311-35.
1987   *Discourse markers.* Cambridge: Cambridge University Press.
1994   *Approaches to discourse.* Oxford: Blackwell.
Schmidt, Richard
1986   "Developing basic conversational ability in a second language," in:
        Richard Day (ed.), *Talking to learn.* Rowley, MA: Newbury House,
        237-326.
1993   "Consciousness, learning, and interlanguage pragmatics," in: Gabri-
        ele Kasper and Shoshana Blum-Kulka (eds), *Interlanguage prag-*
        matics. New York and Oxford: Oxford University Press, 21-42.
Scollon, Ronald
1979   "A real early stage: An unzippered condensation of a dissertation of
        child language," in: Eleanor Ochs – Bambi Schieffelin (eds.), *Devel-*
        opmental pragmatics. New York: Academic Press, 214-227.
Sherzer, Joel
1974   "Namakke, Sunmakke, Kormakke: Three types of Cuna speech
        event," in: Richard Bauman – Joel Sherzer (eds), *Explorations in the*
        ethnography of speaking. Cambridge: Cambridge University Press,
        263-82.
1983   *Kuna ways of speaking.* Austin: University of Texas Press.
Shibatani, Masayoshi
1985   "Passives and related constructions," *Language* 61:821-848.
Shuy, Roger W.
1973   "What is the study of variation useful for?" in: Ralph W. Fasold –
        Roger W. Shuy (eds), *Analyzing variation in language.* Washington,
        D. C.: Georgetown University Press, 312-27.
1990   "Warning labels: language, law, and comprehensibility," *American*
        Speech 65,4:291-303.
Sibata, Takesi
1971   "Kotoba no kihan ishiki," *Gengo Seikatsu* 236:14-21, May (Special
        Issue: Words that bother us). (English quotations and page references
        are taken from this article translated as "Consciousness of language
        norms," Chapter 22 in Fumio Inoue and Daniel Long (eds) of the
        collected sociolinguistic works of Takesi Sibata, *Sociolinguistics in*
        Japanese contexts, to appear, Berlin: Mouton de Gruyter, 373-79.)

Silverstein, Michael
1981   "The limits of awareness," *Sociolinguistic Working Paper #84*. Austin, TX: Southwest Educational Development Laboratory.
Simon, John
1982   "Why good English is good for you," in: James C. Raymond (ed.), *Literacy as a human problem*. University, AL: University of Alabama Press, 55-72.
Sinclair, John – Malcolm Coulthard
1975   *Towards an analysis of discourse*. Oxford: Oxford University Press.
Skinner, B.F.
1957   *Verbal behavior*. New York: Appleton.
Slobin, Dan
1982   "Universal and particular in the acquisition of language," in: Eric Wanner – Lila R. Gleitman (eds), *Language acquisition: The state of the art*. Cambridge: Cambridge University Press, 128-70.
Smith, Henry Lee, Jr. – Clara Stratemeyer
1963-67 *The linguistic readers*. New York: Harper and Row.
Snow, Catherine – Charles Ferguson (eds)
1977   *Talking to children: Language input and acquisition*. Cambridge: Cambridge University Press.
Stalnaker, Robert
1978   "Assertion," in: P. Cole (ed.), *Syntax and semantics 9: Pragmatics*, New York, Academic Press, 315-32.
Stanlaw, J. – Alan Peshkin
1988   "Black visibility in a multi-ethnic high school," in: Lois Weis (ed.), *Class, race and gender in American education*. Albany: State University of New York Press, 209-29.
Starks, Judith
1983   "The Black English controversy and its implications for addressing the educational needs of Black children: The cultural linguistic approach," in: John Chambers, Jr. (ed.), *Black English: Educational equity and the law*. Ann Arbor: Karoma, 97-132.
Stewart, William
1970   "Toward a history of Negro dialect," in: Frederick Williams (ed.), *Language and poverty*. Chicago: Markham, 351-79.
Stross, Brian
1974   "Speaking of speaking: Tenejapa Tzeltal metalinguistics," in: Richard Bauman – Joel Sherzer (eds), *Explorations in the ethnography of speaking*. Cambridge: Cambridge University Press, 213-39.
Stubbs, Michael
1986   *Educational linguistics*. Oxford and New York: Blackwell.
Tannen, Deborah
1989   *Talking voices: Repetition, dialogue, and imagery in conversational discourse*. Cambridge: Cambridge University Press.
1990   *You just don't understand: Women and men in conversations*. New York: Ballantine.

Tarone, Elaine
1983 "On the variability of interlanguage systems," *Applied Linguistics* 4:142-63.
1988 *Variation in interlanguage.* London: Edward Arnold.
Tarone, Elaine – Merrill Swain
1995 "A sociolinguistic perspective on second-language use in immersion classrooms," *Modern Language Journal* 79:166-78.
Thakerer, Jitendra N. – Howard Giles – Jennie Cheshire
1982 "Psychological and linguistic parameters of speech accommodation theory," in: Colin Fraser – Klaus R. Scherer (eds), *Advances in the social psychology of language.* Cambridge: Cambridge University Press, 205-55.
Thomas, Beth.
1988 "Differences of sex and sects: Linguistic variation and social networks in a Welsh mining village," in: Jennifer Coates – Deborah Cameron (eds), *Women in their speech communities.* London: Longman, 51-61.
Toelken, Barre
1979 *The dynamics of folklore.* Boston: Houghton Mifflin.
Trudgill, Peter
1972 "Sex, covert prestige and linguistic change in the urban British English of Norwich," *Language in Society* 1,2:179-95.
1974 *The social differentiation of English in Norwich.* Cambridge: Cambridge University Press.
1983 *Sociolinguistics: An introduction to language and society. (Revised edition).* London: Penguin Books.
Tucker, G. Richard – Wallace E. Lambert
1969 "White and Negro listeners' reaction to various American English dialects," *Social Forces* 47:463-8.
Van Dijk, Teun A.
1987 *Communicating racism: Ethnic prejudice in thought and talk.* Newbury Park, CA: Sage.
1993 *Elite discourse and racism.* Newbury Park, CA: Sage.
Van Valin, Robert
1991 "Functionalist theory," *First Language* 11,31:7-40.
Wardhaugh, Ronald
1969 *Reading: A linguistic perspective.* New York: Harcourt, Brace, and World.
Wardhaugh, Ronald – H. Douglas Brown (eds)
1976 *A survey of applied linguistics.* Ann Arbor: University of Michigan Press.
Weeks, Thelma E.
1974 The slow speech development of a bright child. Lexington, MA: Lexington Books.
Weijinen, Antonius A.
1968 "Zum Wert subjektiver Dialektgrenzen," *Lingua* 21:594-96.

Weinreich, Uriel – William Labov – Marvin I. Herzog
  1968   "Empirical foundations for a theory of language change," in: Winfred
          Lehmann (ed.), *Directions for historical linguistics: A symposium.*
          Austin: University of Texas Press, 95-188.
West, Candace – Don H. Zimmerman
  1983   "Small insults: A study of interruptions in cross-sex conversations
          between unacquainted persons," in: Barrie Thorne – Cheris Kra-
          marae – Nancy Henley (eds), *Language, gender and society.* Rowley,
          MA: Newbury House, 102-117.
White, Lydia
  1989   *Universal grammar and second language acquisition.* Amster-
          dam/Philadephia: Benjamins.
Widdowson, Henry
  1998   "The theory and practice of critical discourse analysis" (review arti-
          cle), *Applied Linguistics* 19,1:136-51.
Wiemann, John M. – Victoria Chen – Howard Giles
  1986   "Beliefs about talk and silence in cultural context," *Paper presented
          to the annual meeting of the Speech Communication Association.*
          Chicago, November.
Williams, Frederick – Jack L. Whitehead – Leslie M. Miller
  1971   "Ethnic stereotyping and judgments of children's speech," *Speech
          Monographs* 38:166-70.
Wolfram, Walt
  1974   *Sociolinguistic aspects of assimilation: Puerto Rican English in New
          York City.* Arlington, VA: Center for Applied Linguistics.
  1991   *Dialects and American English.* Englewood Cliffs, NJ: Prentice-Hall.
Wolfram, Walt – Ralph Fasold
  1974   *The study of social dialects in American English.* Englewood Cliffs,
          NJ: Prentice Hall.
Wolfram, Walt – Natalie Schilling-Estes
  1994   "On the social basis of phonetic resistance: The shifting status of
          Outer Banks /ay/," NWAV23. Stanford, CA, Stanford University,
          October, (abstracts, n.p.)

Author index

Subject index

Major sections which treat a topic are given in bold.

CPSIA information can be obtained at www.ICGtesting.com
Printed in the USA
BVOW010154170513

320936BV00004B/14/P